TERROR AND CONTAINMENT PERSPECTIVES OF INDIA'S INTERNAL SECURITY

TERROR AND CONTAINMENT PERSPECTIVES OF INDIA'S INTERNAL SECURITY

By

K.P.S. GILL

GYAN

ISBN : 978-81-212-0712-6

Published, 2018

Published by

Gyan Publishing House
5, Ansari Road
Daryaganj, New Delhi-110002
Phone: 011-47034999, 9811692060
www.gyanbooks.com
E-mail: books@gyanbooks.com

Printed at: G. Print Process, Delhi.

Contents

	Preface	5
	List of Contributors	7
	Introduction	9
1.	**Endgame in Punjab: 1988-93** *K.P.S. Gill*	23
2.	**Terrorists, Human Rights and the United Nations** *Arundhati Ghose*	85
3.	**The Kargil War: Preliminary Explorations** *Praveen Swami*	99
4.	**A New Strategy for the LoC and Low-intensity Warfare in Kashmir** *Bharat Karnad*	141
5.	**Free Speech in an Age of Violence: The Challenge of Non-governmental Suppression** *Ajai Sahni*	161
6.	**Technology, Terror and a Thoughtless State** *K.P.S. Gill*	183
7.	**Counterinsurgency Warfare: The Use and Abuse of Military Force** *Vijendra Singh Jafa*	211

8. **Terrorism, Institutional Collapse and Emergency Response Protocols** 251
K.P.S. Gill

9. **Security and Development in India's Northeast: An Alternative Perspective** 295
Ajai Sahni & J. George

10. **Kargil: A Window of Opportunity** 319
Sudhir S. Bloeria

Index 361

Preface

The single most critical issue for India's developmental agenda today, and even perhaps for its long-term survival, is the crisis of internal security and the rising scourge of terrorism. An increasing proportion of our national resources, efforts and attention are being diverted to the task of containment of a multiplicity of proliferating crises. These have crippled the economies of vast regions, paralysed governance, administration and the judicial system, disrupted the basic task of education, interrupted the growth process, and crippled responses to the gigantic challenge of nation-building. The history of independent India, moreover, has demonstrated that we, as a nation, have not acted with foresight or with any clear vision, to prevent emerging and potentially debilitating conflicts, but have stumbled from one crisis to another, coping as best we can with disasters that have already been realised.

It is now accepted as a virtual truism, by policy makers and administrators alike, that our national security policies must be 'proactive'. Yet we are far from translating this idea into concrete processes and institutional mechanisms on the ground. The very first element in such a translation is the enormous task of documentation, analysis and understanding. It is imperative that we create an appropriate context for the coherent and objective assessment of policy alternatives, and for strategic formulations that go beyond the *ad hoc*, knee jerk responses that have been the unfortunate hallmark of crisis management in India. Unfortunately, this is a critical task that has, so far, been substantially neglected, both by governments and by the intellectual community at large.

The Institute for Conflict Management, established in 1997, is an effort that seeks to initiate processes that could help fill this vacuum, this glaring lacuna in our national responses. It has already created an enormous data pool on internal conflicts in the South Asian region, built the largest Website on the subject in the world and produced a substantial body of analytic literature, including a quarterly journal, *Faultlines: Writings on Conflict and Resolution.*

Terror and Containment represents a selection of this substantial output. It brings into sharp focus many of the less obvious aspects, causes and consequences of several contemporary conflicts in the Indian subcontinent. Crucially, it puts the disturbing and escalating phenomenon of terrorism, and the state's vacillating responses to it, under a critical microscope, identifying conceptual, policy and strategic failures, and defining the basic principles and mechanisms of a consistent and effective response to this greatest affliction of our age.

K.P.S. Gill

November 18, 2000

List of Contributors

1. K P S Gill is the publisher and editor of *Faultlines*, the founding President of the *Institute for Conflict Management*, and was a member of the National Security Advisory Board (NSAB). An officer of the Assam cadre of the Indian Police Service, he served in a number of theatres of civil strife and low intensity warfare, and, as Director General of the Punjab Police, led the successful campaign against terrorism in that state. Among other activities after his retirement from the Police, he writes on internal security, political and developmental issues for a number of newspapers and magazines.

2. Arundhati Ghose was a career diplomat with the Indian Foreign Service (IFS), and retired as India's Ambassador and Permanent Representative to the United Nations Office at Geneva. She is presently a Member of the Union Public Services Commission, Government of India.

3. Praveen Swami is Chief of Bureau, Mumbai, for *Frontline* magazine and has extensively reported on terrorism in Punjab and J&K. He covered the war in Kargil as well.

4. Bharat Karnad is Professor in National Security Studies at the Centre for Policy Research, New Delhi, and was a Member of the National Security Advisory Board. He was formerly Adviser on national security expenditure to the Tenth Finance Commission.

5. Dr. Ajai Sahni is the Director, *Institute for Conflict Management* and Executive Editor, FAULTLINES.

6. V.S. Jafa serves in the Indian Administrative Service (IAS) and is a former Chief Secretary of Assam. He studied the Northern Ireland conflict as a Visiting Fellow at the University of Oxford (1986-87); as John D. and Catherine T. MacArthur Fellow and a Visiting Fellow at the Massachusetts Institute of Technology (1988-89), he researched the revolutionary, ethnic and religious roots of violence, counter-insurgency and counter-terrorism in the context of the theory and practice of conflict resolution. He is a lso a Consulting Editor with FAULTLINES

7. Dr. Ajai Sahni is Executive Director, INSTITUTE FOR CONFLICT MANAGEMENT and the SOUTH ASIA TERRORISM PORTAL; and Executive Editor, FAULTLINES.

8. Prof. J. George is Professor & Head of Department of Economics, and of Disaster Management, at the Harayana Institute for Public Administration (HIPA), Gurgaon, and a founding member of the INSTITUTE FOR CONFLICT MANAGEMENT.

9. Dr. Sudhir S. Bloeria is an IAS Officer of the J&K cadre. He served as SDM Kargil between 1974-76 and Development Commissioner, Ladakh during 1978-1981, and is presently Principal Secretary, Health & Medical Education, Government of J&K. He is the author of the book The Battles of Zojila-1948, New Delhi, Har Anand, 1996 and Pakistan's Insurgency vs. India's Security: Tackling Militancy in Kashmir, New Delhi, Manas, 2000.

Introduction

South Asia is, to use the colloquialism, a 'bad neighbourhood', possibly one of the worst in the world today. Violence and political instability are endemic, and there is, at once, a great crisis both of ideologies and of leadership throughout the region. Worse, the collapse of long established geopolitical equations has set in motion a new 'great game' through which regional and extra-regional powers jockey for domination in the vacuum created by the collapse of the Soviet Union.

This volatile scenario has to be assessed and understood in the context of other and fundamental changes that have taken place in the nature of conflict between nations. Today, national and strategic ambitions do not find expression exclusively, or even predominantly, in conventional military operations or capabilities. The territorial and strategic ambitions of both regional and extra-regional players in South Asia are, consequently, increasingly finding expression in a wide range of what are euphemistically referred to as 'Operations Other Than War' (OOTW), or 'non-standard', 'irregular' and 'low-intensity' wars that prey on domestic discontent.

Terrorism lies at the core of this new paradigm of international conflict, even as it is adopted by a number of political groups as their prime instrumentality for the expression of domestic discontent. The situation is compounded by easy access to a diversified arsenal of sophisticated small arms, explosives and enabling technologies, as well as the training and organisational skills for their devastating employment against the security apparatus of established nation states.

Three of the states in the region are presently under a complex and extreme threat from the dynamics of terror. Of these, Pakistan is also among the most prominent sponsors of terrorist movements in the world today, a safe haven and training ground for every brand of Islamic fundamentalist militancy, an ideology-neutral supporter of every violent movement directed against India and, at the same time, a state that teeters on the verge of collapse as the forces of disorder threaten, in a Frankensteinian plot, to destroy their own creator. India and Sri Lanka, on the other hand, are the most prominent targets and victims of the rising tide of terror. No nation in the region, however, is free of its malignant shadow. The overflow of terrorism from India's Northeast, and the Gorkha question are critical destabilising elements in Bhutan; the 'Maoist' insurgency and the conflict between the Terai and the Hill people torments Nepal; the demagoguery and belligerence of revanchist Islamic parties that periodically spills over into violence, and the massing of Pakistan-backed fundamentalist elements, has already sown the seeds of a widening terrorism in Bangladesh.

The governmental response to these varied movements and tendencies in each of these countries has been far from adequate. Indeed, no single government in this region has yet been able to define a coherent and internally consistent policy on terrorism, and each vacillates between the alternating extremes of conciliation, even appeasement, on the one hand, and over-reaction or excessive use of force, on the other.

In many ways, India, with the largest number and widest variation in the character of terrorist movements and low-intensity wars on its soil, is a paradigm case, an accurate representation of the magnitude of the challenge, the escalating potential of future violence, and of all that has gone wrong in the state's response. In just the past two decades, more than sixty thousand lives have been lost to terrorism in Punjab, Jammu and Kashmir (J&K) and the ferment in the Northeast. In addition, thousands of others have died in caste, communal and Extreme Left (Naxalite) violence that flares up with unremitting persistence, leaving no part of the country unaffected. And yet, the nation continues to stumble virtually from crisis to crisis, its constantly expanding internal security forces combining imperfectly with its Army, in unending fire-fighting operations.

Shortly before the Communist regime in the German Democratic Republic (East Germany) collapsed, the last President of the Soviet Union, Mikhail Gorbachov, had visited East Berlin and warned of the imminent disintegration of the ancient regime of Stalinist authoritarianism in words that have a prophetic and universal ring. "He who acts too late," Gorbachov said, "is punished by life."

With the state in India, however, acting too late is virtually an art form. The maze of delays, of deliberate deferments and constraints, the elaborate farce of inconclusive 'decision making', the evasion of responsibility, the diffusion of accountability, and the sheer bloody-mindedness of the bureaucracy has kept the nation in a state of paralysis, even on the life and death issues of terrorism. Thus India, today, has neither law nor a coherent policy framework to address a challenge that has been with it, to a lesser or greater extent, for all of five decades, and that has been a compelling threat to the interests and integrity of the nation for at least the last two decades. And for all the prolixity on 'proactivity', India's strategic and tactical responses have invariably followed, and not presaged or pre-empted, terrorist actions. Tragically, it is not the decision-makers on whom life visits its cruel retribution for these failings, but on the people and the nation at large.

And retribution has, indeed, been cruel. While the staggering numbers of the dead and the maimed are its most distressing index, they do not exhaust the depth and the intensity of the tragedy inflicted. Millions have lost their homes to the terror; economies, trade, commerce, the supply and exchange of essential goods have all been disrupted; nothing more than the grinding tasks of survival and subsistence from day to day remains the lot of the people in affected areas. But it is not only the present that is destroyed. The future itself is being undermined. Children are brought up in an atmosphere of incertitude and brutality, exposed at an early age to the possession and use of arms, and to the recurrent spectacle and savagery of death by violence. Among the first targets of most terrorist movements has been the institutional structure and paraphernalia of education, and schools are shut down, teachers intimidated or killed. In their stead, new institutions dominated by the ideologies of extremism are built up to fill the vacuum and to teach the lessons of hatred and strife.

Each terrorist movement has also met with the collapse of virtually all the institutions of civil governance and criminal justice administration in the affected areas. The oldest insurgency in India - the secessionist campaign in Nagaland - dates back to almost half a century. Yet, not even a preliminary exercise in restoring the basic functions of government in large areas has been initiated. Indeed, a substantial proportion of the State (as of others under the sway of terrorism) is effectively, though informally, 'handed over' to an alternative and illegal terrorist regime that levies 'taxes' and evolves its own arbitrary systems of 'civil' and 'justice' administration. In Punjab, I recall that, while no such unquestioned 'domination' was ever established by the terrorists in any clearly defined geographical area, the collapse of the institutions of civil governance was complete, and it was only the uniformed services that survived to impose, in whatever measure possible at different times, the authority of the government and the law. Officers in all branches of government and administration were guilty of the most wilful and gross dereliction of duty throughout the period of terrorism. It is significant, moreover, that after peace returned to the State, these very officers secured the best and most favoured positions. The message is abundantly clear, the prevailing system rewards, rather than punishes, acts of cravenness. This fact is not unique to Punjab, but undermines responses to terrorism in all theatres in India. In 1997, I had written to the then Prime Minister on the many institutional deficiencies in India's counter-terrorism edifice, and many of the issues raised there have been reiterated again and again, at different fora, but to little effect. The essence of this failure is a system that has no penalties whatsoever for acts of omission and dereliction of duty. In the years since the Punjab campaign ended in victory for the Indian state, nothing has been done to ensure that the institutional collapse in the face of the terrorist challenge in that State is not replicated in other theatres, notably J&K and the Northeast. Consequently, a regime of absolute irresponsibility and lack of accountability remains the norm.

This institutional collapse is even more complete - and perhaps far more damaging - with regard to the judiciary in terrorist affected areas. It is nigh impossible to secure a conviction in any case of terrorism in a disturbed area - and the problem here is not the absence of suitable anti-terrorism legislation, but of the courage and will to implement even the ordinary laws of the land. It is, in fact, not necessary to look at the Punjab experience for confirmation of this. In J&K, after more than ten years of terrorism and thousands of innocent lives lost, just a single conviction has been secured for a terrorist crime.[1] The argument that this is a consequence of the infirmity of the existing laws does not hold water - the same laws enabled a Court in Chamba in Himachal Pradesh to convict one offender on January 20, 2000, sentencing him to life imprisonment on the charge of conspiring with Kashmir-based terrorists in a massacre. The massacre had occurred on August 2, 1998,[2] and the relatively swift judgement demonstrates that it is not the judicial system that is flawed or lacking in the power to punish. It is the lack of commitment, of will and of courage within members of the judiciary that is the basic problem. An effective war against terrorism in the absence of effective judicial institutions - indeed, in the face of judicial officers who are actively hostile to the agencies of the state - becomes increasingly difficult and sometimes even forces a resort to extra-constitutional measures. Yet, the policies and reforms that are so obviously needed simply never come.

What is true of India is true, by and large, for all the regimes in the region. The infirmity of the institutions of civil governance, the absence of transparency and accountability, and the collapse of will and confidence is endemic and is, indeed, often greater in the smaller and more fragile democracies among India's neighbours.

Pakistan is, of course, a unique case in this context. The very circumstances of its creation have created within it a uniquely perverse political dynamics that appears to be pushing to a logical and tragic conclusion today. To those who have studied political violence in this region and over time, these consequences were inevitable. The idea that cultural or communal differences were sufficient basis for nationhood was powerfully articulated in British India by Mohammad Ali Jinnah's Muslim League, and resulted in the bloodbath of Partition. The history of Pakistan since then should be a cautionary tale for all those who seek to construct their identities out of exclusion and hatred for others.

The 'two-nation theory', on which the very existence and notion of Pakistan is premised, was not just a question of Hindus and Muslims alone. It expressed a general thesis that all such communities and populations, between whom linguistic, cultural, religious, ethnic or any other significant differences exist, cannot live together, resolve problems amicably, and share broad developmental, national and human goals - and hence that such communities are best 'partitioned', that is, politically separated. Over the years, consequently, notions of religious, ethnic and cultural distinctness and isolation have become more and more constricted, reduced to a multiplicity of mutually exclusive and antagonistic identities, even as sectarian violence grows immensely, both in its incidence and brutality. The result has been the diversion of an overwhelming proportion of Pakistan's energies and efforts to the politics of confrontation and violence, directed both against its own people and its neighbours, and a diversion of national resources from the urgent and fruitful tasks of development, to the unending and constantly magnifying necessity of maintaining internal order and feeding military or quasi-military adventures abroad.

Less than three per cent of the population of Pakistan now comprises of non-Muslims, and the proportion declines each year. But the intolerance and the rage that created that nation must find new victims. It was this bigotry that resulted in the first dismemberment of that country and the creation of Bangladesh. It is the same malevolence that seeks out new enemies among sub-groups of the Muslims themselves - such as the *Ahmadiyas* and the *Shias*. Today, every regional and cultural group in Pakistan - the *Punjabis*, the *Sindhis*, the *Pashtuns* and the *Baluchis* - sees the other as an enemy, and all these together persecute the *mohajirs*, the immigrants who, five decades ago, left their hearth and home in India to follow their dream of an Islamic 'land of the pure'. In the meanwhile, desperate leaders, 'democratic' and military authoritarian alike, can hold the country together only by channelising the hatreds and frustration of the common people against an external enemy - consistently India, for a time, the Soviets and the regime they backed in Afghanistan, and increasingly, a number of 'enemies of the Faith' throughout Central Asia and Eastern Europe.

All this was the inescapable consequence of the very concept of a nation created out of a philosophy of exclusion, and of sectarian antipathies. Sectarian divisions inevitably compound themselves, becoming progressively narrower with the passage of time. These consequences are clear for all to see.

Yet, the same thing is happening in most of the other nations within the Asian region, and their governments are paralysed in the face of escalating disorder. Worse still, while international concern has certainly increased, the power players of the New World Order are yet to disengage from ambivalent policies and programmes that variously tolerate, encourage or explicitly support terrorism in certain areas, or certain terrorist groups, even as they condemn or confront others. In this, they ignore the inescapable truth that the rising scourge of terrorism is a threat not only to this region, but to all humanity.

Terrorism is a method that recognises no limits of law and knows no constraints of morality, of honour, of human compassion, or even of the minimal rules of warfare. Crucially, it transcends all international boundaries, and returns to consume the very systems and societies that create, support and sponsor it, even as it destroys those who tolerate or succumb to it.

For some years now, a part of the political and intellectual world has been seduced by the improbable idea of a clash of civilisations, of a final determination of the superiority of one culture, ideology or Faith over all others. And terrorist violence is sometimes seen as a legitimate instrument in this final, millennial, struggle by those who are absolutely convinced that their vision of the world is the only one possible. But no nation, culture or civilisation can conceivably benefit from terrorism. This is the pitiless enemy of every nation state in the world, of all cultures and of civilisation itself.

Terrorism, moreover, is not the problem of its victim societies alone. Its impact reverberates across the globe. A victory for terrorism anywhere in the world is a victory for terrorism everywhere.

This is why this evil must be fought collectively, by all nations, all cultures and all civilisations. When we speak of defeating terrorism, we do not speak of the right or wrong of a specific ideology or Faith, or of any nation's claims in a particular dispute. We speak only of the rejection of an extraordinarily inhuman and barbaric method of warfare as an instrument of resolution.

Our failures to find effective remedies to the rising epidemic of terror - both domestic and international - is rooted, in large part, in a failure of understanding, a failure to think things through and to assess and analyse the linkages between proximate and apparently inconsequential actions and interventions, between our various acts of omission and commission, and the larger perspective and dynamics of organised political violence by non-state actors. It is, in effect, a failure to systematise the available and cumulative data, information and knowledge of the phenomenon of terrorism, and to examine it with detachment, and within the context of a coherent paradigm of interpretation. This, indeed, is the reason why so many of our policies and strategies appear to cancel each other out; and why, despite the accumulation of large and increasing numbers of high sounding agreements, declarations and conventions in international fora, the actual practice of individual nations and governments remains dissonant with the intent and spirit of a consistent counter-terrorism perspective. It is only when the study of terrorism and low-intensity warfare, in all its aspects, including the military, tactical and strategic, the political, legal and diplomatic, the human and the psychological, is raised to the level of a rigorous discipline that policies and practices will begin to be based on an adequate and coherent analysis of the complexities involved. When this happens, our counterterrorist initiatives will begin to approximate the measures that are actually needed to contain, if not eliminate, the greatest scourge of the new century.

The present volume is an effort to goad decision-making on conflicts in and around India in the direction of coherence and rationality, and to elicit, both from governments within the region, and from what passes under the fiction of the 'international community', responses that are proportionate to the enormity of the actual challenge that the world today faces from terrorism. Each of the papers here constitutes an independent effort to further our understanding of the complexities of the problem the inconsistencies of our past responses, and the imperatives of the future.

Three of the chapters in this volume constitute my own work. Endgame in Punjab is the first and, at this point of time, perhaps the only effort to look objectively at the course of terrorism in that State within the context of the objective circumstances on the ground and the actual data. It encapsulates, moreover, the primary experience of having lived through and commanded the campaigns that eventually and comprehensively defeated the terror. Crucially, moreover, it documents the critical and often disastrous impact of inconsistent, albeit sometimes well-intentioned, policies on the course of the terror, and on the lives of its unfortunate victims. It is my belief that, if India had a rational and efficient form of governance in place (and this is manifestly not the case), the experiences of Punjab could have produced critical impact in other theatres of low-intensity warfare, had they not been so comprehensively neglected, both by political leaders and Force Commanders. The other two papers examine specific aspects of the general neglect and incoherence that has characterised governmental policy. The first of these focuses on the comparative technological responses to terrorist tactics, strategies and innovations; the second, on the structures, policies and protocols of institutional response to terrorism, or, more accurately, the absence thereof. In both cases, the reality is disappointing. Nevertheless, the basic blue print of the inevitable course that policy and strategy will have to adopt is defined here, and it is entirely impossible that governments and bureaucracies will be able to blind themselves to the compulsions of history indefinitely.

Arundhati Ghose's work is a pioneering effort to document the pattern of distortion and abuse to which international agencies, including the United Nations and the larger human rights platform, have been cynically subjected by those who ally themselves with terrorist and secessionist movements in various parts of the world. It is, moreover, the stirring testament of an individual who has suffered a grievous personal loss to the depredations of the terrorists.

The Kargil War has spawned a very large body of literature. Within this corpus, Praveen Swami's writings are immensely influential. Swami has covered the entire course of terrorism in the Punjab and in Jammu and Kashmir, not in the usual and superficial reportage that characterises the works of most journalists who jet in and out of the theatres of engagement, or of those who become part of one or another of the local lobbies, but in a rigorous and disciplined approach that has taken him back again and again to the same events even after they have lost their sensational or titillatory potential. Unsurprisingly, he has often been well ahead of the more opportunistic among his colleagues in identifying and documenting subtle shifts in strategy and policy on both sides of the conflict, and has been unrelenting in his assessment of both failure and success. It is, thus, his deep understanding of the situation in J&K, the context of terrorism and Pakistan's historical role, and of the policies, strategies and tactics that preceded the outbreak of open hostilities in Kargil, that give his paper a ring of authenticity that is missing in most writings on the subject.

Bharat Karnad's is a hard look at Kargil from another perspective. Strictly strategic in its context, it examines a scenario where India adopts Pakistan's own strategies of destabilisation and undeclared warfare to force the latter to reach a permanent solution on Kashmir. The paper is immensely controversial, and demands close attention from military strategists and policy planners alike.

Sudhir Bloeria's 'Kargil: A Window of Opportunity' probes a parallel theme, and suggests that India should look to the Northern Terriroties, "the huge land mass - more than seventy thousand square kilometres... illegally occupied by Pakistan in 1947." The harsh natural conditions here have been exacerbated by an even harsher political regime of centralised control from Islamabad, and there is many an opportunity that can be exploited by a proactive Indian policy. Bloeria also argues that the strategy can be compounded if India shatters the Pakistan economy by making that nation spend more and more on defence. These are certainly ideas that demand a deeper exploration by the Indian strategic community.

Kashmir is, again, the focus of Navnita Chadha Behera's work, although from an entirely different perspective. Behera looks at the ethnic and cultural diversity of the State and highlights the narrowness of the perspective that focuses overwhelmingly on the politics of the Kashmir Valley and its Muslim majority, to the detriment and neglect of a diverse political, cultural and religious spectrum that spans the Jammu and Ladakh regions.

Vijendra Singh Jafa has focused on two different aspects of distorted responses to terrorism in his chapters. The first of these outlines the lessons of the abuse of military force in various theatres of counter-insurgency warfare across the world, and applies the derivative principles to the specifics of the military campaign in Mizoram. This chapter is impressive in its scholarship, and an honest and disturbing examination of India's policies and strategies in the Northeast. Equally disturbing and relentless is his second chapter in its analysis of the double standards and outright duplicity of the Western and super powers in their various interventions in the less stable parts of the world, and the tragic impact such mischief has had on India and Pakistan.

Mamang Dai's 'Arunachal Pradesh: The Myth of Tranquility' turns the spotlight on a State that has long been hidden from public scrutiny, and that is believed to be a haven of peace. The popular impression is clearly mistaken, and large parts of the State have virtually been handed over to the militants. Worse still, Mamang documents a regime of collusion and complicity that brings the role of the State's political leadership into question. Here again we discover the beginning of the patterns of moral and political compromise that have pushed the other States of the Northeast into the vicious cycle of terror.

The book also contains three chapters by Ajai Sahni on entirely distinct but critical issues. The first of these explores censorship and the suppression of the freedom of speech and expression from an unexpected angle. In general, analysts approach the issue of freedom of expression from the perspective of governments trammelling the democratic rights of citizens. Sahni looks at the issues that arise when terrorists and other non-governmental agencies impose arbitrary restrictions, according to their own proclivities and 'moral codes' of conduct, on citizens' fundamental rights of expression, and on their educational and cultural preferences. In another chapter, Sahni and J. George debunk established presumptions of the supposed economic 'neglect' of India's Northeast and raise critical questions regarding the dynamics of the 'underground economy' of collusion, corruption and extortion that emerges in areas of widespread terrorism. Sahni extends the logic of this analysis to the problem of Left Wing Extremism in his third chapter, as he explores the possibilities of reversing the retreat of civil governance in the face of the 'Naxalite' onslaught.

The sheer range of the different works in this book is a measure of the complexity of the issues connected with terrorism. The exercise of analysis and understanding that must inform our counter-terrorism policies and practices is clearly immense, and expanding exponentially. Terrorists, today, are "planning the unthinkable"[3] in seeking access to, or the deployment of, weapons of mass destruction, including nuclear, biological and chemical weapons. The task of strategists and policy makers is, consequently, to develop the capabilities to 'confront the unthinkable'. Scenario projection and the meticulous exploration of every possible option is an integral part of the process of identifying and evolving appropriate policies and strategies.

The enormity of the task is well-expressed in a recent Report that attempts to assess "terrorism's spectacular future".[4] "Terrorism evolves," the author notes, as he confesses that, when his group began their researches in the early 1970s, they could not even conceive of some of the scenarios that have been realised today and that, only decades ago, would have been dismissed as a novelist's imaginings. "Today's lurid speculations turn into tomorrow's headlines, making it hard to dismiss even the most far-fetched scenarios."[5]

The constellation of forces in South Asia augurs huge transformations, and, as is the case with all great shifts in history, these will be attended by enormous turmoil and human suffering. Today, a "multipolar balance of terror stretches over a 6,000 mile arc, comprising some of the most unstable countries on earth," and includes "Syria, Iraq, Iran, Pakistan, India and China."[6] To these, rightly, should be added the whole of the Middle East as well as the breakaway nation states of Central Asia and Eastern Europe that were created out of the fragmented Soviet Union. This is the expanse across which two centuries and more of Western domination is being questioned and, present appearances notwithstanding, will be challenged.

While trade, diplomacy and a continuous revision of geopolitical equations will each play their roles, terrorism will also be among the significant instrumentalities of transformation, even as it impacts on the relations between nations within the Asian region, and on the processes of political changes within these countries. There will, moreover, be an enormous leap in the lethality of terrorist actions, and fundamental changes in terrorist organisational structures, technologies, strategies and tactics. These will require corresponding, and to the extent possible, pre-emptive counter-terrorism responses that can only be based on deeply analytical, rigorous and scientific studies of past and present trends, as well as emerging ideological, geopolitical and technological imperatives. The present work is an initiative in precisely this direction.

NOTES AND REFERENCES

1. There have been other convictions. For instance three Pakistani intruders, arrested from Rajouri district, were sentenced to eight years of imprisonment under the Terrorist and Disruptive Activities (TADA) Act by a court in Jammu on October 25, 2000. According to a news report, this is the fourth conviction in Jammu and Kashmir under TADA. But this conviction was for the offences of crossing the border illegally and possession of arms and not for any acts of violence. Greater Kashmir: Srinagar, October 29, 2000
2. "Massacre conspirator convicted for life," *The Times of India*: Delhi, January 22, 2000.
3. The expression is taken from Peter R Lavoy, Scott D. Sagan and James J. Wirtz, Eds., *Planning the Unthinkable: How New Powers Will Use Nuclear, Biological and Chemical Weapons*, Cornell University Press, Ithaca & London, 2000.
4. Brian Michael Jenkins, 'Foreword', in Ian O. Lesser et. al., *Countering the New Terrorism*, Rand, Washington, 2000, p. iv.
5. *Ibid.*
6. Paul Bracken, *Fire in the East: The Rise of Asian Military Power and the Second Nuclear Age*, Harper Collins Publishers India, New Delhi, 1999, p. 2.

ONE

Endgame in Punjab: 1988-93

K. P. S. Gill

I

The movement for the creation of Khalistan was one of the most virulent terrorist campaigns in the world. Launched in the early 1980s by a group of bigots who discovered their justification in a perversion of the Sikh religious identity, and supported by a gaggle of political opportunists both within the country and abroad, this movement had consumed 21,469 lives before it was comprehensively defeated in 1993.[1] Thousands of others were injured and maimed, hundreds of thousands were permanently scarred by their experience of dislocation, the gratuitous loss of loved ones, and an unremitting terror that they endured for more than a decade.

The campaign that eventually crushed this menace, as dramatic as it was significant in its strategic inventiveness, has received little systematic attention. Apart from the reportage and commentary it attracted in the mass media during its execution, the only sustained attention it has received has been in the form of propaganda by the front organisations of the defeated terrorist movement, and by apologists masquerading as human rights activists purporting to present a "history" of the "sufferings of the Sikh people".[2] Neither group has shown, or could be expected to show, even a cursory respect for facts or evidence. Not only has this manifestly slanted debate excelled in the invention of political fictions, it has failed abjectly to explicate, analyse and evaluate the wealth of strategic experience that this campaign generated.

One of the dominant myths that these propagandists have tirelessly, and in some measure successfully, circulated is the idea that terrorism in Punjab was defeated, not because, but in spite of the use of armed force against the militants. No evidence is ascribed to shore up this claim, but a variety of nebulous theories - essentially populist and politically correct slogans — are propounded regarding a 'people's victory' or a 'political solution' that brought peace to the strife-torn province.

The defeat of terrorism in Punjab, and I have said this before,[3] was unambiguously the result of the counter-terrorist measures implemented in the state by the security forces. Moreover, the use of this coercive force was (and is) not just a necessary expedient, but a fundamental obligation and duty of constitutional government, and its neglect inflicts great and avoidable suffering on the innocent and law abiding. This is not simply an assertion of subjective belief, but a fact that is well borne out, as I shall attempt to demonstrate, by the overwhelming weight of evidence generated during the Punjab campaign. Specifically, I shall seek to demonstrate that each time a 'political solution' was sought through a dilution of the operations carried out by the security forces, through negotiations with terrorists and their front organizations, and through measures referred to as "winning the hearts and minds of the people" — usually an euphemism for a policy of appeasement of terrorist elements — terrorism escalated, as did the threat to the integrity of the nation, and the innocent victims of terrorism multiplied.

Counter-terrorist and counter-insurgency operations in Punjab also challenged established traditions of response to situations of extreme and widespread militancy. By and large, once political violence escalates beyond a certain limit (which may vary from situation to situation, and according to political perceptions), conventional wisdom conceives of the army as a refuge of last resort. This was, and remains, the case in most campaigns within India, as it is in most areas of major civil strife in other parts of the world. Even those who strongly advocate the exclusive use of the civil police to confront all internal security challenges and see a "fundamental conflict" between internal security duties and "the professional instincts, traditions and ethos of the military" concede that a resort to the army is a legitimate "last line of defence" even within "the strict limits imposed in a constitutionalist liberal democratic system".[4]

Within India this advocacy of, and inevitable resort to, the army in circumstances of widespread disorder is also based on an implicit (even occasionally explicit, though not publicly proclaimed) assumption: the presumed subversion of the local police force in any situation of large-scale insurgency or civil strife. Divided loyalties or the "unreliability" of the local police have been used to justify the withdrawal of the government's faith in this force in theatres of low intensity conflict in various states of India's North-East, in Jammu and Kashmir, and, for several years, in Punjab as well.

The Punjab campaign, however, eventually demonstrated not only that the civil police was an effective counter-terrorist force even in the most extreme circumstances, but also that the presumption of bad faith was completely unfounded. The role of the army and of para-military forces was, of course, critical in the final phases of this campaign, but it was the Punjab Police that spearheaded the anti-terrorist offensive — and this is clearly borne out by the relative casualties these various forces suffered Fig. 1.

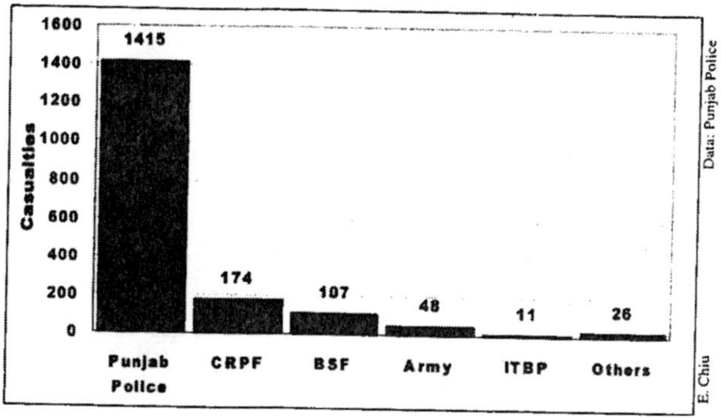

Fig. 1. Force Casualties in Punjab - 1981-96.

Both the devastating consequences of various "political solutions" and of a resort to conventional military strategies against terrorism are borne out startlingly by even a cursory review of the pattern of conflict and response that prevailed in the initial phases of the terrorist movement in Punjab. Counter-terrorist strategies at this stage vacillated between the extremes of paralysis and over-reaction, even as political responses and policies ranged from opportunism through cynicism to panic. It was only towards the end of the Eighties that mounting violence and a mix of exhaustion and alarm made at least some political leaders and regimes — though certainly not all — more amenable to a realistic appraisal of the threat and to the dictates of reason.

It is not my intention to review this initial phase in detail. Certain elements, however, demand elaboration, to the extent that they define the context of the events and strategies that evolved later.

Terrorism in Punjab has, on occasion, been projected as a natural consequence of the unfulfilled collective aspirations of the Sikhs, as "an idealistic movement for the creation of a state... among the Sikhs of the Punjab".[5] The fact, however, is that the movement for Khalistan was created out of a pattern of venal politics, of unscrupulous and bloody manipulation, and a brazen jockeying for power that is too well documented to be repeated. It will suffice to state here that each of the major political players in the state and the national arena participated in the creation of this calamity, and the Congress (I) and the Akali Dal were the most culpable formations.[6] This, indeed, was the first stage where a pernicious pattern of political intervention contributed, not to the resolution, but to the creation and nurturing of terrorism.

Nor indeed, were any 'Sikh aspirations' involved in the movement for Khalistan. Far from being a revolution against 'oppression', this was actually a rebellion of a privileged quasi-feudal caste-based orthodoxy that saw its privileges shrinking. It was, moreover, entirely unconnected with any element or principle of Sikhism, and was based, rather, on a corruption and perversion of everything that Sikhism has historically represented. In it, "the institutions of the Sikhs, both religious and political, ...[were]... hijacked by a small clique, a self-interested oligarchy, representing a particular ethnic cluster, a small endogamous segment of Punjab's social fabric; a narrow caste group that...[sought]... to define Sikhism and Sikh identity in terms of its own constricted vision."[7]

This convoluted pattern of politics, of competitive communalism and brinkmanship in the Punjab, produced the larger than life image of Jarnail Singh Bhindranwale. An image that owed its proportions as much to the political leadership of that time as it did to the media and, eventually and overwhelmingly, to his seizure and control of the Golden Temple — the most hallowed shrine of the Sikhs. Whatever the causes, it is a fact that, by 1984, Bhindranwale's murderous creed had captured the imagination of a significant number of Sikhs, particularly in rural Punjab.

The years preceding 1984 are particularly inglorious for the Punjab Police and its leadership. Their failure to act against extremist elements was comprehensive. It was, nevertheless, understandable. Before the 1980s, terrorism had only been experienced in India in regions that were regarded as 'peripheral' to the 'national mainstream'. The North-East had long been troubled by bloody insurgencies, but was generally viewed as an amorphous 'disturbed area' that invited a certain pattern of armed intervention, primarily through use of military force. Having served a quarter of a century in that region, I had seen these campaigns at close quarters and had long regarded them as an inappropriate model for intervention — one that reflected not only political short-sightedness, but also a strategic failure of monumental proportions. In Punjab, however, the shock of terrorist tactics — unfamiliar in the extreme — produced a paralysis that was compounded enormously by the conduct of politicians at the very highest level. To expect a sagacious, balanced and adequate response from district police officials against extremism that is clearly, directly, sometimes openly, encouraged by leaders at the highest levels of governance, is to ask for the impossible. In any event, in the absence of a clear mandate and a firm leadership, the police, directionless and demoralised, quite simply, refused to engage.

I was not present in Punjab at this juncture, but there was ample evidence of this abdication of responsibility even when I was transferred to the state in September 1984 — a full three months after Operation Blue Star. I held joint charge as Inspector-General (IG) of the Punjab Armed Police (PAP) and IG Operations. In both capacities, my jurisdiction comprehended counter-terrorist operations right across the state, and I was astonished to discover that simply no records were being maintained in connection with terrorist crimes, no investigations were carried out, and almost invariably, no documentation existed of any action taken. There was widespread reluctance on the part of Punjab Police officers to involve themselves in anti-terrorist work. Many of the interrogations had to be carried out by officers at a senior level, as Station House Officers [SHOs] and subordinates at the police stations were clearly unwilling to be associated with the process for fear of identification and reprisals. As IG Operations, records relating to terrorist crime and profiles of terrorists were essential to my work, and it was only after this stage that a slow and painstaking process of record-keeping and analysis was established.

Political mischief, a mounting campaign of demonstrations and *bandhs* orchestrated to coincide with terrorist actions, increasing and unpunished incidents of extremist violence, the evident impunity with which terrorists acted, and the total uncertainty and apathy that attended the actions of the law enforcement machinery, had, by 1984, created an atmosphere of terror and collapse of the state that was far in excess of anything that the situation itself warranted. Between 1981 and 1983, the terrorists had killed 101 civilians. Of these, 75 were killed in 1983 itself [1981: 13; 1982: 13] — an event that, in the prevailing state of hysteria, inspired one commentator to refer to this as "The Year of the Armageddon";[8] disturbing though the numbers were, this evaluation was more than excessive. Indeed, even in the years preceding the advent of terrorism in Punjab, the number of murders in the state were seldom below 500 in any year, and tended to maintain a secular upward trend [1981: 555; 1982: 575; 1983: 591].[9] More recently, in the three years after terrorism was brought under control in Punjab there have been a total of 2,081 murders unrelated to terrorism [1994: 687; 1995: 686; 1996: 708]. These numbers are not regarded as being extraordinary, and have attracted no exceptional comment in the media, nor was there any sense of a "breakdown" in the state.

Without doubt, the impact of terrorist killings — as a result of their sheer brutality, irrationality and randomness — is far greater on the public mind than that of an ordinary criminal act. It is only natural for a poorly informed and sensation-hungry media to devise frenzied headlines. But for the police administration to act as if these represented an objective evaluation of the threat potential is inexcusable.

But the police, no doubt stupefied by the sheer unfamiliarity of the challenge, was also not permitted to act; nor did it dare to act on its own against the manifest intent and stratagems of political powers. The result was that, in the months preceding Operation Bluestar, terrorist violence mounted to claim 158 civilian lives between January and May 1984.

The sheer intensity of police paralysis at this time has been substantially documented. Right since the Daheru incident in 1981, when an ill-prepared police party, when shot at by a group of terrorists whom they had gone to arrest, abandoned its weapon and fled, there had been acts of dereliction without number. Nevertheless, there is one incident that bears repetition, as it reflects the abysmal depths to which the spirits of the law enforcement agencies had plummeted.

> A single incident epitomises their impotence. On February 14, 1984, a group of militants attacked a police post at some distance from the entrance of the [Golden] Temple. Six policemen, fully armed, were 'captured' and dragged inside. The 'police response' came twenty-four hours later in the form of a senior police officer who went to Bhindranwale in the Akal Takht and begged him to release his men and return their weapons. Bhindranwale agreed only to hand over the corpse of one of the policemen who had been killed. He later relented and released the remaining five men who were still alive. Their weapons, including three sten guns, and a wireless set, were not returned. No one asked for them. No action was ever taken in the case of the murdered policeman.[10]

I cannot imagine any police force in the world reacting to such an outrage with such utter cravenness, in such complete and impotent prostration.

Nevertheless, even under the prevailing circumstances and with the victims of terrorism multiplying rapidly, I cannot believe that what was done under Bluestar could be justified. It is my firm conviction that with the right leadership and a clear and unambiguous political mandate, the police morale could have been revived [as it was, much later, and in a situation that was far worse] to secure effective action; and that concerted police action, with suitable para-military and army backing, would have produced better results even at this stage. Instead, in an ill-planned, hasty, knee-jerk response, the Army was called in: artillery battered the revered edifice of the Golden Temple Complex, and tanks rolled across the holy *parikrama*. The army, however, was not to blame for this botched operation; it was acting on specific directions from the Prime Minister's Office, and had been given little choice or time to prepare.[11]

The damage Bluestar did was incalculable. This was compounded by Operation Woodrose, the Army's 'mopping up' exercise all over Punjab that sought to capture Bhindranwale's surviving associates and to clear all *Gurudwaras* in the state of extremist elements. Woodrose suffered from all the classical defects of army intervention in civil strife — an extraneous and heavily armed force suddenly transported into unfamiliar territory; mistrustful (in this case, exceptionally so) of the local police and intelligence, but with no independent sources of information; dealing with a population, large segments of which had become hostile; and operating under a political fiat that not only condoned, but emphasised the use of punitive force. Operating blindly, the army arrested large numbers of people, many innocent, others perhaps sympathetic to the militant cause, but by no means associated with any terrorist or criminal activity. Lacking in adequate information to distinguish effectively at the local level, the indiscriminate sweep of Woodrose pushed many a young man across the border into the arms of welcoming Pakistani handlers. And then, even as Woodrose drew to an end, the evil was incalculably compounded by the pitiless massacre of Sikhs in what were perceived to be Congress-I government-sponsored riots of November 1984.

I regard Operation Bluestar and the November 1984

massacres as "the two most significant victories for the cause of 'Khalistan'...not won by the militants, but inflicted.... upon the nation by its own Government... These two events, in combination, gave a new lease of life to a movement which could easily have been contained in 1984 itself."[12]

After the army, it was the turn of the 'political solution'. The Rajiv Gandhi government, having, in its first days, remained a mute spectator to the anti-Sikh riots, decided to force the ravaged state through a hasty and ill-timed election. Negotiations were initiated by the central government in mid-1985. The Akalis, led by Harchand Singh Longowal, assisted by S. S. Barnala and Balwant Singh (of whom Longowal and Balwant Singh later fell to assasins), showed great eagerness to reclaim their hold on events in the state. But the Centre's 'strategy' went well beyond the 'moderates' in the Akali Dal, and the government also initiated a dialogue with representatives of the All India Sikh Students Federation (AISSF), at that time a frontline terrorist grouping. I was asked, initially, to be present at the meetings between the AISSF and the government's intermediaries, and subsequently, to intervene. Eventually, the AISSF representatives expressed their willingness to join the electoral process, but demanded a short deferment of the projected dates in order to prepare. The Akalis who were negotiating separately with the government, however, objected strongly, fearing that the AISSF, given this time, could sweep the elections. The talks with the AISSF broke down on this trivial difference, mainly because of the Centre's inclination in favour of the Akalis.

The entire move to install the Akalis in power was most unwise. It was based on an erroneous premise that, just as the Marxists [Communist Party of India (Marxist) (CPI-M)] had tackled Naxalism [CPI (Marxist-Lennist) terrorism] in West Bengal, the Akalis would fight Sikh terrorism in Punjab. This was a complete misreading of the relationship between the Akalis and the extremist. I was strongly opposed to the elections of 1985, and repeatedly expressed my reservations, because I was convinced that there was no real difference between the fundamental thinking of the Akalis and the terrorists — and that the Akalis completely lacked the desire and the will to contain terrorism. I was equally convinced that terrorism would return with a vengeance within six months of the Akalis forming the government — and events soon demonstrated that even this projection was an overestimation.

The elections eventually took place — but only after Longowal's assassination — on August 20, 1985. Sympathy, and the lack of any serious opposition in the elections on September 25 returned the Akali's, now led by Barnala, with a sweeping majority (73 out of 117 seats).

One of the first acts of the Barnala government was the appointment of the Bains Committee which released, *en masse*, over 2000 extremists at that time under detention. The impact on terrorist violence was palpable — not only because those who were released simply resumed their activities, but also because others saw in this act a restoration of the immunity they had enjoyed in the pre-Bluestar phase. 1985 had seen a total of 63 civilians and eight policemen killed by militants. As the Bains Committee began its work, in just the first three months of 1986, 102 civilians and 10 security men fell to the terror.

Barnala also surrendered the Golden Temple to the terrorists once again. The shrine was restored to the Akali controlled Shiromani Gurudwara Prabandhak Committee (SGPC) on January 22, 1986. In less than a month, the terrorists, led by the Damdami Taksal, were in complete control. The SGPC, in fact, had to shift the venue of its *Sarbat Khalsa* (the general assembly of all Sikhs) to Anandpur Sahib, because it was in no position to hold the event within the Temple precincts. Once again, murderers swaggered across the *parikrama*; proclaimed offenders, wanted by the police for the most heinous crimes, planned and directed their activities from the security of the hallowed complex; assassins installed themselves in the highest religious offices. By the end of April , a '*Panthic* Committee' had been constituted to coordinate all terrorist activities, and a 'Declaration of Khalistan' was issued by the Committee from the Golden Temple (April 29, 1986). A day later, the Barnala government ordered a mock search in the Temple with ample advance notice. It was an ill-conceived and ill-planned raid (occasionally, if inappropriately, referred to as 'Black Thunder-I') mounted by the National Security Guard (NSG). The sum total of the impact of this Operation was the use of stun grenades that resulted in the burning of a bookshop near the gate of the Temple, the beating up of two *granthis* after they had been chased off the *parikrama*, and the interruption of an *akhand path* due to the disturbances. Not unexpectedly, "no one of note was caught"[13] in this action. The incident, however, was sufficient to provoke a split in the Akali Dal, and, from that point onwards, Barnala's existence was entirely dependant on the Congress-I's support. Nevertheless, after their very brief 'absence' the terrorists simply returned to the Temple and resumed control. The saga of complicity and cowardice that abandoned the Temple and the state to the depredations of the terrorists demands independent documentation. The simple fact, however, is that during Barnala's brief and feckless tenure of a little over 19 months, the lives of 783 civilians and 71 security men were sacrificed in an ill-conceived political gambit that was predestined to failure.

The 'political solution' had borne its bloody fruit.

But the harvest was to continue a great deal longer. The violence escalated continuously as both the political and the police leadership failed consistently to define an unambiguous response to terrorism. Indeed, there was no concerted and consistent bid to confront the problem squarely, no political strategy, and no clarification of the principles of administrative, judicial and executive response to the scourge.[14] The police response, to the extent that it was mandated by the political executive, was itself muddled. Dictated by traditional notions of use of force in situations of civil strife, the dominant thinking emphasised the 'minimum use of force' against the unconstrained violence of the terrorists. This thinking persisted among many police officers at the senior-most level even after the introduction of the sophisticated Kalashnikov assault rifle [the AK-47] into the terrorist armory after May 1987.[15] With the supply of Kalashnikovs to the terrorists, Pakistan had clearly increased the stakes of its covert war in India, and terrorism, at this point, entered a completely new and deadlier phase. The impact was immediate and dramatic. Explosives were yet to play a major part in the terrorist strategy in the state. Though crude bombs extracted a steady toll of innocent lives, it was only after 1990 that sophisticated explosives became an essential component of the terrorist combat gear supplied by

Pakistan. The scale of killing, consequently, was directly connected with the gun-power available to the terrorists — and did not recede to the pre-1987 level until the terrorists were finally crushed towards the end of 1992. Nevertheless, there was a comprehensive failure to understand the magnitude of the shift the induction of this new weapon represented. At that time, the police and para-military forces were armed, in the main, with World War II vintage .303 rifles, or the equally obsolete bolt-action 7.62s. The Central Reserve Police Force (CRPF) were marginally better off, with 175 Self Loading Rifles [SLRs] per battalion. But even the SLR was no match for the sheer lethality of the Kalashnikov. With counter-terrorist operations under my charge, I pressed urgently for an upgradation of weaponry at this point. A large number of Light Machine Guns [LMGs], acquired in the pre-Independence era, were lying unused in their original packing in the armories of various police stations all over the state. My demand that they be deployed in the war against terrorism was met with shrieks of horror from the school of thought — comprehending a majority among the central and state leadership, administrators and senior police officers — that adhered to the dogma that a 'civil' police force could not be equipped with 'military' hardware, irrespective of the circumstances. This curious dogma, in the prevailing situation, translated into the proposition that the police must remain inept, inefficient and ineffectual, simply because they were a 'civil' force. It was only after strong personal insistence on my part, and against the prevailing wisdom of those in authority, that these weapons were eventually brought out and mounted on key police stations, as well as on escort vehicles of Station House Officers (SHOs) and other frontline police officers.

Even worse than the failure to come to terms with the magnitude and nature of the terrorist challenge was the inchoate and utterly confused philosophy of the 'political solution' that still dominated even the thinking of the police leadership. The then DGP openly expressed the belief that the police could not wipe out terrorism, but was only in a position to "control it".[16]

In the meanwhile, 'political solutions' remained very much in vogue even after the dismissal of the Barnala government in May 1987. Earlier, with the appointment of Siddharth Shankar Ray as

Governor, and of Julio Ribeiro as DGP in early April 1986, the Centre had begun to publicly advocate the 'hardline' against the terrorists. By May, 1986, moreover, while the lame duck Barnala government continued to preside over Punjab, law and order was directly overseen by the Centre and a policy of competitive brinkmanship between various parties at the Centre and the state ensued. The Centre continued with the two-faced tactics of attempting to strike 'deals' with various factions of the militants, even as it sought to mount pressure on them through police action. The selective immunity consequently granted to some terrorist groupings, the shifting strategies of 'negotiation' opened out with various known extremists, including, prominently, the 'Jodhpur detenues' — surviving associates and supporters of Jarnail Singh Bhindranwale who had been arrested during Operation Bluestar — and a range of unprincipled political stratagem constantly muddied the waters for the police.

Nevertheless, the police had begun to commit itself for the first time in this long-drawn war — and the conflict had certainly escalated to the level of warfare now. Between May, 1987 and April, 1988 terrorists killed 1533 people in Punjab (a monthly average of over 127), including 109 policemen. In turn, 364 terrorists were also killed. But the vacillating and directionless policies of the government, and the complete inability, indeed visible reluctance, of the state to impose the rule of law - even in cases of the worst acts of terrorism and where the perpetrators were apprehended by the police - swelled the ranks of terrorist forces. Terrorism, which had, in the past, largely been restricted to the districts of Amritsar and Gurdaspur, now had another four districts- Hoshiarpur, Jalandhar, Ludhiana and Faridkot — firmly in its clutches.

The government, however, persisted in its opportunistic quest for just any kind of deal with the terrorists to the very end. On March 4, 1988, 40 high profile prisoners — the Jodhpur Detenues, including Jasbir Singh Rode — were released as part of another compromise with terrorists. They simply walked into the Golden Temple, where Rode was installed as the *Jathedar* (head priest) of the Akal Takht [which was part of the deal]. Shortly thereafter, the terrorists began to build up internal defences within the Temple around the *parikarma* [which certainly was not].

The terrorist response to the Government's "goodwill gesture" was unequivocal. An unprecedented 288 people — including 25 policemen — were killed in March and another 259 [including 25 policemen] in April.

With nothing left to trade, and 2866 lives [2207 civilians, 177 policemen, 482 terrorists] already sacrificed at the altar of the false god of 'political solutions between October, 1985 and April, 1988, the Centre decided that it was finally time to enforce the laws of the land. This time, however, it was not the army that was called in. Operation Black Thunder[17] was executed squarely under the charge of the Punjab Police — backed up by the elite anti-terrorist force, the National Security Guard [NSG] and para-military forces. Its objective was identical to that of Operation Bluestar — to clear the Golden Temple of the entrenched terrorist forces. Unlike Bluestar, however, this was achieved in a clean, economical and near-bloodless action, executed under the fullest glare of the media — both national and international — within a week between May 11 and May 18, 1988.

II

In the overall context of terrorism in Punjab, Black Thunder was only a minor operation. Nevertheless, its impact, in certain aspects, was critical. Though only a fraction of the terrorists operating in the state were apprehended in the Temple, it generated crucial structural transformations in the terrorist movement. After Black Thunder, and the macabre exposures relating to the activities of the extremists in the Temple, the movement for Khalistan could never recover the facade of religiousity that had attended it in its early years, and became increasingly and manifestly criminalised. Moreover, the *Gurudwara* as sanctuary and safe-house for terrorists and their leaders ceased to exist. It had been shown to be uniquely vulnerable to a pattern of police action that would not agitate the devout, and would inevitably force the renegade into police custody. The damage done to the extremist cause was tremendous.

> ....the most significant.... was the loss of the Golden Temple and the Gurudwaras as shield and sanction. Rape, extortion and murder had been the business of the

> terrorists from the very beginning of the movement; but in its initial phases, and right up to the Black Thunder period, the top leadership was apparently distanced from these activities, concentrated as they were in the Golden Temple. Their depravity and vice in the hallowed place remained unknown to the larger mass of Sikhs; and while lesser terrorists were often seen to 'stray from the path', the highest motives could still be ascribed to the militant leadership
> Divested of the sanctuary of the Golden Temple and the Gurudwaras, the leadership was forced to live life as fugitives in the Punjab countryside; on the one hand, their own deeds exposed them, and on the other, the deeds of their followers compromised them even further, since they were now believed to be condoned, even encouraged, by these leaders.[18]

I had assumed charge as Director-General of Punjab Police less than three weeks before Operation Black Thunder.[19] After the successful execution of the Operation, I found, under my command, a police force far from triumphant in this victory; deeply divided and demoralised; ill-equipped, organisationally, materially and mentally, to confront the larger challenge of eradicating terrorism from the entire state. I had been serving in the state, but for a brief interregnum (October 1985 - June 1986), since September 1984, in various capacities that gave me state-wide jurisdiction, and I was more than familiar with the difficulties encountered by the forces in Punjab. Specifically, the problems that required immediate redress, and the steps taken to tackle them - albeit gradually, and in a process that was often frustrated by the lack of means and support from the political leadership — included:

(i) Inadequacy of the police stations to react to terrorist violence on their own: The problem here involved manpower and training, weapons, transport and communications. In most cases of terrorist action, the local *thana* (police station) would call for back-up from headquarters or the para-military forces, and no action would be taken till better equipped reinforcements arrived. The inevitable delay rendered subsequent action more or less infructuous. It was clearly necessary to minimize response time at the local level by an enhancement of the *thana's* capabilities. An across-the-board upgradation of all police stations was, of course, financially unviable and would have proven extremely wasteful. An exercise was carried out to identify the police stations most affected by terrorist activity, and to define the specific weaknesses of each of these. Many required upgradation in terms of the officers in charge, and officers up to the rank of Deputy Superintendent of Police were placed in charge of some sensitive thanas instead of Sub-Inspectors. Then came the question of the necessary wherewithal to confront the terrorist. With the right person in charge, additional manpower and improvement in working conditions, communications equipment, and mobility were the next priorities. But none of these would be of any use without the necessary firepower.

Shortly before Black Thunder, a decision had already been taken to equip the CRPF with SLRs and Automatic Loading Rifles (ALRs), and also to increase the number of holdings of LMGs, and the weapons were airlifted from Delhi to Punjab in April itself. The effect of this upgradation of weaponry was immediately visible in the increased capabilities of this force to repulse terrorist attacks, and to confront the militants on a relatively equal footing. Unfortunately, the Punjab Police was still equipped with the old .303s. To the extent that I conceived of this force as the core of the anti-terrorist campaign, this was clearly unacceptable. In 1987, as stated before, unused LMGs lying at various police stations in Punjab had been brought out and mounted on sensitive police stations, as well as on the escort vehicles of the station house officers of various sensitive *thanas*. The LMG, however, clumsy and heavy as it was, was hardly a suitable counter to the AK-47; nor could a couple of LMGs in each police station secure the necessary counter to the thousands of AK-47s then in circulation with the terrorists.

Even after Black Thunder, it remained difficult to

convince the Centre on the urgent necessity of providing the Punjab Police with better weaponry and other equipment. Shortly after taking over as DGP, I had communicated my views on three critical areas of weakness in this regard. The first related to the core problem of upgrading each police station in terms of the specific challenges it was required to confront, with graded improvements in force strength, transport, communications and weaponry. The second problem arose with regard to the protection of individuals who required special security. Such protection was generally poor, and there were numerous cases where people who were being protected were shot down along with their security guards. The third problem related to the force's limited capabilities to carry out night operations.

Unfortunately, while limited *ad hoc* sanctions were made for improvements in communications and transport, resistance to improvements in weaponry persisted. However, some limited improvements were engineered in other critical parameters. A phased recruitment of an additional 25,000 men in the Punjab Police, took the total strength up to 60,000. Limited facilities for housing for police personnel in protected enclaves were created. And some improvements at the *thana* level were initiated through devices that were largely dependant on man-management and on squeezing the most out of the limited resources available to the police. The objective of the entire exercise of reorganisation and upgradation of the *thanas* was to make each police station capable of reacting immediately and independently to any act of terrorist violence in its jurisdiction, and this was, in substantial measure, secured in all sensitive police stations within the year 1988 itself.

(ii) Extremely unfavourable ratio of operational to static and non-productive force in manpower utilisation: It is a matter of unending amazement to me that when I took over, between 40 to 50 per cent of the 35,000-strong Punjab Police force was, on any single day, tied down to static and entirely unproductive duties. The bulk of this number was immobilized at innumerable *nakas* (barricades) all over the state, particularly in the cities and at checkpoints on the highways. These barricades, at best, helped create the illusion of security among the general public through massive and visible police presence; at worst, they provided terrorists with easy targets for drive-by shootings, or for a 'weapon-snatching' raid. Even in my early days in Punjab, I had taken up the matter with some of my colleagues, but to convince officers of the Punjab Police that this was a waste of human resources was difficult. Even those who were convinced said that it was impossible to dismantle and disband the pickets, since the political leadership thought this to be the best strategy for policing.

Nothing could be more wasteful of the available manpower. If ever a terrorist was apprehended or shot in an encounter at these barricades, it was only the result of inordinate stupidity on his part. Not only was the concept of police pickets and barricades passive and manpower intensive, it was completely cost ineffective and irrelevant in terms of the results it secured. In the months following Black Thunder a large proportion of the personnel trapped at these *nakas* was rapidly reallocated to create an operational force that comprised as much as 85 per cent of the total personnel available.

The reallocation of forces and infrastructure also involved a number of innovations, one of them being the formation of mobile-cum-*naka* contingents — essentially mobile units which would move in terrorist areas to ensure significant police presence. Another innovation, and one that created an enormous psychological impact on the ground, was the concept of 'focal point patrolling' under which all available vehicles in the district were brought to a single location, creating an impression of massive force and a level of saturation and mobility that did not, in fact, exist. Meetings were called by senior officers, at the levels of IG and the DG, late in the night, and in the most sensitive areas; since all subordinate officers in the district were required to be present at such a meeting, many vehicles and a substantial force would cluster at these locations. The impact of a significant, even though transient, mobile police presence in areas which had previously seen little police action, and at night, was enormous.

(iii) Infiltration of the police by elements sympathetic to the terrorist cause, and deep communal divisions within and between various police and para-military units: Communal propaganda that was rife in the state for the past many years had certainly had an impact on the forces. The PAP had a fairly large number of sympathisers in its ranks, as did sections of the Punjab Police. On the other hand, the para-military forces, drawn as they were from outside the state, and with only a small proportion of Sikhs in their ranks, tended to display a strong anti-Sikh bias. These attitudes inevitably spilled over into the general public, and the common man reacted on a purely communal basis to the personnel of each of the security forces operating in their areas. The inherent contradictions of the prevailing situation led to a lot of suspicion and mounting tension between the Punjab Police and contingents of the various para-military forces in the state. Indeed, in June 1986, Punjab Police personnel had clashed openly with the CRPF at Amritsar, and, at one point, it appeared that there would be an exchange of fire.

There were two distinct elements in this problem: the one, of course, involved individuals who had been swayed by the sustained fundamentalist propaganda of the past decade; the other was structural, involving the interaction, or, more accurately, the lack of interaction between various security forces operating in the state.

It was essential to segregate compromised elements within the Punjab Police and PAP from anti-terrorist work, and to reduce their involvement in sensitive duties. It was equally essential to do this discreetly, in order not to exacerbate communal sentiments. A continuous exercise was carried out to identify and allocate personnel, whose loyalties were suspect, to duties that would not undermine anti-terrorist operations. Another priority was to ensure that officers selected to lead in various theatres of the low intensity war in Punjab were free of communal bias, and acutely conscious of the dangers posed by fundamentalist thinking to the social fabric of the state.

The structural conflict between various wings of the security forces appeared to be a more complex problem, but yielded to solutions that were fairly simple. During my charge as IG PAP & Operations at Amritsar I had already initiated, at the local level, a process of correction. The core of the problem was that the various forces were acting in isolation from, often in competition with, each other. There was no sharing of information, and deep-rooted suspicion of the actions of the other units. The Punjab Police, moreover, was extremely resentful of the presence of the CRPF, and over the fact that it was the local force that was being painted as villains by the general public. There was also the natural tendency for each force to regard its own work as the most important. It was clearly necessary for each force to know what the other was doing, and was clear about its own and the other's role. This was simply not happening. For instance, even where the CRPF caught a terrorist and handed him over to the PP for interrogation, the intelligence acquired through questioning would not be shared with the CPPF. To counter this trend, joint interrogation teams were created, and a system established to share available intelligence between all forces engaged in the anti-terrorist campaign. In Amritsar, moreover, a process had been initiated dovetailing the operations of the Punjab Police and the CRPF. Over a period of time, the two forces began to fight as one, achieving levels of coordination and cooperation under fire that made their earlier hostility and suspicion seem irrational, even unreal. These strategies were now extended with similar salutary effect across the state, and one of the most important components of this exercise was the induction of selected officers from outside the Punjab Police cadre to take care of Operations at all levels. At one time, the IG Operations was from the CRPF and was also looking after the Punjab Police, permitting greater coordination of forces and a systematic re-organisation on the ground.

(iv) Near-complete absence of systematic intelligence gathering and analysis: Successful counter-terrorist strategies are based on accurate and detailed intelligence on terrorist networks and activities. It was only towards the end of 1984 that the framework of something resembling an effective counter-terrorist intelligence apparatus was set up in Punjab. As stated earlier, even the routine practice of record keeping in connection with terrorist crime was entirely neglected by the Police administration in the early years of the terrorist movement. The skeletal structure of an intelligence operation was created under my charge as IG Operations after September 1984. Officers were 'borrowed' from the para-military forces and from the PAP, records relating to terrorist crimes were prepared, and investigations started. After Black Thunder, intelligence operations went much deeper. It was no longer adequate to carry out an analysis of terrorist movements at the state level; what was required was details at the ground level in each police jurisdiction — down to the level of each police station in the main affected areas. Police stations were first identified and categorised as A, B and C grade, on the basis of the intensity of terrorist activities. Then a village-wise analysis was carried out. Certain villages were seen to be much more active in their support to terrorism, not only in terms of recruitment to terrorist ranks, but also by way of giving shelter and providing information and material assistance to the terrorists. Gradually, unique patterns emerged from the surface uniformity of terrorist operations across the state. Gangs and their main operatives were identified, their strength determined, their primary, secondary and tertiary spheres of operation defined, their relationships of cooperation and hostility with other gangs documented. Detailed information was also gathered on sources and flows of weapon supplies, networks of safe-houses, harbourers and sympathisers, cross-border routes of ingress and egress, and a large body of corroborated data based on surveillance operations, informers, interrogations and the progressive infiltration of many of the terrorist gangs. By early 1989 itself, a fairly clear, accurate and continuously updated picture was available on the jurisdiction, membership, activities, strategies and networks of each of the major gangs operating in the state. A continuous system of documentation and analysis, and of dissemination of all received intelligence was also introduced shortly after my assumption of command as DGP, and periodic intelligence reports were received by all senior officers of the police and para-military forces in the state.

(v) Absence of a coherent strategy of response to terrorist activity: Successes in counter-terrorist operations prior to 1988 were largely the result of extraordinary initiatives on the part of individual and exceptional police officers. By and large, the terrorists controlled the field, striking at will, and often simply walking away from the scene of the crime. Occasional pursuit and engagement by courageous security men produced occasional successes. Nothing approximating a systematic and independent response strategy at the state level could be identified.

On the basis of the enormous intelligence exercise initiated after Operation Black Thunder, however, it became possible to carry out operations that were area, gang and terrorist specific. The initiative progressively passed out of the hands of the terrorists, and into those of the security forces. No doubt, the terrorists retained the capacity to organise unpredictable and entirely random strikes against soft targets; six years after the defeat of terrorism in Punjab, they still possess this capacity. What they lacked, however, was the impunity of operations that they commanded in the past. Each major strike by the terrorists was followed up with major counter-terrorist operations. The responsible group was targeted not only in the Punjab, but in their safe-houses all over the country. The detailed information available of their possible escape routes — including shelters with the extended families of each terrorist, extended families of terrorists who had been killed in the past, key sympathisers and harbourers — made it possible to mount surveillance and concerted pursuit operations that, even where they did not result in immediate arrest, paralysed individual terrorists and prominent groups, reducing their capacity to act in future.

(vi) The failure of police leadership: The police was being 'led from behind'. Senior officers sought to run operations by remote control, minimising their own exposure to risk. The result was that, while deployment of forces was worked out on paper, there was little or no direct assessment at the senior level to see that orders were implemented on the ground, and no accountability for failures to check terrorist activities within their jurisdiction. As the same attitude percolated down to the field level, even the most routine police and security functions began to be totally neglected. The low casualty figures among security force personnel and terrorists in the pre-1988 phase tended to reflect, at least in part, a tacit arrangement between a majority among the police and the militants that they would not cross paths. Two parallel elements constituted the strategy to create an active and accountable police leadership. One involved a radical policy of postings and promotion through which sensitive areas and critical anti-terrorist operations were headed by officers (often very young officers) who were willing to confront danger and take strong personal initiatives, and most of whom volunteered for these high-risk assignments. A number of courageous officers from other state cadres and from the para-military forces were also brought in at crucial positions, while those whose motivation, loyalty or bravery was suspect simply 'opted out' for softer postings, often on deputation outside strife-torn Punjab.

But even the finest men cannot be asked to risk their lives for a leader who will not lead from the front. Deeply conscious of the honour and responsibility of commanding these men in a crucial war for the nation's unity and integrity, I made it my practice to move constantly across the state, in areas worst affected by terrorism. I had been touring the

> state continuously as IG Operations & (PAP) (September 1985 - October 1986) and as ADG Law & Order (June 1987 - April 1988), directing and appraising anti-terrorist operations — and the response had been most encouraging. These tours constituted a pre-dominant part of my routine throughout the anti-terrorist campaigns in the state, with, on the average, more than twenty-five days of each month spent on the road, journeying again and again, deep into the terrorist heartland.

The combined impact of these measures was enormous and immediate. At one stage, there appeared to be a general consensus — in the media, the public, the political leadership, and even among police officers — that the police were demoralised, cowardly and incompetent to face the challenge of terrorism. I soon found that their 'demoralisation' was, in reality, only the absence of clear directives from above; their 'cowardice' was only confusion caused by conflicting commands, administrative sanctions and political pressures; and their 'ineptitude' reflected only the absence of a coherent strategy and a clear mandate for action.

> People in Punjab's villages spoke of a situation where the police refused to move out of their barricaded police stations after dark; the force's will to fight terrorism, it appeared, had been completely broken.
>
> The appearances were deceptive. What had been lacking was a clear mandate, and a freedom to carry on the battle without crippling political interference. Throughout the era of the ascendancy of terror, virtually every hard-core terrorist had a political patron; police responses were distorted to such an extent that effective reaction was precluded even in cases where policemen and their families had been specifically targeted by the terrorists. But the will was far from lacking. Within five years, this very force was to spearhead one of the most dramatic victories in the history of world terrorism. The men who were said to have been cowering in their police stations chased the terrorists deep into their own territory; and chased them to their deaths.[20]

These five years, however, saw many reverses, a great deal of perverse, pernicious political meddling, and enormous sacrifice by nameless, faceless and now forgotten *jawans* and officers of the forces that fought the terror.

In the days following Black Thunder, the terrorists ravaged Punjab. 343 civilians were slaughtered in May alone. They included 30 migrant labourers working on the Sutlej-Yamuna canal in Ropar district; another 45 migrant workers gunned down in Punjab and Himachal Pradesh; and 20 killed in a bomb blast outside a temple in Amritsar. These reprisal killings were a demonstration that Black Thunder had not decimated their numbers in significant measure, nor undermined their capacity to strike at will.

But the police made demonstrations of its own. The swift redeployment and reorientation of forces bore immediate results, and the civilian casualty rate fell rapidly. The first six months of 1988 had seen 1266 civilians killed, yielding a monthly average of 211 casualties; in the second half of 1988, 688 civilians were killed — a high figure, but nevertheless a radical improvement — with the monthly average down to 114. The terrorists, moreover, began paying a heavy price. On July 12, 'General' Labh Singh, the head of the Khalistan Commando Force (KCF), at that time one of the most active terrorist gangs, died in an exchange of fire with the police. Avtar Singh Brahma, another dreaded terrorist, was among the 68 terrorists killed that month.

By January 1989, the terrorists had been pushed into a thin strip along the border, with over 70 per cent of their strikes restricted to just three of the twelve districts in Punjab — Gurdaspur, Amritsar and Ferozepur. This proportion was to remain a constant throughout 1989 and well into 1990.

It was only natural to focus attention on this area. In March 1989 a massive composite Special Operation — bringing together the forces of the Punjab Police, the CRPF and the Border Security Force (BSF) — was launched in the entire Mand area (a patch of marshland primarily lying in the Amritsar and Ferozepur districts, but flowing over into Kapurthala and Jalandhar as well), Ajnala, Jandiala, Tarn Taran and Batala (along the river Beas). In a single month, 5280 villages and 8859 farm houses/*behaks/deras* were covered in cordon-and-search combing operations. These special operations became a regular feature in the terrorist heartland, yielding a steady stream of arrests and seizures of arms, ammunition and explosives, and mounting pressures on the extremists that they found it progressively harder to bear. The impact was compounded by highly focused intelligence-based operations, as well as by the effective use of 'spotters' — captured terrorists who helped identify former associates. By May 1989, the anti-terrorist drive had completely blunted the capabilities of leading terrorist groups to strike at soft targets. The organisations that that had been reduced to a negligible presence included the Khalistan Liberation Organisation (KLO), the Bhindranwale Tiger Force of Khalistan (BTFK) and the Babbar Khalsa, the last of which had perhaps the most dedicated and resourceful, and the most dreaded, cadres.

Security operations, however, were not the only problem the terrorists had. Black Thunder had already revealed that a majority of recruits to the terrorist cause were found among common criminals. Their exclusive motivation was crude profit, or the supplementary fruits of the illegal power militancy conferred: access to women, to status within the village, and, at the lower levels, to the minor perquisites of the 'trade' — a motorcycle, dry fruits, liquor — essential components of the idea of the 'good life' in rural Punjab. Inevitably, the movement became highly criminalized and alienated from even those segments of the general population that may, in the past, have supported them. The top terrorist leadership — the two 'Panthic Committees', one that was eventually headed by Dr. Sohan Singh [Panthic Committee (SS)], and the other dominated by Gurbachan Singh Manochahal and Wassan Singh Zaffarwal [Panthic Committee (M)] — was by now based entirely in Pakistan. Both groups were well aware of these developments. Nevertheless, beyond making various 'statements' to cadres in India (as evidenced by 'Press Notes' and by correspondence recovered from terrorists who were arrested or killed) , and issuing exaggerated threats of reprisal against those who were 'defaming' the movement through acts of extortion, rape and the murder of innocents, they chose to do nothing. Their own power, and profits depended on these criminal activities, and they were themselves too deeply compromised for these statements to be taken as anything other than propaganda, and they had simply no impact on the ground.

These were not the only signs of trouble in the rag-tag armies of 'Khalistan'. Violent turf wars broke out between various gangs. There was, of course, already a deep and basic difference at the highest level of leadership, divided as it was between two irreconcilable 'Panthic Committees' (a third 'Panthic Committee', propped up by the Damdami Taksal, was also to emerge later, in September 1989). Pakistani handlers had made repeated attempts to mediate in order to bring about some sort of rapprochement between these groupings, but were entirely unsuccessful. The differences were hardly 'ideological'; indeed, neither group — or for that matter, no individual or grouping in the movement for 'Khalistan' — was in a position to project anything that could pass off as a coherent ideology. The disagreements were largely a result of the bloody history of conflicts between the various proteges of each Panthic Committee. Equally significant was the distinctive constitution and strategy of these groups: The Panthic Committee (SS) drew its cadres from a relatively educated urban/semi-urban class, and executed operations primarily against marked targets (though there were innumerable exceptions in which the general public was victim to their violence). The Panthic Committee (M), on the other hand, drew its support from rural Punjab and was dominated by the illiterate and semi-literate; by and large, their 'strategy' was to create as much chaos as was possible through completely indiscriminate killings. With their emphasis on 'soft targets', groupings allied to the Panthic Committee (M) were responsible for a preponderance of the major terrorist actions in the 1988 and 1989 period, although its major striking arm, the BTFK, had suffered enormous losses by mid-1989.

All this, however, was at a plane well above the murk and depravity that marked the daily dealings of terrorist groups. Here, the hard currencies of exchange were control over the narcotics trade and gun-running; disputes did not arise out of ideologies, religious principles, or tactical disagreements; personal ambition and greed were the motives in ascendancy.

These factors helped the security forces tremendously, as traditionally sympathetic sections of the population in Punjab grew progressively disillusioned with the terrorists. The disillusionment extended to the rank and file of the terrorists as well, many of whom had visited Pakistan and seen the decadence and corruption of their 'Chief Generals', and others who saw the outright criminality of their immediate leadership within Punjab.

The terror in the state had, till this point, been absolute. Public cooperation with the police was meagre, and even in the case of orchestrated public executions by small terrorist gangs, there was virtually no protest or resistance from the people at large. But all this began to change towards the middle of 1989. Since at least some of the police weaponry had been upgraded after Black Thunder, there were a substantial number of discarded .303 rifles available in police armouries. A Village Defence Scheme (VDS), and a system of appointing Special Police Officers (SPOs) was devised. The objective was to arm volunteers in vulnerable villages to resist terrorist action at the local level. The scheme was far from an immediate success. When I visited a village in Jalandhar District after a number of killings there, I called the village elders and suggested that the police could arm volunteers so that they would not be as susceptible to sudden terrorist raids in future. The response was outright refusal. The villagers were afraid that the terrorists would selectively target the armed villagers, or even the entire village, if any sign of resistance was shown. Nevertheless, repeated visits over the following months and persistent efforts by senior officers eventually bore fruit, and some villages responded positively. Volunteers were trained in weapon-handling, and a number of gun license-holders were also involved; detailed tactical plans were drawn up for the defence of each village; bunkers were built; initially, small police contingents were also provided at night to buttress the local initiative. SPOs, often army or police veterans, were placed in charge of each village operation. A great deal of effort was expended to ensure that an effective apparatus of self-protection was created, and that the scheme did not degenerate into a cosmetic exercise in morale building. By April 1989 itself, 2350 weapons had been distributed in 451 villages, and the VDS was to play a significant role to the very end of the war against terrorism.

There were other signs, small but nonetheless significant, of the turning tide. On June 6, a bus was hijacked by terrorists near village Talwandi Ghowan, PS Kathunangal, in the Majitha Police District, Amritsar. The Hindu passengers were forced off the bus and were about to be executed, when two Sikhs, Avtar Singh and Rajwant Singh, intervened to save their lives. They were shot dead, and two other passengers were seriously injured. The incident generated a great deal of revulsion against the terrorists among Sikhs in Punjab. Then again, just a month later (July 7), when a terrorist opened indiscriminate fire in the Tarn Taran bazaar, he was over-powered and beaten to death by the shopkeepers — an event virtually unimaginable even a few months earlier in this heartland of the terrorist movement.

The combined impact of the pressure exerted by security forces and the slow but definitive changes in the public response provoked a panic among the leadership in Pakistan and their Pakistani handlers. In March, Manochahal sent written instructions to his followers directing them, among other things, to make hideouts in other states because of the pressures in Punjab; he also instructed his top leaders to go underground to avoid any further killings, as it was becoming increasingly difficult to get new recruits. In April, another letter followed up with instructions to create hideouts in Delhi and in far-away Bidar in Karnataka; a key operative, Satnam Singh 'Chinna' was ordered to remain underground, lest he was killed. Wassan Singh Zaffarwal similarly issued warnings against the infiltration of government agents in his gangs and urged his 'Generals' to step up falling recruitment. By May, militants were being advised to use new routes to smuggle weapons across the border. Jammu & Kashmir, Rajasthan and Gujarat were identified, and major recoveries of weapons intended for Punjab were shortly to be made in Rajasthan. By July, moreover, a number of hard-core and listed terrorists had moved out of the Punjab and set up operations in the Terai region of Uttar Pradesh, not as a measure to expand their areas of operation, but to escape the increasing pressures in Punjab.

The pressure also forced a change in tactics and weaponry. Militants in Punjab were advised to increasingly resort to the more surreptitious device of the timed or remote controlled plastique explosive device rather than the AK-47, which required them to be present at the moment of execution. Explosive handling became an integral part of training in the camps across the border after

April, and some of the first significant seizures of plastique explosives and sophisticated IEDS and timing devices were made in May. See Fig. 2.

The flood of weapons in the state also assumed new and disturbing proportions. Till this point, weapons acquisition had to be financed by the terrorists themselves through extortion and narcotics smuggling. Suddenly, in July, messages were sent out that weapons "which had accumulated in Pakistan for which no payment is to be made" could be acquired by the simple expedient of sending "large numbers" of terrorists across the border.

Since the beginning of the year, the terrorists had mounted a sustained propaganda campaign to pressurise SPOs, Punjab Home Guards [PHGs] and policemen from rural Punjab to resign their jobs on pain of death, and to stop participating in the campaign against militancy in the state. In March alone, some 60 Home Guards surrendered their arms and left their jobs. A steady trickle of such desertions was to continue in the months to follow. What was amazing, however, was that despite a mounting campaign of targeted killings against them, the number remained insignificant. This remained true even after September when the campaign was extended to organised attacks on the members of the families of policemen — despite mounting losses, the force gave no quarter.

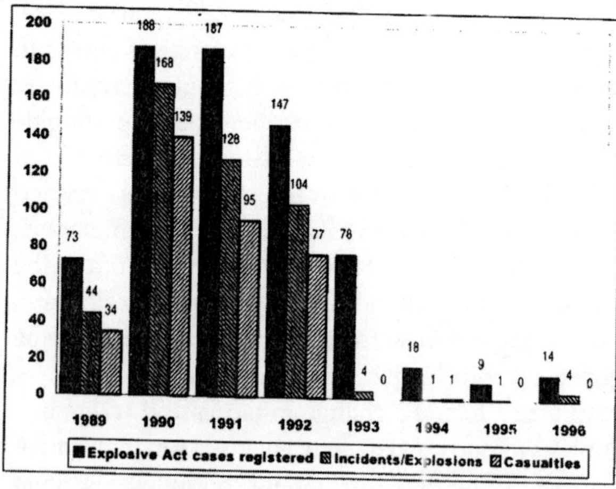

Fig. 2. Trends in terrorist acts involving explosives in Punjab.

The augmentation of the terrorist arsenal led to a substantial escalation of terrorist activities. But civilian casualties were held firmly down throughout 1989, even as the losses inflicted on the terrorists, and by them on the police, mounted. Pakistan was strenuously and openly directing the terrorist campaign at this stage, to the extent that terrorist training camps were being organised even within 75 metres of the international border (in the Ferozepur sector). Border crossings remained a continuous and daily occurrence along the 533 kilometre long international border Punjab shared with Pakistan, and could never really be effectively checked, despite 122 kilometres of fencing that had been erected by August 1989.

However, exhaustion, the impact of a continuous depletion in their ranks, declining trends in recruitment and critical casualties among their leaders had taken their toll. Inspite of every effort on the part of their Pakistani patrons, the morale of all the terrorist groupings active in the state had taken a beating. Tentative feelers were now being sent out. One by one, all the major terrorist factions approached me for a face-saving solution. They wanted to negotiate surrenders — and were willing to do so on their knees, as long as they were not publicly humiliated, and as long as they could escape the extreme penalties their actions over the past years would attract under the normal course of justice.

Their various proposals were routed by me to Delhi.

In the meanwhile, the campaign continued. By the end of the third quarter of 1989, a fairly high rate of civilian, terrorist and police casualties notwithstanding, the militants had been pushed inexorably into a corner. Almost 76 per cent of all terrorist incidents in 1989 were contained within four police districts along the border (out of a total of 15 police districts in the state)[21]: Majitha, Tarn Taran, Batala and Ferozepur. More significantly, of the fifteen police districts in the state, 10 were only marginally affected by terrorist activities, with several months in the year passing without a single killing there. At the end of the year, four of these districts had an average civilian casualty rate of *less than* two a month; in another six districts, casualties ranged between 2-5 a month. It was only in the four 'core districts' that the average rate ran into the double digits.

Even within these districts, the terrorists' sway was not absolute. By the 4th quarter of 1989, just 13 police stations accounted for nearly 65 per cent of all terrorist crime [and 64 per cent of civilian casualties] in these critical districts. And out of the 217 police stations in the entire state, nearly half the killings had taken place within the jurisdiction of just these 13 police stations.[22]

I was then, and still remain, absolutely convinced that terrorism, at this juncture, could have been wiped out in the state of Punjab within another six months of sustained campaigning.

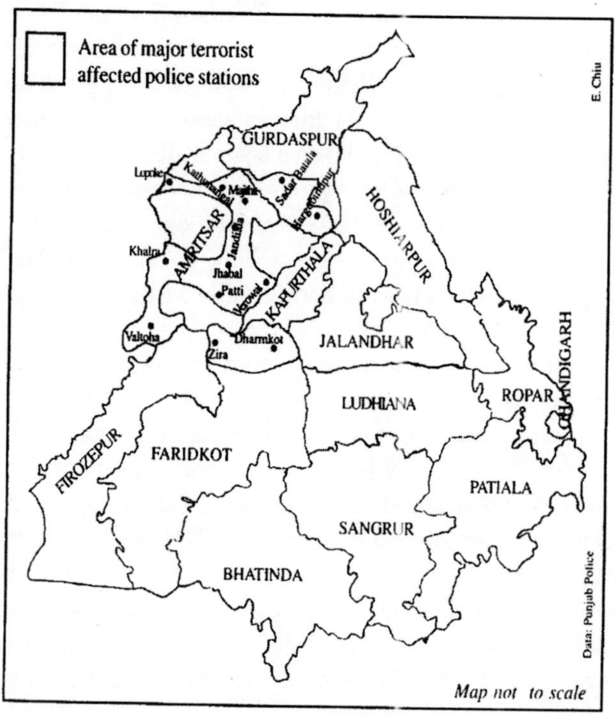

Fig. 3. Major Terrorist Affected Areas in the 4th Quarter of 1989.

III

Politics, however, was destined to intervene once again. At a time when the militants were imploring the government for a general amnesty with greater passion and urgency than had ever attended their demands for Khalistan, the Centre refused to respond. A general election was now imminent, and a deeply discredited regime, swamped under charges of corruption and nepotism, sought to play on popular insecurities. Terrorism became the critical issue of its election campaign — the Congress-I alone, it proclaimed, could defend India against the menace of militancy. At this juncture it appears that the party leadership believed it could profit by allowing the sore to fester a little longer. Once it returned to power, of course, the Punjab problem would be sorted out soon enough.

The moment passed. Soon it became amply evident that the Congress-I would not return to power at the Centre. The offers of conciliation petered out as the militants decided to bide their time.

The announcement of elections itself had a destabilising impact in Punjab. Unmindful of the critical juncture at which the anti-terrorist campaign stood, and the inherently unstable character of the equation that had been established, the Rajiv Gandhi government decided to press ahead for elections in the parliamentary constituencies in this state as well.

The All India Sikh Students Federation had, by now, decided to complement its underground activities with an over-ground role. It combined with Simranjit Singh Mann's pro-militant United Akali Dal [UAD], and the extremist front organisations swept the poll, with 10 of the 13 seats going to candidates backed by the alliance. Before demitting office, Rajiv Gandhi ordered the release of Simranjit Singh Mann, and of Harminder Singh Sandhu and Atindar Pal Singh of the AISSF. All cases against them were arbitrarily dropped to give expression to what was then, perhaps, a proposition unique to Indian justice administration, that a man elected to Parliament may not be tried for any crime that he may have committed.

The war against terror, as with all wars, is fought as much in the minds of men as it is on the field of battle. The V P Singh government that took oath of office on December 6, 1989, brought with it preconceptions, attitudes and a pervasive confusion that surrendered the initiative to the terrorists even before they engaged.

The defining incident with regard to this Government's policy on terrorism occurred within the first week of its installation. The daughter of the newly appointed Home Minister was kidnapped in Kashmir (on December 11, 1989) by what was then an incipient terrorist movement in that state. The government's response was absolute capitulation — and, within days, Kashmir simply exploded into a full-blown insurgency that is still to be brought under control.

The message to extremists all over the country was abundantly clear: This government had neither the will nor the understanding to define and implement a cogent and resolute policy against terrorist violence.

V P Singh's policy orientation to terrorism in Punjab was, in all its simplicity, comprehended by the expression frequently used by him: 'healing hearts' he believed, was all that was needed. Two of his most prominent advisors, ethnic Punjabis, but completely alienated from the peculiar politics of the state and inconceivably ignorant of the nature and magnitude of the terrorist threat, were quite convinced — and apparently succeeded in convincing their Prime Minister that terrorism had long been kept on an artificial respirator by the Rajiv Gandhi regime. With the election of the Janata Dal government, it would simply 'wither away'. All that was required was a little symbolism, a few sympathetic, sentimental gestures, and the violence, the terror, would melt away.

The first gesture came a day after the swearing in, when V P Singh visited the Golden Temple. This was followed by a public meeting at Ludhiana on January 11. No concrete strategy, approach or plan for the resolution of the state's problems was defined either on these occasions, or later. The government simply embarked on a policy of prevarication and drift reflecting an abject failure of political understanding and will.

While the government dithered, terrorist-affiliated overground organisations initiated an unprecedented secessionist campaign that was to reverse all the gains of the preceding years. For over five years (since Bhindranwale's death) the movement had been divested of a public voice, speaking only the language of the bullet and the bomb. Even those among the people of Punjab who may have been sympathetic to the extremist cause had only two possible roles to play — either to take up the gun themselves, or to harbour and support those who did — and in each, they were pushed well beyond the pale of the law.

But now elected Members of Parliament spoke openly of 'Khalistan'. Harminder Singh Sandhu, immediately after his release, had declared that Khalistan was the exclusive goal of the AISSF, and that his organization would talk to the new V P Singh government "only through the aegis of the United Nations".[23] By January, Mann had also declared that there was no question of holding talks with the Centre. Soon, he was talking of a plebiscite or referendum to be held under UN supervision to determine the status of the Sikh people.

A closely coordinated and aggressive agitational programme was simultaneously launched in collaboration with escalating terrorist activities. A document recovered after a BSF encounter on February 17, containing a 13-point directive from Wassan Singh Zaffarwal to Mann revealed the essence of this strategy. The operative part of the directive was that while the common goal was unquestionably Khalistan, *morchas* could be launched to achieve other limited objectives, such as getting the Sikhs registered as a separate *qaum* (nation) under the Indian Constitution, or pressing for the implementation of the Anandpur Sahib resolution, or other specific goals that would help systematically further the cause.

The 'Federation' (the UAD-AISSF combine) now launched an enormous public campaign, backed by high levels of coercive mobilization, that was to create numberless problems for the police and security forces. Calls for *bandhs* became a daily occurrence; *jathas* were sent to court arrest and *gherao* police stations after every police action or arrest of a terrorist. But that was not all. New events were created from day to day — *bhog* (commemorative prayer) ceremonies for every terrorist killed by the police; numberless anniversaries, *shaheedi samagams*, of 'martyrs'; foundation-laying and inaugural rites for commemorative gates, *nishan sahibs* and *gurudwaras* constructed or to be constructed in honour of felled extremists — memorials that had, in the past, never been erected except in the names of the greatest saints of Sikhism. Each of these events became an occasion for the most inflammatory rhetoric, as political and religious leaders addressed the people in the most immoderate terms possible, constructing a false mythology of sacrifice and martyrdom around the death of every common criminal whose reign of terror, extortion and purposeless violence was brought to an abrupt end in an encounter with the security forces. Progressively, moreover, the Gurudwaras in the villages of Punjab — while they could not recover their status as safe-havens for the terrorists — lent themselves to the dissemination of subversive and violently communal propaganda.

It was from these religious and quasi-religious platforms that the new spokesmen for Khalistan began to justify the unjustifiable. Precisely how far they went can be estimated from a statement Mann issued after 13 Bihari migrant labourers — who had no conceivable connection with or interest in the ongoing strife — were gunned down by terrorists at Zira in Ferozepur on May 27, 1990. The killings were condoned by Mann on the grounds that the '*Bhaiyyas*'[24] in the CRPF were 'committing excesses' on the Sikhs in Punjab and were also responsible for excesses committed under Operation Blue Star.

This incendiary mix of politics, religion and intimidation culminated in a campaign of disruption that pinned down ever-increasing numbers of security personnel, progressively reducing the force available for operational duties. Police stations and senior police officials were *gheraod*; roads and railway tracks were blockaded; *bandhs* and strikes paralysed life in urban areas. It was not long before calls for such action emanated — not from their 'front organisations' — but from the terrorists themselves, and were enforced through threats of 'dire consequences' that were widely advertised through press notes (dutifully published by the Press), posters and the public address systems of Gurudwaras. After a point, when a terrorist was killed, the people of the area to which he belonged were simply and routinely directed to observe a 'protest *bandh*' in the advertisements for his *bhog* ceremony itself.

The mobilization of massive crowds for these orchestrated events was a masterful exercise, entirely independent of the popular will. Village *sarpanches* were simply directed to bring a specified number to the tractors-trolleys and trucks that were 'requisitioned' to take the crowds to the day's *gherao* or *bhog*. The public address system of the village *gurudwara* made announcements at night, directing the villagers to report at the appointed hour, with the unequivocal rider that disobedience would be met with dire consequences. Hundreds of trucks[25] and tractor-trolleys carried the captive protestors from one demonstration to another, day after day, throughout this period. Threats were also widely circulated before every protest *bandh* in urban areas. The messages were clear, and compliance, total.

This, of course, is not to say that popular support was totally absent at this stage of the movement. Indeed, such support grew continuously as the mix of religion and politics, the rhetoric of the *bhog* ceremonies and the *shahidi samagams*, touched a sympathetic chord among simple rural folk.

This strategy of quasi-political mobilisation was backed up by a massive and well coordinated campaign by another group of terrorist front-organizations masquerading as human rights activists. 'Fact finding committees' comprising sympathisers or pro-militant politicians were set up after each police operation.[26] At a time when an average of over 200 people were being killed in a month by the terrorists, these 'human rights' activists pretended that every action by the security forces was unjustified. Every terrorist was killed in a 'false encounter' (there was no such thing as a 'genuine encounter' in their lexicon, the words 'false' and 'encounter' went together by definition). Every arrest victimized the innocent. Every action by the security forces was an 'excess', an 'atrocity'. The countryside was rife with stories of these alleged 'police atrocities'; but in every case, they were 'known' to have happened in 'a village nearby', to have been witnessed by a person invariably other than the narrator; they transpired in an indeterminate area of the mind that could not be identified on any map of Punjab, but which existed, at once, everywhere and nowhere.

It was an extraordinary and highly successful campaign. And one that could not, for a single moment, be dissociated from the wave of increasingly focused violence that now began to spill out of the border districts into the space created by the over-ground political activities of the pro-militant groups. This enlargement of the sphere of terrorist activities resulted in a thinner spread of the security forces on the ground. The disruption these tactics caused was far greater than anything the terrorists had, or could have, achieved in the past. Moreover, with the increasing over-ground activities of militant groupings, there was a progressive blurring of lines between the legitimate and the illegitimate. Terrorists openly attended meetings and gatherings called by the UAD and AISSF leaders; and if the police intervened, loud protestations of 'police harassment' were made at the highest levels.

For the police, these were harrowing times. Large numbers were withdrawn from operational duties to cope with the daily campaign of disruption. These demonstrations became effective and highly impenetrable covers for the movement of terrorists and their arsenal, since the police could not engage with a sprinkling of extremists within large gatherings of common citizens, making their task even more difficult. Worse still, The terrorists now directed a virulent and intensifying campaign of intimidation and murder against the security forces, especially in the lower ranks. The objective was to provoke mass desertions, and the strategy was implemented in a highly systematic manner. Initially, a number of intelligence operations were set up by the militants, gathering information on police personnel and their families. Thereafter, threats were issued that, if these personnel did not 'resign', they and their families would be liquidated. The threats were backed by a rising graph of killings of police personnel and their families. The year 1990 alone saw 506 policemen killed — a majority of them while they were at home on leave. 19 members of their families were also killed by the terrorists — a number that was to rise sharply to 134 in 1991, as the terrorists made the families of policemen their favoured soft target in a concerted bid to demoralise the force.

The targeting of police families was the most unsettling of terrorist strategies. Soldiers all over the world risk their lives — but they do so in the security that their loved ones, their parents, their wives, their children, are secure from violence, and that their own actions are in defence of the welfare of their families and community. This is the case, not only in conventional warfare, but also in traditional low intensity conflicts and counter-terrorist campaigns where the army or para-military forces are inducted from regions and communities outside the area of strife. In Punjab, however, the police, the SPOs and the PHG Volunteers were all drawn from the state itself, and predominantly from the very areas worst affected by terrorism. Their actions, their participation in counter-terrorist operations, indeed, the very act of wearing a uniform, exposed their families to unbearable risks, and subjected these men to tensions and pressures that fighting forces are ordinarily not required to confront.

And yet, they did not succumb in any significant measure. With 60,000 men in the Punjab police, another 15,000 PHG volunteers and more than 10,000 men mobilised under the VDS and SPO schemes, barely 600 had abandoned their posts by the end of 1990, a majority among them from the relatively poorly equipped PHG and SPOs. Only a handful of desertions took place in the police, primarily among newly recruited constables.

This is all the more remarkable in view of the State's equivocal posture regarding counter-terrorist operations in this phase, the increasing criticism of police actions by 'human rights' bodies, the media, and even by government agencies and officials, and the extraordinary inducements the terrorists offered for cooperation. Terrorist organisations, at this point, were making fresh recruitments at salaries between Rs. 3000 and Rs. 5000 per month, with a range of perquisites, including huge compensations to families in the event of death, superior weapons and sweeping powers of life and death in their areas of control. The temptation to cross the line must have been overwhelming, especially at a time when (towards late 1990 and through 1991) the victory of the militants was widely believed, both among the people and the more weak-kneed among the political leadership and administration, to be 'inevitable'.

The *morchas*, the *dharnas*, the *bandhs*, the 'human rights' propagandists, the targeted and escalating terrorist violence — all these could have been tackled without difficulty, were it not for the policy of confusion — or perhaps more correctly, the completely absence of any coherent policy — pursued by the government. V P Singh's Prime Ministership was not marked by any significant initiatives in Punjab after the first flourish of symbolism. Instead, the mounting tide of violence and open political subversion was compounded by irrational and arbitrary force withdrawals. When his government was sworn in, there were 288 companies of para-military forces in Punjab, well below the estimated optimal allocation of 306 companies plus 36 companies required for special operations. In March, with an explosive situation emerging in Kashmir, and unmindful of the increasing chaos in Punjab, this number was brought down to 274 companies; out of these, a further 27 companies were allocated under a special contingency plan to the Army, leaving just 247 companies for operations in Punjab. The companies allocated to the Army were gradually released by September, restoring para-military force levels at 274 companies. But several further 'adjustments' were necessitated by the Babari Masjid crisis in Ayodhya, and it was only in November that the force levels stabilised at 283 companies.

The bogey of Assembly Elections in the state was, moreover, kept constantly alive throughout this phase, perpetuating an element of political uncertainty and constant political jockeying between both the over-ground and underground militant groupings. It was only in September, with the extension of President's rule, that the question was briefly settled, only to be reopened shortly after by the Chandrashekhar government.

Meanwhile, the scope of political activity among parties and organizations of (relatively) moderate propensities had been completely eliminated. On May 14, the terrorists made an attempt to kill Gurcharan Singh Tohra, the SGPC President — and a 'moderate' Akali only if the definition was stretched to its very limits — on the Ludhiana-Patiala highway near village Paḥwa. Tohra, an ex-MLA, H S Rajia and a gunman were injured, while the driver of the vehicle died on the spot. Rajia succumbed to his injuries in hospital. Less than a month later, Balwant Singh, an ex-Finance Minister of the state, was gunned down in Chandigarh. The traditional Akali parties simply went into hibernation, and no other national or regional party had, at this juncture, a functional state wing in Punjab.

In any event, the V P Singh government collapsed under the weight of its own internal contradictions after eleven brief and inglorious months of ceaseless crises, including the nationwide conflagration over the Mandal Commission and reservations for backward castes that it conjured virtually out of the dustbin of the government's archives.

The new Prime Minister, Chandrashekhar, heading a minority government with outside support from Rajiv Gandhi's Congress-I, was to preside over another mockery of governance for a further seven months. In Punjab, he took over virtually where V P Singh had left off, broadcasting his willingness to "talk to anyone", including the terrorists.[27]

The Prime Minister's offer of talks was greeted with predictable contempt. Manochahal, voicing what was then the general view held by the militants, issued a 'statement' that any such talks could only be about Khalistan, and would have to be held in Geneva. Wassan Singh Zaffarwal declared that the only issue that was to be negotiated was the proposed boundaries between India and Khalistan. These sentiments were echoed faithfully by the 'human rights' lobby, including General Narinder Singh of the Punjab Human Rights Organization (PHRO), who asserted that no talks for anything less than Khalistan could be held with the Government.

The terrorists, in any event, knew that the government was trying to negotiate on its knees. With its own survival in question from day to day, it had nothing substantive to offer. Moreover, the militants had enormously strengthened their position in Punjab. Only the incurably deluded could possibly believe that they would give away anything as long as they thought they were in a position of control. The spiral of violence had to be broken before any space could be created for a constructive political initiative.

Unfortunately, the political arena at that time appeared to be dominated by the simple-minded or, perhaps, the simply reckless. I was asked to make arrangements for talks with representatives of prominent militant groups. This was done — though I saw fit to warn the Prime Minister that none of them could be trusted to adhere to any commitments they might make in exchange of specific concessions from the government. On the very first meeting, among the first demands to be raised was for my removal from Punjab. The Prime Minister capitulated, and I was transferred to Delhi on December 18, 1990.

I was not privy to any of the discussions the Prime Minister had with the militants. The inescapable fact, however, is that these 'negotiations' had absolutely no impact on the ground. If anything, terrorist violence escalated.

The army had been inducted into the state in November itself in what was called Operation Rakshak I. Plans for the Operation had been detailed much earlier, but after my removal from the state, their eventual execution did not follow the structure of inter-force command and co-ordination that I had envisaged. The result was that Operation Rakshak-I followed the pattern of conventional Army interventions in internal disturbances, certainly exerting substantial pressure on militancy in the border districts— where the bulk of deployment had occurred — but failing to alter the course of militancy in any significant measure. In fact, what Operation Rakshak-I did was to partially squeeze militancy out of the border districts and into virtually the entire state (these trends are discussed in greater detail below).

The Chandrashekhar Government played out its final gamble in Punjab when it forced the state to join the rest of the nation in the mid-term elections slated for June 1991 (though the elections were to be staggered in such a fashion as to allow Punjab to go to the polls well after the process had been completed in the rest of the country). In April, the government announced that elections to the parliamentary and state Assembly constituencies in Punjab would be held simultaneously. The terrorist groupings split down the middle, with those broadly owing allegiance to the Damdami Taksal deciding to participate, and the second group affiliated to the Panthic Committee (SS) deciding in favour of enforcing a boycott.

A large number of the 2146 candidates who filed nominations for the Assembly and Lok Sabha elections were overtly or covertly supported by terrorist organizations. By the time the nominations closed, in any event, even the groups officially boycotting the elections had hedged their bets by surreptitiously putting up candidates. 211 of the candidates had clear terrorist links, and 34 were at that time behind bars. 41 candidates had 'history sheets' (police records) that enumerated offenses including political assassination, hijacking and murder; another 48 were relatives of prominent listed terrorists.

Many of the candidates had refused police protection, declaring that they would make their own arrangements for 'security'. They now began to move openly around the state with large groups of illegally armed terrorists as their 'bodyguards'. In the meanwhile, the Panthic Committee (SS) let loose a campaign of liquidation that was eventually to claim the lives of 27 candidates. On June 7, an explosion damaged the cavalcade of the Minister of State for Home at Gill Road in Ludhiana (the MoS was contesting the Ludhiana Parliamentary seat). On June 15, 74 train passengers were massacred. Yet, the ill-planned and unconscionable gambit for elections in Punjab was not abandoned. It was only after Narasimha Rao was sworn in as Prime Minister of June 21 that this unseasonable elections was eventually aborted.

The irrationality of the decisions inflicted by the Chandrashekhar regime on Punjab persisted to the very end. Despite the enveloping mayhem in the state, the Army had, inexplicably, been withdrawn from the state by this time, and para-military force levels had been cut drastically.

It was during the General Elections of 1991 that Rajiv Gandhi was assassinated. The Congress-I rode back to power on a wave of sympathy, and Narasimha Rao was sworn in as Prime Minister. But the chaos created by the preceding 18 months, during which the declared policy of two successive and singularly incompetent governments was 'winning the hearts and minds of the people', could hardly be contained by an electoral victory at the Centre. The years 1990 and 1991 unambiguously belonged to the terrorists.

Almost as many civilians were killed by terrorists in these two years, as in the preceding 12 — the entire span of the terrorist movement in Punjab. Between 1978 and 1989, there were 5070 civilian casualties; in 1990 and 1991, they were 5058.

The area of conflict now covered the entire state. After Black Thunder, terrorist crime had been confined mainly to the border districts. But by the end of 1991, the 'terrorist heartland' had extended itself from 13 police stations in four border districts

[64.6% of terrorist crime in the 4th quarter of 1989] to over 47 police stations that now accounted for 61 per cent of the greatly enhanced terrorist crime in a widely dispersed area. Only four of the 15 police districts registered a monthly average of civilian casualties below 10. This was easily cancelled out by another four, where civilian casualties were in excess of 20 per month. In Ludhiana, this figure stood at over 44 per month. [See Fig 4]

While the levels of terrorist violence in the border districts remained high, the command centre of terrorist operations shifted gradually to the Malwa region, with Ludhiana and Sangrur as its core. The greater dispersal of terrorist activities was, in substantial measure, intensified by Operation Rakshak-I which exerted a great deal of pressure in the border areas. In the absence of a co-ordinated policy of containment, the top terrorists were gradually 'squeezed out' into the Malwa and Doaba belt. Four border police districts (Tarn Taran, Majitha, Batala and Ferozepur) accounted for 878 killings by terrorists in 1991, as compared to 774 in 1989; this, however, represented a significant decline as against the 1341 civilian casualties inflicted in these districts in 1990. But 1991 also saw 535 civilian killings in Ludhiana (1989: 58; 1990:161), 278 in Sangrur (1989:8; 1990:65), and a total of 2591in the state (1989: 1168; 1990:2467). Distress migrations, which had come down to a mere trickle of ones and twos in a month in 1989, rose to 2524 families through 1990 and 1991 (averaging over 105 families per month).

Viewed in isolation, these figures may suggest that the police and had, once again, withdrawn into a defensive shell in the face of this widening arc of terror. This was far from the truth. Indeed, it was a paradox of the Punjab situation at that time that, while the police (both state and central forces) engaged continually, and while terrorist casualties rose constantly, the killings of civilians also registered sustained and alarming increases.

This was largely due to the renewed successes in terrorist recruitment, which had virtually come to an end in 1989. At that time, the strength of listed and unlisted terrorists was estimated at no more than 1,200. By the middle of 1990, this number had risen upwards of 5,000, and rose above this level throughout 1991, despite the continuous and escalating losses suffered by militant groups. In 1989, under a relatively stable political dispensation,

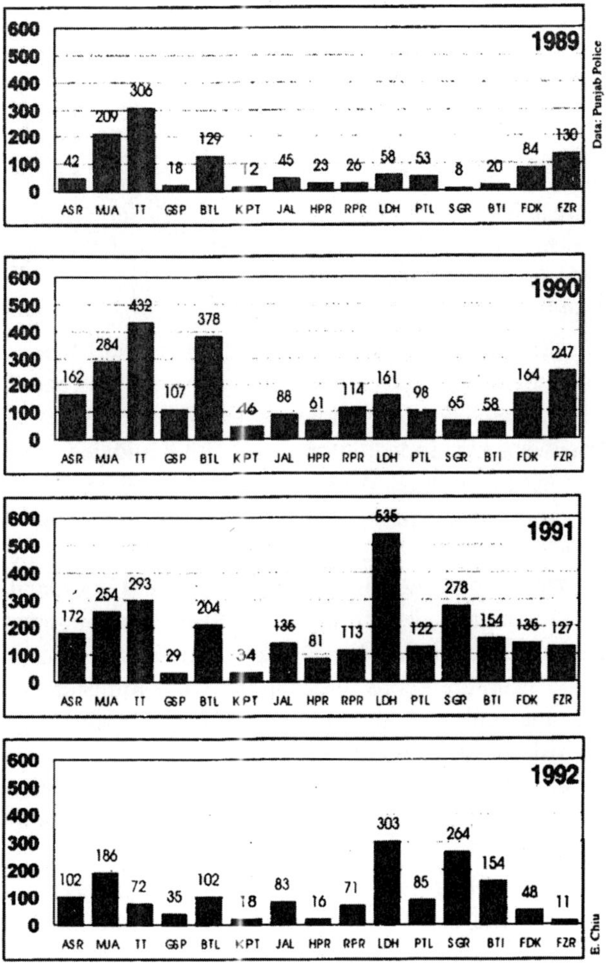

Note: The number of police districts in Punjab was increased to 20 over the period 1990-93. However, all data has been aggregated over the 15 'original' jurisdictions that existed in 1989 to allow for continuity and comparision.

Fig. 4. District-wise trends in civilian casualties.

703 terrorists had been killed, and militancy appeared to have been on the verge of total defeat. In 1990, 1320 terrorists lost their lives, in 1991, another 2177 fell under the 'benign' dispensations of two 'hearts and minds' regimes — and yet, the terrorist movement grew from strength to strength.

While Pakistan had put her whole might behind the Punjab terrorists, the response of the Indian government was marked by indecision, an abject lack of political will, and a yawning policy vacuum. All institutions of the state were in full and open flight; only two forces were operative: the terrorists and the security apparatus, with every other wing of governance paralysed.

There were severe onslaughts on the morale of the security forces by the militants and their over-ground sympathisers. A sustained agitational and propaganda campaign was backed by narrowly targeted terrorist violence. Close relatives of police personnel were kidnapped, intimidated and liquidated, even as police casualties mounted. Worse still, criticism of the police came not only from the media — which had capitulated completely before the 'Panthic Code' that had been enforced by the militants, and that was accepted by the official media, AIR and Doordarshan, as unquestioningly as by the national and regional newspapers (with a single isolated exception)[28] — but from the government as well, on occasion finding its source in the Prime Minister's office itself. For the rank and file, fighting the nation's war at grave personal risk and with enormous losses, there was not a single source of encouragement or succour beyond their own officers. The forces, nonetheless, fought on doggedly, valiantly, and in complete isolation.

There is one final aspect of this phase that requires attention. At this time, the claim that militancy in the state somehow represented the inchoate popular aspirations of the people — specifically of the Sikhs — had acquired substantial force through the over-ground campaign organized by sympathisers. But it was, overwhelmingly, the Sikhs themselves who were the victims of terrorism (See Fig. 5). Moreover, and this is critical, it was the Sikhs — in far larger numbers than ever comprised the terrorist armies — that stood against the movement for Khalistan. 65 per cent of the Punjab police, of course, were Sikhs. But more significantly, there was increasing and organised resistance among civilians against terrorist violence. What had been an occasional instance of individual courage and initiative throughout the Eighties now replicated itself in numberless acts of heroism and sacrifice that challenged the tyranny of the militants. A single index of this swelling popular resistance is the success of the VDC and SPO schemes — initiatives that found few takers in 1989, but which had assumed enormous significance between 1990 and 1991. There were 1075 village defence committees and some 596 SPO pickets functional in the state by the end of 1990, accounting for more than 15,000 volunteers. Despite the overwhelming and highly focused militant assault against them, and the peculiar vulnerabilities of these voluntary forces, the VDCs and SPOs stood their ground even at the end of 1991. The total desertions over these two traumatic years — including VDCs, SPOs, PHGs and the Punjab Police — numbered barely 600.

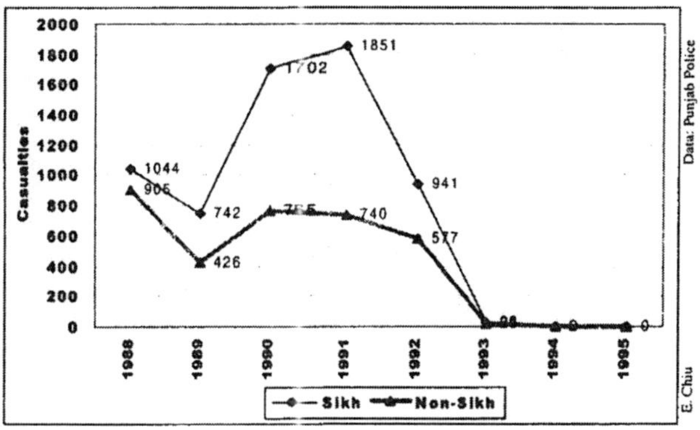

Fig. 5. Sikh and non-Sikh Casualties inflicted by Terrorists.

But the people of Punjab were betrayed by their political leadership and by the Government. The one truth that stands out above all others during this phase is that a confused, irresponsible and ill-informed government that follows a policy of conciliation, even capitulation, in the face of terrorism is the cruelest affliction that a troubled people can be called upon to endure.

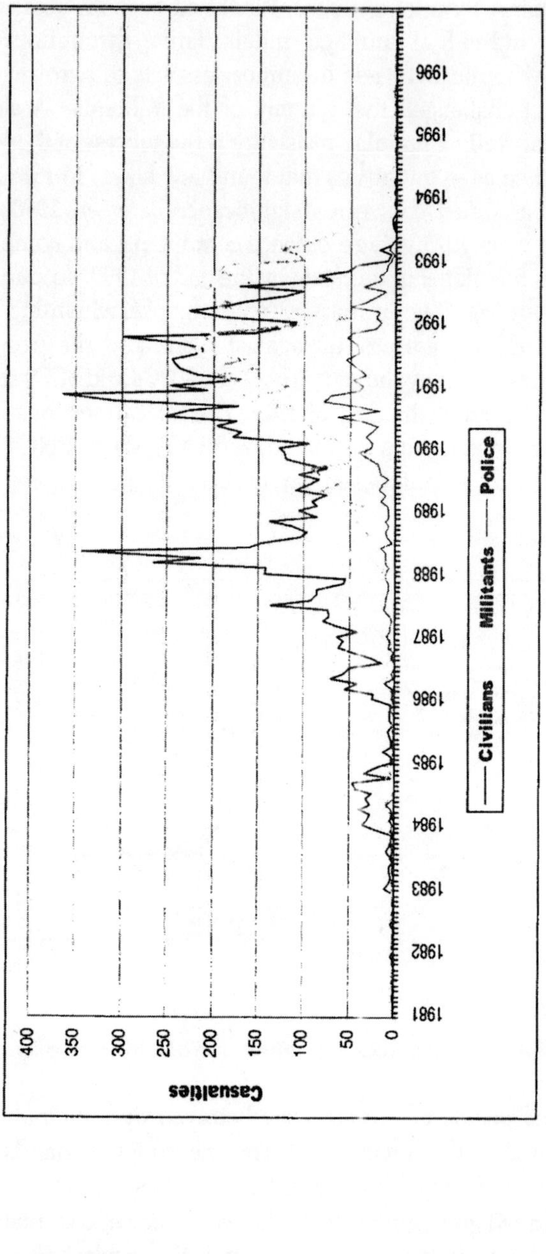

Fig. 6. Civilian, Police and Terrorist casualties in Punjab - 1981-1996.

IV

When the Narasimha Rao Government took over at Delhi, the terrorists were on a roll in Punjab. Their successes over the past eighteen months had spawned dozens of new militant groups and revived many others that had long been defunct. Their armies had grown five-fold. Large masses of the people gathered on their every command. A multiplicity of 'Panthic Committees' claiming to represent the collective will of the 'Sikh people', issued grand proclamations on all subjects — codes of conduct, treatises on morality and 'religious' duties, decrees against the Government and its agencies, stern warnings to the faithless and recalcitrant; they directed punitive strikes and murderous displays of force against those who failed to show due deference to their arbitrary will. True, more of their ranks were being killed; but ever more stood ready to step into the breach. There was an air of absolute certainty, of consummate confidence, that their 'war' against the Indian State was in its terminal stages, that their goal, 'Khalistan', was imminent. 'Governments in exile' appointed themselves in America and the UK; 'Prime Ministers' and 'Presidents' of 'Khalistan' waited in the wings for the impending victory. Brutal turf wars between terrorist groupings grew in number and intensity, keeping pace with the sweep and power of their actions against the people of Punjab and the security forces, as their final goal appeared tantalizingly within reach.

For those who were not there — in the middle of the turmoil, witness and victims to the slaughter, confounded by, or resisting, the swelling enormity of the terror — it is difficult to recall or imagine how close the situation was to complete disintegration.

Nevertheless, the degree to which this anarchy had fed upon the regime of political license, of submission and appeasement of the preceding dispensations became clear as soon as an unequivocal policy was enunciated and implemented on the ground.

When Rao took over as Prime Minister, the very possibility of 'political solutions' in the Punjab had ceased to exist. The various Akali factions, including those openly sympathetic to the militant cause, had been completely marginalized during the aborted elections of June 1991, when the terrorists decided they would rather 'represent' themselves. Simranjit Singh Mann had himself been forced out of that election, though many militant nominees were to contest under the cover of his faction, the UAD (Mann). The other main political leader of the militant cause, Harminder Singh Sandhu of the AISSF, was long dead by this time, murdered by terrorists of the Khalistan Commando Force (KCF), an affiliate of Sohan Singh's Panthic Committee, in January 1990. The 'traditional' Akali parties had, of course, withdrawn into a shell of compliant self-preservation. In any event, with the numerous and continually multiplying factions of political and terrorist groupings in the state, there was no identifiable 'leadership' with whom a dialogue could be initiated, even if the inclination had existed. The terrorists themselves, of course, had no reason to negotiate at this point, convinced as they were that they were poised on the very edge of victory.

An escalation of terrorist violence, at this stage, was inevitable. June itself had seen 245 civilians and 54 security men killed. July, August and September cost another 659 civilian and 123 security men. In October, the violence peaked, with 297 civilian and 53 police casualties. The political compulsions of the Rao Government made a response inevitable, with mounting pressure exerted on the Centre by the Punjab state units of the Congress-I and the Communist Party of India.

In November 1991, the Centre finally took action. The army was re-inducted in Punjab and the forces were given an unambiguous mandate - order had to be restored in the state, and grounds prepared for the election that fell due in mid-February, when the existing Parliamentary sanction for President's rule came to an end. Despite my strong personal objections, I was transferred back to the State as DGP shortly thereafter.[29]

But the elections, this time, were not an enterprise in political adventurism, not a gamble, not a retreat of responsible governance in the face of lawlessness, but an integral element of a coherent strategy for the restoration of Constitutional governance in a state where all its institutions had, for close to a decade, been paralysed or rendered impotent. They were based on a clear recognition that democratic institutions and processes were meaningless in a situation of enveloping terror, and that peace was a precondition

— and not a necessary consequence - of the exercise of popular franchise.

This recognition was translated, in its first expression, into the provision of adequate force in the state, backed by an uncompromising policy of non-interference. Law and order was entrusted to the professional agencies of the state within whose constitutional mandate they fell. There was no back-seat driving from Delhi, no dubious political moves and manoeuvres, no deals with terrorists and their over-ground agencies, undermining strategic and security initiatives. The Government vested a certain, clearly defined, responsibility on the security forces; and the forces did not fail the nation.

What emerged now, was one of the most unique experiments in multi-force counter-terrorist strategic initiatives and integrated command structures.[30] Unlike previous operations, the army and the police (both state and para-military) acted in complete concert, with a clearly defined institutional structure of cooperation and consultation. An officer of the rank of Inspector General (IG) from the Punjab Police was attached to each Corps of the Army deployed in Punjab. A Superintendent of Police (SP) was assigned to each Brigade. Police contingents were attached to every Army battalion, so that comprehensive and coordinated actions could be taken independently by each unit in all emerging circumstances. There was total sharing of all intelligence, to the extent that police control rooms had representatives of the Army present, so that relevant intelligence was passed on a continuous basis to every concerned unit. This interaction was carried right up to the highest level, and I personally coordinated actions with each Corps Commander at Ambala, Bhatinda and Jalandhar. It is a measure of the commitment of the officers of every force involved in this phase of the war against terrorism that no considerations of sub-group loyalty were permitted to undermine the integrity of operations; the entire idea of 'competitive command' — where various agencies vie with each other for 'victories' — which inevitably characterized joint operations in the past, was simply dispensed with, and a new structure of 'cooperative command' emerged. Throughout this final phase of counter-terrorist operations in Punjab, the entire period during which the army was present in the state under

Operation Rakshak-II, I do not recall a single occasion on which this system of cooperative command was compromised by personality clashes or by force loyalties.

The pattern of Army deployment during the run-up to the elections was also significantly innovative. Traditionally, Army commanders have preferred massive presence in specific sensitive locations. During this phase and right through the election period, however, the Army was deployed all over the state; more importantly, it was split up to section level in order to saturate the entire countryside.

Adequate force was also provided for the protection of candidates in the forthcoming elections — a total of 220 para-military companies. An entire platoon was assigned for each candidate's security: a section deployed at the candidate's residence, another as personal escort, and a third that preceded the candidate as an advance party to each scheduled meetings. Once again, the objective was clearly defined — the disorders and selective killings that resulted in the cancellation of the elections of June, 1991 were not to be allowed to be repeated. Despite the commitment of such a large force to these security duties, patrolling also had to be intensified; nevertheless, counter-terrorist operations were still sustained across the state.

The impact on the ground was immediate. In November itself, the number of civilians killed by terrorists fell to 154. Of these, 110 were killed in the first fortnight; the second fortnight, when the Central Government's initiatives were implemented in Punjab, saw just 44 civilian casualties. A number of major terrorist groupings immediately decided to protect their top echelons by advising them to shift outside the state, or even out of India, or to go into a temporary hibernation during which they were instructed to tone up their internal structure and improve operational capabilities.

The elections of February 1992 also forced the militant camp into innumerable strategic failures. The most monumental of these was the decision to impose a boycott on the elections. Goaded by their foreign mentors, as well as by their funding and support groups among non-resident Sikhs in USA, Canada and UK, the terrorists began to believe that if they could force another postponement on the elections, or, failing this, keep voting percentages down below 10 per cent, they would discredit India's democratic credentials. If few voters exercised their right of franchise, they were led to believe, they would be able to convince the international community that this amounted to a 'referendum in favour of Khalistan'. Of all the prominent militant leaders and 'ideologues', the only one to oppose this move for a boycott was - surprisingly, since he was the strongest advocate of a boycott in June, 1991 — Sohan Singh; but his position drew such violent opposition even from his own supporters that he was forced to temporarily flee his safe haven in Pakistan.

Unlike the boycott of June 1991, moreover, there was also eventual unanimity in the militant camp that no Akali faction would be permitted to participate in the elections of February 1992. (Only a single, utterly unknown, faction of the Akali Dal, led by Kabul Singh, eventually participated in the elections).These objectives were secured by a campaign of intimidation. The entire state was saturated with posters, handbills, leaflets, press notes, statements and paid advertisements in selected newspapers, as well as by direct threats to candidates, voters and election officials, warning of reprisals against any act of cooperation with, or participation in, the election process. A 'total curfew' on pain of death was announced by the militants for February 18 and 19 to discourage voting. On February 8, three teachers assigned to election duties were gunned down, and another six were put to death on February 10. In order to terrorise urban voters, 18 explosions were engineered between February 5 and February 19, and attacks against political campaigners claimed 16 lives before the elections. In a final 'warning', 13 spinning mill workers were massacred at Barnala on the night of 17/18 February.

Nevertheless, not a single candidate standing for this election was killed. The election itself passed peacefully, except for one incident in which a grenade was thrown on a Congress-I election office in Ludhiana, killing one person, and injuring twelve.

The voter turn-out was low, no doubt. But it installed an elected government with a comfortable majority in the state. Most importantly, it was a functional government — not a puppet regime. From this point onwards, law and order — and, naturally, counter-terrorist policy — was firmly within the sphere of the state government's responsibilities (unlike the Rajiv Gandhi-Barnala arrangement of 1985-86). For the first time, an extended period of political stability, and planning with at least a five-year perspective, became manifestly possible.

The essence of the state government's policy on terrorism under Chief Minister Beant Singh was an extension of the principles implemented by the Centre in the preceding months. The institutions of Constitutional democracy and governance were to be progressively revived, and to this end, the reign of terror was to be brought to an end. Counter-terrorist operations would not be undermined through any negotiations, pacts or bargains with terrorist groups; nor would the political executive interfere with legitimate police operations, investigations and actions. In my entire tenure under this government, I recall only one instance in which a political 'recommendation' was routed to me; it was in connection with a case of murder, and I wrote on the file that when politics began to intervene in a murder investigation, that would be the end of law and order in the state. There was no subsequent attempt at interference in the duties and responsibilities vested in the police.

The greatest impact of the 1992 elections was that they, once again, banished the terrorists — indeed, the entire movement for 'Khalistan' — into the netherworld of an unambiguously criminal identity as the mask of politics was ripped away. Their over-ground political organizations stood comprehensively discredited in the eyes of the people by this time — essentially as a result of the militants' own stand against them. Had the terrorists themselves — or through their nominees — participated in the elections, they may still have enjoyed the substantial immunities that come with a legitimate political position, and would have been able to participate in a range of over-ground activities which could tie down the security forces — as they had done in the past — and help blur the lines between their criminal and political identities. Now, however, they had entirely forfeited their political voice, and could speak only through the bullet and the bomb — a language that the security forces were well equipped to contend with.

They realized their blunder soon enough. In a desperate damage control exercise, they sought to re-activate the traditional

Akali factions to initiate programmes of mass agitation. A militant-inflicted 'unification' under the banner of the Shiromani Panthic Action Committee (SPAC) sought to bring all over-ground pro-militant and Akali factions on a single platform. The people were exhorted to boycott the Members of the newly elected Legislative Assembly, to prevent the entry of ministers and MLAs in their villages, and to not approach any minister in connection with personal grievances or any other work. The people, frustrated with the many years that they had suffered without redress, ignored their calls; the elected representatives, voting percentages notwithstanding, began to serve precisely the functions that they are intended to in a democratic framework. Within weeks of the election, the supposed mass base of the movement for 'Khalistan' had vanished without a trace.

But the violence persisted. In the days following the elections, 24 voters were killed in separate acts of reprisal in Sangrur, Bhatinda, Ropar, Jalandhar and Ludhiana. In March, the terrorists adopted a new strategy of massive strikes in urban industrial complexes. On March 10, terrorists gunned down 15 executives of a private company in Sangrur. In two strikes at Ludhiana, on March 14 and 18, the terrorists killed 34 industrial workers. On March 21, a similar operation in Ahmedgarh killed 14.

Each shift in terrorist strategy was immediately countered. In the post election period, the army no longer maintained the saturation levels that it had sustained through the elections. The troops, while still deployed in the state, were returned to barracks, and called out only for specific operations — especially to provide rapid-response teams to back up police action, and to provide the outer cordon in search operations. The responsibility for dealing with the new pattern of terrorist actions, consequently, fell squarely on the police. There were some 140 to 150 urban centres in Punjab. Senior officers who were pushing files at Police Headquarters in Chandigarh were mobilized to confront the new challenge, and each of them was assigned four to five such centres. Each centre was divided into sectors along a grid, and vehicles and manpower were allocated for patrolling and pursuit duties along strategic points. With this single device, the threat to urban industrial concentrations was contained.

In April, the terrorists shifted attention to targeted killings of security personnel. The first quarter of the year had seen 54 security men killed. In April alone, the terrorists killed 51 and injured another 73. By August this strategy was to be extended to the most intensive campaign against the police and their families. When Sukhdev Singh Babbar, chief of the Babbar Khalsa International (BKI) — by this time the most powerful terrorist grouping in the state — was killed in an encounter with the police on August 9, 63 family members of policemen were killed in retaliation — forty eight of them between August 9 and 11 itself. In addition, 37 policemen also lost their lives, bringing up the total of these targeted killings to 100 out of the 167 persons killed in the state in that month.

In addition to the police, the terrorists were also targeting political leaders and government officials. There was a car bomb attack on one state minister at Amritsar in May. The son of another minister, and the brother of a third were killed. The most gruesome among this series of targeted actions was the kidnap and subsequent murder of M L Manchanda, the station director of All India Radio at Patiala, on May 27. Manchanda's torso was found in Patiala and his head in Ambala.

The response came in the form of three strategies. The first of these was based on the immediate identification of the perpetrators of the latest outrage, and the application of the fullest force to secure their arrest or elimination.[31] The Manchanda killing is a case in point. The Babbar Khalsa had immediately claimed the killing, in order to impose the militant 'code of conduct' on the government's broadcast agencies. Gurdial Singh Babbar, one of the perpetrators of this outrage, was pursued and killed in an encounter on the same day (May 27), and Amrik Singh Kauli Babbar, who master-minded the kidnapping and killing, met the same fate on June 2.

The second strategy focused on the most important terrorists. An analysis of terrorist strikes had shown, curiously in view of the increasing scope and range of terrorist activities in the state over the past two years, that inspite of their improved striking capacity and mobility, militancy in a majority of cases was highly localized. Even the most important terrorist leaders were found to operate within a radius of no more than 15 to 20 kilometres from their respective villages. With this knowledge, and with continuous intelligence from a variety of forces, it became possible to immobilise, and eventually arrest or eliminate these elements. Consequently, instead of wasting resources on every petty criminal and opportunist who had joined the terrorist ranks, the available manpower and infrastructure was focused disproportionately on the leaders, the planners and the ideologues of the movement. Among the 139 hardcore terrorists who fell to this strategy in 1992 were a dozen self-styled 'Chiefs' and some 20 'Deputy Chiefs' of various terrorist groups, including Rashpal Singh Chhandran, the Chief of the BTFK (June 12), Gurjant Singh Budhsinghwala (July 29), Chief of the KLF, and Sukhdev Singh Babbar, Mukh Sewadar of the BKI (August 10). (One of the last major successes for the security forces was to come in January 1993, with the death of Gurcbachan Singh Manochahal, Chief of the Panthic Committee (M) and the BTFK (M) in an encounter with security forces at Village Rataul in Tarn Taran.)

The third element of the strategic response came, in the wake of the August killings of policemen and their families, in the shape of Operation Night Dominance. Once again, an analysis of the pattern of terrorists activities indicated that an overwhelming majority of the killings in the villages took place in the late evening or very early morning. All senior officers were directed to take personal charge of operations at night. From this point on, these officers would be leading night-ops three or four days in every week — *and* performing their normal duties during the day.

The collective impact of these initiatives was clearly evident by the time the year 1992 came to a close. The situation was so vastly different as compared to the chaos that prevailed at the end of the previous year, that it was possible to speak of a total reversal against the terrorists. The total number of civilians killed in the state in 1992 stood at 1518, as compared to 2591 in 1991, reflecting a fall from a monthly average of 216 to 127. This, however, was not all. The lowest figures in 1991, in the months of November and December, stood at 154 and 126. In 1992, if the year was split into two halves, the monthly average fell to 87 in the second half. In the last quarter, this average stood at 60. In December itself, the total civilian casualties stood at 44. They were never to rise to these levels again. Indeed, in the whole of 1993, civilian casualties *totaled* just 48.

This was not all. A complete transformation had taken place at the psychological level among the people. After the elections of February 1992, the terrorists had failed entirely to elicit any demonstration of support or cooperation from the people of the state. *Bandh* calls, *bhog* ceremonies and other directives emanating from terrorist quarters evoked no response from the public.

The coercion and intimidation that had resulted in the low voter turnout in the elections of February 1992 were also exposed when elections to 95 Municipal Committees in the state concluded peacefully on September 6, with a voter turnout of over 75 per cent. These trends were endorsed when Panchayat Elections were held in the state's 12,342 villages in January 1993, with a voter turnout of 82 per cent. The termination of the Village Panchayats, and their replacement by Khalsa Panchayats had been one of the critical objectives of the terrorist movement.

The transformation went far beyond the return of grassroot democracy and a refusal to cooperate with the militants, to comprehend an enveloping sense of relief. A state that had, for at least the preceding seven years, simply shut down before the sun set, was rediscovering the experiences of peace and normalcy. The markets throbbed with life in the evenings, and cultural events were organised and attended by thousands of people. Distress migrations under threat from terrorists had slowed down to a trickle even at the beginning of the year — a total of 73 families migrated during the first three quarters of 1992. In the last quarter there were no such cases of migration. More significantly, the trend was reversed as people returned to their homes even in areas such as Makhu, Zira, Jhabal, Bhikiwind and Moga, located deep in what was, only a year ago, the terrorist heartland.

Fresh recruitment to the terrorist ranks had come virtually to an end by January 1992 itself. The police strategy, at this juncture created a 'fourth option' for the terrorists: the first three were conventional measures of respons — the possibilities of arrest flight or armed engagement. A fourth option was offered at this stage of the confrontation: the terrorists were told that, if they chose surrender, they would be welcomed and embraced with warmth. By the end of 1992, 537 terrorists had surrendered to the police, six of them hardcore. Another 379, including 11 hardcore terrorists, were to lay down arms in 1993.

All the major terrorist organizations — the KCF (Wassan Singh), the KCF (Panjwar), the Babbar Khalsa, the BTFK — had, by this time, suffered irreversible losses. The smaller organizations — Dashmesh Regiment, Khalistan Armed Force, Khalistan Guerilla Force, Khalistan National Army, Khalistan Liberation Army — had been virtually wiped out. The entire surviving terrorist leadership including Wadhawa Singh and Mehal Singh of the Babbar Khalsa, Paramjir Singh Panjwar of the KCF, Pritam Singh Sekhon of the KLF, and Narain Singh of the KLA, now fled to Pakistan to join their resident ideologues — Wassan Singh Zaffarwal of the Panthic Committee (Zaffarwal) and Dr. Sohan Singh of the Panthic Committee (SS).

The war was over. What remained were mopping up operations. They need not detain us here.

To return, however, to our original theme, let us look at some of the numbers once again (See Fig. 6). 5058 civilians and 1003 policemen were killed in 1990 and 1991, and the state was brought to the verge of disintegration. A total of 1566 civilians and 277 policemen fell to the terrorist bullet through 1992 and 1993, and peace had been completely restored, political parties — including the now revived 'traditional' factions of the Akali Dal — had participated in Municipal and Panchayat elections that had secured unprecedented voter turn-outs, and a Constitutional government was squarely in charge.

Was this result achieved — and this is an impression that is sought overwhelmingly to be created in the 'human rights' debate on terrorism in Punjab — by inflicting an unacceptably high loss of life in terrorist ranks? 3497 terrorists were killed through 1990 and 1991, casualties to the muddleheaded and vacillating policies pursued by the V P Singh and Chandrashekhar governments. At the end of this period the 'armies of Khalistan' stood 10,000 strong. A total of 2911 terrorists were killed through 1992 and 1993, and there was no more than a tattered rump of survivors left, most of them skulking in Pakistan; the 'armies' were discovered to be nothing but opportunistic criminals who took advantage of the pervasive disorders; but when risks outran profits, they abandoned the masquerade of 'revolution' and returned home with whatever they could salvage of their illicit gains.

The 'liberal' mind has always remained ambivalent when confronted by the fact that the State, among other things, is a coercive instrument, and that it must, from time to time, exercise its option of the use of force — albeit of judicious, narrowly defined and very specifically targeted use of force — if it is not to be overwhelmed by the greater violence of the enemies of freedom, democracy and lawful governance. To fail to exercise this legitimate coercive authority is, thus, not an act of non-violence or of abnegation; it is not a measure of our humanity or civilization. It is, rather, an intellectual failure and an abdication of responsibility that randomises violence, alienating it from the institutional constraints of the State, and allowing it to pass into the hands of those who exercise it without the discrimination and the limitations of law that govern its employment by the State. In doing this, it makes innocents the victims of criminal violence, instead of making criminals the targets of its own legitimate and circumspect punitive force.

NOTES AND REFERENCES

1. It is interesting to note that terrorist movements in the Western world that received overwhelming international attention, including a strong academic focus, inflicted comparatively minor damage. Terrorism in Northern Ireland during the peak years of 1969-76 cost a total of 1,686 lives. The Leftist "revolutionaries in Italy", including the Red Brigade, killed 1,182 over the period 1969-87. Indeed, for India, terrorism in Punjab inflicted far greater damage than its three open wars against Pakistan — the death toll in which totalled some 2700 army personnel. But Indo-Pak hostilities and conventional warfare have produced immense volumes of literature in stark contrast to the neglect of low-intensity warfare that has dominated the past decades.
2. Cf., for example, Sangat Singh, *The Sikhs in History*, Uncommon Books, New Delhi, 1996; Inderjit Singh Jaijee, *Politics of Genocide: Punjab 1984-1994*, Baba Publishers, Chandigarh, 1995; Gurtej Singh, *Tandav of the Centaur:Sikhs and Indian Secularism*, Institute of Sikh Studies, Chandigarh, 1996.
3. K.P.S. Gill, "The Dangers Within: Internal Security Threats", in Bharat Karnad [ed.], *Future Imperilled: India's Security in the 1990s and Beyond*, Viking, New Delhi, 1994, p. 117.

4. Paul Wilkinson, "The Role of the Military in Combating Terrorism in a Democratic Society", in *Terrorism and Political Violence*, Vol. 9, No. 3, (Autumn, 1996), Frank Class, London, p. 5.
5. Joyce Pettigrew, "Achieving a New Frontier: Rural Political Patterns and their Impact on the Sikh Independence Movement", *International Journal of Punjab Studies*, Vol. 2, No. 1, January-June, 1995, p. 89.
6. The Akali role, in particular, has been extensively documented in, K.P.S. Gill's, *Punjab: The Knights of Falsehood*, Har-Anand Publications, New Delhi, 1997.
7. *Ibid.*, p. 29.
8. Chand Joshi, *Bhindranwale: Myth and Reality*, Vikas Publishing House, New Delhi, 1984, pp. 126-150.
9. *Crime in India*, [Annual] 1981, 1982, 1983, and 1993, 1994, 1995, National Crime Records Bureau, Ministry for Home Affairs, GOI.
10. Gill, *Knights of Falsehood, op. cit.*, p. 95.
11. *Ibid.*, pp. 96-97.
12. *Ibid.*, pp. 95-97.
13. Julio Ribeiro, the then Director General of Police, quoted in Raminder Singh, "Khalistan Declaration: Last Straw", India Today, May 31, 1986, p. 29.
14. Indeed, such a comprehensive strategic approach and context is still lacking in all theatres of terrorism and low intensity warfare all over the country.
15. When the fist seizures of AK-47s were made; a total of 36 AK 47s were recovered from terrorists over the period May-December, 1997.
16. Julio Ribeiro quoted in Pradeep Mathur, "The Retreat of Ribeiro", *Probe India*, February, 1987, pp. 6-9; even after Black Thunder, he continued to publicly advocate this view, declaring in his capacity as advisor to the Governor of Punjab that "The police can only fight terrorism: not solve it." [*India Today*, August 15, 1988, p. 52]. I am yet to understand the semantic niceties of this curious distinction. But I do believe that it was deeply demoralising for a force that was being asked, at that time, to risk its life for a cause that prominent individuals in its own leadership regarded, in some measure, as being futile. Nevertheless, Rebeiro, divorced as he was from the ground realities of counter-terrorist operations in the field, continues to advocate this point of view even more than a decade later. Cf. Julius Rebeiro, *Bullet for Bullet*, Viking Press, New Delhi, 1999.
17. Originally referred to as the 'Gill Plan'.
18. Gill, *Knights of Falsehood, op. cit.*, p. 100.
19. On April 21st, 1988.
20. Gill, *Knights of Falsehood, op. cit.*, pp. 105-6.
21. The number of police districts was subsequently increased in phases to 20 by 1993. However, all statistics have been aggregated, throughout this paper, over the original 15 jurisdictions for the purposes of continuity and comparison.
22. The thirteen police stations were: 1. Sadar Batala, 2. Sri Hargobindpur, 3. Kathunangal, 4. Lopoke, 5. Majitha, 6. Jandiala, 7. Patti, 8. Jhabal, 9. Valtoha, 10. Verowal, 11. Khaira, 12. Zira and 13. Dharamkot.
23. *The Indian Express*, December 6, 1989.

24. *Bhaiya*: [Lit.] Brother. But used in this context as a derogatory appellation usually for poor migrants from Uttar Pradesh and Bihar.
25. A very large number of these trucks were owned by terrorists themselves, or by their families and agents. A major proportion of extorted and looted money throughout the Eighties was invested in this trade. By 1990, some of the prominent extremists owned entire fleets of trucks. Moreover, by this time, 24 truck unions in the border districts were under the direct control of the militants, and others throughout the state were either influenced or sufficiently intimidated to secure the requisite co-operation. These resources and this power brought in the large numbers of transport vehicles that were needed to mobilise rural crowds for *dharnas, shahidi samagams* and *bhog* ceremonies.
26. The 'human rights' campaign and the affiliations and activities of various 'human rights organizations' in Punjab demand separate documentation and treatment, and stand out as a significant example of the manner in which, and the extent to which, the human rights movement has been subverted to serve ends that conflict directly with its original intent and purpose.
27. Cf. *India Today*, December 31, 1990, p. 37.
28. The Punjab Kesri group, which remained a prime target of the terrorists throughout the period of terrorism in the state.
29. On November 11, 1991 I had strong reservations against returning to Punjab since I had been transferred out at a time when I was certain the situation could have been brought under control in a matter of a few months. Thereafter, matters had been allowed to drift from bad to worse, inflicting unacceptable losses of life and suffering on the people of the state, and making the task of the forces immeasurably more difficult.
30. It is my intention to detail the elements of inter-force coordination and command in a subsequent study.
31. In this, we were greatly helped by the terrorists themselves who had adopted the practice of immediately claiming responsibility for crimes committed — since supplies of weapons and financial support from foreign and NRI backers was directly linked to the number and importance of killings committed and claimed by a particular militant or group. The significance of this kind of propaganda increased after 1989-90, with the emergence of competitive militancy that resulted from the mushroom growth of terrorist groups and Panthic Committees. Throughout this period, 80 to 85 per cent of all terrorist crime was 'claimed' within a week from its commission, primarily through 'Press Releases'. Claims of responsibility were occasionally delayed for tactical reasons: to avoid police pressure on a particular group, their harbourers in a particular area, or to avoid public reactions in the case of killings of individuals who had significant popular support or public standing. False claims were hotly contested, with evidence in terms of details of the operation being supplied through subsequent 'statements' issued by the actual perpetrators.

TWO

Terrorists, Human Rights and the United Nations

Arundhati Ghose

I was India's Ambassador and Permanent Representative to the UN Offices in Geneva at a time when the issue of militants and known terrorists utilising the UN as a platform to gain some kind of legitimacy came into sharp focus. It was this personal experience that forms the basis of what I write here.

I

Human rights issues in the UN are handled not just at the level of the annual meetings of the UN General Assembly in New York, but more specifically, through the Economic and Social Council of the UN (ECOSOC), by the Commission on Human Rights which meets annually in Geneva, by the Centre for Human Rights which has its headquarters in Geneva and operates under the High Commissioner for Human Rights, and by the various instruments and mechanisms set up by these bodies. The Sub-Commission for the Protection of Minorities has also legally evolved a role for itself. It is a subsidiary body of the Commission, composed of independent experts, who are supposed to advise the inter-governmental forum and to bring to its attention patterns of gross violations of human rights anywhere in the world. Since, however, the experts are elected by the Member States of the Commission, the politicisation which rules the Commission has crept into the Sub-Commission as well. It has developed an agenda of its own and its own mechanisms. Its studies and reports are rarely considered by the inter-governmental fora. The main characteristic of the Sub-Commission is the interaction between its members and non-governmental organizations (NGOs), who use this opportunity to bring their complaints to the attention of the experts and of the international community.

In addition to these bodies there are the Treaty Bodies. The Human Rights Committee oversees the implementation by States of the obligations they have undertaken under the International Covenants on Human Rights. Other expert bodies have also been set up to monitor the implementation, again by States, of the different Conventions to which they are party. These include the Convention on the Elimination of Racial Discrimination (CERD), The Convention on the Elimination of Discrimination against Women (CEDAW), The Convention against Torture (CAT), among others. Members of these various expert bodies are elected by the States. All these bodies and mechanisms, such as Working Groups and Special Rapporteurs (both country specific and issue specific), give the idea of an impressive network at the international level, even of activity at the global level, against the violation of human rights anywhere in the world. This would, however, in my view, not be an accurate picture and before I turn to the specifics of the actual practice regarding debates and interventions on human rights issues at the international level, I would like to make at least three general comments.

* Firstly, since the treatment of human rights issues is handled in the UN by Member States, there is a high degree of politicization of the subject. The usual pattern of the meetings that I have observed consists of accusations or charges made by countries of the North — the European Union, the US, Canada *et al* — against violations of human rights by States of the South. The North-South divide is fairly evident in the discussions. Rarely have I heard a country of the North criticising another country from

Europe or the US for violations of human rights. Rarely do Governments get together to deal with a human rights issue in a non-politicised way. Part of the problem lies, of course, in the fact that, in almost all western countries, human rights at the international level are handled as a foreign policy issue rather than an issue which affects all society.

* Secondly, flowing from this, the focus is on violation of human rights by the State and its agents. Though some countries regularly raise the issue of 'terrorism', the role of non-State actors is rarely, if ever, acknowledged. India has frequently raised the issue of militant groups sponsored by Pakistan, but this is seen as a part of the ongoing, perennial and to many countries rather boring Indo-Pak exchanges on Kashmir and human rights violations in others' territories.
* Thirdly, and perhaps, most important is the role of NGOs in the Human Rights field. There is a veritable industry of human rights organizations—not even the Centre for Human Rights is aware of the antecedents of the thousands who participate in the meetings of the Commission, the Sub-Commission and the Working Groups. These NGOs are powerful, as they are given almost equal speaking time on any subject on the agenda and there appears to be no dearth of funding for these organizations. There are, of course, some who are seriously concerned with human rights violations—if only by States—and base their charge on well documented or well researched situations. But such NGOs are few and far between. There are NGOs that are funded, directly or indirectly, by governments to project their own government's point of view. There are NGOs who regularly brief their government representatives, before and during meetings and who sometimes act as domestic pressure groups on the government concerned to raise a particular issue about a particular country.

Most pernicious is what I came to learn was a general practice of many NGOs accredited by ECOSOC after having been vetted by the UN Committee on NGOs, 'lending' and sometimes even 'letting' their banner to individuals and groups who have not been accepted by ECOSOC. Since the

Centre itself has no control on the applications for participation, any person put forward by an accredited NGO — be he a genuine human rights activist, an expert in a particular field of human rights, or a brutal militant guilty of heinous crimes in his home country — is permitted to gain some form of international recognition with the UN offering an international platform for their complaints against the State. My observation of the human rights meetings has led me to the conclusion that the State, especially a State from the South, is automatically held less credible, less truthful, and less reliable than individuals or NGOs who make charges against them.

My own feelings were initially ambivalent. There *are* legitimate cases — the pro-democracy movement in Burma, Kurds in Turkish Kurdistan, the Tibetans, as also many States that are dominated by settlers (often white and of European extraction), such as inAustralia, Canada, the US and much of Latin America — genuine indigenous peoples whose lives and cultures have been all but wiped out by the State. But my ambivalence was quickly corrected, when I found the effort and money put into deflecting these criticisms. Indeed I found it extremely rare that any country from the so-called North would admit to human rights violations in their home States. These nations were now even willing to share with the other members of the international community information regarding how they dealt with issues such as police brutality, custodial deaths, discrimination on the basis of colour etc.

What could, therefore, have been a forum to help States rectify and ameliorate situations of human rights violation in all societies is, I believe, in danger of becoming a sterile forum of North-South confrontation. Even, perhaps, a forum where bilateral quarrels are fought through the use of propaganda and exchanges of charges and counter-charges — for example between India and Pakistan. Not very productive, particularly if one recalls the individuals whose human rights are being violated, and who may look forward with some hope to the more than 50 mechanisms of international institutional appeal and relief created by the human rights industry and the NGOs.

Perhaps one should go back a little in history to try and trace how this degeneration occurred. How the primary human rights forum in the UN system became the politicised and rather ineffective organ it is today. And how, at the high level of elected member-States of the UN, the Human Rights Commission has become a convenient platform for known terrorists and criminals not only to air their views, but also to gain international recognition.

It was the Member States, particularly those of the Non-Aligned Movement, who took both apartheid in South Africa and Israeli practices in the occupied Arab lands to the human rights fora. Not that the activities in these fora were directly effective, but they kept the pressure on South Africa and Israel — and on racial discrimination — focused. This, I believe, established the so-called "country approach" as individual member States, with the help of the NGOs, found the fora convenient to attack the behaviour and practices of their adversaries. Human rights were introduced in the East-West talks during the Conference on Security and Co-operation in Europe [CSCE] in 1972-73, and human rights have, since then, become an effective foreign policy tool in the hands of the Western powers. The initial objective was to introduce the idea and standards of human rights — beginning with the freer movement of peoples, information and ideas — into interstate relations. The Helsinki Final Act of 1975, which became the CSCE's first constitution, codified and established *inter alia* the principle of respect for human rights and fundamental freedoms. But in recognising "respect" for these rights as "an essential factor" in the "development of friendly relations and co-operation" among the States, it directly linked progress in human rights to the political and military dimension of international relations.[1] Eventually, at the Meeting of the Conference on the Human Dimension at Moscow in 1991, interference in 'internal affairs' became a legitimate action in defence of human rights and fundamental freedoms. The successor to the CSCE, the OSCE (Organisation for Security and Co-operation in Europe), today has as one of its priority tasks, the monitoring of "the human dimension record of OSCE States in *close co-operation with* NGOs. The aim is to persuade a State with problems in this area to follow the OSCE's advice and remedy the situation"[2] (Emphasis mine). Enforcement, it was recognized by the OSCE, was with the UN Security Council.

Given the success of the CSCE process, efforts were immediately set afoot to replicate this pattern globally within UN fora. But the global arena had many other players, and the impact of Western powers trying to introduce the methodologies of the CSCE process in, for example, the Commission for Human Rights had unexpected and unforeseen consequences.

Using both experiences, the "country approach" and the CSCE approach, and often depending on NGOs to bring instances of human rights violations to the international level, the focus of debate in the commission shifted.

II

On July 4, 1997, my nephew, Sanjoy Ghose, a development worker who was fairly well known in developmental circles in India was abducted by a militant group, the United Liberation Front of Asom [ULFA], from his base in Majuli, an island in the State of Assam in India's North-East. The ULFA, through its 'Commander-in-Chief' Paresh Barua, claimed that Sanjoy had been "arrested" and would be "tried" according to ULFA "laws". This same Paresh Barua spoke on the telephone to Sanjoy's wife, promising to release Sanjoy to a representative of the International Committee of the Red Cross [ICRC] if the NGO Sanjoy was heading - AVARD-NE moved out of Assam.

These contacts led to a farrago of lies from ULFA, not only to the family, but also to genuine human rights NGOs concerned with Sanjoy's fate and the ICRC. I was in Delhi for most of July, trying to work out arrangements for Sanjoy's release with the ICRC, as instructed by ULFA. The ICRC's own contacts seemed slim, they appeared to be relying on the BBC correspondent in Calcutta as a go-between with ULFA. The entire effort came to naught, when the Indian Army intercepted a message between ULFA cadres, which claimed that Sanjoy had been killed while trying to escape, by falling off a cliff somewhere in Arunachal Pradesh. The family has heard nothing directly from either Sanjoy or ULFA since.

I was, at that time, India's Ambassador at Geneva. I was aware that ULFA representatives had been attending various human rights meetings, including meetings of the Commission on Human Rights. In fact, Anup Chetia, the 'General Secretary' and Sasha Chowdhury, the 'Foreign Secretary' of ULFA made statements to the 53rd (1997) session of the commission, under banners provided to them by ECOSOC accredited NGOs — the *Society for Threatened People*, a Germany-based organization which works in close collaboration with the German Government, and a UK-based NGO called *Liberation*. It is interesting to note that the so-called 'authorised representatives' of *Liberation* frequently included representatives of various Khalistani separatist groups and of the Liberation Tigers for Tamil Eelam (LTTE).

I was also aware that an unaccredited NGO called the *Unrepresented People Organisation* (UNPO), a Dutch-based organization, had been in contact with ULFA leaders, who according to UNPO, wished to join that organization. It was never clear to me where these ULFA representatives got their funding; staying in Geneva, one of the most expensive cities in the world, would have required considerable finance to sustain the presence of the ULFA representatives for such prolonged periods. Even Arabinda Rajkhowa, the 'President' of ULFA, stayed for several days in Geneva in July 1997, when Sanjoy had already been kidnapped, participating in a meeting of the Sub-Commission's Working Group on Indigenous People, purporting, no doubt, to represent the 'indigenous people' of Assam.

I approached the diplomatic representations of those countries whose NGOs had 'given' their banner and sponsorship to ULFA. It soon became evident that these accredited NGOs accepted any person as a 'representative', provided he was from a Third World country, without checking the antecedents of the individual or the group and frequently with no knowledge of the context in which the group operated. It appeared to be enough that an individual or a group was protesting against the policies of the government of their home countries with charges, however wild, being accepted at face value. The role and responsibility of many Western governments and their NGOs in permitting the gross abuse of the system by sponsoring criminals, even from a democratic State that runs on the basis of the rule of law, is enormous.

On my return to Geneva on 13th August 1997 I found the

Sub-Commission on Human Rights in session, and Anup Chetia, the so called 'General Secretary' of ULFA slated to speak at the meeting on atrocities allegedly committed by the Indian Army in Assam. By this time, Delhi Interpol had issued a red corner alert for the ULFA leaders, including Anup Chetia, on charges of murder and extortion. Yet I found Chetia had not only free access to the UN building and the sub-commission meetings, but on one occasion was sitting at ease in the delegates' coffee lounge, apparently quite confident of his 'immunity' and security within the UN premises.

The matter was immediately taken up at several levels — not because I was personally involved, but because instructions had been received by the Indian Embassy in Berne to take up the matter with the Swiss Interpol for Chetia's arrest and repatriation. The Interpol apparently does not have the powers of arrest, and they approached the Geneva Police [the cantonal system in Switzerland requires that the cantonal police make the arrest]. The Geneva police approached the Swiss Mission in Geneva for advice and, according to the Swiss Ambassador, some church NGO as well. In the meantime, I had approached the Director of the UN offices in Geneva[3] and the UN security immediately swung into action. On questioning Chetia, however, they found that he had a perfectly valid Bangladeshi passport under the name of John David Salomar and a perfectly valid Swiss visa to enter Switzerland. It might be noted that the British-based NGO *Liberation* had sponsored both names 'Anup Chetia' and 'John David Salomar'.[4] It was, however, common knowledge in the NGO community milling around the corridors of the UN, that the person in question was Anup Chetia, since he was introducing himself as such. After questioning by the UN Security [the Geneva police cannot enter premises unless specifically requested by the UN] Anup Chetia vanished. Not only did he not speak at the sub-commission, he stopped coming to the UN building altogether. (It is learnt that he was in Switzerland, in the outskirts of Geneva, at least till October 1997).

The legal wrangle then began between the Swiss authorities and the UN legal office and the Centre for Human Rights. The relations between the 'host country' [to the UN] and the UN are finalised by an agreement. According to the Centre for Human Rights, the agreement between Switzerland and the UN contained no reference to treatment of NGOs. The UN legal adviser in Geneva referred the matter to UN headquarters in New York. The latter's reply was somewhat ambiguous, in that it drew on the host country agreement between the UN and the US, in which it was stated that the host country cannot stop any representative of an NGO from attending a UN meeting. A caveat was added, however, that this did not convey immunity of any sort on crimes which may have been committed by the individual concerned, The Swiss Permanent Mission chose to interpret this letter as giving all NGO representatives immunity from arrest and refused to take any action against Chetia. In spite of interventions from the Swiss Foreign Office and Swiss Interpol, in addition to pressure from Government of India offices, Chetia remained free in Switzerland, albeit in hiding, till he himself decided to leave.

Apart from the personal distress and overtones, this incident brought to light the anomalies that had crept into the UN human rights system. While there was sympathy and co-operation from most quarters, there appeared to be little the UN or the Governments could do to prevent a named criminal from attending a UN meeting with impunity. As I have mentioned earlier, representatives of the LTTE, the Khalistanis and other violent armed groups gained repeated access to this international platform, sometimes through the active encouragement of some ECOSOC-accredited NGOs but more often through ignorance, lack of interest in the context in which these groups operate, and the stereotyped image of Third World Governments as uniformly repressive and guilty of human rights violations.

For some time now, there have been discussions in the UN on the issue of terrorism. However, as some NGOs point out President Mandela and President Arafat have been called "terrorists" at one time. There is also ambivalence in the NGO human rights community towards armed groups who abuse human rights norms. There appears to be a cautious recognition that the violent activities of armed groups, particularly against civilians and for political ends, have placed genuine human rights groups in a quandary. To quote from a statements made by a leading human rights activist in India,

Ravi Nair: "Even without arguing for a general condemnation of violence as a political strategy, or passing judgements on the 'merits' and 'demerits' of the ideologies of the armed opposition groups, it bears recognition that in the main such activities do not enjoy widespread support and legitimacy..... the 'apparent silence' of some human rights groups on the abuses by armed opposition groups is met with a hostile reception. The activities of the human rights groups can then be construed as partisan and unfair, if not fundamentally misplaced, leading to an increasing loss of credibility and further marginalization, even with the victim groups.... Should abuses by armed opposition groups be classified as abuses or violations, the latter being used in the case of governments? *The difference is not merely semantic but needs to be maintained in the light of the effort of the government to have the international community pay greater attention to the acts of armed opposition groups...*" [Emphasis mine].

The statement continues, "Simultaneously there is a need to discuss the nature of the response by the human rights community to abuses by armed opposition groups... We must not underestimate the legitimisation function of human rights activity". Nair, after debating the possible dilution of the mandate of human rights groups by covering abuses by armed groups talks cautiously of "working out a graded response to armed opposition group abuses". He concludes that "the expansion of the mandate of human rights activity to include abuses by armed opposition groups" might overload their 'mandate' to the point of complete ineffectively. "If, however, the overall rationale of human rights activity is seen not just as bringing the government in line with constitutional norms and international human rights standards but contributing to a wider political discourse... then a continuous engagement with these issues is inescapable."[5]

This 'cautious response' is possibly common to the international human rights community as a whole, which would explain how, inadvertently, the UN human rights system is being used by armed groups as an international platform, in an attempt to *gain legitimacy*.

However, some lone voices have been raised — not in the highly politicised Commission, but in the Sub-Commission. Asbjorn

Eide the Norwegian expert on the Sub-Commission called for "second generation human rights organizations... which (should seek) to bring to an end the violations carried out by non-governmental entities". He refers to "a direct cult of violence as a way of political participation... and in some cases direct support from the outside to militant groups." Eide sees the danger in not speaking out against these groups in undoing "the human rights edifice" which has been built up over the years.[6] However, even Eide was not prepared to admit that some of these groups found space for themselves, and a form of legitimacy, by participating in UN human rights fora under the banner of accredited NGOs, until the events relating to Chetia's participation in August 1997.

The situation is not under control, though efforts are being made by member states to ensure that NGOs are held accountable for their actions in these fora. There is still a long way to go before the NGOs, particularly the ones based in the West, can understand the dangers to which their actions in sponsoring militant groups in the UN can undermine the very fabric of the norms of human rights behaviour they are trying to build.

NOTES AND REFERENCES

1. Representatives of thirty-five nations gathered in Helsinki, Finland, in 1975 for a Conference on Security and Co-operation in Europe. The Final Act of the Conference, known as the Helsinki Accords, sets forth a number of basic human rights:
"The participating States will respect human rights and fundamental freedoms, including the freedom of thought, conscience, religion or belief, for all without distinction as to race, sex, language, or religion.
"They will promote and encourage the effective exercise of civil, political, economic, social, cultural, and other rights and freedoms all of which derive from the inherent dignity of the human person and are essential for his free and full development.
"Within this framework the participating States will recognise and respect the freedom of the individual to profess and practise, alone or in community with others, religion or belief acting in accordance with the dictates of his own conscience.
"The participating States on whose territory national minorities exist will respect the right of persons belonging to such minorities to equality before the law, will afford them the full opportunity for the actual enjoyment of human rights and fundamental freedoms and will, in this manner, protect their legitimate interests in this sphere.

"The participating States recognise the universal significance of human rights and fundamental freedoms, respect for which is an essential factor for the peace, justice and well-being necessary to ensure the development of friendly relations and co-operation among themselves as among all States."

2. Dr. Wilhelm Hoynck, *From CSCE to OSCE: Statements and Speeches of Dr. Wilhelm Hoynck, Secretary General of the OSCE — 1993-96*, Secretariat of the Organization for Security and Co-operation in Europe, Vienna, p. 23.
3. Vide my letter of August 22, 1997. Our Deputy Permanent Representative, H.K. Singh, had already written on the issue to Jose Bengoa, the Chairman of the Sub-Commission for the Prevention of Discrimination and Protection of Minorities vide his letter of August 14, 1997.
4. Maggie Bowden, the General Secretary of *Liberation*, subsequently sent an equivocal "apology" regarding the incident [Vide her Fax of June 23, 1998 to Michele Fedoroff, NGO Section/DESA]. She insisted, however, that *Liberation* was deceived, and did not act on any "bad motives":

   "Liberation accepts that Anup Chetia deceived us and we genuinely regret this. We obviously were not in a position to check passports or to detect forgeries, neither do we have the practical or financial facilities to vet every single individual with an application where the application is made for and on behalf of an organization. In this case the application applied for was on behalf of Assam Watch, which is a Human Rights organization, and has been affiliated to Liberation for the past four years."

   She does not explain, however, how or why the same individual was simultaneously sponsored under two identities. Instead, with a rare disingenuousness she "trusts that the matter can now be consigned to the past".
5. Ravi Nair's acceptance speech at Thiruvananthapuram on receiving the M A Thomas National Human Rights Award, 10th August, 1997.
6. Eide Asbjorn, "Towards a second generation of human rights action", Intervention at the Sub-Committee for Human Rights, 14th August, 1995. The statement was highly critical of "violations carried out by non-governmental entities, some of which are more extensive than those carried out by governments." Some excerpts are of particular interest:

   "These acts of terror and indiscriminate killings are often sought to be justified by principles which in themselves sound innocent enough. One of the key words used today is that of self-determination of peoples. Used in the abstract it seems innocent, but when applied in practice it is often a basis for extreme brutality pursued with a conviction that the brutality is justified for some higher purposes....

   "...there are many transnational influences which have an impact on this [terrorist] violence, and against which the government cannot defend itself. At one end, there is in some cases direct support from the outside to militant groups...

   "Then there is a massive flow of small arms, and arms traders who make a lot of money out of these violent movements, and here drug traffic is a close associate since it is often used to fund the procurement of arms. There is an international mixture of legal and illegal traffic in arms and drugs which is given much too little attention in the human rights discourse. But beyond this is a moral and ideological support, across borders, for some of those militant movements, in recent years couched in the language of ethnic or religious self-determination. We should be very careful in our choice of language and ponder what consequences it has, unless we want to undo the human rights edifice which has painstakingly been built up over the fifty years since the United Nations was formed....."

THREE

The Kargil War

Preliminary Explorations

Praveen Swami

... the clock shall go on ticking, louder and louder, because it now has nuclear energy infused into it[1].

There is something fundamentally repugnant about the idea of a post-mortem of the Kargil War, premised as it is on the assumption that the conflict has died. In reality, the war of the summer of 1999 is just part of a much wider conflict, driven by forces which are far from spent.

Writing in 1990, with Jammu & Kashmir (J&K) in the middle of a cataclysmic upheaval, analyst Sumit Ganguly addressed the possibilities of a war between India and Pakistan. He argued, among other things, that the Indian state would be able to contain the rise of terror in the Kashmir Valley. It would, Ganguly pithily suggested, "restore order, if not law". But the real danger he foresaw was that an "extended insurgency in Kashmir is likely to lead to continuing small-scale border skirmishes between India and Pakistan, with the ever-present possibility of inadvertant escalation".[2] Elsewhere in his paper, Ganguly pointed out that escalation could well have nuclear implications.

The Kargil War has some important, if depressing, elements of preordination in it. This paper is an exploratory attempt to understand why it came about, and what lessons need to be learned from it. It seeks to examine the legitimacy of Indian claims that the Kargil War ended in an unequivocal victory, as well as the broader political theatre that drove the conflict. Above all, it argues that the Pokhran II nuclear tests of March 1998 prepared the ground for the most serious military engagement in South Asia since the war of 1971.

An important caveat, however, needs to be explicitly stated. Much of the material for this paper was gathered during my work as a journalist covering the war. In the absence of cogent and reliable empirical data from independent sources, a preponderance of this material is based on information made available by military and intelligence agencies, as well as other informants. As more material on the facts and events of the Kargil War emerge in the weeks and months to come, some or many of these facts may prove to be incorrect. I believe, however, that the fundamental thrust of this paper will stand scrutiny, as will at least the contours of the information that has been compiled, if not its ornamental details.

At the time of writing, an enquiry has been ordered into the intelligence and military failures that enabled Pakistan to occupy and hold some 1,000 square kilometres of Indian territory. It is far from clear just what the scope of such an inquiry will be, and whether it will serve any meaningful purposes other than generating electoral capital. An insightful article by the scholar, A.G. Noorani has pointed to the examples of the Shimon Agranat inquiry into the Israel-Arab War of 1973, and the Franks Committee Report on the Falklands War, as examples of the scale and independence of the investigation that is desperately needed to examine the causes and conduct of the Kargil War.

> The nation must stoutly refuse to give any respite to men who have served it so badly. The only ones to emerge with credit are the men of the armed forces who have performed bravely against heavy odds. Their morale will not suffer, but will rise if the politicians who put them in this situation on account of their incompetence are brought to account. V.K. Krishna Menon resigned as Defence Minister on November

7, 1962, even while the India - China War was on. At the height of the First World War, Churchill was removed as First Lord of the Admiralty on May 26, 1915, following reverses in the Dardanelles campaign.[3]

The Three Phases of Battle in Kargil

It is now fairly well established that the first physical contact with Pakistani troops and irregulars in the Kargil sector was established on the Jubbar heights, on May 3[4]. Appropriately for a war characterized by the Indian security establishment's negligence, and on occasion incompetence, the contact had nothing to do with military reconnaissance or patrolling.

Tashi Namgyal, Morup Tsering, and Ali Raza Stanba, three shepherds from the tiny village of Garkhun, had made their way up the Banju heights with their flocks of sheep. Shepherds in the Kargil mountains routinely pool their livestock together, assigning groups of two or three villagers by turn to graze the animals on the high meadows. Namgyal and his friends are a little coy about just what led them up towards the Jubbar heights quite so early in summer, but the most plausible explanation is that they hoped to use the time to engage in the region's favourite sport, poaching mountain goats. Tsering carried with him a pair of powerful field binoculars, purchased years earlier in Leh, a tool of particular use for hunting.

By the morning of May 3, Namgyal had moved some five kilometres up the Jubbar Langpa [*nullah* or mountain stream]. As he scanned the mountain with Tsering's binoculars, he saw groups of men in Pathan suits, digging earth and putting up makeshift bunkers. Although it was possible neither to establish their numbers nor strength, Namgyal promptly informed officers of the 3 Punjab Regiment, stationed locally. Initial reactions to Namgyal's story appear, by local accounts, to have been more than slightly blas. According to 15 Corps Commander Lieutenant General Kishan Pal, two patrols subsequently despatched on May 4 and May 5 to Yaldor and Kha Baroro detected seven intruders on the Kukerthang ridge and two at Kha Baroro. Two further patrols were sent up in the night on May 7. The one sent to Kukerthang lost one man in an ambush, while the second patrol lost two soldiers and suffered several injured in a second ambush in the morning on May 10. Clearly, the patrols had not gone out expecting serious resistance[5].

Army officials have so far been less than forthcoming about just when patrols were sent out in other areas of Kargil, and what precisely their fate was. Lieutenant Saurabh Kalia's ill - fated patrol is now affirmed to have moved down the Kaksar Langpa on May 14 although officials had first claimed it had, in fact, left on its mission ten days earlier. There is as yet no verifiable account of what other patrols were sent out and just where they encountered or engaged Pakistani units. The scale and character of military response to the information first provided by Namgyal is just one of many issues that needs to be established through independent and rigorous inquiry. All that is known is that by the middle of May, the Army was discovering fresh Pakistan-held positions on an alarmingly regular basis, spanning the entire Kargil sector from the Mushkoh Valley in the west to Chorbat La in the east.

The 15 Corps Commander Lieutenant General Kishan Pal has given at least some indication of the conceptual framework that underpinned the Army's early responses. In his first press conference on the Kargil War, called before air strikes commenced, Pal described the territory occupied by Pakistan as "unheld areas". In a subsequent interview, he explained just what he meant by this novel formulation. "If I don't take notice of them", he said, "it will make no difference.... If they come off the heights in the summer, they will be slaughtered. And if they don't leave them in the winter, they will freeze to death"[6]. The true significance of these observations has been little understood. Evidently, the military leadership believed the intrusion at that stage to be little other than a very localised nuisance, an abortive enterprise to push in irregulars into an area of Jammu & Kashmir until then unaffected by insurgent activity.

The middle of May, however, saw at least some degree of unease set in. Pal ordered helicopters engaged in Wide Area Surveillance Operations [WASO] to fly lower, an effort to locate small Pakistan units entrenched on the mountains which would be undetectable from altitude. Three helicopters engaged in WASO were shot at with machine guns. Two were hit, but mercifully managed to return to base safely. Shortly afterwards, Cheetah helicopters used for WASO began to be equipped with machine guns mounted on their skids, a tactic first experimented with in Kupwara in spring. By most accounts, this tactic was only of limited defensive utility. Given the lack of a broad appreciation of the strength and purpose of Pakistan's thrust into Kargil at this stage, small numbers of poorly-acclimatised troops with thin artillery support were pushed up the mountains in a desperate effort to vacate its positions. No weekly breakdown of casualties has so far been made available, but the figures may cast interesting light on the results of Army strategy during this first phase of its Kargil operations.

Both Union Defence Minister George Fernandes' glib pronouncements during the first phase of the Kargil War and the fact that the first meeting of the Cabinet Committee on Security (CCS) was not summoned until May 25, say not a little about the chaotic management and poor strategic appraisal that characterized this period.

The meeting of the CCS led to the commencement of the second phase of the Kargil War. The morning after, Indian combat jets bombed Pakistan-held positions throughout the arc from the Mushkoh Valley to Batalik. For much of the media and public opinion, this signalled the real begining of the Kargil War; but the initial air campaign provided less than illustrious results. The loss of a Mig-21 fighter flown by Squadron Leader A. Ahuja to a Stinger missile on May 27, minutes after a Mig-27 flown by Flight Lieutenant K. Nachiketa went down accross the Line of Control with engine trouble, was followed a day later by the destruction of a Mi-17 helicopter fitted with rocket pods in the Drass sub-sector, resulting in the death of all four crew. Indian planners had clearly not anticipated the use of Stinger missiles by Pakistani air defence. In the wake of the losses, combat aircraft were compelled in general to fly at higher altitudes, using defensive measures to deflect the heat-seeking Stinger missiles. The use of Mi-17 helicopters as weapon platforms was subequently severely restricted.

What uses, then, did the air offensive serve? Chief of Air Force Staff, Air Marshall A.Y. Tipnis, at a press conference in Srinagar, made it clear that "the consequences of the restricted use of air power had been made clear to the Government". By this, Tipnis presumably meant that combat aircraft were not being used for the tasks for which they were designed. Attacks on major Pakistan supply, bases and artillery positions were ruled out by the fact that such an offensive would have meant flying across the LoC. None the less, the use of air power had two significant consequences. First, it signalled to Pakistan troops and irregulars on the Indian side of the LoC that the battle had been joined in earnest. Any expectations that an effete enemy could be held at bay until the winter began to set in were now dispelled. Second, and perhaps most important, sagging Indian troop-morale received not a little aid from the air strikes. Soldiers struggling up the mountains now moved in the knowledge that their adversaries, too, were facing sustained and lethal bombardment.

It is perhaps not coincidental that the first major Indian victory, the capture of the Tololing heights facing Drass, followed the use of air power. Troops of the Rajputana Regiment succeeded in pushing their way up this 4,950-metre summit, and further on to the highest summit visible from Drass, Peak 4,510. The push, followed six weeks of sustained artillery bombardment, and demonstrated to poorly acclimatised and sometimes demoralised troops that the war in the high Himalayas, could in fact, be won. The subsequent assault on Tiger Hills west of Drass, and Peak 5,062 overlooking the Sando Langpa, the gateway to the LoC at Marpo La, proved similarly successful. These victories were the subject of considerable media hype. Officials claimed they had considerable strategic importance, since Pakistani forward observation posts overlooking the highway had now been vacated.

While there was some element of truth in this claim, the fact remained that much of the war remained to be fought. In early July, the picture in several other sectors was less comforting. The body of Major Mariappan Sarvanan, killed in a May 28-assault on a Pakistani position at Height 4,250 in Batalik, had yet, to be recovered. This made it clear that Indian troops had yet to move to higher positions, from where the enemy fire preventing Sarvanan's body from being collected could be engaged and neutralised. Mechanised Infantry officer Major Rajesh Adhikari, killed in the Mushkoh Valley at a height above 4,000 metres, was also listed as missing, a similar indicator of Indian progress. No significant success in India's efforts to regain its forward position on the LoC in Kaksar, Bajrang Post, had been reported at all. In some areas, the Indian attack had faced severe reverses. On June 10, troops of the 12 Jammu & Kashmir Light Infantry and the Desert Scorpions Paracommando unit who had taken a commanding position above the Yaldor Langpa found themselves sandwiched between two fresh lines of counter-attacking Pakistan troops. This established that, contrary to Army claims, Pakistan's resupply lines were still open.

Despite slow progress in several areas, however, India's formidable military machine was clearly at work. This second phase of the battle might best be described as one of consolidation. The 56 Brigade, brought in early in the battle to relieve the 121 Brigade in the Drass sub-sector, had begun to establish itself west of the Munar Langpa. Initial logistics problems, which had on more than one occasion left troops without adequate food, clothing and ammunition, had been resolved. West of Tingel Langpa, another new formation, the 79 Brigade, had taken charge of fighting in Mushkoh. Further troops were pouring in, and over five additional Brigades were in position before fighting was to conclude. At least some officials who were discredited in the early phase of fighting had been removed from their positions. Artillery positions had been reinforced with Bofors guns and Pinaka rocket launchers.

This phase of consolidation, mirrored by sustained air and ground bombardment, prepared the way for the final push that began in early July. Among the most spectacular victories were claimed by soldiers from the Garhwal Rifles, the Bihar Regiment, the Gurkha Rifles and the Grenadiers pushing their way along the flanks of the Batalik heights. The 5,287-metre summit of Khalubar, east of Yaldor, fell on July 2, and the entire mountain was cleared within three days by the Gurkhas. West of the Urdas Langpa, Peak 4,812, which Indian soldiers call Dog Hill, rapidly followed. Holding these flanks, troops could now begin to cut off Pakistan reinforcements making their way down from their rear base at Muntho Dalo, which had been hit by successive waves of air strikes through the previous weeks.

Luck played a significant role in the capture of Jubbar. Troops had succeeded in making their way up the Urdas Langpa to Banju, the minor peak which guards the Jubbar ridge line. The final assault up the ridge would have been murderous, had a shell not hit a massive Pakistani ammunition dump near the Jubbar peak. The route up Jubbar, on to Peak 4,924 and beyond, to Peak 4,927, was now clear. Progress had been rapid on the eastern side of the Garkhun Langpa as well. The push from the village of Yaldor, on the Yaldor Langpa, to Peak 4,821 on Kukerthang had been a protracted one, claiming heavy casualties. But the mountain was finally taken, and the 5,103-metre Tharu followed soon after. With the heights reclaimed, troops could now dominate the Garkhun Langpa, and the villages of Baroro and Kha Baroro. Further Pakistani movement to reinforce positions along the Gargurdu, Garkhun and Yadlor Langpas was now near-impossible.

Interestingly, progress in the Batalik area provided the first irrefutable evidence of Pakistan's military presence on the Indian side of the LoC. Naik Inayat Ali of the 5 Northern Light Infantry (NLI), captured on July 2, told interrogators that his entire unit of 200 had been wiped out in the course of fighting in the Batalik area.[7] Earlier evidence of such involvement had emerged. The US-based magazine, *Time* reported that troops "from the northern light infantry were used because of their high-altitude experience and because they are from the region".

> They were encouraged to look like *mujahideen*, and they discarded their uniforms for traditional *shalwar kameez*, or tracksuits, grew beards and wore traditional white religious skullcaps. The soldiers say that when they reached the heights in February, some genuine *mujahideen* were at the abandoned Indian positions. But these men left after a few days because they could not survive in the high altitudes. They are now used for reconnaissance and as porters.[8]

In an interview, one Pakistani soldier provided a lucid account of his deployment in the Kargil sector, and of the Army's logistical support[9]. Much of what he stated bears out Namgyal's account of his May 3-sighting in Jubbar.

At the time Pakistan troop withdrawals were announced on

July 11, the battle for Batalik, and the third phase of the Kargil War in general, was, contrary to official claims, far from over. Pakistan troops retreating from Jubbar had been reinforcing at two heights over a kilometre inside the Line of Control, Peaks 5,121 and 5,327. Assaulting these heights could have proved costly. To the east of Yadlor lay Muntho Dalo, the 5,065-metre pyramid which acted as Pakistan's principal supply base for the Batalik sector. Although Muntho Dalo had come under sustained bombardment until at least July 9, the final physical occupation could again have taken time. In the event, Pakistan's withdrawal from Muntho Dalo allowed Indian troops to occupy the position almost without resistance. No counter attacks appear to have been encountered from the reinforcements that had begun to gather at Peaks 5,121 and 5,327.

Pakistan's movement out of the Drass area also prevented what could have been a series of small but bitter skirmishes along the Tiger Hills belt. At least one Pakistani position on the western face of Tiger Hills remained intact until the withdrawal, and there had been concerted counter-attacks on Peaks 5,100 and 4,875. Interestingly, the Tiger Hills area also appears to have received significant reinforcements of Pakistan regulars until July 8. On that day, the bodies of at least two Pakistani soldiers, Captain Imtiyaz Malik of the 12 NLI and Captain Karnal Sher of the 165 Mortar Regiment, were reported recovered from the hills. Pakistan continued to dispute claims that its soldiers were there in the first place, a proposition that, by this point, was somewhat ludicrous. But there is little doubt that the early withdrawal helped India retake positions like Marpo La. Somewhat mystifyingly, the Army announcement of the capture of Marpo La was preceeded weeks earlier by a signed official claim that its positions there were already occupied by Indian soldiers.[10]

But it was in the Mushkoh Valley and Kaksar that the Pakistan withdrawal had its most significant impact. The assault down the Mushkoh valley that commenced on 7 July claimed 23 soldiers the next day, and heavy casualties were subsequently reported. Much of the worst fighting came along the Mun Thang, the stream that drains Peak 4,342 above the Mushkoh Valley. The fighting was at an air distance of between five and six kilometres from the Line of

Control, but Pakistan troops were not likely to be present at depth in the region since temperatures in the glaciers north of the Mushkoh Valley would rule out holding positions for any length of time. The counter attacks on Tiger Hills and Peak 5,100 appeared designed to relieve pressure on Pakistan positions in Mushkoh.

Kaksar was also certain to see bitter fighting. At least three attempts to storm the Pakistan-occupied Bajrang Post and Peak 5,299 which dominates the Kaksar stream, had been beaten back since fighting began. A major offensive that commenced on July 6 showed few results until the withdrawal from the area commenced, and while Indian troops had been engaged in virtual hand-to-hand combat a fortnight earlier, Pakistan succeeded in reinforcing its positions. Officials had been desperately petitioning New Delhi for a limited retaliatory incursion across the Line of Control in this area, since the only local ridge-line-route to Peak 5,299 and to India's lost forward-area Bajrang Post lies on the other side. The option was a succession of near-suicidal assaults up the mountain face, certain to claim large numbers of soldiers.

Pronouncements of unconditional victory are clearly problematic, made in the context of the ground situation at the time of Pakistan's withdrawal. Although Indian troops had made significant advances, and Pakistan troops and irregulars had sustained significant casualties, the fact remained that there was more than a little fighting still to be done. The withdrawal saved time for India, and, inevitably, significant economic and human costs. Yet, I shall argue, the structure and conditions of the withdrawal have rendered what most likely would have been an unconditional military victory into a profoundly complex and problematic one. The war on the Kargil heights ended not as the triumph the Union Government would have us believe it was, but as punctuation in a larger conflict over the future of Jammu & Kashmir.

Safe Passage: The Politics of the Victory That Wasn't

It is not entirely clear how the end of the third phase of the Kargil War could be described, as it has been, as a glorious triumph. Pakistan's troops and irregulars were clearly under no military compulsion to retreat at the time they chose to do so, although they faced crippling losses. Nor did Indian military threats to other Pakistan forces or territory bring about the withdrawal. Former Prime Minister Chandra Shekhar is one of the few politicians who has had the courage to strip the US-authored end of the Kargil War of its triumphalist raiment which the Union Government had conferred upon it:

> In the begining, the Defence Minister talked about considering the idea to give safe passage to the intruders. It was ridiculed and rejected. Now the same is being implemented. Whatever may be the claim, in reality it is a ceasefire and safe passage.[11]

The spring of 1998 had seen the reinvention of George Fernandes as a hands-on Defence Minister, suitably dressed in combat fatigues and located on the Siachen heights — an image carefully manufactured for, and nurtured by, television. He was a fitting representative of the defence policies of the new supposedly-nationalist regime that had taken power in New Delhi. Playing out his role to the hilt, he visited the frontlines to shore up morale, despatched recalcitrant bureaucrats to oblivion, and finally fixed his lance and saddled his horse to charge the evil dragon threatening India's security, China.

Fernandes' deservedly notorious Kargil War pronouncements illustrate the complete surprise the government's strategic establishment was taken by when combat broke out in early May. On May 14, the very day Lieutenant Kalia's patrol had disappeared and Indian reconnaissance parties were encountering a plethora of Pakistani positions, Fernandes visited Leh for a meeting of the Ladakh Autonomous Hill Development Council. He described the shelling that had broken out in Kargil as "sporadic", a somewhat curious description for a barrage that claimed since the 121 Brigade's Artillery Dump near Kargil along with several other installations, and said the Indian Army was "well prepared" to deal with the situation. At New Delhi the next day, he promised intruders would be evicted "in forty eight hours". One day later, the Indian news agency, UNI reported from Dhanbad that Fernandes claimed the Army "had cordoned off the area entirely" and that Indian objectives would be realised "within the next two days".[12]

Given that the Indian Army had just commenced pumping in additional troops, the charitable interpretation of the Union Defence Minister's pronouncement is that it was a lie. A second possibility is that Fernandes had been misinformed of the situation by the top leadership of the Indian Army, a proposition rendered implausible since no one has so far been punished for so outrageous a crime. The less generous explanation was that neither he, nor the Ministry of Defence, had bothered to investigate with any seriousness just what was happening in Kargil. Nor, it is now evident, did anyone else in the BJP-led coalition government. It was not until May 25 that the first meeting of the apex Cabinet Committee on Security was called, a day after Jammu & Kashmir Chief Minister Farooq Abdullah visited New Delhi to beg the Prime Minister to take the Kargil issue seriously. It was only after this meeting that the Prime Minister recovered from his Lahore trance to realize the situation in Kargil was "war - like". More than fifty soldiers were by then dead.

Fernandes now attempted to cover up the errors of his Ministry and the defence establishment. On May 29, he claimed that Indian troops had flushed out infiltrators from the Drass sub-sector, and "restored the sanctity of the line of control". This was an outright lie. At the time of this statement, it is now clear, Indian troops were nowhere near the top of the Tololing heights in Drass, let alone the lower saddle of Tiger Hills. Marpo La, India's key forward position on the Drass sub-sector LoC, was only to be reached after Pakistan's withdrawal. A day earlier, the Union Defence Minister had attempted to defend the government's handling of the Lahore process. His effort was to exonerate the government's dialogue partner, Nawaz Sharif. "In this entire episode", Fernandes said on television, "the Pakistan Army has hatched a conspiracy to push in infiltrators, and the Nawaz Sharif government did not have a major role.... The Inter Services Intelligence (ISI), which we know initiates such activities, has not played any role".

Government confusion snowballed as criticism of its handling of Kargil grew. On June 1, Fernandes made his infamous offer of safe passage for Pakistani irregulars and troops back to their side of the Line of Control, a statement that was to have an enormous impact on the structure of the diplomatic dialogue that followed. "Get your troops out of our soil", he proclaimed, "or watch them being thrown out," but adding that, if Pakistan Foreign Minister Sartaj Aziz "wants to discuss how the intruders are to leave, we can discuss their safe passage". The Prime Minister, apparently oblivious to the outrage Fernandes' statement had provoked, endorsed this position while commissioning INS Mysore in Mumbai on June 2. "We can discuss their safe passage if such a request was made", Vajpayee said, "it could be considered". Both statements, despite subsequent denials, served a purpose. They suggested that the diplomatic forces set in place after Vajpayee's bus journey to Lahore offered potential for the resolution of the military conflict in Kargil.

At least two important assumptions could be detected in the noises emanating from the Union Defence Minister and Prime Minister. The first was that there was significant friction between Pakistan's military and civilian centres of power. Pakistan Prime Minister Sharif and, indeed, the ISI were deemed to have had nothing to do with the incursion, in Fernandes' view a purely Army-led maneouvre. The Kargil War was, thus, the outcome of a struggle for supremacy between the centrist Sharif and a *Jehadi* Army establishment, seeking to derail the process of normalization initiated by Prime Minister Vajpayee's bus journey to Lahore. This assumption, for obvious reasons, served the interest of the Union Government in no small measure. But second, and more important, the ascendancy of this interpretation ensured New Delhi had no cogent notion at all of why Pakistan had carried out the incursion, and what it sought to achieve by forcing a conventional engagement.

Fernandes' assumptions, by his own account, were founded in part by intercepts of conversations between Pakistan's Chief of Army Staff, General Pervez Musharraf, and Chief of General Staff, Lieutenanat General Aziz Khan. It is unclear who made the conversations available to India, but the transcripts have a strong element of authenticity. They record conversations between Musharraf and Khan on May 26, 1999 and May 29, 1999, while the Pakistan Army Chief was in Beijing. It is unclear just how Fernandes, and the Union Government, arrived at the conclusions they did on the basis of the conversations. Musharraf told his subordinate, referring to Prime Minister Sharif, that "so many times we had discussed, taken your blessings". "And yesterday also I told him", he continued, "that the door of discussion, dialogue must be kept open and [as for the] rest, no change in ground situation". He also made clear that Pakistan Foreign Secretary Samshad Ahmed had been briefed on the Kargil conflict, along with the Corps Commanders, at a later stage.

Musharraf made explicit Pakistan's objectives in a second conversation on May 29, preceeding the initiation of a serious diplomatic engagement on the war. This time, Aziz Khan told Musharraf that he would ensure Pakistan Foreign Minister Sartaj Aziz would give "no understanding or no commitment on [the] ground situation" during their imminent talks with New Delhi. Aziz would be instructed to argue that "we have been sitting here for long". "Like in the beginning, the matter is the same — no post was attacked, and no post captured. The situation is that we are along our defensive Line of Control... On this line", Khan concluded, "we can give them logic, but in short, the recommendation for Sartaj Aziz *sahib* is that he should make no commitment in the first meeting on the military situation". "And he should not even accept a cease-fire, because if there is cease-fire, then vehicles will be moving [on the Srinagar-Leh route]." In the May 26, conversation, he reported further that Sharif was "confident, just like that":

> Samshad [Haider] as usual was supporting. Today, for the last two hours, the BBC has been continuously reporting on the air strikes by India. Keep using this — let them keep dropping bombs. *As far as internationalisation is concerned, this is the fastest this has happened* [emphasis added]. You may have seen in the Press about United Nations Secretary General Kofi Annan's appeal that both countries should sit and talk.[13]

Pakistan, then, was quite content to allow Sartaj Aziz's visit to New Delhi to collapse: indeed, failure was its very purpose. As Aijaz Ahmad has pointed out in the second of his remarkable analyses on the Kargil conflict, three alternate military outcomes had come to be by mid-June.[14] First, India's response would be compelled, for a variety of reasons, to be so restrained that Pakistan forces would be able to sustain their positions until the onset of winter, generally after October 15. Second, India would be so resolute in its determination to retake the Kargil heights, a resolve driven by the certainty of electoral disaster if they were not regained, as to contemplate acceeding to requests by the armed forces to cross the LoC, provoking a full blown war. This, as I have argued earlier, is supported by the actually - existing ground position in several areas in the Kargil sector, particularly Kaksar. Third, India would seek some form of international assistance to ensure Pakistan would vacate the Kargil heights, and Pakistan, in turn, would be able to demand some kind of at least minimal *quid pro quo* on the larger issue of the future of Jammu & Kashmir.

By mid-June, it was clear to India's government, with military experts warning of a prolonged conflict on the Kargil heights, that the first of these possibilities was dangerously close to realization. That, in turn, had made the second possibility, of a full scale Indian assault across the LoC, dangerously imminent. Chief of Army Staff General V.P. Malik had begun to drop dark hints about approaching the Cabinet for permission to mount an attack into Pakistan, and at his June 13-press conference in Srinagar, Prime Minister Vajpayee refused to rule out crossing the LoC, saying only that he could not be expected to discuss strategic issues in public[15]. Some pretence of avoiding international intervention was made, with India rejecting United Nations Secretary General KofiAnnan's offer to despatch an envoy. But finally, while proclaiming the somewhat vapid communiqu emerging from the Cologne G-8 Summit a grand victory, though it only called for an end to hostilities without naming Pakistan as an aggressor, India asked for measures to be taken against its neighbour, including a blockade on economic asssitance from the International Monetary Fund (IMF).[16]

It seems clear in restrospect that this was also the stage where the Indian government made its finally decisive and desperate appeal for US assistance. The contents of Prime Minister Vajpayee's letter, conveyed by India's National Security Advisor Brajesh Mishra to his US counterpart, Sandy Berger, on June 16, are not known, but it is probable, as the *Washington Post* reported, that it made it clear that an assault across the LoC could not be delayed further:

> While President Bill Clinton was in Geneva in June making a speech to the International Labour Organization, his National Security Adivsor Samuel R. 'Sandy' Berger slipped out to receive an alarming letter from Indian Prime Minister Atal Behari Vajpayee.
>
> Vajpayee's message was that India might have to attack inside Pakistan if Pakistan did not pull back troops who had seized Indian outposts in the disputed territory of Kashmir.
>
> It stoked already high US fears that India, which has lost more than 100 troops trying to dislodge the Pakistanis, would storm across the ceasefire line that divides Kashmir or open a second front elsewhere on its border with Pakistan, widening the first armed conflict between the rivals since both tested nuclear weapons last year.[17]

If Clinton had now chosen to squarely involve himself in the Kargil War, he had no intention of marginalizing Sharif, or of opening the way for the even more rabidly chauvinist elements to come to power in Pakistan. Nor was Pakistan as isolated as India wished to believe. On June 29, well before the Pakistan Prime Minister's fateful journey to Washington was announced, State Department spokesperson James Rubin made it clear the US did not intend to influence the IMF. China had earlier announced plans to build a factory to produce combat aircraft in Pakistan, and the Organization of the Islamic Conference (OIC) had sprung to Sharif's defence.

> The Indian media reported it all, but in the small print as it were, refusing to draw the conclusion that in virtually every respect and in all the usual quarters it was business as usual and that Pakistan's "great isolation" in the "international community" was restricted to the scale of its operations in Kargil beyond the LoC, which of course even the Pakistan government must have anticipated before launching the operation. *For them, the question had always been how far will the condemnation go, in material terms, and what else, other than the condemnation, could they get* [my emphasis].[18]

In retrospect, the weekend of June 26-27, was central to the diplomatic resolution of the Kargil War. After concluding intense discussions with the Commander-in-Chief of the United States' General Command, Anthony Zinni, and Deputy Assistant Secretary of State Gibson Lanpher, who had been in Islamabad over the preceding week, Pervez Musharraf told journalists in Karachi that Sharif would soon be meeting Clinton. *The Sunday Telegraph* reported on June 27, that the structure and timing of a Pakistan withdrawal had been the central thrust of the discussions between Zinni and Musharraf. And *Dawn*, in turn, went on to assert that Pakistan had insisted on reciprocity, demanding a time-bound process of discussions with India for the resolution of the Kashmir problem in return for "assisting the *mujahideen* to (return to) home bases".

> Pakistan, on its part, would be prepared to consider as part of the permanent solution the inclusion of the entire Valley and the Muslim parts of Jammu in the Azad Kashmir territory — a settlement on the line of the Owen Dixon plan.[19]

Whether something of the kind was, indeed, discussed when Sharif and Clinton met on July 4 is not known. Certainly, the wording of their joint statement does promise that Clinton would "take a personal interest in encouraging an expeditious resumption and intensification of these bilateral efforts [for resolving all issues dividing India and Pakistan including Kashmir] once the sanctity of the Line of Control has been fully restored".[20] It is also now known that Lanpher and Sharif's special envoy, Niaz Naik, had spent time in New Delhi conferring with both Prime Minsiter Vajpayee and Brajesh Mishra, who were presumably told of the content of the Musharraf-Zinni meeting. Consider the subsequent sequence of events. Naik left New Delhi for Islamabad on June 27, the same day Musharraf announced his Prime Minister would shortly be leaving for Washington. Sharif, in turn, abruptly terminated his visit to Beijing the next day, having concluded the most important of his meetings with the Chinese leadership. Clinton, finally, altered the dates of his planned vacation to enable the final meeting with Sharif at Blair House.

Though Vajpayee, under intense domestic pressure, refused

to travel to Washington, the Blair House summit was, nevertheless, nothing short a US-engineered summit on South Asia. Pakistan and US officials sat together across the table to hammer out an agreed text, based on the crucial Musharraf-Zinni negotiations. Berger, meanwhile, constantly discussed the wording of the emerging joint statement with Brajesh Mishra, as the Indian Prime Minister waited to receive a final telephone call from Clinton. It is also now clear that some of the exploratory work for the Blair House text may have been concluded during the three visits to Pakistan by R.K. Mishra, editor of the Ambani-owned *Business and Political Observer*, who was acting as a back-channel emissary of the Vajpayee government.

Indian officials and BJP leaders have been as desperately claiming a diplomatic victory as a military one. Nothing could be further from the truth. Pakistan's alleged isolation notwithstanding, the fact remains that it has secured its core objective of bringing the US into a strategic dialogue on the larger question of J&K. Notably, the US has not, in the course of the entire conflict, had a word to say about the fact that, for the past ten years, Pakistan has been routinely violating the LoC by sending terrorists across it, with tragic consequences for the peoples of J&K. Continued terrorist violence, with enormous losses of civilian lives, is evidently acceptable to whatever constitutes the 'international community': the holding of fixed territory, and the prospect of a frontal conventional engagement with the concomitant possibility of nuclear engagement is not.

An escalation of violence within J&K is now inevitable (an issue I will return to below). How the Indian establishment will cope with this, however, remains to be seen.

Kashmir as the Context of War and Peace in Kargil

Indian bureaucrats and officials appear to have no plausible explanation for Pakistan's objectives in the Kargil War. Persistant claims that Pakistan sought to cut-off Siachen by disrupting the Srinagar-Leh highway are less than cogent. India's has another perfectly usable route to Leh and on to Siachen, the highway from Kulu over the Rohtang pass. Nor is it probable that Pakistan would have provoked a full-scale conventional engagement simply to secure a territorial bargain of some kind. Broader political objectives were clearly at play, impelled by developments both in Pakistan and in India, objectives which India's political and security establishment failed to comprehend and engage with.

It has passed largely unnoticed that the Kargil War intervened in an ongoing political dialogue on the future of J&K. Pakistan's own perception has been that the US-authored withdrawal from the Kargil heights would lead to some kind of progress towards a second partition of J&K. This demand for the logic of Partition to be taken to its 'inevitable' conclusion has structured Paksitan's recent policy. Aijaz Ahmad has perceptively noted, regarding negotiations between Musharraf and Zinni:

> *Dawn*, the oldest of English dailies in Pakistan, went further and wrote: "Pakistan had insisted on reciprocity. For example, a promise by the Indians for time-bound discussions on Kashmir in return for assisting the *mujahideen* to home bases. Pakistan, on its part, would be prepared to consider as part of the permanent solution the inclusion of the entire Valley and the Muslim parts of Jammu in the Azad Kashmir territory — a settlement on the line of the Owen Dixon Plan.... That "the Valley and the Muslim parts of Jammu" should be included "in the Azad Kashmir territory" is of course Pakistan's maximum demand which India is most unlikely to concede. But that some variant of this solution, interim and much softer, is being prepared seems beyond doubt, as we can surmise from the contours of the plan for the reorganization of Jammu & Kashmir that Farooq Abdullah's Regional Autonomy Committee had released already, on April 13..."[21]

Chief Minsiter Farooq Abdullah's Regional Autonomy Report lies at the core of recent events, and underlines more vividly the reality of the threat to a democratic and secular J&K than Pakistan's pleadings to the US. Released by the Regional Autonomy Committee (RAC), the Report calls for the historic regional formations of Kashmir, Jammu and Ladakh to be broken down into new entities. In some important senses this holds out more fundamental threats to the prospect of a secular and democratic J&K than any number of Lashkar-e-Toiba terrorists.

The RAC recommended the creation of eight new provinces, each of which would have an elected Provincial Council. In Kashmir itself, if the RAC has its way, there would be three new Provinces. The Kamraz Province would be made up of the districts of Baramulla and Kupwara, the Nundabad Province of Budgam and Srinagar and the Maraz Province of Anantnag and Pulwama. Although all of these three Provinces have some historic resonance, their coming into being makes little sense. The people of the districts have, indeed, been arguing for more local power, but not for new administrative boundaries built along non-existant faultlines.

Ladakh, if the RAC has its way, would be subject to a brutal application of the National Conference's communal cleaver. The mountain region would be broken up into two new provinces, consisting of just one district each, those of predominantly Buddhist Leh and predominantly Muslim Kargil. Already sundered by the exclusion of Kargil from the Ladakh Autonomous Council set up in 1989, a decision for which no cogent explanation has ever been forthcoming, the transfiguration of the two districts into Provinces would serve only to sharpen communal and ethnic boundaries. Had protests by local chauvinists in Kargil been disregarded in 1989, the deepening fissures between Buddhists and Muslims in the region may have been averted. As things stand, voting in the region since 1996 has largely been on communal lines, and many political groups in Leh have been calling for a united Buddhist nominee to contest this year. Indeed, Buddhist chauvinists in Leh even opposed the use of the district to house refugees from Kargil, a sign of the depth of communal bitterness that has already developed.[22]

But the most dramatic impact of the RAC recommendations would be on Jammu. Here, the RAC Report makes no effort to hide its authors' motives. The district of Doda, and the single Muslim-dominated *tehsil* of Mahore from the adjoining district of Udhampur, would be made into a new Chenab Valley Province. Largely Hindu Jammu, Kathua and Udhampur districts would become the Jammu province. Poonch and Rajouri districts, for their part, would form the Pir Panjal province. The existing Province of Jammu would, thus, be turned into three provincial blocks divided along the geographical faultlines of Hindu and Muslim majorities. Perhaps the best index of the RAC's deep communalism is that not a sentence in their Report even seeks to explain these decisions. All that exists by way of reason, if it can be called that, is a suggestion in paragraph 32 that "the prevailing classifications of Provinces/Divisions are hampering the processes of social/ human development... The Committee is also of the view that this arrangement is coming in the way of democratic participation at the grassroots level within the state".

On more fundamental issues, the Report offers even fewer insights into the RAC members' thinking. Why development could not be achieved within the existing district and Province boundaries is nowhere explained. On how the creation of new Provinces would aid development, there is no serious discussion at all. Indeed, the RAC only calls for changes to be made to the Constitution of J&K to enable the new Provincial or District Councils to be made, without spelling out what they might be. Nor are the powers of the new Councils and their specific responsibilities spelt out. Since this was presumably the purpose of setting up the RAC Committee in the first place, it is hard to escape the conclusion that it did not do its work.

The history of the RAC offers not a little insight into how some of its more outrageous recommendations came into being. The RAC was set up shortly after the National Conference government came to power in October 1996, with Chief Minister Farooq Abdullah as its chairman. Academic Balraj Puri was appointed as its working chairman. The members consisted of Finance Minster Mohammad Shafi Uri, Members of Legislative Assembly (MLAs) Syed Mushtaq Bukhari and Mubarak Gul, and Ladakh representative Pinto Narbu. The *raison detre* of the RAC was to ensure that National Conference demands for greater autonomy for J&K as a whole did not alienate minorities in the State, since they would be given guarantees of regional autonomy.

Puri was, however, besieged with demands from National Conference leaders and other politicians for both new Provinces and Districts. He flatly refused. The RAC's terms of reference said simply nothing about new Provinces, asking only for recommendations which would "promote better involvement and participation of people in different regions for balanced political, economic, educational, social and cultural development (and the) evolving of instrumentalities, like local organs of power at all levels". The RAC was also to examine the powers that local organs of power were to be vested with, and "whether any changes in the State Constitution would be needed to bring them about". Late last year, Puri circulated his proposals for regional autonomy, which essentially consisted of strengthening existing institutions at the Panchayat, block, district and regional level. Much of the emphasis in his Report was on removing the State Government's powers to nominate members to local bodies. One third of all Panchayat members, for example, are government nominees, along with representatives of the Scheduled Castes, Scheduled Tribes, and what state laws describe as 'Other Classes'. District Development Councils, in an institutional arrangement unique to the State, have an entirely nominated leadership. Puri sought to replace this burlesque with real democracy.

But National Conference members on the RAC, although they had expressed no reservations with drafts that were circulated, rapidly distanced themselves from Puri's Report, claiming it did not have their support. On January 21, 1999, Puri was informed that his term, along with that of the RAC, had expired. Then, on March 4, the State Government issued orders retrospectively extending the term of the RAC. The order revived the terms of all members except, mysteriously, the working chairman. In just three months, the new Report was assembled. Curiously, the final RAC Report tabled in the J&K Assembly, bears neither the signatures of its chairman — the Chief Minister — nor of Narbu.

The strange history of the RAC, and its equally bizarre recommendations, suggest that meaningful democratic change is the last thing on the National Conference's mind. Indeed, the proposal to set up smaller Provinces will erode the powers of the existing ones, since each in itself will simply not have the resources to engage in large-scale developmental work. Nor will local bodies like Panchayats and block-level bodies be democratized and empowered. The sole outcome of the RAC proposals will be to enable National Conference politicians in the Jammu region to represent themselves as defenders of local Muslim communities against a largely fictional hegemony of Jammu's largely Hindu urban trading communities.

What then, was on the RAC's mind? In the wake of the Pokhran nuclear tests in 1998 May, and the subsequent ill-fated romance between Prime Ministers Nawaz Sharif and Atal Behari Vajpayee, the US political establishment offered some insights into its vision of a final settlement on J&K. This came in the form of a report, *Kashmir: A Way Forward*, circulated by the high-profile think tank, the Kashmir Study Group. The Kashmir Study Group is controlled by a non-resident Indian, Farooq Kathwari. Two Indian establishment figures, former Foreign Secretary N.K. Singh and retired Vice Admiral S.K. Nair, have been associated with the Kashmir Study Group, although both deny they endorse the report's thrust. *Kashmir: A Way Forward* advocated that "a portion of the former princely state of Jammu & Kashmir be reconstituted as a sovereign entity enjoying free access to and from both India and Pakistan". Widely circulated among politicians in the State, the Report said the new entity would have its own legislature, citizenship and internal law and order force, with its defence guaranteed by both India and Pakistan. The portion referred to was self-evidently the Kashmir valley itself, that being the area under most bitter dispute. Interestingly, Kathwari visited India shortly after the report was released, and met a wide spectrum of the political hierarchy.

The Kashmir Study Group-proposals in effect meant a sundering of Kashmir from Jammu, and a division of the State on communal lines. In 1950, Owen Dixon, the United Nations mediator on Kashmir, had suggested an essentially similar plan. The Dixon Plan called for the international border to run broadly north of the Chenab river, cutting apart predominantly Muslim Doda, Rajouri and Poonch from Jammu, and joining them to the Kashmir valley. Hindu Kathua and Jammu would have stayed with India. The proposal, for a variety of reasons, and not all of them predictable ones, in the end proved unacceptable to India's political establishment. The United States' revival of the idea had obvious significance in the context of a meeting between two right wing Prime Ministers. Shortly afterwards, Pakistan Foreign Minister Sartaj Aziz chipped in with an intriguing off-stage performance calling for a district-wise referendum in J&K, a sharp but little-noticed departure from his country's historic position[23]. Finally, figures on the Hindu Right, ranging from Dogra royal family patriarch Karan Singh to Ramesh Gupta, businessman and brother of Udhampur's Bharatiya Janata Party Member of Parliament, Chaman Lal Gupta, called for varying forms of seperation of the Province of Jammu from Kashmir[24].

Significantly, former Pakistan Prime Minister Benazir Bhutto has been making express what appears to be a US-approved formula for what she describes as a "deliberate, incremental advances" for a final settlement in J&K. Bhutto advocated that "the two sections of Kashmir should have open and porous borders", a proposition remarkably similar to that advocated by Kathwari's Kashmir Study Group. Prior to a final period when "the parties commence discussion on a formal and final resolution to the Kashmir problem, based on the wishes of its people and the security concerns of both India and Pakistan":

> Both sections would be demilitarised and patrolled by either an international peace-keeping force or a joint Indian-Pakistani peace-keeping force. Both legislative councils would continue to meet seperately and on occasion jointly. The people on both sides of divided Kashmir could meet and interact freely and informally. None of these steps would prejudice or prejudge the position of both countries on the disputed areas.[25]

But as important as national and international-level sponsors of the enterprise to create a US-backed protectorate in J&K are actors firmly entrenched in the State's own political apparatus. Since at least 1996, influential figures in the National Conference have been pushing hard to transform the character of Jammu, a communally diverse but culturally coherent region which is the principal barrier to Kashmir-centred secessionist claims. Rajouri MLA and School Education Minister Mohammad Sharief Tariq, Surankote MLA Mushtaq Ahmad Bukhari, Mendhar MLA and Agriculture Minister Nisar Ahmad Khan, and Uri MLA and Finance Minister Mohammad Shafi Uri are among the powerful figures who have been arguing for a restructuring of the basis of regional identity in the state. All the four National Conference leaders come from the predominantly Muslim areas of Jammu broadly north of the Chenab river, slated to be part of Pakistan had the Owen Dixon plan succeeded. In 1996, National Conference leaders from the region demanded the creation of a new Pahari (mountain) region, separating the predominantly Muslim Rajouri-Poonch belt from Jammu province, and integrating it with Uri to the north in the Kashmir province.

Similar demands for separation from Jammu province have come from the National Conference in the sprawling district of Doda. Indeed, in the wake of last year's tragic massacre of Muslim villagers at Karara in Doda, local MLA Khalid Suhrawardy chose to share a platform with the Jamaat-e-Islami's Sayyidullah Tantrey.[26] Both parties are bitter enemies in the Kashmir Valley. These alliances are in part driven by short term political considerations. The demand for a Pahari region, for example, was designed to undermine the influence of Gujjar and Bakerwal leaders in the region, communities who have traditionally backed the Congress (I). But they also rest on the wholly ridiculous proposition that these regions have no common culture with Jammu. Clearly, events since 1998 have driven political forces committed to some variant of the Owen Dixon plan to believe that it was possible to engineer a renewed partition of J&K. The string of communal massacres that has exploded on the landscape of J&K over the past two years forced new movements of population across the river Chenab, preparing the grounds for such a partition.[27] These developments had serious military and strategic consequences. In New Delhi, however, there was little comprehension of these events, and even less interest: what passed as India's Kashmir policy in the spring of 1999 could, at best, be described as a polite bureaucratic yawn.

From Pokhran to Kargil, via Lahore

It has strangely been little commented upon that US diplomacy was placed firmly in the context of international concern on J&K in the wake of the Pokhran II tests. Indeed, the blast of hot air that emanated from Pokhran II, nuclear and polemical, blew firmly north towards Kargil.

On June 4, 1998, not many weeks after Pokhran II, a Joint

Communique of the five permanent members of the United Nations Security Council addressed for the first time in decades the question of J&K. If Indian observers were elated by the fact that the Security Council did not make explicit reference to the need for third-party mediation in the Kashmir conflict, or to Kashmiri representation in the India-Pakistan dialogue, US diplomats made it clear that Kashmir had *de facto* been made a subject for international attention. After the release of the Communique, for example, US Defence Secretary William Cohen suggested that multilateral discussion on India was necessary, despite the fact that "India has strongly objected to any kind of international consideration of that issue". All Parties Hurriyat Conference (APHC) chairperson Syed Ali Shah Geelani, in his second post-Pokhran address at Jamia Masjid in Srinagar, displayed a clear understanding of what was to follow. "Whenever there was international pressure on it", he argued, "New Delhi agreed to bilateral talks.... But when these were held, New Delhi made these exercises purposeless by repeating that Kashmir is an integral part of India.... Now that there are apprehensions of a nuclear war, the world powers must intervene".[28]

Those apprehensions had not a little to do with Union Home Minister Lal Krishna Advani's curious decision to make a linkage between the Pokhran II tests and the future of J&K. On May 18, after emerging from the government's first major policy meeting on J&K, Advani argued that India's "decisive step to become a nuclear weapon state has brought about a qualitative new state in India-Pakistan relations, particularly in finding a lasting solution to the Kashmir problem". "Islamabad", he said, "has to realise the change in the geo-strategic situation in the region and the world" as a consequence of the Pokhran II tests. Although "we adhere to the no-first-strike principle", Advani continued, "India is resolved to deal firmly with Pakistan's hostile activities".[29] Several secondary BJP leaders followed in their leader's footsteps, with former Union Minister Madan Lal Khurana inviting Pakistan to join battle "at a place and time of its choosing". Such machismo evaporated rapidly after Pakistan's own nuclear tests at Chagai, but the ideas that generated it continued to shape policy.[30]

Pakistan's military strategists clearly understood that

Pokhran II offered them an opportunity to force a conventional military conflagration in J&K, and ensure international intervention on the issue. India's security establishment, by contrast, largely refused to even engage with this possibility. In some senses, it could not. To acknowledge that the Pokhran tests had been a strategic misjudgement would have been to admit the absurdities of the BJP's core politics. Under pressure from the US, both the Pakistani and Indian governments began what has come to be known as the Lahore process this February. At the outset, it was clear the Indian government was considerably more desperate for results from the dialogue than Pakistan. Pakistani Prime Minister Nawaz Sharif's famous 'half hug' greeting stood in sharp contrast with his Indian counterpart, Atal Behari Vajpayee's soap-opera mawkishness. Pakistan Army Chief Parvez Musharraf's absence at the Wagah border along with his service colleagues, too, made it clear the military establishment he represented was less than enthusiastic about the new dialogue. As one observer noted of bus diplomacy in the wake of the Kargil War, the "hawks in India have clearly been taken for a ride by the hawks in Pakistan".[31]

This political blindness to Pakistan's emerging objectives had several military consequences. In the autumn of 1998, Pakistan shelling along the LoC escalated to levels unknown since the war of 1971. Kargil town itself was devastated, and 17 civilians lost their lives. In a desperate effort to ensure the conflict did not escalate to the point where it would sabotage nascent efforts for a rapprochement with Pakistan, Indian Army Chief V.P. Malik is believed to have been instructed to ensure his troops did not retaliate to Pakistan-fire with heavy calibre guns, including 155-millimetre Bofors howitzers. Pakistan Army Analysts in all probability, drew the obvious inference. If India was both unwilling and unable after Pokhran to risk an escalation along the LoC despite deliberate and escalating provocation, larger enterprises could now be considered by Pakistan's military establishment. By at least some accounts, a limited territorial incursion by Pakistan to force an international intervention on J&K had been considered, and rejected, several times in the past. No conventional restraints now operated.

Events from August 1998 underlined the absence of a strategic paradigm within which Pakistan's post-Pokhran objectives could be read. In the autumn that followed the Pokhran II series of tests, credible reports emerged of Pakistan-backed terrorists having acquired shoulder-held surface-to-air missiles (SAM). The then Air Force Chief, M.K. Sareen, offered the use of Jaguar aircraft with photo-reconnaissance kits for surveillance. Perhaps driven by a misplaced sense that J&K was his force's exclusive concern, V.P. Malik declined the offer. Both Vajpayee and Fernandes, the sources said, believed that intelligence inputs on the SAMs were fiction. While the SAM story may perhaps have indeed been dubious, events after Pokhran II should themselves have made the case for heightened surveillance. Had use of the Jaguars been institutionalised last year, the first movements of irregulars and troops across the LoC would almost certainly have been picked up early.

For reasons which have still to be explained, no preparations appear to have been made in the Kargil area even for the kind of shelling seen in 1998. Heightened exchanges of artillery continued throughout the winter of 1998 - 1999, and several Indian forward posts faced sustained bombardment. Yet, no special stocking of supplies and ammunition appear to have been carried out. Had the Zoji La Pass, which blocks the route from Sonmarg to Leh, not opened early this year, India would have faced serious logistics and troop problems in Kargil. While Malik bears some responsibility for these failures, he appeared to have been facing his own problems. Through last year, some officials say, the Indian Army Chief's repeated calls for upgrading signal intelligence capabilities, and for the introduction of new direction finding and interception facilities, met a wall of Defence Ministry disinterest. The new equipment Malik asked for arrived late, and in very small quantities.[32] There has been no denial of this sequence of events by Army authorities so far.

The Research and Analysis Wing's Aviation Research Centre [ARC] also proved generally hostile to requests for cross-LoC area surveillance through this period, saying it needed political clearance for such use of its 40-aircraft fleet, which includes an especially fitted Boeing 707 and several twin-engine Beechcraft. These aircraft are designed to fly at extremely high altitudes to avoid detection. It is unclear whether any specific request for surveillance in the Kargil area or elsewhere along the LoC was made. The fact that no such flights were carried out in itself raises several questions.

Within J&K, the ARC had proved more co-operative. In October and November 1998, just as training for the Kargil offensive was underway at Olthingthang, ARC aircraft were stationed at Jammu to verify reports that large numbers of terrorists had gathered on the mountain heights of Doda. The photographs obtained, police officials engaged in the operation say, were "extremely useful". But no flights were carried out along the Line of Control, presumably because the ARC was not ordered to do so.

What this set of events makes clear is that in the wake of Pokhran, there was no cogent understanding of the new strategic opportunities for Pakistan. After the initiation of the Lahore process, the political establishment in New Delhi and an often submissive military leadership concurred that Pakistan's sustained aggression in J&K would now be slowly subverted. US pressure, business interests, and, above all, the *a priori* assumption that nuclearization would ensure conventional peace were among the many asinine reasons offered for the ridiculous assumption that Pakistan would choose to ignore the best opportunity it had in two decades to force an international initiative on the future of J&K. This postively imbecilical faith in nuclear deterrance rested on profoundly flawed assumptions. As N. Ram has pointed out:

> Claims that peace, in terms of preventing major conventional conflicts, has been assured in the sub-continent have become stock-in-trade with the champions and apologists of India's nuclear weaponization, especially following the first successful foreign secretary - level meetings and the Lahore exercise. Kargil seems to demonstrate precisely the opposite: given nuclear weaponization, esclation is built into a bilateral situation marked by tension, animosity and distrust; a crisis can escalate into a conventional conflict; and a conventional conflict poses the risk, unless very great care is exercised, of going out of control and escalating further.[33]

Predictably, officials in New Delhi responded with disdain when hard reports first came of a major offensive being planned by

Pakistan in the Kargil area. It has now been widely reported that the Leh station of the Intelligence Bureau (IB) sent out two specific warnings in the third week of October 1998. The head of the Bureau's Leh office said in his first report that irregulars were being trained at two camp's adjoining Pakistan's forward headquarters at Olthingthang. The group, his report made clear, planned to cross the border inApril 1999. The Leh reports were based on information provided by a Skardu-based informant reporting to the young and well regarded in-charge of the IB's Kargil post. The Leh station's second report, again based on field intelligence from the Kargil post, pointed to the use of remotely-piloted photo-reconnaissance vehicles being used by pilots along the Srinagar-Leh national highway. Both reports, IB officials say, reached the office of the their Director, Shyamal Datta, and were presumably passed on to the Prime Minister's Office (PMO). While there has been no denial of the existance of the reports, there has been a studied silence from the high quarters they eventually reached.[34]

Emerging and plausible evidence suggests the Kargil field operative of the IB shared the information from Olthingthang with the Kargil-based 121 Brigade's Military Intelligence (MI) apparatus. Officials claim Major Bhupinder Singh of the Brigade Intelligence Teams (BITS) and Major K.B.S. Khurana of the Intelligence and Field Security Unit [IFSU] were kept aware of the IB's flow of information. BITS and IFSU are belived to have set up two reports on the Olthingthang build-up, the first in September 1998, classifying the information as non-reliable, and a second, later in the winter, marking it as highly reliable. Despite flat denials by the Army that it was made aware of the IB's reports, these claims appear plausible, since field-level information is routinely shared among several concerned agencies. If Khurana and Singh did indeed send up such reports, it is certain they would have been received both by the 15 Corps Headquarters in Srinagar, and by Army Headquarters. With what seriousness they were taken is, of course, another business altogether.[35]

More corroborative evidence was to follow. Azhar Shafi Mir, a Hizb-ul-Mujaheddin operative, was arrested by Border Security Force (BSF) troopers in the Poonch area on December 20, 1998. What he told BSF interrogators was enough to arouse an unusual interest in the intelligence community in Srinagar. Mir had tired of a long career as a Hizb-ul-Mujaheddin footsoldier, and set up shop as an auto-rickshaw driver in Muzaffarabad, the capital of Pakistan-occupied Kashmir (PoK). His vast experience in J&K, however, led the ISI to push him back into the State. In mid-1998, he was picked up in Muzaffarabad on fabricated charges of rash and negligent driving. Mir was then offered a simple choice: spend an indefinite period in jail, or head back into India. By August, Mir was completing his training in a camp on the Munshera-Gilgit road. The camp, he said, housed 110 Hizb-ul-Mujaheddin recruits, some 30 of them Pakistani and Afghan nationals. On September 1, 1998, five sections from this camp were launched across the LoC at Athmuqam. After a somewhat precipitate retreat, provoked by fear, Mir was launched again, this time with a stern warning that cowardice would mean death.[36]

Mir's group was in itself unexceptional, but its objectives were startling. It was tasked, in the words of his interrogation report, "to cause extensive damage to the Bandipore-Gurez road, and to ensure the isolation of the Army Division in Gurez so that a full-fledged front could be opened against them.... Similarly, the group would cause extensive damage to the Kangan-Leh road to prevent vital supplies from reaching forces in the area". This left little to doubt. It hardly served the interests of terrorists in the Uri-Gurez area to cut off the Indian Army's 19 Division, since those soldiers would continue operating against them locally. The objective, clearly stated, was to prevent reinforcements from being moved from the Gurez area and elsewhere into "somewhere on the Kangan-Leh road". This could only have meant the Dras and Kargil areas. Maps of these areas had been found on the body of Ali Mohammad Dar, a Hizb-ul-Mujaheddin commander killed in Srinagar by the J&K Police's Special Operations Group on August 9, 1998.

Sadly, there was no effort to interpret and act on this body of information. While some officials did express concern, with the Officiating Commander of the 15 Corps, Major General A.S. Sihota, warning on January 11 of the "possibility of Pakistan trying to capture some of our posts",, no institutional introspection took place.[37] Posts that were not engaged in returning Pakistan fire fire appear to have been vacated in winter, as they had been for years, with no sense of the bitter consequences that would follow. Army officials have been obfuscatory in the extreme about just when posts were vacated, resorting, on occaision, to crude and easily falsifiable claims. Some transparency on this issue, like others, is desperately needed. In the absence of hard evidence, however, it seems probable posts were held in most areas until relatively late this winter. The first snows fell in the Kargil sector on October 16, 1998, just one day after the formal closure of the Zoji La for civilian movement. But after two days of moderate snowfall, there was a respite until the night of January 4. January and February saw only light and intermittent snow, not enough to force positions off the Kargil heights. March 8, however, witnessed severe weather, and it is plausible that most high-altitude positions, like the Bajrang Post in Kaksar and others around Marpo La in Drass, were starting to run short of supplies by this time and were probably vacated with an intention to reoccupy them in summer. This would have been the time the intrusion began to be put in place.[38]

Interestingly, high-altitude positions in the Drass sub-sector, where fighting had been among the most bitter seen through the Kargil region, were routinely held through the winter until 1982. Troops of the BSF had been assigned control of the Drass sub-sector until that year. Even positions like Marpo La at 5,353 metres and Sando at 4,268 metres were occupied by BSF soldiers despite near-impossible operating temperatures. An altered political and strategic environment appears to have led the Army, which replaced the BSF in 1982, to decide that no significant purpose would be served by holding on to high altitude pickets in the winter. Despite growing border tensions, and regular artillery exchanges in the Kargil area from 1997, a certain inertia of the imagination evidently ensured that there was no review of the earlier policy. Had troops been positioned on Marpo-La and Sando through the winter, intrusions by Pakistan irregulars and troops could have been detected early. Equally important, Indian troops would have then held commanding positions, making it difficult for Pakistan to supply its positions on Tololing, the Tiger Hills and the Mushkoh Valley.

Significantly, the BSF appears to have continued with its pre-

1982 policy in areas it was assigned in the Kargil area. BSF troops remained on the Bravo-1 post on Chorbat-La through the bitter winter cold. Positions over 4,500 metres at Alpha Tekri and Punjab Tekri, both in the Kargil sector, were also held. Had BSF troops not been at Chorbat La, Pakistan's effort to cut off Turtok by moving a brigade down the Mian Langpa gully may well have met with success. The BSF troops at Chorbat La were under sustained fire, but have succeeded in repulsing attacks. For reasons which are not entirely clear, Army regiments to which the BSF's companies are attached chose not to stay up at their positions in the winter. The 3 Punjab Regiment, to which the BSF company at Chorbat La is attached, does not for one appear to have separately held any significant number of posts in the area. While the soldiers and officers of the regiment can in no way be held responsible, their top leadership clearly has some questions to answer. Secondly, while a succession of alleged experts have been claiming special Siachen - style equipment will be needed to sustain such winter positions, it is worth noting that the BSF uses no special equipment at its posts, and supplies them using little other than mules and porters.[39]

Writing in *The Sunday Times*, defence journalist Manoj Joshi has argued that the mere fact of reports having being filed means little "because they are couched in generalities" and that only a high level probe can "determine whether there indeed was forewarning of what was to come".[40] Leaving aside the minor point that the field offices of RAW have made no claims that they detected plans of a Pakistan instrusion, Joshi's argument requires consideration. It is, indeed, true that the flow of intelligence is neither tidy nor unidirectional. But this, rather than being a failure of some kind, is inherent in the business of intelligence gathering. Disparate intelligence flows acquire coherence only when analysed through ideological, strategic and political filters. Those clearly did not exist. Joshi cites the opinion of a former special secretary with RAW, V. Balachandran, stating that the problem may not have been so much as an "absence of intelligence" as inadequate "strategic assessment". To put it simply, information might have been there in bits and pieces, but there was no one to put it together and make sense of the larger picture.[41]

But why was there "no one to put it together and make sense of the larger picture"? Observers have been curiously reticent to place blame where it belongs. The deeply held ideological beliefs of the political and bureaucratic establishments have not been understood with clarity. These ideological beliefs shaped the filtering of information, and the process of vesting certain inputs with importance and consigning others to the dustbin. For the political hierarchy of the Rashtriya Swayamsevak Sangh (RSS) and the BJP, nuclear deterrance has been something of a credo. In his March 15, 1999, statement, Vajpayee outlined a not-so-new doctrine for India.

> Now both India and Pakistan are in possession of nuclear weapons. There is no alternative but to live in mutual harmony. The nuclear weapon is not an offensive weapon. It is a weapon of self defence. It is the kind of weapon that helps in preserving the peace. If in the days of the Cold War there was no use of force, it was because of the balance of terror.[42]

This was the body of beliefs that cost India more than a thousand casualties — dead, injured, or maimed for life. Ahmed has pointed to the actual and profound implications Pokhran II had for the Right-wing political establishment in Pakistan.

> Pokhran II was a gift to Sharif as the Afghan War had been for Zia ul- Haq. Since 1971, Pakistan had been trying, unsuccessfully, to overcome its strategic inferiority in conventional warfare. By opening the way for nuclear parity and competitive weaponization, the Vajpayee government gifted to Pakistan a strategic parity that it could not otherwise achieve. To the extent that the possession of nuclear weapons capability by both sides tends to put serious constraints on a full-scale conventional war, to that same extent it facilitates the institutionalisation of low-intensity, localised wars. The more the two countries move toward nuclear weaponization, the more Kargils we shall have. In this sense, the present reality in Kargil is not only the other face of the rhetoric of Lahore, it is also a precise, necessary, repeatable consequence of Pokhran.[43]

The Kashmir War After Kargil

The real war is the one in J&K: in this larger conflict, Kargil is just something of a footnote. But Kargil's impact on security in the rest of J&K might be mildly described as a calamity. 58 battalions of the Army engaged in counter-terrorist operations have been withdrawn for border deployment in the war's wake. 36 of these have been withdrawn from Kashmir and 22 from the Jammu Province. Just 14 Central Reserve Police Force (CRPF) and 6 BSF battalions have been moved in to take their place. A further six have been sent in for the Amarnath Yatra, and these may stay on until the 1999 Lok Sabha elections. With the prospect of a permanent manning of the LoC, no one has any cogent idea of just how the shortfall will be met in the long-run. During the 1998 Lok Sabha elections, moreover, 354 additional companies, each of approximately 125 men, had been deployed in J&K. This time round, at least 500 companies will have to be brought in to even meet the 1998 security levels.[44]

At least two significant elements of the war in J&K have already become evident. First, since last summer, the mountain heights of the State, areas of little political significance, have seen large concentrations of Pakistani and Afghan terrorists, as well as an assortment of other "freelance seekers of martyrdom".[45] Received military wisdom has it that these groups lack the motivation or resources to fight a losing battle in the Kashmir Valley. But a more plausible possibility also exists. By building-up numbers on the heights dominating Doda, Banihal, the Rajouri-Poonch belt and Kupwara, terrorist groups will dominate the principal lines of access to the Kashmir Valley. Read in the context of recoveries of increasingly heavy weapons in recent months, ranging from mortar and anti-aircraft guns to a Grail anti-tank missile launcher, some argue that current deployment patterns suggest terrorist groups are preparing to support Pakistan troops in a conventional engagement.

The second key element of terrorist activity in months to come is certain to be the engineering of a deterioration in communal relations, pushing Muslims out of Hindu-dominated areas south of the Chenab river, and Hindus from the predominantly Muslim areas to its north. Such migrations will give a *de facto* demographic legitimacy to Pakistan's objective of securing some variant of the Owen Dixon plan. These processes have been in place at least since 1997, although they gathered momentum after the Pokhran II tests and Advani's promise of a "pro-active" policy in J&K. In a broader sense, revanchist groups in Pakistan believe the communal war they are engaged in is merely part of a larger struggle against supposedly-Hindu India. These faultlines, ironically but unsuprisingly, are precisely those that shape the *mentalite* of the Hindu Right.[46]

Even as much of J&K finds itself without security cover, there is substantial evidence that cross-border infiltration of terrorists has been unusually high in summer 1999. Field intelligence officials in Kupwara and Baramulla estimate that at least six hundred terrorists have moved in since March, often occupying positions at heights above 4,000 metres. Anantnag, too, has seen sharp rise in the numbers of Pakistan and Afghan terrorists active in the district, with over two hundred reported to be based in the district. While most groups of terrorists have been avoiding frontal engagement with state forces, there is little doubt that the period since the Kargil conflict broke out has seen a marked escalation in violence in the State.[47]

A secondary thrust of terrorist activity 1999 summer unveiled itself with the murder of Deputy Inspector-General S.K. Chakravarty, Joint Director G-Branch Mahendra Raj, and Sub Inspector K. Bhaskar during a raid on the BSF's Sector Headquarters at Bandipore on July 13. Evidently, the increased targeting of security force personnel represents, at once, a shift in strategy as well as a radical enhancement in weapons capabilities and the proficiency of the foreign militants who have come to dominate the movement in J&K. This has been a progressive trend of the past three years, as the steadily worsening ratio of security force personnel to militants killed demonstrates. This ratio has declined from 1:5.79 in 1997, through 1:4.54 in 1988, to 1:3.20 in 1999. Worse, with the thinning out of security forces in the wake of Kargil and the escalation in Pak-backed militant activity, this ratio fell to 1:2 in June 1999 year, as compared to a ratio of 1:5 in June 1998.

If the massacres and violent attacks this summer mark a

vertical escalation in the conflict in J&K, there are also signs of a generalised horizontal escalation in the Leh region. Last month's arrest of a twenty-five member terrorist cell from the Turtok area of Leh, led by local resident Ali Bhutto, has made it clear that conflict can be expected in this until-now quiet region. Bhutto's arrest, outside Leh, has been treated with little concern. But terrorism had similar low-key origins elsewhere as well. In Poonch, the first sign of an offensive was the arrest of Ayub Shabnam in May 1990. Shabnam, who went on to spend five years in jail, was believed to be responsible for the training and distribution of weapons to several local operatives. But he, like Bhutto, had little knowledge of Pakistan's broader objectives. Few took the incident seriously, until Poonch went up in flames after 1993.

Bhutto was picked up along with his cell, which included two police constables, in a series of raids that began on June 7. The group had hidden 25 Kalashnikov assault rifles, one heavy machine gun, one general purpose machine gun, a sniper rifle, a rocket propelled grenade launcher and several kilogrames of explosive material, brought in by Bhutto's Skardu-based brother, Ibrahim Sangsang. Sangsang, interrogators of the Turtok cell discovered, had made several trips across the LoC in 1998, handing over weapons to relatives and associates in five villages. All the five villages, Turtok, Pachathang, Thakshi, Thang and Chalungpa were captured by India in the war of 1971. Bhutto's father had been instrumental in asking villagers, against Pakistan Army advice, to stay in India on the grounds that it was wrong to leave the land of their birth. Interestingly, dozens of villagers in nearby Bogdang village were issued rifles by the Pakistan Army in 1971 to wage a guerilla war against advancing Indian troops. Few complied, and the rifles were instead put to use poaching mountain goats.[48]

Ibrahim Sangang's story illustrates the rich relationship between broad ideological factors and purely local issues in the emergence of terror. Sangsang had, by local accounts, been intimate with local officials and the military authorities, even having been sponsored to visit New Delhi for a Republic Day parade in 1987. But by 1994, Sangsang found himself embroiled in a series of legal disputes. Most emerged from a criminal assault on a police officer, the outcome of a violent dispute over the use of a diesel generator set that powered several villages. Under pressure from the criminal justice system, Sangpapa fled across the LoC, where the ISI appears to have offered him a better deal as against several years in jail. But several larger factors appear to have been at play in the five villages. The Noor Baksh sect that historically dominated the region, an eclectic Sufi-inspired faith drawing both from Sunni and Shia custom, has been under sustained seige from ultra-conservative Ahl-e-Hadis prosletysers. The Ahl-e-Hadis have been closely associated with terrorist groups in J&K, notably the Lashkar-e-Toiba and the Tehreek-ul-Mujaheddin.

The near-unchallenged growth of revanchist religious groups both in Pakistan and in J&K is certain to prepare the real ideological agenda of events to come. In J&K, as the RAC Report illustrates, the National Conference has begun to tear away from its historic character as a secular, modernizing force, and recast itself as a Muslim communal formation. The tendency has been most marked in Jammu where, as I have pointed out earlier, leaders of the far-right Jamaat-e-Islami have shared platforms with the National Conference. These trends will be reinforced from across the border as, most disturbingly, the future of Pakistan's establishment elite has never been more unsure than in recent years.

> Back home, economic hardship and the inability of a corrupt government to bring relief has made Pakistan's Islamic fundamentalists more popular with ordinary folk and — crucially — with the military, which for decades has helped the Westernized elite to curb Islamic fervour. As Jamaat [e-Islami] leader Qazi Hussain Ahmad pointed out at a well-attended convention in Islamabad in October, the income gap between junior and senior officers has been widening as the economic crisis worsens.[49]

In the first of his seminal articles on the Kargil War, Aijaz Ahmad had written, "The Pakistan we are dealing with was born not once but twice". He outlined the crisis of identity that emerged from the creation of Bangladesh, and the reinvention of Pakistan not as the home of sub-continental Muslims, but of a mythically pure Islam, subsidized by West Asian wealth.

Nothing worked as magically in restoring the self-confidence

> of the Pakistani state and its privileged classes as the infusion of petrodollars. But this new sort of money brought with it a new and curiously effective commodity as well: petro-Islam. A hybrid thing, born of centuries of ferocious conservatism so characteristic of the desert, but also of the unprecedented levels of wealth that was newly gained but was the product neither of a settled history nor of accumulated labour but of chance, that the black gold flowed here rather than elsewhere. It was a curious kind of Islam, equally ferocious in its piety and in its consumerism.[50]

To those who have noted the organic links between the emergence of a new middle class through the 1980s, and the rise of the Hindu Right through India,Ahmad's description of petro-Islam will be disturbingly familiar. In both India and Pakistan, the forces of reaction are far from spent, driven, as both now are by nuclear power. The end of the war on the Kargil heights, it is almost certain, is profoundly unlikely to mark the beginning of peace.

NOTES AND REFERENCES

1. Aijaz, Ahmad, "Mediation by any other name' *Frontline,* July 30, 1999, p. 22.
2. Sumit Ganguly, "Avoiding War in Kashmir", *Foreign Affairs,* Winter 1990-1991, p. 72.
3. A.G. Noorani, "Questions of accountability", *Frontline,* July 2, 1999, p. 24.
4. Praveen Swami, 'Unknown heroes of Batalik', *Frontline,* July 30, 1999, p. 7.
5. Dinesh Kumar, "What it took and the run up to Operation Vijay', *Times of India,* July 19, 1999, p. 10.
6. Praveen Swami, "War in Kargil", *Frontline,* June 18, 1999, p. 4.
7. Praveen Swami, 'The final assault and the withdrawal', *Frontline,* July 30, 1999, p. 6.
8. Ghulam Hasnain, "Under Cover of Night" in *Time,* July 12, 1999, p. 21.
9. 'In Enemy Territory: A Soldier's Story', in *Time,* July 12, 1999, p. 21.
10. Letter of Army Public Relations Officer Colonel Shruti Kant. See , "Of Strategic Follies", *Frontline,* July 16, 1999, pp. 116 - 17.
11. "Kargil has witnessed an invasion", *The Hindustan Times,* July 18, 1999, p. 15.
12. For an excellent compendium of Fernandes' statements on the Kargil War, including those cited here, see "Govt. doublespeak on Kargil", *The Tribune,* June 5, 1999, p. 1.
13. Transcripts of conversations between General Pervez Musharraf and Lieutenant General Aziz Khan, released by the Union Ministry of Defence,

New Delhi. Also see Praveen Swami, "A Long Haul Ahead", in *Frontline*, July 2, 1999, pp. 12 - 13.

14. Aijaz Ahmad, "Mediation by any other name", in *Frontline*, July 30, 1999, p. 20.
15. Praveen Swami, "Pak Shelling Near Venue of PM's Visit in Kargil", in *Business Line*, June 13, 1999, p. 1.
16. Seema Guha, "Pak unlikely to heed G-8", *The Times of India*, June 22, 1999, p. 1.
17. "The US Angle", reproduced from *The Washington Post*, in *Frontline*, July 16, 1999, p. 11.
18. Aijaz Ahmad, "Mediation by any other name", in *Frontline*, July 30, 1999, p. 20.
19. Cited in *Ibid.*, p. 18.
20. Sridhar Krishnaswami, "A firm American demand", in *Frontline*, July 30, 1999, p. 16. For the full text of the Clinton - Sharif joint statement, see "The Joint Statement", in *Frontline*, July 30, 1999, p. 17.
21. Aijaz Ahmad, "Mediation by any other name", in *Frontline*, July 30, 1999, p. 18.
22. Balraj Puri, "Signs of Distress", in *Frontline*, July 16, 1999, p. 127. Puri notes that "When 150 refugees from Kargil took shelter in Buddhist - dominated Leh, they were greeted with demands for their repatriation. The youth wing of the Ladakh Buddhist Association warned that "our people will be the last to play host and extend hospitality" to illegal intruders.
23. Balraj Puri, *op. cit.*, p. 126.
24. Praveen Swami, "'Pro - Active' After Pokhran" , in *Faultlines*, May, 1997, Bulwark Books-ICM: New Delhi.
25. Benazir Bhutto, "Comment" in *The New York Times*, June 8, 1999, republished as "For a Camp David for Kashmir", in *Frontline*, July 2, 1999, p. 22.
26. Praveen Swami, "Blood on the Chenab", in *Frontline*, April 11, 1998, p. 20.
27. Praveen Swami , "Pro - Active' After Pokhran", *op. cit.*
28. Praveen Swami, "Kashmir at a Crossroads", Frontline, July 3, 1998, p. 14.
29. Praveen Swami, "Flashpoint Kashmir", Frontline, August 28, 1998, p. 8.
30. Praveen Swami, "The Bungle in Kargil", Frontline, July 2, 1999, p. 5-6.
31. Amit Baruah, "Pakistan's strategy", Frontline, June 18 1999, p. 15.
32. Praveen Swami, "The Bungle in Kargil", *op. cit.*, p. 6-7.
33. N. Ram, "The Pokhran - Kargil Connection", Frontline, July 2, 1999, p. 9.
34. Praveen Swami, "War in Kargil', *op. cit.*, p. 6 and 9.
35. Praveen Swami, "The final assault and the withdrawal", *Frontline*, July 30, 1999, p. 10.
36. Praveen Swami, "War in Kargil", *op. cit.*, p. 6 and 9.
37. A.G. Noorani, "Questions of accountability", *Frontline*, July 2, 1999, p. 26.
38. Praveen Swami, "The final assault and the withdrawal", *Frontline*, July 30, 1999, p. 10.
39. Praveen Swami, "Strategic follies", *Frontline*, July 2, 1999, p. 12.
40. Manoj Joshi, "Our soldiers succeeded. Where did we fail?", *The Sunday Times*, July 18, 1999.
41. Cited in *Ibid.*

42. Cited in Prakash Karat, "Kargil and beyond", *Frontline*, July 16, 1999, p. 16.
43. Aijaz Ahmad, "The many roads to Kargil", *Frontline*, July 16, 1999, p. 25.
44. Praveen Swami, "Another summer of killings", *Frontline*, July 30, 1999, p. 29.
45. N. Ram, *op. cit.*
46. See Praveen Swami, "'Pro - Active' After Pokhran", *op. cit.*
47. Praveen Swami, "Another summer of killings", *op. cit.*, pp. 27-29, details this summer's massacres and other data used in this section.
48. Praveen Swami, "The other victims of Kargil", *Frontline*, July 16, 1999, pp. 128-129, recounts events relating to the Turtok terrorist cell.
49. Ahmed Rashid, "Raise the Crecent", in Far Eastern Economic Review, Hongkong, December 3, 1998. Internet download: no page number available.
50. Aijaz Ahmad, "The many roads to Kargil", *op. cit.*, p. 21.

FOUR

A New Strategy for the LoC and Low-intensity Warfare in Kashmir

Bharat Karnad

Marcus Tullius Cicero, the Consul of Rome in the reign of Julius Caeser, pronounced on an elementary truth about inter-state relations when he said that between war and peace there is nothing. Either two countries live amicably with each other or they engage actively in hostilities geared to achieving complete military victory. In the latter case there is a winner and there is a loser and little doubt about which side is what.

By the 17th century, however, in a Europe ravaged by religious wars things were not as clear cut any more and a third, very contemporary, alternative to war or peace, namely, neither peace nor war gained international sanction. The Dutch jurist, Hugo Grotius, in attempting to codify the "rules of just warfare"[1] first made the distinction between declared and undeclared wars, deeming the former legal and the other as not necessarily illegal.[2] The "undeclared war" option, whose ambit covers most of what has come to be identified as low intensity conflict and proxy wars, moreover, received approval in treaty law in 1868 with the St. Petersburg Declaration on the basis of the by then well established principle of 'military necessity'or kreigraison.[3]

On the other hand, United Nations General Assembly (UNGA) Resolution 380 (V), 1950, condemned as a form of aggression the "fomenting of internal strife". Some twenty-four years later, the UNGA, vide Resolution 3314, seeking to define aggression, further elaborated (Article 3) that "the sending by or on behalf of a State of armed bands, groups, irregulars or mercenaries, which carry out acts of armed force against another state of such gravity [such as invasion, bombardment, blockade] or its substantial involvement therein" amounts to aggression. The same Resolution also expressly outlawed military assistance to insurgents—a prohibition contained in an earlier UNGA Resolution 2625, as well. Thus, the conclusion from just these two sets of laws is that aggression of the covert, less conspicuous and formal kind indulged in by sovereign States is at once justified and banned!

This opening digression on international law was necessary to indicate that like any other law, the law of war too is an ass. It confounds more than it clarifies. In attempting, for example, to safeguard the sovereign prerogative of States to pursue national interests by any and all means at their disposal, under the rubric of military necessity, international law undermines the very concept of sovereignty by approving instrumentalities that would put nation-States, especially those that are socially and ethnically heterogenous, at grave risk.

Such contradictory laws would be of no great account were it not that the Government of India's entire approach to outstanding territorial disputes with its two neighbours, Pakistan and China, is overly legalistic and politically naive. It exposes the country's position on Kashmir, for instance, to the vagaries of a manifestly jumbled set of laws, thereby increasing the country's vulnerabilities. Worse, it seems unmindful of the basic fact of international life that powerful countries make the laws and, when it suits their purposes, twist them to subserve their interests. In the event, sticking to the letter of the law, as New Delhi has done has only produced perverse results: it has turned the "correlation of forces" in the subcontinent on its head; the lesser State is in the driver's seat. Pakistan has ended up enjoying the power of initiative, the power to direct the course of events in Kashmir and the decisive power to engineer a *denouement* to its exclusive satisfaction even as the Government of India (GoI) is locked into a mainly reactive-defensive-passive mode and the Ministry of External Affairs (MEA) harps unconvincingly about the legalities of accession, the conditionalities imposed by the 1949 UN Security Council Resolution and the bilateral obligations under the 1972 Shimla Agreement. Underlying the official Indian thinking is the presumed rigour and efficacy of international law, which in real terms is non-existent.

As may be readily seen, Pakistan has cannily exploited precisely this grey area. Incapable of military victory over India, it has chosen over the last twenty years to wage an undeclared, relatively low-key conflict in the hope that this will progressively weaken the Indian grip over Kashmir and, by raising the cost in human lives and in material terms, New Delhi's will to hold on to that province. Kargil suggests a further honing of the Pakistani strategy into a two-pronged approach of applying pressure from the inside by orchestrating sustained insurgent activities within Kashmir, complemented by the external pincer constituted of military actions by regular forces, but in *mufti*, to capture territory along the Line of Control (LoC) with the aim of slowly nibbling away at the Indian portion of Kashmir and pushing the LoC eastward. Nuclear weapons in its inventory, Islamabad was apparently convinced, would serve (1) as adequate deterrent against India responding forcefully to neutralise violations of the LoC and, in case full-fledged war broke-out, (2) as a low ceiling beyond which India would think it imprudent to escalate, bringing the fight quickly to a standstill and (3) to precipitate mediation by the US and the West.

It is another matter that Pakistan's plans did not pan out. In part because the GoI did not keep to the Pakistani script and ordered a massive conventional parry and thrust to rollback the incursion in the Kargil sector without crossing the LoC, which might have brought the Pakistani armed forces more fully into the war and led to unpredictable turn of events. And because, the GoI simply refused to rise to the nuclear bait dangled by Islamabad and studiously ignored the nuclear threats emanating from high sources there.[5] The dismissal of the Pakistani talk of using nuclear weapons as sheer "lunacy" was particularly telling.[6]

This is what unhinged the Pakistani game-plan, which depended centrally on the threshold being speedily raised to the nuclear eye-balling level.[7] At this stage, Islamabad hoped that the Americans and their Western cohorts, frightened out of their wits by the prospect of a South Asian atomic brushfire war, would impose a peace inclusive of a settlement of the Kashmir dispute congenial to its interests.

What happened instead was that while fears were voiced in Washington and elsewhere about the India-Pakistan imbroglio escalating into a nuclear confrontation,[8] New Delhi's measured, responsible and reassuring stance, both with regard to nuclear weapons and its conduct of military operations in Kargil, increasingly marked India out as a mature country. This impression was reinforced by the fact that this response came notwithstanding the political uncertainties attending upon a caretaker government in New Delhi. On the other hand, Pakistan stood out as an unstable nuclear trigger-happy State, egged on by extremist Islamic elements within its fold, and spoiling for a fight. Western fears of nuclear escalation, in the event, boomeranged on Pakistan, and firmed up Western opinion behind the restoration of the LoC as the basis for any negotiated settlement.[9]

The all-round success attending upon the Kargil episode may well be due to the fact, as the Minister for External Affairs, Jaswant Singh stated, that the challenge of "turning back the aggressor, in defeating all his designs, in reversing the aggression but with the maximum of restraint" was met.[10]

However, if this success is looked upon as validating India's longstanding, mainly reactive, policy on Kashmir, and, thus, as a justification for its continuance into the future, then the country will be condemned perennially to dealing with the Pakistanis on their terms.

Pakistan obviously means business. India's conditions for resuming a dialogue — affirming the inviolability and sanctity of the LoC and ending "sponsorship of cross-border terrorism"[11] — have been summarily rejected.[12] Prime Minister Nawaz Sharif's threat of "many more Kargils" made during the Kargil episode has been followed up by his *confidante* and Information Minister Mushahid Hussain revealing that all that has happened after the *mujahideen* "disengaged" from the embattled sector was that they "relocated their positions... [and being] mobile...can surface in Baramulla tomorrow, Doda or Srinagar."[13] Moreover, by advancing the fiction of the *mujahideen* as having taken on the Indian Army in Kargil,[14] he has the larger purpose, which is revealed in the interview, of etching the supposedly close similarity between Kosovo and Kashmir on the minds of opinion-makers, especially in the West. The onus of pressurizing India is thus, cleverly placed on the US/NATO, who are coming off a successful operation to "demilitarize" Kosovo and to restore, to the Muslim minority, human rights imperiled by the majoritarian excesses of a Milosevic.

Again, it is the same pincer policy at work, except now external pressure is sought to be generated within the international community. Simultaneously, the bilateral track has been rubbished both in terms of its efficacy and the prospect it holds for a Kashmir solution. Pakistan Foreign Secretary Shamshad Ahmed, for instance, has charged that New Delhi uses "dialogue" as only "a tactical ploy" and demanded "an interpreter, as we speak different languages",[15] which last was a riposte to Jaswant Singh who, some time back, propounded a thesis that India and Pakistan, because they share the same cultural space, can do without third party mediation or even umpiring.

Even as India is wallowing in a euphoria of sorts, Islamabad is already on to beefing up its policy of obtaining a Kosovo-like situation within Kashmir by inducting more *mujahideen*, this time, into Jammu & Kashmir,[16] supported from the outside by a Kosovo-type system. At the same time, no opportunity is spared to internationally project a grim picture of human rights, abuses. The Pakistani game-plan is clever, clear and ambitious.

But is there an Indian counter-plan? 'More of the same' is not the answer. It has failed over the last fifty years to pacify the Kashmiri people, or to prevent Pakistan from meddling in the state's Kashmir's affairs. Worse, it has cost the country dear in terms of financial, human and military resources. Nor is relying on American/Western goodwill, seeded by the Indian policy of restraint in Kargil, going to serve any purpose. This goodwill is ephemeral at best and is, in any case, tasked for use as a vehicle for the US counter-proliferation agenda, of which the prime objective is to secure New Delhi and Islamabad's signatures on the Comprehensive Test Ban Treaty.[17] It is a design inadvertently furthered by Pakistan's imprudent nuclear sabre rattling at the time of the border skirmish. So, what is the answer?

A new approach to solving the Kashmir problem, premised on significantly raising the costs to Pakistan of persisting in its present policy of non-acceptance of the *de facto* partition of Kashmir, of the LoC as the international border, and of aiding and abetting Kashmiri insurgent activities, was recently outlined.[18] It recommends that (a) the Pakistani strategy be reciprocated in its entirety, requiring (b) forthrightly taking on Pakistan in the political-ideological realm, (c) informally issuing a brief to the Army to mount sustained small unit and commando actions all along the LoC to establish newer Lines of Control and to otherwise enlarge the Indian sphere at the expense of Pakistan-occupied Kashmir (PoK) and its Northern Areas; and (d) launching an extensive programme of covert assistance to all manner of malcontents within Pakistan.

Some of these and other relevant points will be elaborated upon here, as will the case that an ideological-military offensive is mandated by circumstances, and that this will convince Pakistan that freezing the LoC into an international border is the best possible solution. What is suggested here goes well beyond what is being sold as a "proactive" policy by other strategic analysts, which emphasizes measures including permitting the international Press to cover any hostilities unhindered; highlighting the abysmal human rights conditions in PoK and the Northern Areas; projecting the clandestine trade in sensitive technologies engaged in by Pakistan with North Korea and China; heightening the fear of a "crumbling" State in Pakistan and the threat posed to international security by its inventory of missiles and nuclear weapons; and asking for "a detailed discussion on security issues" with Pakistan as part of the Lahore process.[19] These measures are all very well, but by themselves will not make much of a difference to the course Pakistan has adopted. The iron that needs to be inserted into a genuinely proactive policy is of a different kind altogether.

A New Strategy

In international law, the Line of Control is only a Cease Fire Line (CFL). As a product of a war kept in suspended animation, it carries the expectations of both sides that a final and satisfactory settlement can be obtained if not through negotiation than by force of arms. It is this logic which under-girds Pakistani justification for trans-LoC military actions, like those in Kargil.

What are the chances that consequent upon the military reverses in Kargil, and the virtual American *demarche* to respect the LoC, the Pakistan Government will hereafter cease and desist from waging low intensity warfare in Indian Kashmir, or from initiating a Kargil-like misadventure in future? Nil. This is so because of the balance of forces in the Pakistani polity. The Punjabi-dominated military, civil services and legislature have set the agenda and the increasingly active religious right provides the motivational force and, in war-like situations with India, the sheer numbers of indoctrinated cadres who take to the streets, mobilise popular resentment and otherwise preempt any radical change in a policy centred on Kashmir and enmity with India.

Kargil has also brought to a head the disjunctions within the Pakistan Army. The Army Chief, General Parvez Musharraf, and his Chief of Staff, Lieutenant General Mohammad Aziz, both with Special Forces background, as well as the Special Service Group (SSG), have now to contend with the differing perspectives of the corps commanders of the field army. The differences apparently came to a head around the last week of June 1999 when an infantry brigade was detached from the Pakistani I Corps, an armoured strike formation stationed at Mangla, and moved to the Skardu plains to stiffen the defences in case the Indian Army attacked across the LoC in the Kargil sector. The fear of the nine Corps Commanders was three-fold: that by thus denuding their units of fighting forces, the GHQ, Rawalpindi, was imperilling war plans, (i) by weakening the ability of the mobile strike formations to go on the offensive-defence, i.e., fighting defensively to protect the Pakistani Punjab, but on Indian territory; (ii) by making the country as a whole vulnerable to attacks by India's "poised to strike" three armoured corps; and (iii) by stressing gains in a lesser theatre, putting the heartland at risk.

These factors suggest that the mainstream Pakistan Army may be unable to resist the popular demand for helping the *mujahideen* wage war in Kashmir but, at the same time, are unwilling to prosecute a full-scale war in PoK and the Northern Areas if this means putting at risk the defence of Punjab. Also, the inherent tensions between the SSG and the Corps Commanders can be sharpened by the Indian Army pressing across the LoC in an unconventional war-fighting mode. The three Indian Strike Corps (I, II and XXI) can "fix" the bulk of the Pakistan Field Army south of Suchetgarh. This would free the Indian Mountain Divisions, in small components, to adopt a policy of "grab as grab can" — a peak here, a Pakistani post there — across the LoC, in order stealthily but steadily to push the Line westwards in the Poonch and Rajouri sectors, northwards in the Kargil sector, and northwestwards in the undemarcated glaciated regions beyond Point NJ 9,842. The Pakistani ruse of dressing up regulars in *mufti* and deploying them across the LoC is an excellent example to follow for all actions across the Line. The Pakistani military establishment would certainly find the prospect disconcerting if Indian "irregulars", for instance, in slow stages capture one ridge after another, until they sit astride the mountains overlooking Skardu, Forces Command Headquarters, Northern Areas; or sit atop hills looking down on Domel or Muzzafarabad. This would, in effect, impose "Siachenisation" on the Pakistan Army, which would have to scramble to build up all-weather defences and to garrison strongly-held lines in the mountains.

Such a policy, however, will require the GoI to rid itself of its several inhibitions about what it believes the Shimla Accord enjoins. Its view that senior Indian and Pakistani army officers, deputed by their respective Governments, cartographically marked out the LoC, and, therefore, that there is an implicit ban (perhaps formalised by a 28-year old custom) on the use of conventional armed forces across the CFL will have to be tempered by reasons of "military necessity". The "hot pursuit" option abjured so far by the Indian armed forces, but permissible in international law under the principle of *droit de voisinage or nachbahrrecht*,[20] will have to be activated.

Such a course of action will open up opportunities for

territorial augmentation because the logic of the CFL/LoC offers it. The trouble is this logic seems to be better appreciated by Pakistan than by India. Once Islamabad had determined that there was no chance of peacefully wresting Kashmir from India, its actions — whether in support of the low intensity warfare waged by 'freedom fighters' in the Valley or of the trans-LoC aggression in Ladakh — have been in tune with the longstanding Pakistani conviction and policy that Kashmir rightfully belongs to them, and that they mean to secure it, come what may.

The same cannot be said about India. Prime Ministers, beginning with Indira Gandhi, including Narasimha Rao and right up to Atal Bihari Vajpayee, have in response to the Pakistani stance that Kashmir constitutes the "unfinished agenda" of Partition, claimed mostly for effect that the only unfinished part of that wretched business remains the return of PoK to India. And that there was nothing else to negotiate. But these were statements devoid of serious intent and designed merely to protect leaders against the charge of selling-out. In the event, the Indian Government has ended up treating the LoC as sacrosanct, at great cost to the country.

That the Indian leaders are periodically compelled to take this inane position is traceable to the fact that Indira Gandhi, as the leader of the victorious country in the 1971 War, deliberately forsook the last legitimate chance afforded by international law of imposing a peace which might have included the conversion of the LoC into an international border at Shimla. She failed to press home the advantage because, like Zulfikar Ali Bhutto and all the Indian and Pakistan leaders since, she, too, feared a political backlash for 'giving away' territory and retaining only a part of Kashmir.

Over time, this political compulsion has turned into complacency *vis-a-vis* the LoC, leading to contradictory Indian policies. For example, the pronouncements of Indian leaders if taken at their face-value would mean that New Delhi is as keen in absorbing PoK as Islamabad is in taking over the Indian part of Kashmir. In that case, the LoC loses its standing of inviolability any way, which New Delhi swears by. Because the Pakistanis are no more likely to amicably hand over PoK and Northern Areas to

India than India is likely to transfer J and K to Pakistan, the disputants are left with only two alternatives: go to war and risk an attendent catastrophe now that the milieu is nuclearised, or engage in low-level but sustained military actions — grabbing a peak here, a post there — aimed at continually increasing the size of the real estate in their possession.

Islamabad has cannily opted for this last, risk-free, option; risk-free because the Indian Government, 1972 onwards, has stood national security interests on their head in choosing to regard the LoC as a *de facto* international border and in accepting in its train a whole lot of obligations that are not mandated by international law with regard to a CFL. A shackled Indian military, moreover, is stuck with the difficult task of dealing with well-armed Pakistani troops and guerillas-for-hire *after* they infiltrate *en masse*, as in Kargil; their difficulty enhanced further by the GoI's unmerited respect for the LoC. The military's frustration is, perhaps, what boiled over into the Chief of Army Staff, General V.P. Malik's plea to the government to rethink its attitude on cross-LoC operations.

Whatever we understand the obligations of the bilateral agreements and understandings between India and Pakistan to be, the fact is that most of the world considers the LoC as nothing more than a CFL pending a final solution. This is the political and ground reality and it is this status that has the sanction of international law. The most obvious manifestation of this is the continuing presence of the United Nations Military Observer Group in India and Pakistan (UNMOGIP) set up as a result of the original 1948 UN Security Council Resolution. India has, of course, unilaterally decided that the UNMOGIP's functioning is invalidated by the Shimla Accord, and has restricted its working to a closed compound in Srinagar.[21] But this position is not agreed to by Pakistan nor supported by any major country.

It is this status of the LoC, for instance, which is the basis for the growing Western view voiced by former American diplomats Teresita C. Schaffer and Howard B. Schaffer — each of whom headed the Bureau of South Asian Affairs in the US Department of State — in favour of freezing the LoC into an international boundary.[22] New Delhi will have no trouble backing such a proposal, because that is what, without putting it in so many words, it has been working to realize these many years. The problem is how to persuade Pakistan that this is the only feasible way out of the quagmire?

Talking alone will not do. Experience shows that Foreign Minister and Foreign Secretary-level meetings are all very well but that these have so far resolved nothing except issues on the margins. Nor will ill-considered actions, like striking conventionally across the international border, do anything other than possibly prompt nuclear weapons use by Pakistan. The real challenge is to provide negative incentives to the Pakistanis to settle along the desired line, because positive incentives, such as promises of hugely beneficial trade and economic ties and of cultural exchanges, etc., have failed to convince Islamabad.

The track guaranteed to fetch results is to informally order the army to keep pushing the LoC outwards. Sustained and relatively inconspicuous military actions by small-sized units and commandos backed up by the occasional battalion-strength operation, at varying depths in PoK, recommend themselves as the obvious instrumentality for a policy of incremental additions of territory to the Indian Kashmir. Like its counterpart in Pakistan, the Indian government can, in the meanwhile, offer political cover for such activity by continuing to harp on the Shimla Accord, the LoC, etc. and to simply deny any evidence of the LoC-changing measures.

The optimal use of military manpower in this "slow creep" policy will ideally mean reorganising the army in such a way as to create a Special Forces Command headed by a Lieutenant General-rank officer, the equal of an Army Commander. This has become imperative both because there is an immediate necessity for such a structure to prosecute sustained actions in hostile territory as envisaged in this Paper and, more generally, because future wars are likely to resemble small scale operations which are best prosecuted within the Special Forces ambit,[23] rather than as a lesser branch of conventional warfare characterised by masses of men and machines rolling across plains or fighting uphill in mountainous terrain, as is the present case. All operations to be carried out across the LoC and possibly the Line of Actual Control (with China) would be the responsibility of the GOC-in-C, Special

Forces Command. He would have under him fighting units, most of them extracted from existing Mountain Divisions and, by way of integrating all the available fighting assets when necessary, the paramilitary police forces, such as the Border Security Force, the Central Reserve Police Force, the Indo-Tibetan Border Police, *et al.* As an opposition Member of Parliament, Jaswant Singh, in fact, suggested just such a scheme some four years back.[24]

With the hindsight of what worked, it will be preferable to have units in the proposed Special Forces Command recruited from among mountain-folk. The singular successes notched up in the Kargil heights by elements of the Naga Regiment, the Garhwal Regiment, the Gurkha Rifles, the Jammu & Kashmir Light Infantry, and the Ladakh Scouts indicate that the onerous high altitude acclimatisation regimes can be short circuited when it comes to soldiers who are highland natives. (It takes upwards of three months to properly recondition troops from the plains for fighting in the mountains.)

The other prong in this more aggressive approach will require external intelligence agencies methodically to assist discontented groups within Pakistani society, starting with those in PoK and the Northern Areas — which should not be difficult since the latter are denied basic human rights even according to a judgement handed down by a Pakistani High Court Bench.[25] The Mohajirs in Karachi provide a second fertile ground.[26] Destabilising Karachi, Pakistan's commercial capital and the source of most of its tax revenues, and the Sindh province at large, can be facilitated by linkages with the Muttahida Quami Movement (MQM). Similarly, the Taliban in Afghanistan and their offshoot in Pakistan can be distracted and neutralised by reviving the independent Pakhtunistan movement, and by installing some kind of an air-bridge for military supply of the ousted Rabbani government, comprising the Northern Afghan tribes and factions who are fighting Kabul. Cooperation with Iran to assist the Afghan Hazaras can also be diligently pursued. Separatists in Baluchistan were brutally crushed in the Seventies. Judicious aid could easily resurrect their movement as well.

Such policies are not merely a mirror to the Pakistani role in Kashmir and other parts of India. They serve two specific purposes: first, to demonstrate to Islamabad that, as in the conventional military sphere, India has a decisive edge in the unconventional military field as well. Second, and more important, to compel the Pakistan government and elites to rethink their risk calculus.

The objective simply would be to make Islamabad fully comprehend the costs, both in terms of domestic disorder, and the ever-shrinking territory it would control in Kashmir, as well as the unaffordably high bill it will have to pay to finance military and police effort to tackle such Indian initiatives. Islamabad is already reduced to surviving from one World Bank *tranche* of credit to the next. It sequesters in excess of 90% of its annual budget on debt repayment and the maintenance of its military and civil service. Even if it wished to, it cannot spend more on internal and external security, short of inviting complete economic collapse.[27]

The beauty of this tit-for-tat policy is that Pakistan will not be able to match the Indian effort in either the conventional or the unconventional/covert spheres. Ultimately the Indian weight of numbers and the disparity in all kinds of resources, including military and economic, will begin to tell. In case a frustrated Pakistan, in this pressure situation, hints at using nuclear weapons, the threat will be as incredible and infructuous as a like Indian threat would have been in the Kargil crisis. Such a threat would also have the world opinion ganging up full square against Pakistan.

Islamabad will then be faced with some severe options: to settle permanently for PoK as its part of the final Kashmir bargain, formally accepting the LoC as an international border, or gradually losing strategic portions of the State it now holds and steadily getting enervated economically and internally, in terms of law and order. However, a promise can be held out as a further incentive to Pakistan that in case it agrees to settle on the LoC as the international boundary (rationalization of the border apart), the LoC prevailing at the time of the Shimla Accord would be the settled border, and that India would surrender any territory captured/occupied by its "irregulars".

An activist policy cannot now be avoided. Kargil has fired up the people, so much so that even conservative journals have called editorially for "Avenging our dead."[28] If Pakistan follows through on its avowed policy to nurse the insurgency in Kashmir back to life, then, in international law, this will amount to *animus belligerendi* — conclusive behaviour from which the intention to wage war can be inferred. This, in turn, may be a *casus belli*, justifying almost any Indian counter measures, including resort to use of force or to stratagems of the kind discussed above.[29] The policy fleshed out here will, above all else, satisfy the punitive mood of the people and advance Indian interests in Kashmir without precipitating a general war. Unfortunately, the core problem is something more troubling.

The Ideological Divide

Distrust is endemic to India-Pakistan relations.[30] Its sheer intensity is an intimation of a graver, more enduring ideological rivalry and a deep and unresolved socio-cultural issue: India's fundamental premise that the obvious differences in caste, creed, religion, ethnicity and language, within a vast and gloriously heterogenous society, can be moderated to a point where the perception of common good transcends narrower affiliations, and a nation-State is constituted.

The central idea of Pakistan rests on the contrary and an equally basic assumption that no such reconciliation is possible at least not between Hinduism and Islam. Whatever the merits of the Pakistan-argument — it entirely ignores the reality that sub-continental Islam is as varied as Hinduism and as much a product of syncretic and tolerant cultural impulses — what it ultimately reduces to is the glorification of fairly trivial differences. As Mohammad Ali Jinnah, in 1946, told the visiting Chief of the Imperial Defence Staff, Field Marshal, the Viscount Montgomery, who queried him about the chances of India and the Indian Army remaining united, "How can I talk with the Hindu? He worships the cow; I eat it." The *Quaid*, thus, touched at once on the most profound and petty aspects of the communal divide in India; a divide that, as a result of Partition, has been internationalized.

Seen in this light, Islamabad's diplomatic campaign to portray Kashmir as another Kosovo is pregnant with dire possibilities. The crux of the matter is not that it is an inapt analogy but that, as an American political scientist concluded in a recent analysis of developments in Kosovo, "the new logic of national self-determination, while it may reinforce state sovereignty in ethnically homogeneous states, frequently challenges it in multinational states."[31] The fact that 'multinational' States today comprise a majority of the countries of the world provides some protection against international attempts to intervene in Kashmir, as does the dawning realization in the US and West Europe that self-determination, while fine as rhetoric, can be extremely disruptive of the social fabric woven over the millennia in traditional polities. But this cannot by any means be considered a long-term deterrent. Superpower interests may be differently interpreted at any time.

The war for Kashmir is less military than one of competing ideologies. Tackle Pakistan's ideological stake head on, and the military problem will, of itself, dissipate. What is at issue? The right of the Kashmiris to decide their own future, but a future that is within the Indian whole. After all, had there been no Partition would the people of the erstwhile "princely state" of Kashmir have had the option not to join the Indian Union? Could they have chosen to couple with Afghanistan or China or be independent? Obviously not. The tyranny of choice came only with the reality of Partition. This to say that the incumbent Maharaja's prerogatives with the lapse of British paramountcy had nothing to do with prior linkages between Kashmir and the rest of India, which were and still are as integral to the whole and as organic as of any other constituent province. The history and ties of culture, ethos and even shared religion cannot be suddenly sundered on the basis of arbitrarily imposed criteria, which are spurious at best. It is the Partition criteria, then, which become the lynchpin for the argument that all of J&K stays with India or that it seeks a future as part of Pakistan.

Whatever the merits of the historical case made by either side and the reasons for the absence of a negotiated settlement so far, the fact is that a solution has to be sought in the here and now, and not in the sharply differing versions of the reality that existed in 1947-49. That is one constant. The other is the Partition criteria according to which chieftains of over six hundred small and large kingdoms decided to merge with one or the other of the successor States. The two operative principles followed were those of contiguity and of the religion of the majority of the people within the princely state. The first criterion was straight forward; the second less so because, unlike Pakistan which opted to don an Islamic identity and to adopt Islam as State religion, India remained firmly secular by Constitutional *diktat*. Moreover, however many Muslims chose to migrate to Pakistan, the bulk of them stayed behind. In other words, Partition was not a clean communal break, necessitating full and complete transfer of Hindus and Muslims from one Dominion to the other, but merely a dissociation by a rump State.

Muslims may have many grievances against the Indian State, but nothing distinguishes these from the grievances that other sections of society also have against the same State. Low literacy levels, for example, plague many regional, caste, tribal and other sub-groupings, as they do the Muslims (assuming they can all be treated as similarly disadvantaged, like-thinking, people, which is simply not the case). And Kashmir, if anything, has received a much better deal than many others. Here the investment of the Indian taxpayer's money is so great, that barring some North-Eastern States, it is the most highly subsidised State in the Republic— nearly three-quarters of its revenues emanate from the Centre, up from less than four per cent in 1950-51.[32]

To argue in this fashion may beg the question, since demography was the basis of Partition. But the logic of demography has itself altered radically since Maharaja Hari Singhs's Accession decision of September 1947. At that time Pakistan was, in fact, the State with the larger Muslim population. This and the contiguity principle favoured Kashmir's merging with Pakistan. But that was then. Today, there is an independent Bangladesh, which seceded from Pakistan in 1971. As a result, the Muslim population in India first equalled and, by some accounts, has now exceeded the strength of Muslims in Pakistan. Indeed, if the latest census figures are any guide, the Indian Muslim population stands to surpass that of Indonesia by 2010-2015.

As the soon-to-be largest Muslim country in the world, India's Kashmir policy is instantly endowed with heft. New Delhi's claims on Kashmir acquire unmatched credibility, both in terms of the main Partition criterion because it is now joined to the successor country with the larger Muslim population, and because of the evidence of more than fifty years of good faith efforts to protect Kashmir's autonomy within the Indian Union and to protect its special identity, vide the controversial Article 370 in the Constitution.

It would be of even greater conseqeunce, from the point of view of undercutting the residual Pakistani claims on J&K, if the GoI were to henceforth declare that this country is also the guardian of interests of all Muslims in the subcontinent, including those in Pakistan. This guardianship role is the one coveted for Pakistan by Jinnah. India's assumption of this role can effectively destroy all of Pakistan's pretensions as a leader of Muslim countries worldwide, and at home, would fatally undermine the mischievous Two-Nation theory. Wouldn't it be a soul-destroying prospect for Islamabad to find the Mohajirs of Karachi and Sindh turning to India for protection against the predatory Punjabi State of Pakistan? This can happen, if New Delhi adopts some version of the policy suggested here.

The hitch in all of this is, alas, the Government of India which is unlikely to imperil its secular credentials by so boldly furthering Indian interests in Kashmir by 'exploiting' the fact that India is the largest Muslim country in the world, just as it is the largest Hindu, Sikh and Jain country in the world. Indian foreign policy generally is in a rut and particularly so where Kashmir is concerned. In lieu of any bright ideas, the same old time-worn rhetoric, policy and statements are dusted up. Any surprise that the Kashmiris don't listen and the international community is deaf to the Indian case as traditionally pleaded?

NOTES AND REFERENCES

1. LIPSET, Seymour Martin (Chief Ed.), *The Encyclopedia of Democracy*, Vol. III, London, Routledge; p. 879.
2. DE LUPIS, Ingrid Detter, *The Law of War*, Cambridge, Cambridge University Press, 1987; fn. 34, p.8.
3. *Ibid*; pp. 332-33.
4. *Ibid*; pp. 60, 68
5. See "Pak again threatens to use N-weapons", PTI, *Times of India*, 1 July 1999.
6. "Pak N-threat borders on lunacy: Brajesh", PTI, *Hindustan Times*, 5 July 1999.

7. GoI's view is also that it regarded Pakistan's Kargil incursion as "calculated to provoking India into an escalation." See the text of External Affairs Minister Jaswant Singh's speech "Kargil and Beyond" delivered at the India International Centre, 20 July 1999; p. 4.
8. See the statement by US Defence Secretary William Cohen urging caution on both India and Pakistan, now that both of them have developed nuclear weapons in "India, Pakistan out to flex N-muscle: Cohen", PTI, *Times of India*, 11 July 1999.
9. "US: Pak flouted N-code by crossing LoC", *Pioneer*, 22 July 1999.
10. SINGH, Jaswant, "Kargil and Beyond"; *op. cit.*, p. 2
11. "India sets 3 terms for talks to resume", *Hindustan Times*, 14 July 1999.
12. "Pakistan rejects India's terms for bilateral talks", PTI, *Indian Express*, 22 July 1999.
13. See the interview with Mushahid Hussain , "Mujahideen have been relocated: Pakistan" by Seema Mustafa, *Asian Age*, 21 July 1999.
14. Hussain is quoted as saying: "The Indian Army has received the biggest hammering at the hands of a few hundred mujahideen."; *Ibid.*
15. See Fn. 12.
16. See SHARMA, Arun, "Militants enlist more youth, forces fear fresh violence", *Indian Express*, 22 July 1999.
17. CHANDRAN, Ramesh, "Clinton seeks Senate ratification of CTBT", *Times of India*, 22 July 1999.
18. See my "Kargil: Using LoC to India's Advantage" in *Economic and Political Weekly*, July 19, 1999; "An elastic border", *Hindustan Times*, 15 July, 1999; and, "Pushing LoC Outwards", *The Week*, July 25, 1999.
19. SUBRAHMANYAM, K., "A Proactive Policy: Countering Pakistan After Kargil", *Times of India*, 13 July 1999.
20. DE LUPIS, The Law of War, *op. cit.*, fn 137, p. 72. Also see V.S. Mani, "Kargil and international law - II", *Hindu*, 30 June 1999.
21. A detailed history of UNMOGIP may be found in Pauline Dawson, *The Peacekeepers of Kashmir: The UN Military Observer Group in India and Pakistan*, Bombay, Popular Prakashan, 1995.
22. SHAFFER, Teresita C. and Howard C., "Freeze Himalayan Borders Before Fighting Escalates", *International Herald-Tribune*, 16 June 1999.
23. CREVELD, Martin van, *On Future War*, London, Washington, New York, Brassey's, 1991. This is the most comprehensive treatment of the subject.
24. See his USI National Security Lecture, 1995, reproduced as a book *National Security:An Outline of Our Concerns*, Lancer Paper-7, New Delhi, Lancer Publishers,1996; pp. 64-68.
25. See Mani, *op. cit.*
26. MODY, Anjali, "MQM fast to protest 'atrocities' against Mohajirs", *Indian Express*, 22 July 1999.
27. See Jayshree Sengupta, "Pakistan's sick economy", *Hindustan Times*, 14 June 1999, and Sanjaya Baru, "War and economy: Pakistan's Road to Ruin", *Times of India*, 14 July 1999.
28. Business India, June 14-27, 1999.
29. DE LUPIS, *op. cit*; pp. 9, 259.

30. The Pak Foreign Minister Sartaj Aziz rejected his Indian counterpart Jaswant Singh's condition for dialogue that Pakistan take actions to restore the trust occasioned by the Indian PM Atal Bihari Vajpayee's bus trip to Lahore, saying "Since there has not been any trust between the two countries due to the negative, obdurate and hegemonist Indian attitude, there is no question of any betrayal of trust." See "Vacate Siachen, Chorbat La: Aziz", IANS, *Pioneer*, 23 July 1999.
31. See Carol Skalnik Leff, "The Kosovo Crisis" in *Swords and Ploughshares: The bulletin of the Program in Arms Control, Disarmament, and International Security*, University of illinois at Urbana-Champaign, Vol. II/Numbers 1-2, 1999; p. 3.
32. KARIM, Maj. Gen. (retd) Afsir, Kashmir: *The Troubled Frontiers*, New Delhi, Lancer Publishers, 1994; p. 242.

FIVE

Free Speech in an Age of Violence

The Challenge of Non-governmental Suppression

Ajai Sahni

Words are deeds.[1]

In April this year, the Srinagar station of All India Radio (AIR) stopped the broadcast of an innocuous, though very popular, programme based on Hindi film songs, *Geet Gata Chal*, following threats by a militant group active in the Kashmir Valley. The decision was officially conceded to have been taken under pressure from 'certain quarters'. It came close at the heels of a threat-notice published in a local Urdu daily by a pro-Pakistan militant group that claimed that the programme offended against 'Kashmiri culture'.[2]

From a limited administrative perspective, the decision is not unreasonable, particularly against the background of highly focused terrorist violence against media professionals who offend extremist sensibilities. In February 1999, three cable television entrepreneurs were shot in their legs as a "warning"[3] against their failure to follow the extremists' *Talibanised* code of conduct.[4] There have, over the past decade, been several attacks — many of them fatal — against media personnel, both in the private and state-owned media.

Such trends have not been restricted to the State of Jammu & Kashmir (J&K) alone. One may recall the chilling effect of the kidnap and gruesome murder of M. L. Manchanda, station director of AIR at Patiala in May 1992. Manchanda was decapitated, his torso thrown in Patiala, and his head, miles away, in Ambala. The killing, claimed by the Babbar Khalsa, was an unprovoked, crude and effective demonstration of the terrorists' determination to impose their 'code of conduct' on the government's broadcast agencies. And despite the fact that the perpetrators met their end in police encounters within a few days,[5] the retreat, not only of the official media, but of the Press in general, was complete. Every element of the "Panthic code of conduct" was, thereafter, "accepted by the official media, AIR and Doordarshan, as unquestioningly as by the national and regional newspapers (with a single isolated exception)".[6]

The validity of the 'limited administrative perspective' that contributed to the AIR decision is compounded by the fact that the content of the speech acts that are sacrificed by such a withdrawal may not, on the face of it, appear to be worth the risks or the expense that would be involved in opposing the militants' demands. A programme of Hindi film songs has little overt political value and there is a large constituency, not only in Kashmir or among the terrorists, but among the general public all over India, that regards the increasing prurience of their lyrics and the coarseness of their execution with great disfavour. In view of the crisis of the low intensity proxy war in Kashmir, to make an issue out of something quite so 'frivolous' may seem incongruous.[7]

This argument, however, is defeated by the very context within which it is stated, because the demand to shut down a particular radio programme is only one element in a larger campaign to "set the Valley's cultural agenda in their (the terrorists') own narrow and sectarian terms."[8] This agenda includes the prescription of a "dress code" for women, *fatwas* against cinema halls, as well as against the consumption and sale of liquor, and a rigid code of social and religious practice, each of which has been, from time to time, imposed through violence or the threat of violence.

Terrorist-imposed restrictions on the freedom of speech, moreover, are part of a continuum that comprehends acts of criminal intimidation and incitement to crime, and that often culminates in crime. The Manchanda-killing in Punjab was intended to inflict a specific Panthic code for the electronic media that, at its most innocuous, required women newsreaders and anchors on television to cover their heads; banned the words 'terrorist' or '*atankvadi*' (in Punjabi) and their derogatory equivalents and sought an end to all non-Punjabi language programming. But they also demanded that highly subversive propaganda material be carried on the official media — without amendment or censorship — and sought a number of administrative changes that no democratic and secular government could accept.[9] These demands were elements in a larger and more general "Press Code" that required mandatory publication by all newspapers of the press releases and advertisements sent in by terrorist organisations (and this was faithfully done even where the contents were highly subversive and amounted to criminal incitement and intimidation). At the same time, a Panthic Code of general conduct was also implemented in the State through bullet and bomb.[10]

The dilemma, in the Srinagar AIR case, consequently, goes far beyond the question of discontinuing a single, apparently 'zero value', programme. As one commentator notes, "the fight against militancy was not so much about guns as about the fundamentalist and obscurantist world-view that it represented."[11] And it is this worldview that is inflicted, through violence or the threat of violence, on large populations who are otherwise unwilling to accept the fundamentalist perversion of their culture. By retreating in the face of the threat of violence, the State abandons the very constituency that makes democracy a possibility, leaving them voiceless and vulnerable to coercion.

Nor indeed, in our age, is the problem restricted to the fight against militancy. The assault against the freedom of expression has, in these times, taken on a peculiar virulence and a character with which conventional executive and judicial wisdom has rarely been confronted.

The traditional challenge to the freedom of speech has usually come from a repressive State that seeks to silence criticism, or to suppress ideas that are not approved of by the government of the day, the ruling elite, or by the moral majority. In this regard, there is a long tradition of jurisprudence that has set the bounds of the freedom of expression far from the core of politically valuable speech, and fairly close to the limits of licence. An oft-quoted dictum, both in the US and Indian jurisprudence, is that :

> A function of free speech under our system of government *is to invite dispute*. It may indeed best serve its high purposes when it *induces a condition of unrest, creates dissatisfaction with conditions as they are, or even stirs people to anger*. Speech is often provocative and challenging. It may strike at prejudices and preconceptions and have profound unsettling effects as it presses for acceptance of an idea.
>
> This is why freedom of speech...is...protected against censorship or punishment... There is no room under our Constitution for a more restrictive view. For *the alternative would lead to standardisation of ideas either by legislatures, courts, or dominant political or community groups*. (Emphasis added)[12]

By and large, restrictions on the freedom of speech have, consequently, been defined in the interest of public order since "opinions lose their immunity when the circumstances in which they are expressed are such as to constitute their expression a positive instigation to some mischievous act."[13]

Such an approach, however, fails to meet the exigencies of an increasing number of cases where the threat to peace is not caused by particular speech acts that are abusive, insulting or inciting to violence, but arises out of a response to the voicing of certain ideas that may be disapproved of by specific, often small, vocal and potentially violent groups. Or, in a lesser *avatar*, cases in which restrictions on speech are sought to be imposed on grounds that particular speech acts would 'hurt the sentiments' of particular communal, caste, regional or other special interest groups.

The furore over the film *Fire*, which explored the development of a lesbian relationship within the context of a conservative Indian family, is a case in point. This perfectly pedestrian film was transmuted by the Shiv Sena's violent protests into an icon of the freedom of expression standing against a groundswell of bigotry and intolerance. Significantly, for the chauvinistic groups who attacked the film, the issue was not 'obscenity', but 'Indian culture'. One of the foot soldiers of the Bharatiya Janata Party (BJP), which co-operated with the Shiv Sena in the anti-*Fire* protests, saw evidence of an "Islamic conspiracy" in the portrayal of one of the main characters of the film, Radha, by a Muslim actress.[14] The then Chief Minister of Maharashtra lauded the violence of his Shiv Sainiks, declaring, "What they have done is correct. The film is against Indian culture."[15]

The State of Maharashtra has, of course, played a leading role in the "public censorship" of ideas that are deemed to offend against the so-called ideology of *Hindutva* ever since the BJP-Shiv Sena combine came into power there. There has been a sustained and violent campaign, led by supporters of these two parties and supported by the Vishwa Hindu Parishad, against artist M.F. Hussain's "offensive" portrayal of Hindu deities.[16] Morality brigades have mushroomed, scrutinising, for instance, the lyrics of songs to be played by the Australian band, Savage Garden; and demanding a ban on Eric Clapton's *Cocaine* on AIR — a demand that was immediately conceded.[17]

But the wave of bigotry goes well beyond the borders of Maharashtra, and indeed, of common sense. Thus, we have the BJP — self-appointed votaries and defenders of India's ancient culture — protesting against the representation, on the cover of a diary issued by Delhi Tourism Development Corporation, of a well-known bronze sculpture of a dancing girl dating back to the Indus Valley Civilisation. The diary, on which hundreds of thousands of rupees had been spent, was hastily withdrawn.[18]

Nor indeed, is the lunacy restricted to the Hindu far right. The staging of a play (once again in Maharashtra), *Mee Nathuram Godse Bolte*, which sought to represent the point of view of Mahatma Gandhi's assassin, was blocked by protests, both of the leadership and the lumpen elements, of the 'secular, liberal, democratic' Congress party.[19] In Madhya Pradesh, the Chief Minister of the Congress-I-led government, similarly, sought a ban on a book, *Godse's Murder and After*, by Gopal Godse, Nathuram Godse's brother.[20]

Taking their cue from national political parties, numberless 'social service' and non-governmental organisations and activists have also jumped on to the censorship bandwagon, often using the Courts to further their ends — and to derive the publicity that is usually their predominant motive. A handful of examples demonstrate the sheer sweep of such actions. In 1997, the Miss Tourism International pageant was disrupted as a result of protests by a motley group of some 200 activists of the Bharatiya Janata Mahila Morcha, who barged into the hotel where the contestants were staying, and ransacked the lobby during a rehearsal of the show. The local administration simply withdrew permission for the show, and their decision was upheld by the Andhra Pradesh High Court.[21] Even more interestingly, two population and sex education programmes, *Balance Barabar* and *Kaam ki Baatein*, produced by a Non-governmental organisation (NGO), Population Service International, and Marie Stopes Clinic, and aired on the extremely conservative AIR, were banned on grounds of 'obscenity' on a petition by another unknown defender of public morality, the Azadi Bachao Andolan. The Magistrate's concern, however, obviously went well beyond obscenity, and sought to impose a particular interpretation of public morality: "*Balance Barabar*", he noted, "tilts heavily in favour of sexual freedom in the guise of sexual information without caring for ethical and moral standards. So is the case with *Kaam ki Baatein*." The offending programmes answered public queries relating to common sexual problems and apprehensions — masturbation, homosexuality, the use of Ayurvedic pills for safe sex, adultery, etc.[22] A Delhi Court also restrained the telecast of a TV programme which featured a pair of turbaned anchors who called themselves Tony Singh and Titoo Singh as a result of a petition that claimed that the "feelings of Sikhs in general have been deeply and badly injured."[23] In Rajasthan, the Chief Justice of the High Court converted a letter written by a school girl into a Public Interest Litigation against a satellite television channel; the girl claimed she was frightened by a horror show aired on the channel.[24] Numerous such cases are brought up, from time to time, in provincial courts, and their chilling effect on the freedom of expression is barely noticed, as most such cases go unreported, or secure only passing mention in the media. This impact is compounded many times over by other instances, which do not even reach the Courts, but where intimidatory tactics are used against individuals and groups who fail to conform to the ideas and expectations of potentially-violent groups.[25]

Unfortunately, the subordinate judiciary has frequently been more than willing to support claims of injured sectarian and moral sensibilities, displaying little concern or awareness of the larger context and purpose of the freedom of speech, or of the jurisprudence established by superior courts in clear precedents. To the extent that decisions of the subordinate courts in most such cases are seldom appealed — publishers, TV programmers, film-makers and artists simply want to get on with life and are far from eager to remain mired in an interminable, complex and often futile judicial process — the actual limits on the freedom of speech are ordinarily defined in these numerous, often unnoticed, judicial orders. Indeed, many such cases end at the preliminary stage itself, as producers and artists voluntary cut out the offending portions of their productions in order to escape the pattern of 'punishment by trial' that has now become a fact of life in India's sluggish judicial system.

There has, of course, always been a large sphere of intolerance in Indian society; but while it may not have diminished, there is no reason to believe that it has grown. It has, however, shifted in recent years from the periphery of the social and political stage to its very influential centre. What has grown, as a result, is the institutional tolerance of (specific categories of) intolerance, and this is increasingly reflected in judicial and executive action.

The most significant impact of this regime of intolerance and constraints on the freedom of speech is that it has tended to impose a closure of debate on a wide range of issues deemed to be 'sensitive', politically incorrect, or morally improper. Caste and religion, linguistic, regional and cultural differences, gender and sexuality — the free discussion of controversial aspects of each of these has come under progressively restrictive taboos, even as the entire public space has been left free for obscurantism and bigotry.

We, thus, see the emergence of two opposing dangers. In situations of extreme and widespread disturbance, the Courts and the executive have expressed themselves through acts primarily of omission in favour of the freedom of the most extreme speech, frequently comprehending incitement to terrorist crimes and violence.[26] In situations of peace, on the other hand, the institutions of the state have tended to ally themselves with the intolerant, prohibiting speech acts on the first pretext of an 'injury' to sectarian sentiments or standards of morality peculiar to small and volatile groups. The violent exposition of the doctrines of communal and sectarian hatred, and the suppression of certain categories of speech that are disapproved of by volatile elements, has, thus, been encouraged by a policy of increasing licence extended selectively to those who back their speech acts, or their acts of censorship, with violence.

This, however, is not the consequence of the jurisprudence evolved in the superior judiciary, but of the practice inflicted in numberless and unreported — often uncontested — decisions that reflect little more than the personal predilections and prejudices of individual members of the subordinate judiciary and the provincial administration. These decisions tend to ignore the distinction between a threat to peace that is *caused* by particular speech acts that are threatening, abusive, insulting, or inciting to violence, and a threat to peace that *arises out of* an 'audience response' to the voicing of 'unpopular' ideas, what is described in legal literature as the "heckler's veto".

Clearly, if the purpose of free speech is "to invite dispute"[27], and if even unpopular ideas are to be allowed expression, we must come to terms with the possibility of attempts by militant groups to violently disrupt their public espousal. If a danger to public order alone obsesses the mind of enforcement agencies, then, if a group of dissenters, or simply hooligans, disrupts, or threatens to violently disrupt a meeting in which one or more speakers expresses unpopular opinions, or opinions divergent to theirs, and action is taken against the speakers for breach of peace, such action vests a *de facto* power of censorship on the disrupters. And this is not the sole danger. Once this principle is established, the police may be tempted to disperse meetings or demonstrations, even when the risk of violence is relatively slight; and worse, a biased administrative authority may use the possibility of violence as an excuse to actively suppress and censor the expression of views critical of the government or the *status quo*.

As with other areas on the uncomfortable borderline between

freedom of speech and violence, no simple solution is available to the problem of the hecklers' veto. The law must, of course, preserve peace, but if the democratic ethos were to survive, the law must, equally, guarantee protection against intolerance to those who express divergent opinion.

It is important to note, within this context, that courts may be reluctant to challenge the exercise of executive and police discretion in circumstances of apparent emergency. In any case, by the time the matter reaches the court, and in the event that the speaker is acquitted, the exercise of his right to free speech will already have been successfully stifled. An acquittal does not retrospectively guarantee the right to freedom of expression: the moment may have passed, the protest may no longer have significance and the occasion for the demonstration may have lost relevance. It is, consequently, essential to establish and implement an explicit jurisprudence that judiciously balances competing values.

The problem of hostile audience has notably been taken up by the Indian Supreme Court in substantial detail in what is known as the *Ore Oru Gramathile* film censorship case.[28] The Tamil film *Ore Oru Gramathile* (In Our Village) dealt critically with the sensitive issue of the State's reservation policy, arguing against the Constitutional provisions for reverse discrimination in favour of the Scheduled Castes and Tribes, under which a proportion of seats are reserved for these groups in educational institutions as well as in government service and public sector employment. The State of Tamil Nadu had appealed to the Madras High Court against grant of a censor's certificate for exhibition of the film on the grounds, among others, that the film could create serious law and order problems in the State.

The Madras High Court found great merit in this reasoning and noted that if the film was exhibited it would endanger public order because "it instigates ill feelings and distrust between Forward Castes (*sic*) and Backward Castes, including Scheduled Castes and Scheduled Tribes".[29] The Court cited with approval the observation of members of the Revising Committee on the film that "The overall impact of the film is an exhortation that there should not be any reservation on the basis of caste. This, I fear, will create strong negative response from a section of the public leading to a law and order problem." Similarly, the Court noted that a member of the Second Revising Committee had opined that "the film, if exhibited, is likely to hurt the feelings of some group which may endanger public order."[30]

The Madras High Court also very convincingly placed the issue in the context of India's continuing history of communal and caste violence, observing that the film's advocacy of abolition of the 'reservation system' would lead to clashes "between several castes."

> Already people in the state of Gujarat had suffered immeasurably for a long period on this issue. Several were killed and public properties were damaged. There were agitations in Andhra Pradesh, Tamil Nadu, a land of tranquility, by misguided notions of some, had experience in recent past communal clashes (sic)... Valuable lives have been lost... On the eve of elections, invariably, caste factors have come to play their disgusting role... when the impact of the film is centred around caste factor and when the topic has been mishandled, if a breach of law on this factor occasions (sic), then it will have wide ramifications... If the administration fails to foresee properly the outcome of the dissatisfaction created among Castes and Communities, if would result in public properties and valuable lives of Citizens being lost.[31]

Certainly the danger of violence noted by the High Court was both real and grave. Equally clearly, however, this violence was not being instigated by the speech act in question, which essentially consisted of the peaceful - if politically incorrect - advocacy of reforms in certain laws, and the criticism of certain policies adopted by the government. However inaccurate its representation of the issues, or unpopular the ideas expressed in the film, it was no part of the prosecution's argument that the film constituted incitement to violence, or instigation to crime; nor was the film abusive or intolerably insulting against any individual or group of individuals. The argument, quite simply, was that reverse discrimination on the basis of caste is unfair and results in distortions that could constitute a miscarriage of justice. Those who disagreed with this message were free to stay away from the screening of the film. Or to protest it by peaceful means, in the equal exercise of their own freedom of speech. The very real threat of violence that was spoken of in the Madras High Court judgement was the threat of a hostile audience reacting to a message it preferred to suppress. As the Court itself admitted, the film would affect the "sensibilities of large sections of the general public, who are prone to resort to violence."[32]

What the Madras High Court did in Ore Oru Gramathile was entirely in keeping with the general attitude of Courts in India in the past. By and large, courts chose to refuse to make concessions to free speech in the face of broad demands by the state that public order would be affected. In the Crossroads case of 1950, of course, there had been a powerful liberal statement,[33] and the Constitution had to be amended when judges refused to accept that the interests of public order were linked to the security of the state. Broadly, however, the courts tended to show great generosity in fulfilling the state's restrictive demands. The Supreme Court, for instance, allowed time-bound pre-censorship in the Daily Pratap case, even while admitting that the law was not "designed to directly maintain the public order, or directly protect the general public against any particular evil";[34] and in Ramjilal's case, the State was allowed to punish for the publication activities which had a "tendency to cause public disorder."[35]

In *Ore Oru Gramathile,* however, the Supreme Court completely repudiated this tradition, refusing to accept the threat of public resort to violence as a legitimate ground to deny the censors certificate to the film. The Supreme Court chastised the High Court judgement for having run "afoul of the democratic principles to which we have pledged ourselves in the Constitution."[36] Justice Shetty cited the observation of the Court in Naraindas Indurkhya vs. State of Madhya Pradesh with approval:

> It is our firm belief, nay a conviction which constitutes one of the basic values of a free society to which we are wedded under our Constitution, that there must be freedom not only for the thought that we cherish, but also for the thought that we hate.[37]

Justice Shetty particularly stressed the Constitutional dispensation that "it was not necessary that everyone sing the same song."[38] The state, the judgement asserted, cannot prevent open discussion and open expression, however hateful to its policies, and everyone had a fundamental right to form and express his or her own opinion on any issue of general concern. Free speech in a democracy, the Supreme Court insisted, was not just a strategic safety valve, but was based on the expectation that "a bit of sense may be salvaged from the odious minds striving to be rational."[39] Quoting the European Court in Handyside vs. United Kingdom, Justice Shetty defended the right to unpopular speech, even if such speech "shocked or disturbed the State or any sector of the population."[40] He insisted that the restrictions imposed must be proportionate to the legitimate aim pursued, and any restriction by the State "must be justified on the anvil of necessity and not the quicksand of expediency."[41]

These observations alone were sufficient to overturn many preceding judgements in favour of constraints on speech: the state was now required to show a necessity, and that too, a real necessity, even a clear and present danger, before it was given the power to restrain and punish expression.

The Court, however, went even further, declaring that not only was it incumbent on the State not to restrain such speech, but that it was the duty of the State to actively and positively protect and defend those who exercise the right to unpopular speech. The Court demanded, "what good is the protection of freedom of expression if the State does not take care to protect it?"

> ...freedom of expression cannot be suppressed on account of threat of demonstration and processions or threat of violence. That would tantamount to negation of the rule of law and a surrender to blackmail and intimidation. It is the duty of the State to protect the freedom of expression since it is a liberty guaranteed against the State. The State cannot plead its inability to handle the hostile audience problem. It is its obligatory duty to prevent it and protect the freedom of expression.[42] (Emphasis added).

Whatever the practice resorted to in day-to-day administration by the police and the magistracy, with Ore Oru Gramathile the jurisprudence established by the Indian Supreme Court now stood at par with the most liberal ideologies of the West. Indeed, in many ways, the observations in Ore Oru Gramathile go well beyond the prevailing jurisprudence in the USA and UK, considered leaders in the field.

The American Supreme Court has not clearly delimited the powers and duties of the police where there is a hostile audience on the point of violently breaking up a lawful meeting. However, Feiner vs. New York[43] is one of the leading cases with a bearing on this issue. A speaker at a street corner in Syracuse gathered a small crowd of both whites and blacks around him. He launched into an invective-laden speech in which the US-President was described as a "bum", and the local mayor as a "champagne-sipping bum" who "does not speak for the Negro people." The speaker advocated that the blacks should "fight" for equal rights, and the crowd began to get restive. The police feared that a fight could break out, and after two requests to the speaker to stop, he was arrested for disorderly conduct. The majority of the Court upheld the conviction on the grounds that he had incited to riot, and that there was clear and present danger of disorder - perfectly acceptable grounds in law, though the Court's interpretation of facts could be brought into question. It was, however, the dissenting opinion of Justice Black and Justice Douglas that gave special significance to the case, as they argued that the record did not show any intent on Feiner's part to cause violence despite his exhortation to the 'Negro people' to fight for equal rights. Justices Black and Douglas thought that the police's primary duty in the situation was to protect the speaker, if necessary by arresting members of the hostile audience. By adopting the opposite course, they insisted, police censorship had been imposed.

Though no subsequent judgement of the American Supreme Court explicitly dealt with the hostile audience issue in any detail, it appears that the dissenting opinion of Feiner vs. New York has now gained predominance in the US jurisprudence. In Wolin vs. Port of New York Authority[44] the 2nd Circuit Court indicated that the initial responsibility of the police is to protect the First

Amendment rights as far as possible. Thus, if the police have advance information on the possibility of violence or disruption of a political demonstration/speech, they should ensure the presence of an adequate force to safeguard the freedom of speech and assembly. An order to disperse can only be justified as a last recourse, when there is a clear and present, or imminent, danger of physical violence. In Gregory vs. Chicago,[45] the majority of the US Supreme Court held that the demonstrators could not constitutionally be convicted of 'disorderly conduct' for refusing to obey police requests to disperse when they were confronted by hostile opponents. In the landmark Skokie judgement, where the Supreme Court held that a group of neo-Nazi's could not be prevented from carrying out a flag-march in Skokie village which had a large Jewish population, many of whom were survivors of the Holocaust in Germany, the hostile audience problem was also touched upon, albeit peripherally. The Court observed that, if Skokie officials were so sure that certain hostile groups would be hard to control, the village should seek an injunction against those persons and prohibit their unlawful actions, adding that "if these civil rights are to remain vital for all, they must protect not only those society deems acceptable, but also those whose ideas it quite justifiably rejects and despises."[46] In all, American case law seeks to protect the values of free speech until it is clear beyond doubt that they should be subordinated on a particular occasion to public order.

British case law is far more restrictive, and confers sweeping powers on the police. There is, of course, one major decision that adopts an uncompromisingly pro-free speech position in the hostile audience context: Beatty vs. Gillibanks,[47] where the Divisional Court refused to uphold binding-over orders imposed on leaders of the Salvation Army for holding an unlawful assembly. On a number of previous occasions, their procession had been broken up by the Skeleton Army, and on this occasion, Beatty and some other Salvation Army leaders were arrested when they refused to disperse a procession that police felt would also be violently obstructed. The Court held that the processionists had not caused any unlawful act, and that the disturbances had not been the intended, natural, or necessary consequences of their processions.

Justice Field added, further, and very significantly, that the Skeleton Army would be less inclined to intervene when they appreciated that their obstruction would not terminate the Salvation Army processions, but that if they did continue their violent opposition, the police would deal with them, and not with people exercising their lawful rights.[48]

The case, however, was highly controversial in Britain, and its impact has been progressively diluted by the preventive powers granted to the police to keep the peace which now provide a basis for criminal prosecution even where organisers of a meeting have no intention to provoke disruption. This authority flows from Duncan vs. Jones,[49] in which the appellant had started to address a small meeting outside a training centre for the unemployed in London, at a spot where disturbances had followed another meeting an year earlier. Fearing a repetition, the police asked the appellant to move to another spot, 175 yards away, and when she refused, she was charged with obstructing a police officer in the execution of his duty. Her conviction was upheld by the Divisional Court.

This decision evidently rendered the law on freedom of non-provocative assembly impotent. Here everything turned on whether the police reasonably apprehended a breach of peace - clearly a fragile basis for the protection of civil liberties.

Compared to the sheer scale of potential violence that Ore Oru Gramathile addressed - the possibility of a caste conflagration that could envelope an entire state, and possibly spread across the nation - the dilemma confronting the British and American courts appears almost trivial, and their resolution somewhat equivocal. Ore Oru Gramathile was indeed an immensely revolutionary judgement; but more than a decade has passed since it was pronounced. Over this period, the spirit and essence of that judgement appear to have been swept aside by the rising tide of political violence, and the increasing fragility of the Indian administrative system - both civil and judicial. These changing circumstances may tempt a revision of the principles stated in Ore Oru Gramathile, bringing our jurisprudence in line with the more conservative practice, and the increasing intolerance, of our age.

This would be a grave error, compounding the cumulative

failures of governance and the administration of justice that have already pushed our nation to the knife edge of violence. Indeed, the growing violence of our times is, at least in part, a consequence of declining levels of political debate and a consistent refusal — across party lines — to discuss fundamental and disturbing issues. The result is that these troubling issues are simply brushed under the carpet of a pretence of harmony and conformity until they explode into violence. The whores' ethic of consensus has, today, made it impossible to hold an honest debate on issues connected with caste or religion, to take two prominent examples, and has given rise to the absurd claim that only a Dalit or a Muslim can correctly articulate the interests, the aspirations and the good of the community he 'represents'. Large sections of the population have, consequently, been held hostage to their own exploitative, often bigoted, caste and religious leadership, progressively excluding them from the sphere of liberal democratic thinking and the possibility of social and economic development. Any critical attention from an 'outsider' or a dissident is immediately suppressed, not only by violent opposition from caste groups and religious orthodoxies, but also as a result of the supportive and politically correct protestations of the supposedly liberal, egalitarian and secular political leadership.

These problems are immensely exacerbated in a situation of widespread terrorist violence. Administrative expediency is, in such circumstances, a near-overwhelming argument in favour of the selective suppression of speech acts that may offend fundamentalist and extremist sentiments. But such a regime of expediency would only strengthen extremism. It is now imperative that the state puts its fullest force behind the protection of free speech against non-governmental and extremist censorship and repression. This becomes a basic necessity for the survival of the democratic framework: "If we seek a true victory, we must defeat the fundamentalist ideologies that threaten to plunge the entire region into a conflagration that may well destroy us all. The greater war that we must now engage in is the war for the minds of men."[50]

Rhetoric alone, even the powerful rhetoric of Ore Oru Gramathile, will not suffice to meet this end. Consistent administrative and judicial action, based on a sound understanding of the rationale of the judgement, even in the most challenging of circumstances and at costs that may be regarded as prohibitive, is required. The level of commitment that is needed to implement such a policy on the ground can be understood best in the context of a single extraordinary example — the sacrifices, the costs, the effort and the manpower that went into protecting the Hind Samachar Group in Punjab. The Group was thought by Sikh extremists to be projecting an 'anti-Sikh' stand. One of the earliest acts of terrorism in that state was the assassination of Lala Jagat Narain who headed this Group. A sustained campaign of liquidation targeting the management, the journalists, and eventually even the distribution network - including hawkers and newspaper delivery boys — was carried out against this Group throughout the period of terrorism in the state. 62 persons associated with the Group were killed by the terrorists.[51] The stubborn persistence of the family that controlled the Group, even in the face of this onslaught, is well known: they simply refused to be cowed down, to shut down their paper or to change their editorial stance. What is not known quite as well is the sheer magnitude of the protective umbrella, provided by the state police, under which they functioned, and in the absence of which their courage and obstinacy would have been fruitless, indeed fatal to the very last man. More than two battalions of armed police men and para-military force personnel were, at one time, assigned to the protection of the Hind Samachar Group and its operations - and this included operations down to the smooth delivery - through hawkers and newsboys - of copies of the paper to its readers.[52]

Speech is a curious entity. The most noble ideals enunciated in the Constitution, the stentorian pronouncements of the Supreme Court, the overarching oration of our members of Parliament, may have no impact on the ground — despite the immense significance ascribed to them in our system of governance. And yet, a seemingly obscure idea articulated in a context ripe for its realisation; a chance remark, uttered in some remote province, that seizes the imagination of its people; a symbol, conjured out of the collective aspirations of our faceless masses; each of these has within it immeasurable possibilities of national transformation.

This is the unequivocal presupposition of democracy. And this is why the state cannot, must not, retreat - or allow even the most inconsequential voice to be silenced - in the face of intolerance, of intimidation, of coercion, even of the threat of the most extreme violence.

NOTES AND REFERENCES

1. WITTGENSTEIN, Ludwig, *Philosophical Investigations*, 546.
2. Cf., "Meek Surrender", (Editorial) *The Hindustan Times*, April 6, 1999.
3. AHMAD, Rashid, "Valley stage to new morality play", *Pioneer*, 7.3.99.
4. MISHRA, Law Kumar, "J&K militants target jeans, cable TV", *The Times of India*, February 25, 1999.
5. Cf., GILL, K.P.S., "Endgame in Punjab: 1988-1993", *Faultlines 1.1*, Bulwark Books, May 1999, p. 64-65.
6. *Ibid.*, p. 53. The exception was the Hind Samachar Group, which had paid and, throughout the period of terrorism in Punjab, continued to pay in blood for their stubborn resistance to the extremist *diktat*.
7. The distinction between 'frivolous' and 'serious' speech acts, however, is not as simple as it seems. There have been several attempts in jurisprudence to distinguish between 'high' and 'low' value speech which merit differential protection, and 'zero value' speech, which would merit no protection. It is, however, erroneous to assert that the protection of the freedom of expression should be extended only to political or politically significant speech, and not to other speech deemed to be of lesser social value. Apart from the intrinsic value of speech as a medium of self-expression and self-development, there are a number of problems of distinguishing between what constitutes 'political' or significant speech, and what doesn't. This problem has often been raised in connection with obscenity laws. Thus it has been suggested that almost all sexually related 'speech' "will invariably carry an implicit, if not explicit, message in favour of more relaxed sexual mores... In our society, the very presence of sexual explicitness in speech seems ideologically significant, without regard to whatever other message may be intended." [STONE, 'Restriction of Speech because of its Content: The peculiar case of Subject-Matter Restrictions'. 46 *University of Chicago Law Review*, 1978, p. 111-112]. As a result, American Courts have seen fit to treat topless dancing as a form of expression protected by the First Amendment, though they recognised that "few of us would march our sons and daughters off to war" to protect this form of expression [*Krueger vs City of Pensacola*, 759 F 2d 851, 854 (11th Circuit) 1985]. Indian Courts, however, have been far more conservative in the moral codes they seek to inflict on the nation, and have found it expedient to exercise their power of censorship in a wide range of cases, including the successful prosecution of a Bombay bookseller for the sale of D. H. Lawrence's *Lady Chatterly's Lover*. (AIR 1965 SC 881: 1 SCR 65). Such sweeping powers of censorship are

rooted in the "overbroad" provisions of Article 19 (2) of the Constitution, which define the 'Interests of Decency and Morality' as grounds for restriction of free speech. The fact, nevertheless, remains that "The line between the informing and the entertaining is too elusive for the protection of that basic right. Everyone is familiar with instances of propaganda through fiction. What is one man's amusement, teaches another's doctrine." [*Winters vs. New York*, 333 US 510 (1948)].

8. "Meek Surrender", *op. cit.*
9. The Babbar Khalsa issued a Press Release on May 21, 1992, setting the following conditions for Manchanda's release:
   (i) Letters written by Sukhdev Singh Sukha and Harjinder Singh Jinda (General Vaidya's assassins) to the President of India be broadcast in various languages including Punjabi on Radio and Television at prime time (9.00 pm).
   (ii) All programmes relayed from AIR-Chandigarh, Bhatinda and Patiala should be in Punjabi.
   (iii) Jalandhar Doordarshan would telecast programmes in Punjabi, with preference to programmes depicting 'Khalsa culture' . Only 5 per cent of the total programmes were to be telecast in Hindi, and these were to be screened by a committee of Punjabi scholars.
   (iv) All non-Punjabi officials - including artistes - working in Radio and Television stations should be removed.
   (v) News in Punjabi to be broadcast at prime time and Hindi bulletins be discontinued.
   (vi) A majority of newsreaders and announcers on Doordarshan should be Sikhs.
   (vii) Teleprinters in Punjabi should be introduced.
   (viii) Radio and Doordarshan should adopt a balanced approach and give proper coverage to militants.
   (ix) Apologies should be tendered for telecasting the programme 'Punjab Yatra' which was aimed at defaming the militants.
   (x) In Punjabi bulletins, the word atankvadi should be dropped and instead the word kharku be used. Words such as terrorists, extremists and ultras should not be used.
   (xi) Representatives of militants should be invited to present their views on Radio and Doordarshan.
   (xii) Every programme or News bulletin should commence with *Sat Sri Akal* in place of *Namaskar*.
10. Some 243 persons were killed by terrorists in Punjab between 1990 and 1992 alone under the garb of "social reforms" - or the implementation of their Panthic moral code. [1990: 76; 1991: 121; 1992:46]. Source: Punjab Police.
11. "Meek Surrender", *op. cit.*
12. DOUGLAS, Justice William O., Terminiello vs. Chicago, 337 US 1, 1949. See also: WIGMORE, John, 'Abrams vs. US: Freedom of Speech and Freedom of Thuggery in War-time and Peace-time", 14 Illinois Law Review 1920, pp 554-58; BOLLINGER, Lee C., The Tolerant Society: Freedom of Speech and

Extremist Speech in America, OUP (New York), Clarendon Press (Oxford), 1986; NEIER, Aryeh, Defending My Enemy, New York: Dutton, 1979

13. MILL, J S, "On Liberty", *Britannica Great Books*, Vol. 43, Encyclopaedia Britannica, 1952, p. 293.
14. BAGHEL, Meenal, "Quick Gun Murugans, Revolver Ranis", *Indian Express*, December 13, 1998
15. DUTT, Nirupama, "Playing with Fire", *Indian Express*, December, 1998.
16. *Ibid.*
17. BAGHEL, *op. cit.*
18. DUTT, *op. cit.*
19. Cf. AZMI, Shabani, "Freedom under Fire", *Times of India*, December 17, 1998.
20. "Digvijay seeks ban on book by Godse's brother", *The Pioneer*, October 27, 1997.
21. "Organisers of 'Miss Tourism' move apex court against stay", *Indian Express*, November 3, 1997.
22. "FM producers summoned for 'obscene' broadcast", *The Pioneer*, October 25, 1997 and "AIR pulled up for 'obscenity'", *Indian Express*, October 25, 1997.
23. GILL, K.P.S., "The Devil's Alternative?", *The Pioneer*, August 9, 1997.
24. *Indian Express*, December 7, 1997.
25. Cf. for instance, "Arrest warrant against Mamta Kulkarni", *Times of India*, October 171998; "Book Banned", *The Pioneer*, December 2, 1998; "Udham Singh in dock for mocking Laloo", *The Hindu*, April 21, 1999; "Schools targeted for letters on Kargil", *Indian Express*, July 19, 1999.
26. The issue of extremist speech, incitement and intimidation merit separate and detailed treatment, and I propose to take these up elsewhere.
27. See DOUGLAS in note 12 above.
28. S. Rangarajan vs. P Jagajeevan Ram and others, (1989) 2, SCC, 574.
29. S. Rangarajan vs. Government of India, AIR 1989, 176, Madras.
30. *Ibid.*
31. *Ibid.*
32. *Ibid.*, at 177.
33. *Romesh Thapar vs. State of Madras*, 1950 SCR 594.
34. *Virender vs. State of Punjab*, AIR 1957; SC 896.
35. *Ramjilal Modi vs. UP*, 1957 SCR 860, ('57) ASC 620.
36. *Op. cit.* at 35.
37. SCC p. 816, para 23: SCR p. 650.
38. *Op. cit.*
39. *Ibid.* at 40.
40. EHRR, 1976, p. 737.
41. *Op. cit.* at 53.
42. *Ibid.*, at 51.
43. 340 US 315, 1951.
44. 392 F. 2d.83, 2nd Circuit, 1968.
45. 394 US III, 1969.
46. 578 F. 2d at 210.

47. 1882,9 QBD 308; 1882 15 CoxCC 138.
48. *Ibid.*, 146, per Field, J.
49. 1936, 1 KB 218.
50. GILL, K.P.S., "Battle for the Mind: Nobody can be a Winner in Kargil", *Times of India*, July 9, 1999.
51. This included 2 chief editors; 2 news editors / sub-editors; 12 reporters / photographers and their relatives; 2 drivers; and 44 agents, sub-agents and hawkers. Source: Arvind Chopra, Director, Hind Samachar Group.
52. Details of the actual security cover provided are as follows:

Security Cover for Hind Samachar Group Jallandhur

(i) Security at the Press - permanent guards at Jallandhur. Inspector - 1, Sub-Inspector -3, Head Constable - 6, Constable -60, (above one company strength)

(ii) For escort of the proprietor and his family - Head Constable - 2, Constable -3, (about one section strength)

(iii) Residence of the Proprietor - Sub-Inspector - 1 , Head Constable -3 , Constable - 3, (about one platoon strength).

(iv) Arrangement in the morning at Jallandhur for sending taxis with Hind Samachar Group of News papers going to various destinations - about one half company's strength (say-about 90 Security personnel with escorts vehicles, going with Taxis or escorts persons sitting in the taxi itself).

(v) At various main centres of Distribution in Jallandhur - Wherever hawkers used to come to collect news paper about one and a half Company strength (say 90 Personnel with Gypsys for Mobile Patrolling and guarding of the distribution centre).

(vi) Residents of the main distribution in Jallandhur - about one platoon strength (Say about 24 personnel at the rate of 2-3 armed personnel for distributor's residence).

(vii) Patrolling in the areas where hawkers of Hind Samachar Newspaper used to distribute news paper in various areas - about two company (Say 90-120 armed personnel with Gypsies for Patrolling).

(A) The Arrangement in other Cities/Towns where Taxis Carrying 'Hind Samachar Group of Newspaper's Reached with the news Papers

(i) At the place of arrival of Taxi-One Section-Guard/Patrolling (Main Distribution Centre).

(ii) At Sub-Distribution Centres, Hawkers etc. the arrangement of armed Guards/Escorts were being made according to the sensitivity of the area/town. Normally, it consumed a strength of one company (Say about 60 Personnel), in smaller town and about 3 companies (Say 180 Personnel) in bigger towns.

(iii) The arrangement of Guarding distributors, sub-distributors and hawkers were required everyday during the morning hours- at the time of distribution of the newspaper. However, some distribution centres and residence of distributors which had been declared targets by the terrorists were given permanent guards.

(B) In Borders Districts of Amritsar, Gurdaspur and Ferozepur

Despite massive security arrangements which at times required deployment of about 5-6 company's (300-350 Security Personnel) during the morning hours, foolproof security cover was not possible to be provided. In the first few months of declaring Hind Samachar Group a target, the terrorists killed, a number of hawkers and a few distributors in these districts.

Subsequently, terrorist killings of personnel associated with the Hind Samachar Group became more prominent in the Malwa Areas - i.e., the Ludhiana-Sangur Belt.

(C) General

The arrangement of sending escorts with the Taxis carrying Hind Samachar News Paper was as under:-

Starting from Jallandhur escorts used to accompany the Taxis up to the border of the adjoining districts. The adjoining districts used to provide escorts in the area of its own districts and escorts of Jallandhur used to return back from the inter District Border. Thus almost every district had to keep escorts ready at various inter-district border to take over taxis carrying Hind Samachar News Paper.

The district SSPs in turn used to make similar arrangements for inter Police Station escorts. Thus there was a network of escorts and patrolling provided throughout the state every day to ensure that the voice of media is not curbed by the terrorists. Despite all efforts, sporadic killings of person associated with the Hind Samachar Group did take place.

Source: Information provided by C. Pal Singh, former IG Operations, Punjab, who was responsible for counter-terrorist operations in the state, and under whose over-all charge the security arrangements for the Hind Samachar Group were made.

SIX

Technology, Terror and a Thoughtless State

K.P.S. Gill

Policing in general and counter-terrorism operations in particular have, in India, remained trapped in a low technology cul de sac for decades. Indeed, it would be safe to say that, on the threshold of the twenty-first century, a bulk of the police forces in the country are operating at technological levels that date back to the early twentieth century — or, at best, to the post-World War II colonial era. The primitive *lathi* (bamboo stick) and the bolt-action .303 are often the only instruments of authority that the police wields in an increasingly volatile context that comprehends constantly widening areas of escalating civil strife.

The situation has been compounded infinitely by terrorism and low intensity warfare that have become a permanent feature of India's internal security scenario over the past two decades. In this time, the technologies available to terrorists have improved continuously, albeit along a linear, accretionist scale, dramatically increasing their fire power, mobility, communications and surveillance capabilities. The response pattern of the security forces to these incremental gains has lagged significantly and consistently behind. Virtually no shift in the technologies available to the terrorists in any theatre has been presaged and countered in advance of its introduction into the theatre of conflict — even where the direction of change is clearly predictable and inevitable.

The introduction of cellular phones and later, of Iridium technology, are cases in point. India woke up to the cellular phone technology well after it was already entrenched, not only in the advanced nations of the West, but in most of the market economies of South Asia. The potential for misuse and abuse of cellular communications by criminals and terrorists was not only evident, but substantially documented in many of these countries well before the cell phone found entry into India. And yet, when these instruments were introduced into the terrorist inventory, or to run criminal networks (in some cases even from within the State's prisons), enforcement agencies responded with inept amazement, and it was some time before they began to turn the technology to their own advantage, setting up the requisite facilities to monitor calls on these networks and to identify and locate terrorists and criminals by tagging suspect connections. The legislative response has been even tardier. Far from establishing an adequate regulatory mechanism to prevent abuse of this technology, laws do not even provide for any failsafe methods to ensure that connections on cellular networks are not acquired under false identities, or anonymously.

The matter does not end here. The slow creep of Iridium technology, heralded by a long drawn international media blitz, caught intelligence agencies as completely unprepared and ill-equipped as its precursor, the cell phone. Another potential opportunity had been squandered, with the advantage, once again, surrendered to the forces of disorder and violence.

Similar patterns are visible in weapons technologies available to terrorists. Kalashnikov Assault Rifles, RDX and sophisticated timing devices, shoulder fired rockets and missiles, Unmanned Aerial Vehicles (UAVs) for surveillance and attack — the introduction of each of these in the Indian theatre of low intensity warfare was easily predictable and inevitable, given regional geopolitics and the prevailing supply situation. Yet, on each occasion, the security forces and with them, every other institution of governance, has been caught entirely unprepared.

The responsibility for this failure cannot squarely or

correctly be laid on the security forces, the legislature, or any specific institutions or arm of governance. It is, in substantial measure, structural. The flow of information between the vast governmental apparatus of research and various field and operational agencies, as also state and central legislatures, is mediated — or perhaps more accurately, obstructed — by a bureaucratic maze that destroys all possibilities of proactive, or even efficiently reactive, response. The reverse flow of information from the field — regarding specific problems and challenges emerging from technological shifts in terrorist capabilities — is similarly inhibited.

More than a century ago, George Bernard Shaw had wryly remarked, "The British soldier can stand up to anything except the British War Office."[1] The statement describes perfectly the relationship between the Indian *jawan* and the formless, faceless bureaucracy that defines the conditions and circumstances under which he must serve. Bureaucrats by and large, prefer to deal with problems they understand and feel they can succeed with. In general, they do not understand low intensity warfare and terrorism, are largely ignorant of the ground situations in which forces are required to operate and of the character and role of modern technologies in contemporary conflict. To the extent that this is the case, they tend to undervalue, neglect and ignore threats emanating from this direction, preferring conventional responses, such as the shuffling around of forces in a reassuring demonstration of their own power. That this demonstration feeds nothing more than their own flagging confidence is increasingly evident in the rising casualties terrorists are inflicting, both on civilians and on the SFs themselves and in the widening gaps that exist between technologies and materials accessed by terrorists and those that have been made available to the SFs. Denial, I have had occasion to note in another context, marks the bureaucratic response to the emerging challenges of a world in transition. Bureaucrats lack, and have stubbornly refused to acquire, the specialized skills that contemporary technological changes have made imperative, turning themselves, at a stroke, into ill-adapted anachronisms fated to extinction.[2] The problem is not, as most bureaucrats would immediately argue, one of the allocation of scarce resources. It is primarily a problem of perceptions and of the growing inadequacy of a predominantly 'generalist' bureaucracy in an increasingly specialized world. Most of our administrators and policy-makers lack the requisite technical knowledge, or even the general awareness of technological shifts occurring in the field of conflict and much more, on the outer periphery of technological innovation and research.

At least part of the problem is also the contempt in which the lives of personnel in the uniformed services are generally held. The predominant attitude appears to be that, since these men have volunteered for service in the police, paramilitary forces, or the army, they should accept even the most extraordinary — and often avoidable — risks and hardships without complaint and must expect to be killed. This characterization may sound uncharitable to all but those who have actually been involved in the thankless task of negotiating with the bureaucracy on behalf of the fighting men of this country.[3]

I have, in the past, cited the example of the impact of the introduction, in May 1987, of the Kalashnikov (AK-47) in the Punjab terrorists' arsenal and my requests for an upgradation of the SF's fire-power.[4] The police and SFs were, at that time, armed with the obsolete .303 Lee Enfield rifles, or the equally obsolete bolt-action 7.62s. The Central Reserve Police Force (CRPF) were slightly better equipped, with 175 Self Loading Rifles (SLRs) per battalion — although the SLR was no match for the AK-47. When no new supplies seemed forthcoming, I requested that the large number of Light Machine Guns (LMGs) then lying unused in police armouries all over the state be deployed against the terrorists. Completely ludicrous arguments were advanced to obstruct this move — among them the assertion that such weapons may be used by the police against unarmed crowds and would contribute to the possibilities of 'human rights violations.' This reflected such ignorance of police procedures that, had it not been articulated at the highest levels of governance, it would not even deserve explanation. The fact is, every police station is armed with a mix of weapons and each of these is issued for specific use. Teargas would be issued for mob control; rifles, only when these were required. I cannot imagine a police officer in India who would authorize the issue of machine guns for any kind of crowd control or management of unarmed demonstrations. Suffice it to say that, eventually, after the LMGs were deployed, far from these being used against civilian crowds, the SFs in Punjab never found it necessary to use any kind of firearms for crowd control. This was the case even through the turbulent 1990-91 period when tens of thousands of agitated Sikhs gathered in quasi-religious demonstrations to protest the "martyrdom" of various prominent terrorists.[5] The fact is, better arms and equipment with the SFs do not lead to human rights violations or police excesses. If anything, the reverse may be true, as inadequately equipped forces confront a better equipped enemy and succumb to the inevitable frustrations of a war of attrition which they see themselves fighting with their hands tied down.

Take another example. For the past decade, on an average, nearly a thousand security men have been killed each year — most of them in terrorist conflicts, or while confronting well-equipped criminals from organized networks. India's vast technological resources, research establishments and immense manufacturing capacities are capable, we are constantly reminded, of putting satellites into space, of building nuclear bombs and missiles for their delivery across continent, and of creating supercomputers. Yet they cannot, or have not been tasked to, produce a lightweight, safe and economical bulletproof jacket that could protect its men in action. Instead, police administrators in the past have been forced to depend on their own inventiveness and the resources of the market to fabricate a crude jacket of steel plates. This may weigh as much as 9.5 kilos (the maximum permitted by MHA specifications), inhibits movement and offers limited protection against the high density fire of the Kalashnikov assault rifle. The DRDO has developed a BP Jacket that weighs 7.8 kg and this is now issued to many of the SFs. Is this the best we can do against the imported jackets that come up to a few hundred grammes and are safer?

This is critical. The fighting capabilities of a soldier are not measured in terms of fire-power, mobility and communications alone — though these may be the most important parameters. Indeed, bureaucratic indifference and neglect is reflected most dramatically and persistently in the personal effects and protection that are standard issue to each *jawan*. Dramatic changes in design have resulted in the development of rucksacks that can redistribute weight from the shoulders to the waist and could significantly diminishing both the burden and discomfort of carrying the 5 to 20 kilo standard issue that each *jawan* must bear in various situations and at little incremental cost. But the forces in this country have failed to move beyond the crude World War I backpack — the pitthoo — that cuts deeply and painfully into the shoulders if carried for any length of time. Nor has there been any change in the heavy, clumsy and comfortless boots that *jawans* wear. Only a fraction of the personnel serving in high altitude areas are issued imported alpine jackets; most must make do with the cold comfort of the bulky and relatively ineffective Indian issue. The recent Kargil conflict exposed the somewhat bizarre predicament of the army of a 'nuclear nation' temporarily paralysed by the lack of suitable mountain footwear for its soldiers.[6] Hasty imports were needed to resolve that problem. And yet, India has been fighting the highest altitude war in the world on the Siachin Glacier since 1984; paramilitary forces have also been fighting terrorists at high altitudes in J&K for nearly a decade. Can we not even produce a suitable pair of shoes for our fighting men?

The question is not of technological competence, but of attitudes. The fact is that, even today, the *jawan* is thought of as a sort of combination of *coolie* and cannon fodder, not only by policy makers and bureaucrats, but by many of his own officers as well and by much of the public at large (except in brief periods of national crisis where excessive sentimentality dominates the public response). These attitudes have been able to survive at the threshold of the 21st century largely because a burgeoning population of the rural poor keeps our armed forces supplied with poorly qualified manpower and because we have, till now, been able to measure our strengths purely in terms of crude numbers.

This, however, will not do in the new century. We are now on the verge, not only of an unprecedented acceleration, but of a radical discontinuity in the linear trajectory that terrorist technologies have followed over the past decades. Indeed, we must now prepare for a paradigm shift in the very nature of low intensity warfare and terrorism. The stubborn courage, the dedication, the unquestioning obedience and spirit of sacrifice of our forces may have sufficed in the past, but these will need to be backed with far greater technological competence, equipment and infrastructure — and more importantly, far greater prescience and planning — if we are to succeed against the emerging "capacity for hyperviolence"[7] that is passing progressively into the hands of the terrorists.

The character and potential scale of this "capacity for hyperviolence" has not yet been adequately understood by our bureaucrats and policy-makers. The sheer enormity and swiftness of the changes that threaten us in this sphere make not just the decisions of the past, but the decision-making process itself, entirely obsolete. Alvin Toffler notes in connection with the 'non-state actors' in the emerging international political scenario that:

> Governments find it increasingly difficult to deal with these new actors on the world stage. Governments are too bureaucratic. Their response times are too slow. They are linked into so many foreign relationships that require consultation and agreement with allies, and must cater to so many domestic political interest groups, that it takes them too long to react to initiatives by drug lords or religious fanatics and terrorists.[8]

The terrorists themselves, however, are entirely free of constraints or compunctions.

> By contrast, many of the Global Gladiators, guerillas and drug cartels in particular, are non- or even pre-bureaucratic. A single charismatic leader calls the shots quickly, and with chilling - or killing - effect.[9]

The Global Gladiator's capacity for hyperviolence is, today, finding increasing potential for expression in two distinct trends: i. the rapid, though linear, improvement of technologies available to terrorists and the widening gap between these and the technologies available to counter terrorist forces; and ii. the radical leap in technologies for low intensity warfare — including Weapons of Mass Destruction (WMD) — that is now imminent. Both these will demand unique patterns of response and neither can be neglected, if we are to survive as a nation. Our success will depend entirely on our ability to understand and predict the character and dimensions of these changes and to initiate responses well in advance of their realization.

Linear Developments

The primary sources of arms and communication technologies for terrorists in various parts of the country, till the mid-eighties, were weapon snatching, theft or robbery, raids on police armouries, ambushes on SF patrols and convoys and a trickle of arms and equipment acquired in the black market abroad and smuggled into the theatre of conflict. There was, consequently, a certain symmetry in technologies available to terrorists and those used by the SFs, with an advantage of numbers and assured supplies accruing to the latter.

Pakistan's direct intervention in terrorism on Indian soil — specifically in Punjab — in the mid-eighties brought about an irreversible change in this situation. For the first time, agencies of a nation-state, with their enormous resources and legitimate access to high military technologies, guaranteed supplies to non-state terrorist groupings. For some time, these supplies had to be paid for by the militants, usually in funds mobilized through extortion or the drug trade; after 1989, however, they not only came free of cost, but in a far greater number than ever before. Initially, the sheer enormity of this change was not realized in India beyond the limited circle within the police and military leadership who had to confront and counter the escalated threat. Indeed, even today, when Pakistan's covert agencies are offering weapons to any and every militant group — irrespective of ideology and wherever they may be active, in J&K, the North East, even Bihar and Orissa— there are many in the civil administration who persist in the belief that the problem can be confronted locally and through conventional law enforcement measures based on assumptions of the minimum use of force.

A decade-and-a-half ago, terrorists in India had access to an arsenal that comprehended single shot rifles, pistols, a few SLRs, carbines and sten guns, hand grenades and crude bombs. Today, they have graduated to sophisticated assault rifles, high velocity telescopic sniper rifles, Light and Medium Machine Guns, armour piercing incendiary ammunition, RDX and PETN based explosives with complex triggering devices including trip-switches, remote control mechanisms, light differential relay switches, high frequency based triggering devices, time pencils and electronic timers. They have access to virtually unlimited supplies of ordinary and anti-personnel grenades, anti-tank and anti-personnel mines, grenade-and rocket-launchers, mortars, anti-aircraft guns and Stinger surface to air missiles. Sophisticated communications and surveillance equipment, including Unmanned Aerial Vehicles (UAVs) are also in use. They are now reports that some form of chemical weapons may also have been introduced into their armoury, though these have not yet been used.[10]

The *rate* of improvement in the terrorist armoury, moreover, has undergone continuous acceleration, keeping pace with the most recent developments in the technologies available on the international market — both legal and underground. In contrast, the state's response remains inexcusably sluggish and often erratic, if not entirely whimsical.

In the post-Kargil era, this judgement may seem somewhat harsh, especially in view of the quick decision to upgrade equipment for counter-insurgency operations and the defence of the LoC at a proposed cost of almost Rs. 40 billion. If anything, however, this decision merely confirms the *ad hoc*, knee jerk character of our responses and provides a suitable example for analysis of the standard governmental response in the aftermath of a crisis.[11] The projected 'upgradation,' reportedly to be realized over the next seven years (a fairly long period in terms of present rates of technological change), represents little more than a lavish buying spree that will bring in automatic grenade launchers, sniper rifles and flame throwers from Russia, multi-grenade launchers and mine-protected vehicles from South Africa, under-barrel grenade launchers from Bulgaria, C-90 disposable rocket launchers from Spain, and bullet proof vests from UK and Germany.[12]

This is, presumably, a partial and unconfirmed list of the actual acquisitions to be made. Consequently, it would be infructuous and inappropriate to go into the merits of any of the items on the proposed procurement list. There are, however, several *prima facie* problems with the 'upgradation' plan.

(i) It is evidently based on perceptions of what is required to counter the current patterns of attack to which the SFs are being subjected and the levels of technology presently available to the terrorist. To the extent that these acquisitions are to reach the field in phases over the next seven years, many of them will be outdated and ineffectual by the time this happens. Any long-term acquisition would have to be based on projections — however tentative these may be - of emerging technologies and must attempt to outstrip the terrorists' rate of acquisition of technologies if they are to be effective. I cannot think of a single example where this has been the case in the sphere of counter-insurgency technologies in India.

(ii) To the extent that this is a 'wish list' largely dreamt up by military and civilian bureaucrats at Delhi, many of the acquisitions may prove ineffective or inappropriate in the field. There are already reports in the Press, for instance, that suggest that the anti-mine vehicles purchased from South Africa, some of which have already been deployed in the field, are unsuitable for J&K — their principal destination - since they are "built for the plains and the cabin is so high up that it is almost impossible for the driver to see a road in mountainous terrain. It requires an escort party to show the way."[13]

This is a recurrent theme in technological acquisitions for the army and SFs. Part of the problem, of course, is the pervasive blight of corruption, as a result of which the acquired systems are not subjected to a transparent and objective process of evaluation. The greater problem, however, is a failure on the part of bureaucrats and technical advisors who act at a sanitized distance from the actual theatre of conflict and are, consequently, in no position to make a correct evaluation of the utility of specific systems.

Weapons and technologies have to be situation and threat specific and should facilitate a resolution of an existing or emerging problem in the quickest possible time, with minimum damage. During the Punjab campaign, an elite commando group was deployed for night ambushes in Tarn Taran in 1989. They were expected to have an overwhelming advantage, since they were equipped with night-vision devices. Unfortunately, the experiment was a failure, with the number of casualties canceling out on each side. This was because no one had anticipated the impact of artificial light on night-vision devices and most of the villages in the Punjab are electrified. The commandos went in blind into an engagement where they thought they would have the devastating advantage of sight over their adversaries.

The problem was and frequently remains, that the selection of weapons and technologies is based on theories and books, not on direct discussions with field commanders or on operational requirements and experience.

(iii) Many, if not most, of the technologies that we are shopping for all over the world are available, or can be developed, within the country at costs that would prove to be a fraction of the price of imports. To the extent that they are made to specifications defined in the field and can be continuously modified to confront emerging shifts in the pattern of terrorist movements and attacks, they would meet the short-term requirements of the forces far better than unitary systems imported from foreign manufacturers.

It is important to remind ourselves once again, in this context, that not all the proposed imports are high-ended weapons or communication systems and that many of the very expensive (and reportedly overpriced) items — including the anti-mine vehicles— have already been developed and used within India in other theatres.

The problem, however, cannot be resolved within the present institutional system. The flow of technologies from scientific and research establishments has been fitful and capricious, often as divorced from the ground situation as the 'wish lists' of the Central bureaucracy. The Defence Research & Development Organization (DRDO) alone, I believe, would be sitting on an entire treasure house of technologies that could be translated into force multipliers on the ground. But what actually reaches the forces is defined through the same convoluted, irrational bureaucratic process that robs it of all possible efficacy and condemns immense resources and research efforts to absolute futility.[15]

The problem, moreover, is not just of bridging the immense gap between India's premier defence laboratories and the SFs in the field. Indeed, there is much that could be done at levels of innovation of which students in our technological institutes and colleges are perfectly capable. It is my firm conviction that many of the required technical inputs could be sourced locally, if a mechanism could be devised where students and faculty of these institutions are specifically tasked to solve problems locally confronted by SF commanders. There is a story doing the rounds — apocryphal, no doubt — of a police officer in J&K who used the skills of a local television repair mechanic to fabricate a crude though effective — and very cheap — Direction Finding Device to identify and locate militant wireless facilities.

Unfortunately, none of the SFs or enforcement agencies in India has the wherewithal, the orientation, or, ordinarily, even the authority, to make their own technological choices. More than six years after terrorism was defeated in Punjab, the lessons of that campaign remain poorly understood and largely ignored. Nevertheless, the salutary consequences of programmes that place actual, even though limited, technological initiatives in the hands of the SFs, were more than adequately demonstrated there.

With mounting casualties under a sustained, increasingly sophisticated and devastating terrorist offensive, a small "special cell" was set up in February 1990 under the charge of K. K. Attri, DIG, and in coordination with Dr. Gopalji Misra, Director, Forensic Sciences Laboratories (FSL), Punjab. The Cell was to undertake a continuous and systematic assessment of the operational skills of the terrorists and the technologies available to them. The Cell also established a working alliance with universities, national laboratories such as the CSIO and TBRL as well as with research facilities of the DRDO all over the country. Liaison was also maintained with the National Security Guard (NSG) and the Special Protection Group (SPG).

Traditionally, the FSL had only been involved with casework and the related forensic examination of evidence. It now undertook the study of terrorist weaponry, explosives and initiators and mobility aids, including optical devices, vehicles, etc. On this basis, a thorough threat assessment was made and the deep involvement of Pakistan's covert agencies in arming the Punjab terrorists was also established. This evaluation was collated and disseminated through the operational, monitoring and planning levels in the Police and other wings of government involved in the war against terrorism and contributed significantly to logistics and operational planning of the SFs. This was, to my mind, a unique and unparalleled experiment in this country. It was, however, only a beginning.

The Special Cell also began a process of developing appropriate technologies to confront specific challenges posed by the various weapons, communications and other systems available to the terrorists, as well as solutions to specific problems that arose out of their *modus operandi*. The FSL's work included R&D on bullet-proofing materials, including steel, glass, kevlar and polycarbonates, as well as projects to develop optical, electrical and electronic devices. Some of the innovations proved exceptionally helpful in the fight against terror, either resulting in specific breakthroughs, or minimally ensuring dramatic cost reductions and improved operational effectiveness. They included the following:

1. *The Infra-red Filter Glass Torch:* Toughened glass was coated with a combination of dyes to check the visible light and allow the filtration of infrared radiation. This coated glass was used on dragon lights and allowed for visibility of about 250 metres with the help of night vision goggles during dark nights. A heavier coating on such glass used over aeroplane landing lights increased visibility upto 700 metres. Each such light, fitted into portable wooden boxes, and connected to two 12 volt truck batteries, was found extremely useful for watching terrorist movements at night without giving any indication of the police position.

2. *Infra-red Filter Head — and Parking Lights:* The headlights and parking lights of police vehicles were similarly treated to permit the vehicles to be driven at night without disclosing their position from a distance.
3. *Parabolic Sound Enlarger:* This device allowed tracking of the movement of terrorists during the night in forested areas or across water bodies through the directional focusing of a parabola that amplified sound that could be monitored on headphones.
4. *Mechanical Clock Detector:* To detect mechanical timing devices for bombs concealed in closed packages, boxes or luggage. The device was developed at a cost barely 7 per cent of similar devices available on the market.
5. *Electronic Timer Detector:* While the mechanical clock is relatively easy to detect, the silent electronic timer is a greater challenge. The detector could locate a timer concealed in any kind of packing, behind walls and from a distance of upto 15 inches. In 1992, when this device was developed by the FSL, no similar mechanism was available in the international market. The first such device to be made available commercially came in 1994, with a price tag of Rs. 290,000. The Punjab Police detector cost Rs. 10,000.
6. *Poison Detection Kit:* A simple kit that could be easily operated by a police constable and which gave its results within five minutes, was developed to identify potassium cyanide or arsenic in water or food.
7. *Country-made Bullet Proof Jackets:* Various steels were tested and tempered to develop plates that could protect against the AK-47. Crude jackets, with these steel plates stitched into in strong cloth provided a degree of protection to a large number of SF and police personnel and despite their weight, contributed enormously to their operational efficiency and confidence. These jackets cost a fraction of factory made BP jackets, and the design is still in use in other theatres of LIC.
8. *Bullet Proof Mobile Morchas:* Three plates of 6mm tempered steel were shaped into a simple structure that could be carried and installed anywhere through a hooking system.

Each plate was provided with a firing port. These mobile *morchas* or posts proved very useful during encounters/ambushes and were strong enough to stop AK-47 bullets. A pair of such plates (size: 46"x27") was also sufficient to protect an LCV passenger vehicle or Gypsy.

9. *Bullet Proofing of Vehicles:* Steel easily available on the market was tempered to produce economical bullet proof Gypsies, Jeeps, Ambassador cars, LCVs and police trucks. At the peak of terrorism, Punjab had more than 650 BP vehicles. Bomb protected flooring also saved lives against the increasing use of IEDs and landmines during the later phases of terrorism in the State.

   The impact of such innovations was dramatically illustrated by the development of the BP Tractor. The sugarcane fields in Punjab gave the terrorists excellent cover for ambush and escape and had proven to be a major headache for the police. So great was their advantage that the militants forced farmers on pain of death to sow sugarcane all along the roads and their clandestine routes. After an attack, the terrorists would simply run into the fields and if the police tried to follow, they would simply be picked off one by one. When the first BP Tractors were pressed into operations, this advantage simply vanished and the sanctuary of the sugarcane field was lost, forcing irreversible tactical changes on the terrorists. Later, the terrorists got hold of armour piercing bullets and inflicted a few casualties on policemen in the armoured tractors, thus neutralizing the advantage. By then, however, the time for 'sugarcane terrorism' was over.

10. *R&D on BP Materials:* R&D on materials, including various steels and alloys, glasses, composite materials and polycarbonates, led to the replacement of Kevlar pads on the floor and in the ceiling of Ambassador cars, resulting in a saving of as much as Rs. 100,000 per protected vehicle. Tempered steel, similarly, reduced the cost of bullet proofing of LCVs and police trucks, as compared to the cost of Jackal steel previously in use. The design of innovative door-catches for protected vehicles added to their security under

attack. The replacement of the Ambassador engines by an Isuzu 1800 petrol engines acquired in the second hand market also proved to be a highly cost-effective way of improving efficiency.

R&D on Ammunition: At each stage, exhaustive studies were carried out on various types of ammunition used by terrorists in order to develop appropriate protection against them and save valuable lives.

Simple and Panel Periscopes: Simple periscopes with three backup mirrors were developed for observation from secure positions without exposing the observer. The system survived even if the mirrors were hit twice, as the third angled mirror remained intact.

Protective Viewing Window: A protected, BP viewing window, with a visibility angle of 140°, was fitted into BP patrol vehicles and BP mobile *morchas*. This constituted a quantum leap over the periscopes that had been devised earlier.

Riot Control Shields: made out of polycarbonate shields ranging between 4 mm and 12 mm. The material did not break even if beaten with iron rods and could not be penetrated with a knife. Polycarbonate sheets of 6 to 8 mm thickness could stop 12 bore shots and lead projectiles from small fire arms, including revolvers and pistols.

Some of these innovations would, to those who are focused he hi-technology end of defence research, appear to be crude, ı primitive — though others involved fairly sophisticated R&D ı special materials and alloys. It is, however, impossible for ı distanced observers to estimate the sheer and overwhelming act that each of these developments had in the fight against terrorists in Punjab.

It would be equally difficult for such observers to imagine sheer enormity of the constraints under which these elopments took place. There was unrelenting resistance from bureaucracy and audit institutions to every unorthodox ative, often forcing absolutely ludicrous decisions. A small ıp had been constituted to work on steel wool, which would have been lighter and stronger than the material then being used for bullet proofing. The project had to be given up, largely due to an ingrained fear of innovation. The in-house cost of effective bullet proofing of a vehicle was under Rs. 400,000. Yet, a costlier alternative, involving the established system of open tenders and outside manufacture, had to be adopted, since audit objections would subsequently be raised against a manufacturing activity that did not fall within the department's mandate. Indeed, such strong inhibitors to unorthodox development exist within the prevailing administrative system that it was well nigh impossible to secure funds for such projects.[15]

This system will have to be dismantled if the hyperviolence of future terrorism is to be effectively neutralized. A continuous system of unmediated coordination between field commanders and R&D personnel at various levels will have to be created so that the time lag between emerging trends in terrorism and counter-terrorist initiatives is diminished. This will demand extraordinary efforts, since the technological advantages of state players are being progressively eroded by the terrorists' free access to advanced technologies.

There is, consequently, a need for a dual response that requires both local level facilities and efforts that do not go beyond tinkering with existing technologies, on the one hand, as well as highly sophisticated research at the very limits of contemporary scientific knowledge, on the other.

This, however, will not be enough. It is no longer sufficient to constantly run close on the heels of the terrorist. He must be overtaken and outmanoeuvred if his increasing and potentially devastating power is to be neutralized.

> In general, CT (Counter Terrorism) planners have been successful when they were able to match or exceed the technological skills of their terrorist adversaries... (T) he forces of order no longer enjoy an inherent advantage in the competition with those who would prevent the orderly functioning of society. Therefore, their success will not be a function of privilege or position but rather the reward for their greater ingenuity and resourcefulness.[16]

This requires even deeper levels and more complex structures of coordination and research and a technological perspective that must define — as minutely and accurately as is humanly possible —the direction and character of future weapon systems and enabling technologies that will be deployed in low intensity wars. Once such a perspective has been constructed — and even as it is constantly reviewed and revised — research, developmental and manufacturing initiatives must create the technologies to counter these systems well before they are accessed by the terrorist. In war, surprise is a critical ingredient for victory — and it is imperative that the Indian security establishment is not taken by surprise.

As stated earlier, the mere development or theoretical availability of a technology has no impact on the ground. Systems for its timely production and deployment are just as important. In this, the private sector can and should be co-opted, though some precautions may be necessary to ensure that sensitive technologies are not exploited for purely commercial ends. Nevertheless, it is important to remind ourselves that those who draw their salaries from the state do not have a necessary monopoly on patriotism, nor, for that matter, an exclusive duty to fight the nation's wars.

Our approach, however, must comprehend much more than weapon systems and technologies. While it is well beyond the scope of this paper to discuss the issue in any detail, it is essential to recognise that the manpower resources and training requirements that will create the low intensity warfighter of the 21st century, will be radically different from the ill-equipped and poorly trained *jawan* of the 20th. It must, equally, be recognized that changes in manpower and training policies today will significantly impact on the constitution and character of the security forces several years hence. There is, consequently, no more time to waste in this regard.

Leaping the Abyss

Procrastination is a luxury that we can afford even less in view of the "great leap forward" that weapons of mass destruction now offer the terrorist. The slow-bleeding warfare that has been inflicted upon us, particularly over the past two decades, has cost the nation thousands of lives, billions of rupees. Yet, even at our present levels of engagement, it is entirely possible to contain its impact within levels that are considered — by an increasingly brutalized and unresponsive public and political leadership — "acceptable" and without a compelling proximate threat of national disintegration. All this changes with the paradigm shift that must be anticipated in the technologies of terror in the new millenium.

The Pokhran II tests of May 1998 and the retaliatory demonstration in Chagai, heralded a new phase in the precarious strategic equilibrium that prevails in the Indian subcontinent. A great deal has already been written about this momentous development and the advent of the perilous 'nuclear age' of Asia. The debate, however, remains trapped within the paradigms of deterrence defined by the West over decades of the Cold War and fails to distinguish, or even acknowledge, the unique circumstances that prevail in South Asia.

Critically, current Indian strategic perspectives on the issue end with capabilities to ensure a retaliatory strike that would inflict destruction that the "aggressor will find unacceptable" if nuclear weapons are used against us. This is nothing but the regurgitation of classical deterrence postures and the infamous Mutually Assured Destruction (MAD) doctrine — a doctrine that, no doubt, kept the superpowers out of nuclear conflict for nearly five decades of an intense Cold War that often expressed itself through proxy wars and direct confrontations in other countries. Nevertheless, it is important to understand the circumstances that made MAD so effective in assuring nuclear peace. The first of these was the fact that all nuclear powers of the Cold War period had long standing and entirely stable institutions of governance with clear chains of command and elaborate systems of checks and balances that forced a rational decision on all the players in this confrontation. Secondly, the projected nuclear strikes in case of a conflagration were of such an intensity and number that there were no possibilities whatsoever of either nation surviving; indeed, there was little chance of life — certainly human life — surviving on this planet. In effect, the calculations played out in the war games of both the superpowers engaged in the Cold War ensured an absolute No Win situation. There was no calculus or alternate rational scheme that could tempt either to risk actual use of their arsenal, whatever the aggravation.

The situation is made infinitely more complex by the advent of a range of other Weapons of Mass Destruction (WMD) — including chemical and biological weapons — where the barrier to acquisition is much lower than the one that inhibits access to nuclear technologies. The destructive potential of these weapons is well-known in a restricted circle of scientists and strategic scholars in India, but the larger community of administrators and policy makers remain oblivious of their dangers. A small package of chemical agents, for instance, is estimated to be 40 times more effective as a weapon than a comparable package of conventional explosives.[17] But this is just an insignificant fraction of what biological weapons can do.

> To gain an understanding of the lethality of these toxins, the brevity of their production time-frames, and their ease of concealment, consider that with merely a flask of culture medium and a few anthrax spores, a terrorist with college-level laboratory skill can produce one kilogram of anthrax bacteria in just eight days. One half a gram — about 0.02 ounces — comprises enough doses to kill five million people. Butulinum toxins are equally fatal.[18]

Indeed, "college level laboratory skills" may also be fairly redundant, as "rogue states... wield nuclear, biological, or chemical weapons through the vehicle of terror surrogates as a practically untraceable tool for covert proxy war."[19] A chilling reminder that this is no Cassandra's call is the fact that the list of nations known to currently possess biological weapons includes a number of unstable regimes and many that are present sponsors of terrorism. The list of biological weapons nations includes Russia, Iraq, Iran, China, North Korea, Egypt, Syria, Taiwan, Israel and critically, Pakistan, but "The threat lies not in the length of this list but in the fact that many of these nations reject the political and territorial status quo and are more likely to use such weapons to advance an aggressive agenda."[20]

The assumptions of classical deterrence theory, consequently and obviously, cannot apply to the Indian subcontinent. Classical deterrence may work most of the time against stable nation states, but it has no relevance to the non-state nuclear weapons player, or, for that matter, to a rogue state acting through such a player. These are very real possibilities and may be realized in a number of alternative scenarios, all of which cannot be examined here. Nevertheless, there are two explicit dangers that need to be immediately recognized.

(i) The first of these arises out of the character and the increasing influence and stridency of what is described as 'Islamic Fundamentalism and Militancy' in the region. As with all millennial faiths, the calculus of those who subscribe to such an ideology differs strikingly from what we — and classical deterrence strategies — would regard as rational. Nevertheless, the 'millennial rationality' has its own internal coherence and must be understood and confronted as such.

For those who believe that they are fighting on God's Command and for the establishment of His Empire on earth — and believe this with absolute and uncompromising ardour - the lives of their fellow men and indeed their own lives, do not have the value that is placed on them by liberal-democratic rationality. Nor indeed does the *mujahiddeen* mindset yield to the imperatives of traditional nationalism. It is entirely possible that, were such individuals placed in positions of control over nuclear, chemical or biological weapons of mass destruction, they would accept the possibility of the annihilation of their own nation if they could believe that the 'Empire of God' (or, bluntly, the 'Islamic World') could be expanded.

Such a calculus would, moreover, be applied in a situation that differs radically from classical deterrence assumptions in that the scale of destruction projected is lower. The intended damage would substantially be confined to India and Pakistan, though it may flow across their borders in limited measure. Nevertheless, it would had the potential to "Free" the subcontinent of the power of the "Unbeliever" and open it up to a final "Islamic Conquest" from Central Asia.

It must be recognized that the influence of what is

described as Islamic Fundamentalism is increasing enormously in Pakistan and if present trends continue — especially with the consolidation of the Taliban regime in Afghanistan — it is inevitable that they will eventually seize power in that state, irrespective of the opinions and desires of the more moderate population who may incline towards peace with India.

While no quantitative probabilities can be assigned to the possibilities of the use of WMDs against India by such a future regime, it is essential for acknowledge this possibility and to discover means to defeat the calculus of this millennial rationality.

ii. A second threat, possibly more insidious than the one described above, arises out of the character and patterns of Pakistan's sustained strategies against India over the last decade and a half and is exacerbated by the new paradigm of the combined use of regular forces and terrorists that has been exposed through their recent actions in Kargil. It is certain that — irrespective of the outcome in Kargil — Pakistan will continue in its efforts to expand the sphere of low intensity warfare within India. If any regime in Pakistan were to convince itself that regional, communal and political fragmentation in India had reached a stage where the destruction of a few critical centres of authority would effectively ensure the disintegration of the nation, it is possible that it would gamble on the use of small nuclear devices — the notorious "suitcase bomb" — or other WMDs smuggled in and deployed by terrorists.

Such a calculus is not based on — and does not need — millennial rationality, though such thinking would certainly heighten the dangers. The power elite and an influential segment of the Pakistani establishment conceive of India's disintegration as an end in itself, even if no territorial advantages accrued to it. To the extent that such a strategy would also offer the possibility of at least partially escaping responsibility by crediting such actions to 'Freedom Fighters' within India, it becomes all the more attractive.

We cannot pretend that there are any easy solutions to these problems. Nevertheless, there are general directions that need to be explored if we are to obviate the threat they constitute.

The first of these refers to the boundaries of our strategic perspective. Clearly, it cannot end with an assured retaliatory strike, for the extremist calculus would not necessarily be deterred by such a possibility, nor, indeed, would it be clear as to who such a strike is to be directed against.

Only if those who contemplate nuclear or biological aggression against us are convinced that India would not only survive, but that their own sphere of influence would significantly shrink, would such extremist elements be deterred against an adventure using WMDs against us. Such a deterrent must be based on the creation of political, administrative and institutional structures, processes and procedures that would survive such a catastrophic strike. These must comprehend the identification of possible target cities, plans for evacuation, the containment of a panic that could reach unprecedented proportions, the restoration of order within the surviving populations of these target cities and provision of medical and other relief to them at a scale that has never been envisaged in the past and the preservation of order in the most far flung areas of the country. Equally, they must include a clear chain of surviving command and a plan for retaliatory strikes based on prior identification of possible perpetrators and mandatory punitive protocols. While such identification may not be perfectly adequate, knowledge that such intelligence exists would work as a deterrent on the entire and highly interdependent network of terrorist organizations and their sponsors.

This is, clearly, only a crude outline of what is needed and an enormous exercise would be required to define and implement the necessary plans. Our strategic perspective must, however, at least identify the directions that such plans must follow and initiate the processes that would lead to their realization. Such an exercise has already been initiated in nations where the terrorist threat is at much lower levels in comparison to the situation in India.[21]

There is, in the observations above, an overwhelming focus on the threat of unconventional aggression by Pakistan and by militants based in, or connected with, that state. This is a product, perhaps, of our present situation, as of a personal perception. This threat, however great it may presently be, does not exhaust the dimensions of the dangers of attack by WMDs that India faces. Indeed, our future strategic doctrine must identify potential adversaries and define their varying calculii — every adversary would not use the same calculus and our projected responses must accommodate these variations. Nor, indeed, is it sufficient to base our strategic perspectives on present perceptions of who our potential adversaries are. In a rapidly changing world, these relationships will shift, even as access to unconventional weapons and delivery systems widens. Each such possibility needs separate examination if it is to yield valid strategic options. And a continuous and intense exercise to identify and play out each potential scenario must be undertaken if we are to defend ourselves against every emerging eventuality.

Virtual Wars

There is one more danger that is currently exercising counterterrorism strategists across the world. It is variously referred to as Cyberwar, Netwar, or Information Warfare and Terrorism. Its potential for destruction in the coming century is immense. Scenarios have been drawn up that link narrowly targeted attacks with a cumulative potential to disrupt complex electronic command and control systems across continents.[22] The destructive potential of cyberwarfare is expected to increase exponentially with the progressive computerization of all systems in business, social services, governance and defence. The degree of vulnerability can be estimated by the fact that, during recent tests, computer specialists demonstrated their ability to crash the computer systems of both the New York Stock Exchange and the social security system. One expert estimates that as many as 80 per cent of the Fortune 500 companies have been electronically penetrated by hackers.[23] A 1997 survey by the Computer Security Institute and the FBI's International Computer Crime Squad found that 75 per cent of the respondents reported financial losses due to various computer security breaches.[24]

Even the most secure defence establishments have been hacked, and this includes the US military nerve centre at The

Pentagon where computer systems were reportedly under "an unprecedented and concerted series of external attacks" in March this year.[25] Several successful breaches are known to have occurred, including one by an "18-year old Israeli computer enthusiast with a lot of time on his hands, and two teenagers from California who were using readily available software tools downloaded from the Internet to discredit the Pentagon's computer security."[26] Representative Curt Weldon, who chaired the subcommittee of the US House Armed Services Committee that heard testimonies relating to the US Defence Department computers is reported to have stated, "This Y2K thing is a piece of cake compared to this."

Cyberwarfare, moreover, creates another critical shift in the character of terrorism. The idea of the 'one man army' is more completely realized in the identity of a well informed hacker than it ever has been through any other technology. A single individual, with the right knowledge and skills and working on a simple computer hooked to the internet — a computer indistinguishable from ones commonly used by students, professionals or businessmen and freely available at an extremely modest and declining, price — could realize his own anarchical agenda without help from, or complicity of, any other agency or group. This would make detection difficult, if not impossible and there would be no physical risks even at the moment of 'engagement'. And the damage could be done to massive national infrastructure, commercial, information and defence systems across continents. This single factor has the potential to force fundamental and comprehensive revisions in our concepts and strategies of the future of counterterrorist warfare.

In India, all this may still seem to be in the realm of science fiction. Computers have, of course, entered the office space in every sector of the economy, of governance and of defence. But they are, as yet, far from the integrated systems of command and control whose disruption could bring the life of a nation to a standstill. Indeed, at this point of time, even where computers are integral to critical operations, their disruption would, at worst, cause a temporary setback before operations were resumed under traditional technological and command structures. Cyberterrorism, consequently, remains a distant prospect, given low levels of computerization in most core sectors. 'Information Warfare' is, as a result, widely interpreted by Indian planners within the traditional categories of propaganda, with the difference that, now, a new electronic medium is available.

This situation cannot, of course, persist for long. If India is to follow a vigorous programme of economic development, it will have to adopt contemporary technologies — including computerization and global networking of all critical operations. And as it does so, its vulnerabilities to the malevolent hacker will grow.

It would be foolhardy to believe that we will have time enough to respond when the danger manifests itself. Indeed, it is now that preventive action must be initiated, so that safety is built into the very architecture of the nation's expanding private and public networks — to the extent that this is possible. How this can be done is, of course, a matter for the experts. That it needs to be done, however, is something that bureaucrats and planners will have to realize and concede, before the experts can get down to their jobs.

The cumulative impact of technological change in terrorist warfare is truly terrifying and contains within it the seeds of the destruction of many a nation at the hands of even the most insignificant minorities.

> In a world of satellites, lasers, computers, briefcase weapons, precision targeting, and a choice of viruses with which to attack people or computers, nations as we now know them may well find themselves up against potent adversaries, some no more than a millionth their size.[27]

The politics of rage and vengeance has closed avenues of rational negotiation with radical groups whose motivation no longer attaches value to traditional notions of national or self-interest. The sheer speed of transformations and of potential attack, the multiplicity of potential sources of aggression, the anonymity and degree of dispersal with which a terrorist offensive can be planned and executed, all these will make the world a dangerous and unstable place in the new millennium.

The source of all these dangers is a growing pool of widely

available knowledge — of weapon systems, of information that was traditionally monopolized by governments and of skills to translate such information into subversive action. There is only one possible protection against these and that, again, is to secure greater knowledge, continuously upgraded intelligence, skills and technologies that keep us far ahead of the forces of disorder.

At this point of time, however, we appear to be lagging well behind.

NOTES AND REFERENCES

1. Shaw, G.B., "The Devil's Disciple," cited in Norman F. Dixon, *On the Psychology of Military Incompetence*, London, Jonathan Cape and BI Publications, New Delhi, 1976, p. 110.
2. Cf. K.P.S. Gill, "Bureaucracy must emerge from its maze," *Pioneer*, New Delhi, January 23, 1999.
3. See Manvendra Singh, "Years after request, Army still awaits counter-insurgency equipment", *Indian Express*, New Delhi, December 12, 1997, which describes a five-year wait for 'inexpensive', 'lifesaving' and 'operation enhancing' equipment. Snowmobiles case.
4. K.P.S. Gill, "Endgame in Punjab: 1988-93," *Faultlines*, New Delhi, Vol. 1, ICM-Bulwark Books, May 1999, pp. 13-14.
5. *Ibid.*, pp. 41-44.
6. See J. G. Nadkarni, "The Army needs modernisation: We love quantity," *Indian Express*, August 11, 1999; "How well equipped are the jawans", *Times of India*, New Delhi, June 9, 1999, which speaks of the equipment available to soldiers of the Indian Army, who are, by and large, much better off than the paramilitary and state armed police forces.
7. Alvin Toffler, *Powershift*, New York, Bantam, 1991, p. 417.
8. *Ibid.*, p. 453.
9. *Ibid.*
10. "Militants possess chemical weapons," *Pioneer*, September 27, 1999; "Pak Militants 'May' Use Poisonous Gases," *Tribune*, Chandigarh, September 27, 1999.
11. Mahendra Vaid, "Rs. 4,000 cr worth of weapons, equipment for infantry," *Times of India*, October 22, 1999; Shishir Gupta, "Govt. okays upgradation of weaponry," *Hindustan Times*, New Delhi, October 22, 1999.
12. Vaid, *Times of India, op. cit.*
13. Wilson John, "Army buys second-hand junk for a fortune," *The Pioneer*, October 22, 1999.
14. Cf. for instance, though in a different context, the report that the Indian Air Force ignored indigenous radar technologies for over a decade because an "influential lobby" favoured imports. Joseph Thomas, "IAF Ignored Reconnaissance Radar", in Bharat Verma [ed.] *Indian Defence Review*, New Delhi, Vol. 14, No. 3, July-September 1999, pp. 93-94.

15. Information available to me suggests that most of these projects were wound up after my departure from Punjab. The crisis had passed and the establishment lapsed into its habitual stupor.
16. Stephen R Bowers and Kimberly R. Keys, "Technology and Terrorism: The New Threat for the Millennium," *Conflict Studies 309,* London, Institute for the Study of Conflict and Terrorism, 1999, p. 22.
17. Bowers and Keys, *op. cit.*, p. 16.
18. Joseph W. Foxell, Jr., "The Debate on the Potential for Mass-Casualty Terrorism: The Challenge to US Security", *Terrorism and Political Violence,* London, Vol. II. No. 1, Spring 1999, p. 102.
19. *Ibid.*, p. 99
20. Bowers and Kimberly, *op. cit.*, p. 13.
21. Cf., for instance, the US Department for Defence Plan for Integrating National Guard and Reserve Component Support for Response to Attacks Using Weapons of Mass Destruction, Prepared by the DoD Tiger Team, January, 1998.
22. Matthew G. Devost, Brian K. Houghton and Neal A. Pollard, "Information Terrorism: Can You Trust Your Toaster?," *Sun Tzu Art of War in Information Warfare,* Institute for National Strategic Studies, http://www.ndu.edu
23. Arnaud Deborchgrave, cited in Bowers and Kimberly, *op. cit.*, p. 6.
24. *Sword and Shield - Cyber Crime Rap Sheet*, http://www.sscs.net/cybercrime.html.
25. Michael J. Martinez, "Pentagon Attacks Overblown?", http://abcnews.go.com
26. *Ibid.* See also Barbara Starr, "Pentagon Cyber-War," and Laura Myers, "Pentagon Computers Vulnerable", http://abcnews.go.com.
27. Toffler, op. cit., p. 453.

SEVEN

Counterinsurgency Warfare
The Use and Abuse of Military Force

Vijendra Singh Jafa

I

Since 1945, the majority of the larger armies of the world have spent more time in counterinsurgency warfare than in conventional forms of war.[1] Several governments have, in the recent past, used advanced military technologies to combat rebellions and insurgencies — helicopter gunships, napalm, chemical warfare and electronic devices, to name a few. On the other hand, easy availability of modern arms, better organized and politically educated dissident leaders, hostile neighbours offering arms, training and sanctuary, are some of the factors which have contributed to a growing number of unresolved internal wars in the post-1945 era. In short, protracted small wars, causing immeasurable suffering and pain to an increasingly larger number of people, have become an inextricable aspect of our civilization. What was once a last resort is now adopted as a means of expression.

Independent India has had its own share of insurgencies. The earliest was the Naga insurgency, which dated back to the very moment of independence, entered a distinct military phase in 1954 and still persists. Since the late sixties, political discontent has found expression in a number of other "small wars," including secessionist insurgencies in Mizoram, Manipur and Tripura; activities of the Bodos and the United Liberation Front of Asom (ULFA) in Assam; the Sikh insurgency in Punjab; and Pakistan's proxy war in Jammu & Kashmir (J&K). Numerous other, smaller militant organizations — often clustered around what is termed "Left" ideology — have also raised the standard of revolt against the State in some form or the other, prominently in West Bengal, Andhra Pradesh, Madhya Pradesh and Bihar.

India's experience in counter-insurgency operations has, consequently, been long and marked by a few dramatic and hardwon successes. In achieving these, it has never been the policy of the government to resolve insurgencies by military means alone, although for many years, a degree of military pressure has been used. The ultimate basis of resolution of the Mizo insurgency, for instance, was the creation of a political *quid pro quo* — an arrangement that allowed the groups in conflict to exercise some authority over each other, roughly in proportion to their size. This, perhaps, is what Eisenstadt called "the permeation of the periphery by the center and... the weaker impingement of the periphery on the center."[2] In political terms, it means increased consultation and wider participation in decision-making or "consociational democracy"[3], "coalitions of commitments or alliances, that have in-built incentives to conciliation"[4] or simply "fundamental revisions in the relations between the regime and its people."[5] Bluntly put, it meant Indira Gandhi's master strategy which broke the Mizo rebellion by getting some of the important dissidents amongst the insurgents into the Congress (I) fold and pouring in enormous quantities of money for the enrichment of this class along with the bureaucracy and the new breed of local contractors.

While the simple expedient of buying off the opposition was not significant in Punjab, insurgency there was similarly defeated through a combination of political initiatives that created the mandate for the reorganization and mobilization of the State's police force — backed by the army and paramilitary forces — to fight the terrorists, as well as fundamental revisions in the relations between the regime and its people. This included the progressive isolation of extremist elements in the State, the aggregation of the support of moderate political leaders and at the very height of the terrorist movement, the holding of elections to the state legislature in 1992. The voter turnout in this election was, no doubt, abysmally low, as a result of a sustained intimidatory campaign by the terrorists that involved a large number of pre-election killings and the declaration by them of a total curfew on pain of death to impose their boycott. Almost all the "moderate" Sikh political parties succumbed to these tactics and withdrew from the elections. The election, nevertheless, resulted in the installation of a democratically elected government that oversaw what proved to be the terminal and most savage stage of the terrorist movement. Critics dismissed this government as unrepresentative, inept and corrupt, but it served to restore the lines of civilian control and local mechanisms of grievance redressal that revived options for a distressed people — options that, for well over a decade, had simply ceased to exist. Significantly, this government was a fully "functional government — not a puppet regime"[6] and it soon extended the democratic process through municipal and *panchayat* (village council) elections that secured large-scale participation. In September 1992, despite terrorist threats, elections to 95 Municipal Committees in the State were concluded peacefully, with an extraordinary voter turnout of 75 per cent. In January 1993, *panchayat* elections were held in 12,342 villages in the State with a voter turnout of 82 per cent. Significantly, the police saw to it that the semi-criminal elements that usually took charge of the *panchayats* through a process of intimidation and manipulation were not permitted to do so and a comparison of previous *panchayats* with the ones that came into being through the '93 Election would show that an entirely new breed of politicians emerged.

The State police, moreover, successfully engineered a direct mobilization of large numbers of the people of Punjab in the counter-terrorism effort by creating, training and arming hundreds of Village Defence Committees (VDCs) and appointing ex-servicemen and civilians as Special Police Officers (SPOs). The VDCs and SPOs were usually stationed to protect their own villages. They played a critical role in fighting the terrorists, were specially targeted by them and suffered a large number of casualties. Nevertheless, they continued to stand as a bulwark against the terrorist assault. Perhaps even more significant was their psychological impact in the countryside, as the common people began to see the war against terrorism as their own war, fought by fellow villagers and by close relatives.

However, with the exception of the extraordinary and unconventional use of the civil police in Punjab, the Indian Army has been the primary force in counter-insurgency warfare from the time of the country's independence in 1947. Its tactics and strategy have remained fundamentally conservative and traditional, influenced substantially by accounts of the British experiences in Malaya (1946-49), Kenya (1954-56) and Cyprus (1955-58) that have, in considerable measure, defined the Indian Army's training and response. The writings of British authorities such as Sir Robert Thompson, Julian Paget, Frank Kitson and C.M. Woodhouse have been a part of the Indian infantry officer's *accoutrement* at least since the 1960s. To some extent, the experiences of the French in Indochina (1946-54) and Algeria (1957-61) and the United States in Vietnam (1958-72) have also contributed to the development of the science of counter-insurgency warfare in India. Since the 1960s, training has been given a high priority. Specialized inputs at the counter-insurgency and Jungle Warfare School (established at Haflong and later transferred to Vairengte), the training curricula at the National Defense Academy, the Indian Military Academy, Infantry School, Defense Services Staff College and the National Defense Staff College have also been upgraded to cater to the emerging internal security requirements of the nation in a more sophisticated manner.

Of late, however, there has been an increasing awareness among army officers that Western precepts of counter-insurgency warfare devised by the British, French and American strategists are suitable only for colonial or interventionist armies fighting in foreign lands; that the internal wars that afflict the developing countries are an altogether different military problem. These conflicts arise when ethnic minorities inhabiting geo-politically sensitive border areas move into the process of negotiating new terms of integration with the central authority, or when such minorities take up arms at somebody else's bidding and promise of support. The army's capabilities are severely restricted when dealing in such cases with their own people. Northern Ireland is often cited as a signal example.

This growing awareness has, at least in part, found expression in the increasing development and use of India's Para Military Forces (PMFs) such as the Central Reserve Police Force (CRPF), the Border Security Force (BSF), Assam Rifles and the armed police forces of the States in the national response to insurgencies. The PMFs have been extensively deployed in situations of widespread terrorism, and have acquired considerable experience in counter-insurgency warfare. Although these forces have traditionally worked under the overall command of the army while handling insurgencies in India's North-East, they have shown remarkable levels of success even when they have been on their own. The expansion of paramilitary forces in India between 1965 and 1996, moreover, has been greater than the expansion of the nation's army. Despite the fact that this growth, as Janowitz points out, may be on account of rapid population increase, extensive urbanization and the resulting increase in crime, it has contributed to the regime's stability because of the increased resources available to the government for dealing with political crime.[7]

Nevertheless, in terms of strategic perspectives and control of operations, the army continues to dominate the nation's response to low intensity warfare in most theatres, particularly and overwhelmingly in J&K and the North-East. It is, moreover, in the North-East that insurgencies have proved to be the most intractable and persistent. A wide range of continuously evolving strategies and tactics have been employed by the army in this region and a review of these lies well beyond the scope of this paper. Here, the historical and intellectual context of the military response to insurgency is explored with specific and exclusive reference to the crises and contradictions of the Unified Command structure and the experience with the policy of the relocation of villages in Mizoram. To understand these issues, however, the legacy of colonial policies and the received wisdom on counter-insurgency strategies as conceived of and implemented by Western powers must first be examined.

The Background

The origin of the guerrilla tactics adopted in irregular warfare is ancient, but the ideological, political and socio-economic trappings have been added to insurgency in fairly recent times and perhaps not earlier than the emergence of the communist revolutionary warfare based on the theories of Mao-Tse-tung, Vo Nguyen Giap, Che Guevara and Carlos Marighela in the 20th century. Marx and Engels declared in 1848 that the objectives of communists "can be attained only by the forcible overthrow of all existing social conditions."[8] Force, in their view, encompassed a variety of forms: mass demonstration, general strikes, even relatively passive boycotts, as well as armed uprisings. The *Communist International* set down the conditions for armed struggle succinctly: "An absolute essential condition precedent for this form of action is the organization of the broad masses into militant units, which, by their form, embrace and set into action the largest possible number of toilers."[9]

Mao-Tse-tung added new scope and depth to the armed struggle strategy and tactics and combined guerrilla warfare with regular protracted warfare through which he delivered the decisive blow in the last stages of the Chinese Revolution (1928-49). Most effective was Mao's strategy of establishing liberated bases far away from the ruling-class power centres, making the peasantry the base of the struggle, subversive activities in the cities followed by surrounding and capturing them from the countryside. He summarized his tactics in the celebrated remarks: "Divide our forces to arouse the masses, concentrate our forces to deal with the enemy. The enemy advances, we retreat; the enemy camps, we harass; the enemy tires, we attack; the enemy retreats, we pursue. To extend stable base areas, employ the policy of advancing in waves; when pursued by a powerful enemy, employ the policy of circling around. Arouse the largest number of the masses in the shortest possible time and the best possible methods. These tactics are just like casting a net; at any moment we should be able to cast it or draw it in. We cast it wide to win over the masses and draw it in to deal with the enemy...."[10] Giap agreed with Mao in three main respects: the concept of protracted war, use of regular army as the main tool of the people's war and the primacy of political activity and propaganda over military operations. Guerrilla warfare was useful only in the early stages of the revolutionary war as it was effective both in the mountain and the delta regions of Vietnam and could be waged with good as well as mediocre men and material. Giap had expected Dien Bien Phu war to last "five, ten, twenty or more years."[11] In this readiness for protracted warfare lay his trump card against the USA. He could not hope to win militarily against the Americans, but the longer the Vietcong fought, the more difficult became a prolonged US involvement because of domestic and foreign policy considerations.[12] As Townshend says: "In conventional war, time is expensive to governments; in irregular war it is cheap to their opponents."[13]

Unlike Marxist-Leninist and Maoist philosophy, which regarded armed insurrection as an important phase of the struggle, Guevara thought it was only an initial means and nothing more. Nor did the political party, ideology or political education play an important role in his scheme of things.[14] He drew four fundamental lessons from the Cuban revolution: (1) Popular forces can win a war against the army; (2) It is not necessary to wait until all conditions for making revolution exist; the insurrection can create them; (3) In underdeveloped America the countryside is the basic area for armed fighting; (4) Guerrilla outbreak cannot be promoted against a government which has come to power through popular vote. (He later changed this last view and asserted that conditions for armed struggle existed anywhere in Latin America).[15]

The modern approach to counter-insurgency dates from the publication of Callwell's book in 1896,[16] which drew its lessons of minimum force, firm action and civilian control from incidents like Amritsar (1919) and Cyprus (1931) and became the text-book at the Imperial Defense Staff College between the two World Wars.[17] Clausewitz's 'people's war' was essentially about the role of partisans in conventional warfare.[18] But the sophistication of revolutionary warfare preached by Mao-Tse-tung inspired a cascade of literature on the subject. Among the first notable studies was Thompson's seminal work on the Malayan communist insurgency.[19]

The American Approach

In 1962-63, the Centre for International Affairs of Harvard University sponsored a study that resulted in a small but extremely practical book by a French army officer, David Galula. This was based on his observation (from Hong Kong where he was Military Attache in 1950-53) of the communist Huk rebellion in the Philippines (1946-54), of Greek civil war during 1949-50 as the UN Military Observer and his personal experiences in Algeria (1956-58).[20] Galula and his contemporary American theorists like Pushtay[21] and McCuen[22] were most influential in the formulation of the global counter-insurgency doctrine adopted by the Kennedy administration.[23] But it is one of the greatest paradoxes of modern military history that whereas the US succeeded in an advisory role in the Philippines and Latin America in the 1950s-60s, they failed to successfully apply the same principles when confronted with the communists in Vietnam themselves.

The likely reason was that time-tested principles of flexible approach and the adoption of socio-economic programs to erode the popular support of the insurgents were replaced by purely military objectives and the consequent reliance on massive fire-power and aerial bombardment in Vietnam.[24] USA dropped 13 million tons of high explosives (six times the bombs dropped by USA in World War II) and 90,000 tones of gas and herbicide in Vietnam.[25] This "saturation bombing" principle has also been the undoing of the Soviets in Afghanistan and the Iraqis against their Kurd rebels. Beckett and Pimlott have observed: "Firepower, however, may not be an adequate substitute for.... having men on the ground hunting down the insurgent in his own environment.... In Malay ten minutes by helicopter was calculated as the equivalent of ten hours by foot, but experience has shown that the tendency to become 'heli-bound' in the way that the French were road-bound in Indochina must be resisted. There is little doubt that, in Vietnam, US forces often forgot that it is necessary to get out of the helicopter in order to fight effectively against the insurgent on the ground. The reliance on technology in counter-insurgency, although not entirely misplaced (notably in the increasing use of computers in intelligence analysis and of sophisticated surveillance devices), inevitably carries the risk that it will dominate the conduct of the campaign. Generally speaking, the less sophisticated the army, the better able it has been to defeat insurgency. Indeed, reliance on the helicopter or fire-power may be regarded as pacification rather than counter-insurgency. The latter also requires contact with the people on the ground, for the civilian population will always be the arbiters of success or failure for both security forces and insurgents."[26] In the last twenty years, a new concept in counter-insurgency warfare, called Low Intensity Conflict (LIC), has been a recurring theme in the United States with the US Army and Air Force Joint Center for Low Intensity Conflict as the focal point. But the central issue is the difficulty of agreeing on the definition of LIC and it has provoked disagreements that are much more than semantics. Differences between prolonged counter-insurgency warfare (involving political, economic and military measures) and special operations (involving counter-terrorism, rescue missions, commando operations, raids, etc.) continue to fuel unresolved debates over the meaning of LIC, a doctrine that is supposed to cover all these and much more. At the same time, every serious military study of LIC has concluded that the United States is still no better prepared to counter-insurgencies now than it was thirty-five years ago when it began the long march to defeat in Vietnam.[27] "The fundamental lesson to draw from our misadventures of the counter-insurgency era is the one already emphasized by many — the lesson of the limits of American power," says Blaufarb.[28] The emphasis on 'Rambo-oriented' individuals and units in the LIC and the suggestion that this force should be privatized to avoid Congressional oversight and accountability while maintaining a more genuinely covert profile, has raised new doubts in the background of the Iran-Contra affair. Many military experts in the United States have also come to believe that if USA cannot win against an insurgency, this does not mean that it will disengage: the idea is to deny the enemies the opportunity to achieve a real victory either. The utility of LIC for this limited purpose is seen by them as sufficient reason for its continued development.

The irony of the American situation has been aptly pointed out by Stone:

> In reading the military literature on guerrilla warfare now so fashionable at the Pentagon, one feels that these writers are like men watching a dance from outside through heavy plate glass windows. They see the motions but they can't hear the music. They put the mechanical gestures down on paper with pedantic fidelity. But what rarely comes through to them are the injured racial feelings, the misery, the rankling slights, the hatred, the devotion, the inspiration and the desperation. So they do not really understand what leads men to abandon wife, children, home, career, friends; to take to the bush and live with gun in hand like a hunted animal; to challenge overwhelming military odds rather than acquiesce any longer in humiliation, injustice or poverty..."[29]

British Refinements

The British Army is credited with having developed the best counter-insurgency warfare techniques in the modern world. It may be due to their valuable experience in many such wars since 1945: Palestine (1945-48), Malay (1948-60), Kenya (1952-60), Cyprus (1955-59), Brunei and Borneo (1962-66), Radfan and Aden (1963-67), Dhofar (1970-75) and Northern Ireland (1956-62 and 1969 onwards). Cyprus, Aden and Northern Ireland may not be the best examples of their success, but the British have allowed neither men nor weapons to rust after World War II.

British counter-insurgency theory and practice has been greatly influenced by the campaigns of Field Marshal Sir Gerald Templer in Malaya, Field Marshal Harding in Cyprus, and Major (later General Sir Frank) Kitson in Kenya. The first two cases are good examples of the application of what Thompson later enunciated as the 'five principles' of counter-insurgency: (1) clear political aim on the part of the government; (2) adherence to the rule of law; (3) a co-ordinated plan in which political, economic, social and military responses are clearly laid down; (4) security of own bases before launching military operations; and (5) initial concentration on destroying the political infra-structure of the insurgents.[30]

The key elements of the British strategy were "political primacy, insurgent isolation, intelligence and appropriate military response."[31] This meant: (1) a close political control over the army demonstrated by overall control of a civilian vested with political powers; (2) emphasis on collection and collation of intelligence by the police to take advantage of their local knowledge and to recreate an air of normalcy; (3) isolation of the insurgents from support among the people by giving them a vested interest in the legitimate administration and by influencing their "hearts and minds" (Templer); (4) isolation could sometimes take the drastic form of resettlement of population away from insurgents' activity and influence; (5) elimination of cells of passive support and suspects by temporary detention and intelligence screening; (6) army to pursue insurgents when they are forced by isolation measures to retreat into countryside or slums and urban sprawls; (7) avoidance of civilian casualties to prevent alienating uncommitted people; and (8) sustained military campaign.[32]

Kitson is the best known exponent of the new ideas on special operations (counter-terrorism, raids, rescue and commando operations, etc.) which form much of the basis of the British Army's training in counter-insurgency warfare and his well-known book[33] is considered to be an outstanding professional manual on the subject. Having had counter-insurgency experience in Malay, Kenya and Cyprus, as well as having commanded the 19th Airportable Brigade in Northern Ireland during the 1970s, his qualifications are beyond question. The only problem with his views, however, is that they are based on the assumption that the enemy is the 'Left', the protesters, organizers of strikes and demonstrations in Third World countries and maker of movements for national liberation — in short, a colonial orientation. He sees all types of political protest by the Left, the 'subversives,' as a preparation for armed action. This plants the idea in the minds of the soldiers that the radical elements in the society or the exercise of the democratic rights by the people must be dealt with by military methods.

It is significant that "strengthening of indigenous police and armed forces" to secure their loyalty still remains an objective principle of the post-colonial British Army. The implication is clear: their role is still visualized largely outside the country. Most modern theories of counter-insurgency in the non-communist world have been developed in Britain, France and USA. With the exception of Britain, which has had a kind of insurgency in Ireland (now Northern Ireland) from 850 AD onwards, these countries have not experienced the impact of insurgencies and terrorism within their own towns and countryside as India has during the first 50 years of its independence. All British and French counter-insurgency theories propounded until the 1960s were based on conclusions drawn from uprisings in their colonies.

Inevitably, their concept of counter-insurgency warfare was essentially colonial. In the post-colonial times counter-insurgency warfare has been practiced by superpowers for effective military intervention aimed at securing bases and influence. The techniques are ideally suited for vanquishing or pacifying enemies and there is very little which can be borrowed from these techniques for resolving problems connected with indigenous ethnic insurgencies in the developing world. According to Ekbal Ahmad,

> Contemporary revolutions have been occurring in the non-western world. Yet all the counterinsurgency theorists are westerners. More than their native clients they need ideological and moral arguments to justify their intervention to the natives no less than to the western soldiers who are sent to wage a confusing war on alien soil. Hence the counterinsurgency ideology seldom develops in response to local needs; it is mechanically manufactured or imported and characteristically lacks not only native roots but even the necessary adaptations to the local culture and values...[34]

II

The Question of Command

Civil-military relations and their respective roles in a counter-insurgency operation have been subjects of considerable debate and disagreement in most democracies. The question of overall command has often been a critical one, with the British favouring a Committee at every level comprising a senior military commander, a senior policeman and intelligence officers under the chairmanship of the head of the local administration. The

French have preferred a single commander system, who is usually a military officer, with advisors from the military as well as the civil administration. The British model is based on the democratic model defined by Vagts in which civilian-political supremacy is guaranteed by democratic parliamentary institutions and by the professional ethics of the army itself,[35] which excludes it from involvement in domestic partisan politics.[36] The civilian-political elites exercise control over the military through a formal set of rules that specifies the functions of the military and the conditions under which the military may exercise its authority.

The French follow a slightly democratic variant of the old aristocratic model in which civil and military elites are socially and functionally integrated. These are what Huntington calls the "objective control" (democratic) and "subjective control" (aristocratic) of the military.[37] There is no doubt, however, that a unified command is necessary for fighting an insurgency. Only the problem of co-ordinating civil and military measures is complicated. Regaining the allegiance of the population is both the prelude to destroying the power of the insurgents as well as the ultimate goal of a counter-insurgency operation. In an area of active hostility, the army is inevitably seen by a beleaguered civil population as an adversary in the initial stages of fighting and the situation does not change until well after the army establishes its superiority. The task of increasing the material comforts of the population and rectifying their grievances remains the exclusive business of a civil administration.

The British took the idea of the unified command to its logical conclusion in Malay and Cyprus when their generals became the heads of the government. In a democratic system like India, however, pressure groups like the Civil Service and the Press would be equally vocal against an administration headed by a serving military man, even if the political leadership was inclined to accept it as an emergency measure. For instance, the 1968 decision to post a serving army general as the Commissioner of a Division in Assam so that he could be the overall and unified commander of all agencies dealing with the Mizo insurgency had to be reviewed and set aside within a week under pressure from the Indian Administrative Service. Attempts to secure this unification of command under a retired military officer have also failed to pay significant dividends. Many ex-chiefs and retired generals of the Indian Army have been Governors of States riven by insurgencies but they have, despite such states having often been under President's rules for long durations, failed to resolve insurgencies as effectively as States working under popularly elected governments. This confirms Horowitz's view that such conflicts can be better resolved through a combination of electoral politics, re-distribution of economic resources and military campaigns rather than through military means alone.[38]

In this context, K.P.S. Gill made a unique contribution to counter-insurgency warfare. He is credited with resolving the Punjab insurgency largely through the use of the State's police force — something inconceivable in a sphere in which the regular army has traditionally been the ultimate panacea the world over. If the conflict in J&K is treated in its correct perspective as a protracted Low Intensity War between India and Pakistan, the insurgency in Punjab was the most serious internal conflict in post-independence India in terms of the intensity and frequency of violence, lives lost on both sides, the world-wide propaganda capabilities of the insurgents and the political significance that was accorded to the Khalistan insurgency internationally. The active and direct involvement of Pakistan's ISI from right across the border and from inside India turned it into a formidable conflict. The efficiency and speed with which the insurgency in Punjab was resolved under the command of K.P.S. Gill as the Director General of the Punjab Police has been a subject of considerable debate and discussion for a long time. Gill introduced "one of the most unique experiments in multi-force counter-terrorist strategic initiatives and integrated command structures," what he refers to as the idea of "cooperative command".[39] It is unfortunate that this experiment has yet to receive the attention it deserves from strategists and has not been attempted in any other theatre in India. It must, of course, also be acknowledged that the command structure in Punjab was an organic development based on K.P.S. Gill's emergence as the dominating personality in the counter-terrorism campaign, with an aura of authority that no other wing of the security forces operating in the State cared or dared to question. Critically, it was not a product of state policy, but of the personal strength and vision of a single commander and this, perhaps, is the reason why the experiment has not been replicated in any of the other States rife with insurgency. What is abundantly clear from the Punjab experience, however, is that once the best person to lead the operations has been identified, he should be left free to command.

III

Grouping of Villages as Counter-insurgency Strategy

The years 1967-69 saw the entire rural population of Mizoram (roughly eighty per cent of the total population) uprooted from their homes, to be relocated miles away in what were euphemistically called 'Protected and Progressive Villages'. The army argued that the segregation and control of the population by this method was necessary for a successful counter-insurgency campaign. The general humiliation, loss of freedom and of property and, very often, injury and death involved in this process of so-called 'grouping of villages' were incidental to the military operations in Mizoram (1966-1986), as perhaps they are to internal wars anywhere. But it appeared to many then, as it would appear to many more acutely now, that the policy of 'grouping' was tantamount to annihilation of reason and sensibility and certainly not the best policy to follow against our own ethnic minorities.

The Mizo Insurrection

The context for the policy of grouping of villages was created by the Mizo insurrection which commenced when the Mizo National Front (MNF) declared the "independence" of Mizoram from India in the early hours of March 1, 1966. Laldenga and 59 others issued a statement to justify the extraordinary step that they had taken.[40] The Mizo National Front government had Laldenga as its 'President'. Its other important functionaries were: Lalnunmawia — 'Vice-President', R. Zamawia — 'Defence Secretary', Sainghaka — 'Home Secretary', Lalkhawliana — 'Finance Secretary', J.F. Manliana — 'Chief Justice', and Malsawma Colney — the 'Speaker of the Parliament'. The military hierarchy of the Mizo National Army was fairly well-defined. The MNA was headed by a Chief of Staff and 'Lieutenant General' Thangzuala Sailo held this position in 1966. His Vice-Chief of Staff was 'Major General' Vanlalhruaia. Other members of the general staff were: 'Major General' Thankima, 'Adjutant General', 'Major General' J. Sawmvela, 'GOC-in-C Western Command' and 'Major General' R. Lalngura, 'GOC-in-C Eastern Command'.

At the time of the Mizo uprising in March 1966, the Mizo National Army (MNA) consisted of eight infantry battalions organized on the pattern of the Indian Army, but the number of men in each 'battalion' was about 50 in the hope that future recruitment and training would raise the strength sufficiently to match the Indian Army's infantry battalions. Seven battalions were named after legendary Mizo heroes Vnapa, Khuangchera, Taitesena, Lalvunga, Saizahawla, Chawngbawia and Zampui Manga and one after a Biblical character, Joshua. The battalions were known by their initials, e.g., 'V' Battalion stood for Vnapa, 'J' for Joshua and so on. T, CH, S and K battalions made the Lion Brigade, and V, J, L, and Z battalions the Dagger Brigade. The Brigades had their clearly demarcated area of operation in the early days of insurgency, with the northern half of the district under the Dagger Brigade and the southern half under the Lion Brigade. In the beginning the main body of the MNA consisted of about 2000 men who had gone through various levels of training, and about an equal number of irregulars, known as the Mizo National Volunteer Force (MNVF). The approximate number of weapons MNA had by end of March 1966 (including both the arms smuggled from Pakistan and looted from Assam Rifles, Border Security Force and Assam Police in the early days of the uprising) was: 600 rifles (mostly .303 bore), 20 light machine guns, 75 sten-guns, 25 carbines, 30 revolvers/pistols and about 1500 shotguns including muzzle-loading guns.

The Army's Response

On the night of February 28/March 1, 1966, the MNA simultaneously engaged the 1st Assam Rifles garrisons at Aizawl, Lunglei and Champhai and the 5th Border Security Force (BSF) posts at Tipaimukh, Hnahlan, Vaphai, Tuipang, Vaseitlang, Chawngte, Demagiri, Marpara and Tuipuibari. On March 1, they raided the Aizawl treasury and telephone exchange and made off with ten rifles and some cash. The same day they succeeded in attaining complete surprise at Champhai, killed the sentries at the Assam Rifles quarter guard and took possession of the weapons before the garrison knew what had happened. They took over Aizawl town on March 3 and T.S. Gill, the Deputy Commissioner of the District, took shelter in the Assam Rifles headquarters. Lunglei was invested by the MNA on March 5 and R.V. Pillai, the Subdivisional Officer, was kidnapped. The BSF posts held out despite the severity of the attacks.

The army was asked by the central government to deal with the situation on March 2 and the 61 Mountain Brigade was moved from Agartala (Tripura) to Silchar on March 3 and to Aizawl on March 7 to start operations against the MNF. The overall responsibility for the army operations as well as liaison with the Government of Assam was given to Major General (later Lt. Gen.) Sangat Singh, GOC 101 Communication Zone, with Headquarters in Shillong. The first army battalion (8th Sikh) advanced from Silchar into the hills on March 3 and after some minor skirmishes on the way, linked up with the besieged Assam Rifles garrison at Aizawl on March 7. On March 8, 2nd/11th Gurkha Rifles moved towards Champhai and 3rd Bihar towards Lunglei. Lunglei was secured by the Indian Army on March 14 and Champhai on March 15. On March 14-15, 5th Para were flown in by helicopters into Lunglei. They made a dash for Demagiri on the East Pakistan border and took over this area on March 17.

During the first month of operations, the Security Forces (SFs — this expression will now be used as, by the end of the month, it was a composite army/paramilitary/police force) were able to take back all the posts which had fallen to the MNA in early March. The cost in terms of casualties was heavy. The SFs suffered 59 killed, 126 wounded and 23 missing. The MNA casualties during this period were 95 killed, 35 wounded and 558 (which included unarmed MNVF) captured. The SFs also captured 175 rifles of various bores and types, 332 shotguns, 467 muzzle loading guns, 57 pistols/revolvers and about 70,000 rounds of ammunition. These weapons also included the ones that were seized from the villagers during search operations.

The MNA headquarters was in Aizawl in the beginning of March. On March 3, it moved to South Hlimen, about thirty miles south of Aizawl. On March 18, it was shifted to Reiek, east of Aizawl. By the end of the month, Laldenga and the entire MNF and MNA high command had crossed the border and established their headquarters in Chittagong Hill Tracts of what was then East Pakistan.

During the next eight months, the SFs were joined by two more army battalions (18 Punjab and 9 Bihar), three Assam Rifles battalions (6th, 18th and 19th) and four armed police battalions belonging to the Central Reserve Police and the States. These forces were able to secure the district, subdivisional and block civil administration headquarters and to some extent the main Silchar-Aizawl-Lunglei road by the end of the year 1966.

By the end of April 1966, the MNA dispersed in smaller units and merged with the population. From the safety of their villages they launched guerrilla attacks on the SFs, often inflicting considerable damage and casualties. The routine activities of the SFs, such as escorting road convoys and manning of static posts at administrative centres, SF movements on interior roads, as well as their ignorance of the topography made them easy targets to guerrilla bands. They had very little access to hard intelligence, and the Mizos could not initially be involved in this work as they were too scared of the punishment the MNA might meet out to them. SF operations were, therefore, undertaken on scanty or no information throughout 1966. Between March and December 1966, the SFs lost 95 men and 60 weapons.

The high casualties and the inability of the SFs to effectively check MNA depredations were viewed with some concern. There was only a semblance of Indian authority in the Mizo Hills during 1966, and with the reported arrival of fresh MNA reinforcements from East Pakistan with more arms, it was feared that the situation would not be qualitatively better in the days to come unless a longer-term view was taken of the counter-insurgency operations and its strategic/logistic requirements. The army was under pressure to provide evidence of a higher level of competence than they had shown over the past year. The government was equally under pressure. Hundreds of Mizo families had run away to

Shillong and other places in Assam to escape the chaos at home, and a further and much larger migration of Mizos caught between two fighting armies was feared. There was scarcity of food and other essential commodities in the district as most non-tribal shopkeepers had run away and no fresh goods were finding their way into the district. The convoys being run to bring in food and other goods under SF protection were few and far in-between because of the frequency of ambushes and heavy SF casualties. The Border Roads Organisation (BRO), who had been building strategic roads in the district since 1964, was also finding it difficult to build and maintain roads under such insecure conditions. And to add to the government's discomfiture, there were reports of serious human and civil rights violations and maltreatment of civilians at the hands of the SF in the Indian as well as the foreign press.

The army proposed that insurgency could not be controlled without more troops for operations and without recourse to resettlement of villages in order to isolate the guerrillas from the populace. The country had a difficult choice. Many battalions of the army were already committed in a similar role in Nagaland and Manipur. An indecisive war had been fought with Pakistan in the previous year (1965) and the situation was too uncertain to allow thinning of the troops on the western border. Although a war with China had been fought four years earlier, the massing of Chinese troops on the border, their belligerence in Tibet and the extension of their support to the Naga (and later Mizo) insurgents precluded withdrawal of troops from the northern borders.

There were clearly two options in so far as additional troops for the Mizo Hills operations were concerned: either the army could reduce the period the troops were allowed in family stations between postings in non-family stations on the borders, or the government could agree to the raising of more battalions and consequently, the size of the army itself. On the basis of a re-assessment of infantry battalions which were likely to be involved in counter-insurgency operations in the North-East, it was decided that another infantry division would be added to the army. Plans had already existed for the creation of this division as part of a larger scheme to give the army more teeth in the eastern sector in the event of a major conflict with either Pakistan or China in the future and the Mizo Hills situation speeded up the process.

There was considerable debate on the question of resettlement or regrouping of villages, which the army thought was essential for effective counter-insurgency operations.[41] This proposal was advanced by the army as a solution to two more pressing problems — the attacks on convoys by insurgents living in the villages and high SF casualties. The Silchar-Aizawl-Lunglei road was the lifeline of the district and convoys carrying food and other essential commodities were necessary both to save the population from starvation and for the maintenance of the SFs. The convoys could move only if they were escorted by the SFs and the road was made secure. The insurgents, who had merged with the local population, ambushed the SF escorts or the road patrols and made away with looted weapons, back to hideouts in the villages. Unless, the army argued, the villages within ten miles from the main road were depopulated and were regrouped along the main road and put under constant SFs surveillance, they could not hope to isolate the MNA from the population and make the roads more secure from their attacks. Once isolated, the insurgents would tend to go back to the jungles where the SF would be able to tackle them more effectively. Such a step, moreover, would facilitate better intelligence, as informers would be more forthcoming when the population had confidence in the ability of the SFs to protect them from the rebels. So far they were working on the basis of information gained from observation or from interrogating prisoners. The interrogation was also inefficient because it was very difficult to make sense out of prisoners' stories, especially since there was no advance information available to either check a story or trip up the prisoner when the lying started.

Resettlement of Villages

In a report sent to the army headquarters in October 1966, Lt. Gen. (later Field Marshal) Sam Manekshaw, GOC-in-C Eastern Command, Calcutta, recommended that to be effective militarily, grouping must be extensive and must intern a very large portion, if not all, of the population. He, however, suggested that grouping may initially be undertaken in a 10-mile belt on both sides of the

Vairengte-Aizawl-Lunglei road. The military advantages of this action, according to him, would be to make the road axis secure and thus increase the logistic capacity as well as relatively unhampered road-construction work by the BRO. The grouped villagers could also be gainfully employed to work on the new roads. The 20-mile secure belt thus created would restrict movement of hostile gangs from one sector to another and to and from East Pakistan. Coupled with a 'food denial' programme based on monitoring and controlling food supplies to the grouped villages, the policy envisaged forcing the insurgents into devoting their energies to personal survival rather than armed activity. This would compel the MNA to migrate into ungrouped and depopulated areas, thus diminishing the territory that was required to be dominated by the SF. Manekshaw was also of the opinion that grouping of villages would enable the civil administration to exercise more effective control over a larger population than it was able to do at that time and would eventually lead to destruction of the political infrastructure of the insurgents by isolating the militants from their support among the people. He visualized that the provision of administrative facilities for the newly regrouped villages would include food supplies and fair-price shops, house-roofing material like galvanized corrugated iron sheets, dispensaries and doctors and schools.

Meanwhile, the Government of Assam had also separately proposed to the Government of India the grouping of 75 villages, mainly to the north of Aizawl, with a population of 36,517 and had envisaged these centres as protected villages with basic civic amenities. This proposal was initiated by R. Natarajan, the Deputy Commissioner of Mizo Hills District, who thought that the army scheme was likely to be drastic and that it could be effectively kept in check only if the civil administration could foist a scheme of its own. The Central Cabinet rejected the army proposal on October 20, 1966.

It appears that the main opposition to the army scheme came from B. K. Nehru, Governor of Assam and the Central Ministries of Home and Finance. But the army embarked on a programme of most forceful lobbying of their case during the next few weeks and also launched a major public relations exercise with the

Government of Assam to get them to agree to a scheme of village relocation which would meet their operational requirements and yet be acceptable to the state government. In any case, dithering on such an important policy issue at the behest of the Government of Assam, which was largely held responsible for insurgency in Mizo Hills, was considered bad form in Delhi in those days, particularly when mounting army casualties had become a matter of serious concern. The army's endeavours were fruitful and the scheme was finally cleared by the Government of India on December 5, 1966. The government also specified certain guiding principles.[42]

The army called it 'Operation Accomplishment'. In its 6 p.m. news broadcast on January 3, 1967, the All India Radio announced the decision of the Government of India to group villages in Mizo Hills for security reasons. Lt. Gen. S.H.F.J. Manekshaw and A.N. Kidwai, Chief Secretary of Assam, announced the decision in press conferences held in Calcutta and Shillong simultaneously on that day. The Indian press generally appreciated the gesture of the government to have taken them into confidence in this matter. Formal orders were issued by B.C. Carriapa, Commissioner of Division of Cachar and Mizo Hills and ex-officio Central Government Liaison Officer for Mizo Hills, under Rule 57 of the Defence of India Rules, 1964, which directed habitants of 100 villages within a 20-mile belt astride Vairengte-Aizawl-Lunglei road to move with all their property to 18 specified group centres and authorized the army to remove them, if necessary, by use of "minimum force".

'Operation Accomplishment' was executed by the army with the best possible speed and efficiency. In forty-nine days between January 4 and February 23, 45,107 inhabitants of 109 villages were relocated in 18 group centres on the main road. The army, assisted by the first batch of civilian officers earmarked for the administration of these new centres, carried out screening of the entire population, supervised the layout of the new habitations and house-sites, constructed bamboo and barbed wire stockades along the perimeters, recorded particulars of all individuals and issued identity cards, distributed rations based on a daily scale approved by the government, organized medical cover including vaccination of all population to guard against disease and epidemic and posted army doctors to look after the health of the villagers. Each centre was initially placed in the charge of an officer of the rank of a Major or Captain, with a company of troops to look after the security and protection of the centres as well as road protection duties for the passage of civil and army convoys. These new grouped village centres were designated 'Protected and Progressive Villages' (PPVs) and were handed over to the civil administration during the course of the following three months.

The MNF started interfering in the grouping of villages around the end of January 1967 when the army found two villages, Keifang and Tualbung, partially deserted after they were ordered to move to the Thingsulthliah centre. About 2000 villagers were successfully prevented by the MNA from being grouped. The SF launched their 'Operation Satsriakal' to deal with the MNA and in the ensuing confrontations between January 4 and February 15, 1967, they again suffered heavy casualties. 75 soldiers were killed and 60 wounded and the SFs lost about 40 rifles, 5 light machine guns, 6 sten-guns and other assorted arms and ammunition. MNA losses were 36 men killed, 10 wounded and about 100 apprehended. The SFs also seized some 30 weapons of different types and as well as ammunition from the MNA.

Operations During 1967 and 1968

As was expected, the SFs carried out large-scale offensive operations against the MNF during the whole of 1967 to consolidate whatever they had gained from the grouping of villages. They first combed the depopulated areas on both sides of the road along which grouping had been done to destroy possible hideouts and hidden stocks of foodgrain. There were also regular smaller operations undertaken by the SF posts in the interior that emphasized vigorous patrolling and ambushes. Major operations, involving employment of troops from different sectors as well as helicopter-borne troops, were also conducted in the interior. The pattern generally followed was to lay stops around areas selected on the basis of information and reconnaissance analysis and to flush the areas with troops to make it impossible for any hostile to escape. Thickly wooded areas in the vicinity of villages and watercourses, which were often used by the MNA guerrillas as their camping places, were subjected to special searches.

The 'Operation Blanket' concept, which was tried by 5 Para in 1966 with some success, was also frequently employed. This involved the sending out of self-contained patrols for 10 to 15 day sorties to dominate a group of nearby villages in each mission, in order to give the villagers an impression of almost permanent presence so that they could be rid of MNF influence. Though the operations undertaken during 1967 were not very successful from the point of view of MNF casualties or recoveries of arms, they did, for the first time, result in the relative security of road convoys and reduced SF casualties. They also kept the insurgents constantly on the run as the whole district was patrolled and dominated by the SFs throughout the year.

But the tables were turned again during January-April 1968. The MNA carried out some very successful ambushes against the SFs early in the year and let loose a reign of terror against their own kith and kin who they suspected of assisting the SFs. This resulted in one of the biggest operations, with about twelve battalions taking part, launched in April. Ironically, an SF column was ambushed within a few hours of the commencement of the operation. Nevertheless, in many ways, this was a decisive year from the military point of view.

1968 saw the heaviest rainfall in Mizo Hills in living memory and throughout the summer months the SFs kept tightening their noose between Tuipui and Tuichang rivers, the area where hostile movement was most conspicuous. By the end of the year, about 90 insurgents had been killed and many more taken prisoner, though the SFs also suffered a loss of about 35 of their men. These operations dealt a severe blow to MNF morale and the majority of the guerrillas escaped into East Pakistan, leaving Mizo Hills relatively free from military activity for the next two years, with the exception of some isolated and minor skirmishes.

At the beginning of 1968, it was estimated that the MNF had about 650 rifles of .303 calibre, 25 self-loading rifles of 7.62 calibre, 75 sten-guns, 50 light machine guns and 10 two-inch mortars. During the first four months of the year, they grabbed another 16 rifles of 7.62 calibre, 7 rifles of .303 calibre, 9 sten-guns, 3 light machine guns and 1 two-inch mortar, in successful ambushes on the SFs. The SFs, however, recovered 5 light machine guns, 15 sten-guns and 156 rifles of .303 calibre from the MNF during the operations launched during the year. By 1969, consequently, the MNA were left with about 10 two-inch mortars, 47 light machine guns, 67 sten-guns, 503 rifles of .303 calibre and 40 self-loading 7.62 rifles as their main fighting weapons. The estimates of the SFs regarding the weapons held by the MNF were fairly accurate. The initial figures were compiled on the basis of the interrogations of MNF Vice-Chief of Staff, Major General Vanlalhruaia, who was captured on December 19, 1966. These were substantiated by the MNF Quatermaster General, Brigadier Liandawla, who was captured on December 27, 1966 in Aizawl. This information was further verified from the MNF Lion Brigade documents that the SFs seized on December 31, 1967. These sources and documents also confirmed that the Pakistani army had so far given them 360 rifles, 24 carbines, 35 sten-guns, 30 LMGs and 4 two-inch mortars.

The ostensible reason for the MNF to take to terrorising of the civilian population was either to strike down proven army informers or a move to prevent people from hampering further recruitment. But some MNF cadres later confessed after they came overground that, for many of them, it was also the release of an enormous strain that had been mounting on their nervous systems, a kind of emotional catharsis. They were of the opinion that Mizos were not temperamentally suited to a long drawn-out war and prolonged isolation from their families. This often resulted in discharge of wrought-up emotions and anything, even shooting at a tree, sometimes soothed their nerves.

It is estimated that during the two distinct phases of terror in 1968 and 1973-74, the MNF wiped out about 350 of civilians from their own communities.

The First Amnesty

In August 1968, the Government of India took advantage of the military superiority of the SFs and offered amnesty to the rebels. The terms included pardon for participation in the war against India for those who surrendered with their serviceable arms and cash rewards of Rs. 4,000 for a light machine gun,

Rs. 600 for a mortar or rocket launcher, Rs. 500 for a 7.62 calibre self-loading rifle, Rs. 300 for a .303 calibre rifle/sten-gun/carbine and Rs. 250 for a pistol or a revolver. This resulted in 60 insurgents surrendering with weapons and 1464 without weapons.[43] The insurgents who surrendered revealed that the MNF morale had been shattered by the combined effect of the latest operations, very high incidence of sickness, particularly malaria and inability to get adequate food from the population and general disgust and disillusionment in the rank and file of the MNA and volunteers. In fact, the morale of the MNF was so low during 1969 that Laldenga sent Vanlalngaia, the chief of the MNF intelligence branch, to Mizo Hills to study the possibility of a rapproachment with the Government of India. This initiative was, however, frustrated due to the arrest of this emissary by the SFs. The news of low rebel morale encouraged the government to make several amnesty offers during 1969-70, though the renewed offers did not always elicit the desired level of response.[44]

Further Resettlement

The army took advantage of this success to press home the demand for further regrouping of villages along the Mizo Hills borders with Tripura, Burma and Pakistan. There was again some hesitation on the part of the Government of Assam, but the Government of India went largely by the army's advice and an order for grouping of another 185 villages, with a population of 95,917, to be relocated in 41 centers was issued by the District Magistrate of Mizo Hills under the Assam Maintenance of Public Order Act, 1948, as the earlier order under the Defence of India Rules was found to have some legal flaws.

The second grouping order was executed by the SFs' 'Operation Accomplishment Two' over 1968-69. This was followed by a third grouping of 63 villages with a population of 34,195 at 17 centres. The army, however, carried out a further grouping of 110 villages with a population of 47,056 in 26 centres without any order from the government on the ground that these villagers had expressed a desire to be shifted voluntarily. The government had no choice but to regularize this grouping by an *ex post facto* order issued in 1970. By 1972, there were 102 group centres accommodating 240,000 persons, or more than 80 percent of Mizo Hills' population of 285,000. The remaining 45,000 people lived in Aizawl, Lunglei and Saiha and a few ungrouped villages in the Pawi-Lakher region in the south.

An interesting development had taken place in the meantime. While the last two phases of grouping of villages were being carried out, the general resentment against grouping mounted to such an extent that some Mizos challenged the orders in the Gauhati High Court as violative of the Fundamental Rights guaranteed in the Constitution. The High Court directed the suspension of all further grouping and asked the government to show cause why this order should not be made absolute. The matter was, however, dropped by the High Court after the government had assured it that no further grouping of villages was planned. By this time, however, 80 per cent of the population of Mizo Hills District had already been relocated.

The Resettlement Strategy Examined

When Roman legions marched across Europe and Asia, they had a rather simple way of dealing with the local hostile population: they just carted the natives to their capital and sold them off as slaves. Modern armies have developed more sophisticated ways of dealing with such problems. The concentration camps established during the Boer War were instrumental in isolating the Commandos from their economic and spiritual bases and contributed materially to the British success. This method was used by the Nazis to wipe out almost the entire population of ethnic Jews who were herded into concentration camps. But it was essentially the successful British experiment in resettlement in Malaya (1948-60) which has provided a model for use of such tactics in the counter-insurgency campaigns of the last forty years.

Resettlement and other similar forms of population control have, however, been a favourite counter-insurgency technique with most modern armies. Although the French Army never adopted this as a general policy in Vietnam, resettlement was undertaken in the border areas of Cambodia in 1947 and 1951 as part of their pacification programme with some success in so far as it removed the sources of food, shelter and recruits from the

Viet Minh. The South Vietnamese under Diem continued these efforts. During the Algerian War, the French Army, as part of their *regroupement* policy, uprooted more than one million peasants from their homes and created immense social discontent and suffering. In Vietnam, the *agrovilles* created by the French became 'strategic hamlets' under the Strategic Hamlet Programme of the (US) Army in the 1960s. But this strategy failed largely because of the American adherence to a 'search and destroy' policy rather than the 'clear and hold' concept recommended by Robert Thompson of the British Advisory Mission in Saigon.

The US Army had hired a team of British advisors[45] for the purpose of formulating the resettlement or the 'strategic hamlets' plan and like many other American obsessions, "their creation became the purpose itself."[46] It served no military or administrative objective and in fact, one sceptical US official commented: "If you stand long enough down there, they will throw a piece of barbed wire around you and call you a strategic hamlet."[47] The British Army had, as mentioned above, successfully tested this strategy under Thompson when they resettled about half a million Chinese in Malaya in 1950-51 in new villages protected by military units and wire fences. Incidentally, the Portuguese Army had also experimented with resettlement in Mozambique, Angola and Guinea between 1945 and 1974, by establishing *senzalas do paz* or *aldeamentos* to serve a variety of objectives including the separation of populations from the guerrillas, the accommodation of refugees returning from Zaire, and the release of more land for further white settlement. The Portuguese brought together more than one million Angolans and 15 per cent of the population of Mozambique into the *aldeamentos* with disastrous results. Resettlement was also undertaken on a large-scale in the whole of black rural Rhodesia from 1973 onwards and besides causing immeasurable suffering to the tribal communities, failed to achieve the objective of containing violence.

Tactically, the strategy of resettlement has been used: (a) to isolate the hostiles from villages to deny them intelligence, food, money and new recruits; (b) to achieve full freedom of operation against the guerrillas in the depopulated and unenclosed countryside; (c) to free more troops for operations; and (d) to build up the confidence of the villagers in the SFs' ability to protect them so that they become willing members of the military-intelligence set-up. Strategically, resettlement helps: (a) to protect the population; (b) to unite the people in positive action on the side of the government; (c) to instill in them the will to morally and physically resist the demands of the hostiles so that some responsibility for the defence of the new settlements can devolve on the inhabitants; and (d) to provide a framework for social and economic improvement.

It is evident that in modern counter-insurgency warfare, there is a greater emphasis on 'clear and hold' operations as opposed to 'search and clear' or sweep operations, since the latter, howsoever aggressive, do not achieve the dual purpose of killing insurgents and destroying their infrastructure. Moreover, massive deployment of infantry and air power, which is essential for 'search and clear' operations, is generally wasteful and not within the means of all countries to afford. Even US armed forces failed to get proportionate benefits out of the massive 'search and clear' operations that were launched throughout the intensive phase of the Vietnam War. On the other hand, 'hold' operations have very little effectiveness in counter-insurgency campaigns if resettlement, or similar methods aimed at physical and political isolation of the population from insurgents, is not the basis of the security framework. But resettlement of populations or their control by similar methods has had many other vital implications in recent military history.

Whether in its more extreme form, as practised by the Nazis against the Jews, or in moderate forms of varying degrees as adopted in Malaya, Vietnam, Algeria, Angola, Mozambique and Rhodesia (or even nearer home in Mizoram in 1967-70), patterns of control of populations through concentrating in camps display certain discomforting similarities.

First, they have always been used against people who are racially or ethnically different. The white races have practised control of ethnic populations in the American continent as a means to subdue the natives and to colonize their lands and resources for almost four centuries. In modern counter-insurgency warfare, too, the seminal experiment in resettlement came with the control of the Chinese population by the British in Malaya and this provided a model for its application by other armies.

Secondly, resettlement has often been used to maintain economic and strategic interests and to suppress struggles for democratic advance and national and social liberation. These frankly anti-democratic and anti-national-liberation purposes were pursued by the British Army against Malaya (1948-60), Kenya (1952-55), Aden (1963-68), Oman (1957-59), Cyprus (1954-58), Malaysia (1963-66). Clearly, there is a stigma attached to these tactics in their application in the Third World, where colonialism and ethnic heterogeneity have been among the most common factors responsible for insurgency.[48] It appears unlikely that a section of white citizens in an economically stable country like the USA will take to terrorism or warfare against the state. But it is equally unlikely that, in case that happens, an entire white population would be herded into camps with barbed wire thrown around them.[49] Just as it would be impossible for the British and Spanish governments to agree to a plan of their armies to exercise control over the Catholic population of Northern Ireland or the Basque population of Spain by resettling them in stockaded centres guarded by armed troops. Such extreme measures would always hold good for peoples other than those who belong racially and ethnically to the dominant majority.[50]

Arguably, this is a serious charge that India will be confronted with internally and externally if such a strategy was to be adopted today against an ethnic minority as the reach of the media in the new millenium would be a million times more extensive than what it was in the 1960s. Although the Mizo crisis is over and many of the PPVs have been de-grouped with villagers returning to their native villages, the grouping exercise carried out over 1967-70 has left a huge scar in the Mizo psyche. The romance of Mizo village life disappeared forever. A personalised account of the enormity of the exercise and its impact are provided in the reminiscences of one Army officer who was engaged in the execution of the policy of relocation:

> "Darzo was one of the richest villages I have ever seen in this part of the world. There were ample stores of paddy, fowls and pigs. The villagers appeared well-fed and well-clad, and

most of them had some money in cash. We arrived in the village about ten in the morning. My orders were to get the villagers to collect whatever moveable property they could, and to set their own village to fire at seven in the evening. I also had orders to burn all the paddy and other grain that could not be carried away by the villagers to the new centre so as to keep food out of the reach of the insurgents. For about three hours I tried to convince them that they would have to shift bag and baggage to Hnathial Protected and Progressive Village, as the group centres were officially known. They argued with me endlessly, until I had no choice but to tell them that the soldiers would deal with them if they did not obey my orders. It was obvious they could not carry away even one fourth of the paddy they had in storage. Now, it was a dilemma as I had orders to burn all paddy that could not be carried away so that the insurgents don't benefit from it. Imagine, we were supposed to destroy all that food for which hundreds of families had toiled for months. I somehow couldn't do it. I called the Village Council President and told him that in three hours his men could hide all the excess paddy and other foodgrain in the caves and return for it after a few days under army escort. They concealed everything most efficiently.

Night fell and I had to persuade the villagers to come out and set fire to their homes. Nobody came out. Then I had to order my soldiers to enter every house and force the people out. Every man, woman and child who could walk came out with as much of his or her belongings and food as they could. But they wouldn't set fire to their homes. Ultimately, I lit a torch myself and set fire to one of the houses. I knew I was carrying out orders, and would hate to do such a thing if I had my way. My soldiers also started torching other buildings, and the whole place was soon ablaze. There was absolute confusion everywhere. Women were wailing and shouting and cursing. Children were frightened and cried. Young boys and girls held hands and looked at their burning village with a stupefied expression on their faces. But the grown up men were silent; not a whimper or a whisper from them. Pigs were running about, *mithuns* were bellowing, dogs were barking, and fowls setting up a racket with their fluttering and crackling. One little girl ran into her burning house and soon darted out holding a kitten in her hands.

When it was time for the world to sleep, we marched out of Darzo — soldiers in front, with the Mizos following, and the rear brought up by more soldiers. We had enough troops for the job. If anyone had tried to run away from the column, he would have been shot. We walked fifteen miles through the night along the jungle and the morning saw us in Hnathial. I tell you, I hated myself that night. I had done the job of an executioner. That night when I saw children as young as three years carrying huge loads on their heads for fifteen miles with very few stops for rest, their noses running, their little feet faltering, with pregnant women hardly able to carry their burden up the hill from the Mat river valley — for the first time in my life as a soldier I did not feel the burden of the fifty pound haversack on my own back. It was a miracle that we reached Hnathial without a casualty, or perhaps the Mizos are a very tough people, physically and emotionally. But there was something more to be carried out. I called the Darzo Village Council President and his village elders and ordered them to sign a document saying that they had voluntarily asked to be resettled in Hnathial PPV under the protection of the Security Forces as they were being harassed by the insurgents, and because their own village did not have communications, educational, medical and other facilities. Another document stated that they had burnt down their own village, and that no force or coercion was used by the Security Forces. They refused to sign. So I sent them out and after an hour called them in again, this time one man at a time. On my table was a loaded revolver, and in the corner stood two NCOs with loaded sten-guns. This frightened them, and one by one they signed both the documents. I had to do it as I had no choice in this matter. If those chaps had gone to the civil administration or the courts with complaints, there would have been all kinds of criminal cases against us.

> We had to protect ourselves with these false certificates. We had no choice. All individual officers were expected to carry out their tasks in such a manner that it left no scope for embarrassment to our higher formations."[51]

There is, of course, no doubt that grouping contributed considerably to the success of the army's counter-insurgency operations. But the irony is that the colonial strategies adopted by the British to suppress independent movements and other anti-colonial insurrections in Kenya, Aden, Oman, Cyprus and Malay and which had at one time been decried most vehemently by our national leaders, were used by us against some of our own people in the post-independence era. One hopes that Indian government would not allow use of such outdated colonial military strategies while dealing with our own ethnic minorities who have not been able to finally settle their terms of political association with India. The problem is that in the nation's internal wars against terrorists and insurgents, it is very often not the culpable segment of the population that suffers the most. Those who had set up insurrections in Nagaland, Mizoram, Tripura, Manipur and Assam soon became fleeting, elusive shapes, like the phosphorescent creatures of the deep ocean, directing their confused struggles from the safety of foreign sanctuaries, while the village folk, most of whom knew very little about anything, have borne the brunt of an exasperated, and often clueless, system of governance.

APPENDIX I

Text of Mizo National Front's Declaration of 1966

In the course of human history it becomes invariably necessary for mankind to assume their social, economic and political status to which the Law of Nature and Nature's God entitles them. We hold this truth to be self-evident that all men are created equal, and that they are endowed with inalienable fundamental human rights and dignity of human person; and to secure these rights governments are instituted among men deriving their just power from the consent of the governed and whenever any form of Government become destructive of this end, it is the right of the people to alter, change, modify and abolish it and to institute a new government and laying its foundation on such principles and organizing its power in such forms as to them shall see most likely to effect their rights and dignity. The Mizo, created and moulded into a nation and nurtured as such by Nature's God have been intolerably dominated by the people of India in contravention of the Law of Nature.

The leaders of the Mizo Nation had, many a time, verbally and in writing, put forward to the Government of India their desire of self-determination for creation of free and independent Mizoram for bringing about protection of Human Rights and Dignity, which the Mizo, by nature, ought to have, but the Government of India, violating the Charter of the United Nations and its Universal Declaration of Human Rights reaffirmed in the Principles of Bandung Conference, have ignored the voice of the Mizo people and determined to continue domination and colonization ruling over us with tyranny and despotism by instituting self-designed administrative machinery with which they endeavour to mislead the world to win their confidence.

Our people are despised, persecuted, tortured, manhandled and murdered without displaying justice while they preach and profess before us and throughout the world that they have instituted for us a separate administrative set up in conformity with the principles of Democracy. To conceal their evil and selfish design, religious assimilation and Hindu indoctrination they preach to have established which we cannot accept as it leads to suppression of Christianity.

To prove this, let facts be submitted to the candid world:

1. They have instituted government to rule over us in our own country without any respect for Human Rights and Dignity even in the face of the present candid world which is committed to these rights and dignity.
2. They have been pursuing a policy of exploitative measures in their attempt to wipe Christianity, sole religion, and no consideration has ever been paid to our national way of life.
3. They have been preaching throughout the world as if they have instituted a separate administrative machinery in

conformity with the principles of Democracy to conceal their policy of degeneration of our national morality and of assimilation while what had been instituted for us is a pattern of Colonial administration.

4. They refuse not only to procure supply of food and arrange other forms of assistance in times of famine, but also prohibited us from seeking and receiving assistance from friendly countries, which resulted in the death of many people.
5. They have established a multitude of offices and sent hitherto swarms of Indian officers, who had an immoral life, cruelly appeasing our womenfolk to commit immorality with them by taking advantage of their official capacity and of the position they occupy in the administrative machinery.
6. Taking the advantage of economic frustration of the people they subject us to economic slavery and force us to enter into the door of poverty.
7. Curbing freedom of expression, our patriots are arrested and kept in jails without displaying any form of justice.
8. The export facility which we used to enjoy before the pre-Indian domination has been totally closed.
9. Without exploring our country's economic resources in agriculture, industries and mining and giving no consideration for their development, they maintain suppressive measures against our economic right.
10. Realising the importance of our country to India in its defence strategy, the Government of India is establishing military bases throughout our country and thereby creating an atmosphere of cold war while nothing is done for its economic and social development.
11. Inspite of our repeated appeal for peaceful settlement of our rightful and legitimate demand for full self-determination, the Government of India is bringing exploitative and suppressive measures employing their military might and waging war against us as done in the case of the Nagas and the Kashmiris.
12. Owing to absence of medical facilities in our countries, our

people died without having medical treatment and attention.

For these and all other innumerable causes, we declare to the candid world that India is unworthy and unfit to rule over the civilised Mizo people who are created and moulded into a nation and nurtured a such and endowed with territorial integrity by Nature and Nature's God.

We, therefore, the representatives of Mizo people, meeting on this day, the first of March, in the year of our Lord, 1966, appealing to the supreme Judge of the World for the rectitude of our intention so, in the name and by the authority of the good people of this country, solemnly publish and declare, that Mizoram is, and of right ought to be, free and independent, that they are absolved from all allegiance to India and its Parliament and all political connections between them and Government of India is and ought to be dissolved and that as a free and independent state, they have full power to levy war, conclude peace, contract alliances, establish commerce and to do all other Acts and Things which Independent state may of right. And for the support of this Declaration, we mutually pledge to each other with a firm reliance on the Protection of Divine Providence, our lives, our fortunes, and our sacred Honour. We appeal to all freedom loving nations and individuals to uphold Human Rights and Dignity and to extend help to the Mizo people for realisation of our rightful and legitimate demand for self-determination. We appeal also to all independent countries to give recognition to the Independence of Mizoram.

NOTES AND REFERENCES

1. See Walter Laqueur, *Guerrilla: A Historical and Critical Study*, Boston, Little Brown, 1976 p. 8; also see Lewis H. Gann, *Guerrilla in History*, Hoover Institution Press, Stanford, 1971.
2. S. N. Eisenstadt,"Cultural Orientations and Center-periphery in Europe in a Comparative Perspective" in Per Torsvik [ed.], *Mobilization, Center-Periphery Structures and Nation-Building*, Bergen, Universitetsforlaget, 1981, p. 96.
3. Arend Lijphart, *Democracy in Plural Societies*, New Haven, Yale University Press, 1977, p. 165. According to Lijphart, consociational democracy "assumes that political elites enjoy a high degree of freedom of choice, and

that they may resort to consociational methods of decision-making as a result of the rational recognition of the centrifugal tendencies inherent in plural societies and a deliberate effort to counteract these dangers."

4. Donald L. Horowitz, *Ethnic Groups in Conflict*, Berkeley, University of California Press, 1985, p. 578.
5. William J. Foltz, "Building the Newest Nations", in Roger E. Kasperson and Julian V. Minghi [eds.], *The Structure of Political Geography*, Chicago, Aldine Publishing Company, 1969, p. 285.
6. K.P.S. Gill, "Endgame in Punjab - 1989-93", *Faultlines*, New Delhi, Vol. 1, May 1999, p. 62.
7. See Morris Janowitz, *Military Institutions and Coercion in the Developing Nations*, Chicago, Chicago University Press, 1964, 1977, pp. 36-37. According to Janowitz Indian para-military forces doubled from 100,000 in 1966 to 200,000 in 1974. The total strength of Central para-military and State armed police forces now exceeds the one million mark.
8. Concluding paragraph of Karl Marx and Frederick Engels, *Communist Manifesto*, first published in 1848.
9. "Program of the Communist International" (1928), in *Handbook of Marxism*, Emile Burns [ed.], Moscow, International Publishers, 1935, pp. 1034-35.
10. *Selected Writings of Mao-Tse-tung*, Peking, 1968, See the chapter entitled "A single spark can start a prairie fire", p. 72.
11. Patrick J. Mcgarvey, Visions of Victory: Selected Vietnamese Communist Writings 1964-68, Stanford, 1969, p. 40.
12. Laquer, Guerrilla: A Historical and Critical Study, *op. cit.*, pp. 268-269.
13. Charles Townshend, Britain's Civil Wars: Counterinsurgency in Twentieth Century, London, Faber and Faber, 1986, p. 14.
14. Laqueur, *op. cit.*, pp. 330-331.
15. Che Guevara, *Guerrilla Warfare*, London, Widenfield and Nicholson, 1969, p. 9.
16. C. E. CALLWELL, *Small Wars: Their Principles and Practice*, London, His Majesty's Stationery Office, 1896.
17. Charles Gwynn, *Imperial Policing*, London, Macmillan, 1934, p. 38.
18. Karl von Clauseitz, *On War*, Michael Howard and Peter Paret [eds.], New Jersey, Princeton University Press, 1976.
19. Robert Thompson, *Countering Communist Insurgency*, London, Chatto and Windus, 1966.
20. David Galula, *Counterinsurgency Warfare: Theory and Practice*, New York, Praeger, 1964.
21. J.S. Pushtay, *Counter-insurgency Warfare*, New York, Free Press, 1965.
22. J.J. McCuen, *The Art of Counter-Revolutionary War*, London, Faber and Faber, 1966.
23. D.S. Blaufarb, *The Counterinsurgency Era: US Doctrine and Performance*, New York, Free Press, 1977, p. 217.
24. A famous Washington Post cartoon during the 1960s showed President Johnson exclaiming: "We are there only in an advisory capacity and only last week we dropped fifty thousand tons of advise."
25. Norman Dixon, *On the Psychology of Military Incompetence*, New York, Basic Books, 1976, p. 21.

26. Ian F. W. Beckett, and John Pimlott [ed.], *Armed Forces and Modern Counter-Insurgency*, New York, St. Martin's Press, 1985, p. 10.
27. US Army-Air Force Joint Low-Intensity Conflict Project, 1987.
28. *Ibid.*
29. I. F. Stone, *In a Time of Torment*, New York, Basic Books, 1968, pp. 173-74.
30. Thompson, *op. cit.*, 1966), pp. 50-57.
31. Beckett and Pimlott, *op. cit.*, p. 24.
32. This has been adapted from Beckett and Pimlott, *Ibid.*, pp. 16-45. The British Army's training manual, *Land Operations, Volume III, Counter-Revolutionary Operations* (1975) sets out the following measures for conducting such wars: (1) passing of emergency regulations to facilitate the conduct of a campaign; (2) political, social and economic measures designed to gain popular support and counter or surpass anything offered by the insurgents; (3) setting up of an effective organization for joint civil and military control at all levels; (4) the forming of an effective, integrated and nationwide intelligence organization; (5) strengthening of indigenous police and armed forces so that their loyalty is beyond question; (6) control measures designed to isolate the insurgents from the population.
33. Frank Kitson, *Low Intensity Operations*, Harrisburg, PA, Stackpole Books, 1971.
34. Ekbal Ahmad, "Revolutionary Warfare and Counterinsurgency" in Gerard Chaliand [ed.], *Guerrilla Strategies: A Historical Anthology from the Long March to Afghanistan*, Berkley, University of California Press, 1982, p. 260. This is an extract from N. Miller and E. Aya [eds.], *National Liberation and Revolution*, New York, The Free Press, 1970.
35. According to Samuel P. Huntington, professionalisation of military men contributes to and in fact ensures their political neutrality. See his *Political Order in Changing Societies*, New Haven, Yale University Press, 1968.
36. See Alfred Vagts, The History of Militarism, New York, W.W. Norton, 1937.
37. Cited in Janowitz, *Military Institutions and Coercion in the Developing Nations*, *op. cit.*, pp. 187-88.
38. See chapters 11 to 16 of Donald L. Horowitz, *Ethnic Groups in Conflict*, University of California Press, 1985.
39. Gill, *op. cit.*, p. 59.
40. See Appendix I for Text.
41. A Planning Commission of India Study Team under the Chairmanship of Tarlok Singh, which visited Mizoram in February 1966, also recommended resettlement of villages for the purpose of development. The Team was of the view that about 1000 hamlets with a population of 100 were dispersed all over the district and the provision of schools, medical care and water supply for all of them would be difficult unless they were grouped together along the main roads. This was on the lines of resettlement carried out in East Africa during the early 1960s. It is interesting to note that the Planning Commission did not recommend similar strategies of development for equally dispersed populations in Arunachal Pradesh, J&K, and Himachal Pradesh. It appeared to some that the army in Mizoram had done an excellent PR job.

42. 1. The grouping will cover Aizawl-Serchhip, Aizawl-Vairengte and Serchhip-Lungleh roads in three phases;
    2. Rations, iron sheets for roofing etc. would intially be provided by the army and the cost reimbursed by the Government of Assam;
    3. The villages would be rendered uninhabitable after the v1illagers had shifted to the new centres with their belongings;
    4. Rations will be provided free to all villagers. As the villagers would need, in addition to rations, some money to buy other necessities of life, all able-bodied villagers would be engaged on road construction work; the rules for payment of wages would be liberalised so that payment of wages could be made as frequently as possible;
    5. The villagers would be allowed to keep their crop produce with them even after they moved to the centres. Also suitable precautions would be taken to ensure that stocks left behind did not fall into the hands of the hostiles;
    6. The army would complete the grouping by the end of February 1967 and hand over the administration of the newly created group centres to the civil authorities by the first week of April 1967. At the time the centres are handed over to the civil administration, they would have stocks of food for 15 days and medical supplies for one month to tide over the transition problems;
    7. Among other arrangements at the new centres, adequate educational facilities and places of congregational worship would be provided;
    8. When the responsibility for the administration of the grouped villages is made over to the civil administration, the Government of Assam would make arrangements for supply of food and other essential articles to the villagers, as well as as the transport for moving these materials. Army would, however, provide for their safe escort;
    9. The civil administrators and staff including the medical officers would be carefully selected and placed in position well in time to take over the administration from the army;
    10. Measures for agricultural development, utilization of land near group centres for cultivation and establishment of subsidiary industries should receive the highest priority;
    11. The GOC-in-C Eastern Command would brief selected press correspondents about the implication of the scheme. They might also be allowed subsequently to visit the Mizo Hills district to see things for themselves so that they could project a correct and balanced picture;
    12. In view of the fact that the majority of the population to be moved were Christians, the operations should commence only after Christmas 1967 and the New Year day.

43. There were broadly three reasons why so many people surrendered without arms. One, those who surrendered without arms were mostly from the MNVF who were not allotted any weapons because there were not so many weapons to go around. They were, however, free to carry weapons which they had themselves bought from the illegal arms market or captured from the SFs. Secondly, those who were suspected of being potential

deserters were deprived of their weapons. And, lastly, many hid their arms in the jungles before surrendering to be able to go back to fighting if the resettlement terms offered by the government were not suitable.

44. The majority of ex-rebels I interviewed told me that at least half of the total MNA force would have surrendered with arms, and the back of the insurgency would have been effectively broken, if the cash rewards were about five times of what was offered. The reason given was that higher cash rewards would have increased the financial security and the means to make a fresh beginning in life; nobody who had taken to arms wanted to return to a life of poverty and deprivation.
45. Malaya veteran Sir Robert Thompson headed the British Advisory Mission in Vietnam from 1961 to 1965.
46. R Thompson., *Defeating Communist Insurgency*, London, Chatto and Windus, 1970, p. 124.
47. U.S. Army officer, in R. Marston, "Resettlement as a Counter-Revolutionary echnique", Journal of the Royal United Services Institute, London, Vol. 124, No. 4, 1979, pp. 46-49.
48. Samuel P. Huntington, *Political Order in Changing Societies*, New Haven, Yale University Press, 1968, p. 42.
49. In the event of such treatment being meted out to the Blacks, Indians (they have been confined to reservations for three centuries) and the Inuits, it would not in all probability inspire a strong public outcry in the USA, as would perhaps happen in the case of the whites, if they were to be herded, hypothetically speaking, in a concentration camp. As the situation stands today, a crime committed by an individual 'black' is construed by the white majority as a serious reflection on the whole community. A crime committed by a white does not lend itself to similar construction. The dangers of such a situation should be obvious in all multi-ethnic societies.
50. The preface to the British Army's training manual - Land Operations, Volume III - Counter-Revolutionary Operations states that between World War II and 1 January, 1969 Britain's armed forces were engaged in no less than 53 'counter-revolutionary actions' in different parts of the world. These military interventions were mainly to repress social unrest, workers' strikes, national independence movements and struggles, and some even democratic movements to throw out autocratic rulers. On the basis of this vast experience, the manual sets out its approach for handling similar situations in other overseas territories. One of the important techniques set out in the manual is 'control measures to isolate the insurgents from popular control.' But this strategy to isolate the insurgents has been used against non-British, and mostly third world, polulations outside the British isles. It has not been resorted to in Northern Ireland.
51. Acknowledgement for this excerpt is due to my wife, Jyoti Jafa, who recorded this conversation in her Mizo Hills diary. The identity of the officer remains undisclosed for obvious reasons.

EIGHT

Terrorism, Institutional Collapse and Emergency Response Protocols

K.P.S. Gill

"Complacency is the true friend of the terrorist."[1]

The past year has been particularly harrowing for those who are concerned with India's internal security, as a series of terrorist acts and patterns of covert aggression, including the massive incursion of Pakistani troops and state-backed mercenaries into Kargil, destabilised existing internal security equations. A recurring feature of the strategic and tactical shifts visible in the patterns of terrorism and Pakistan's widening proxy war, particularly those centred around the conflict in Jammu & Kashmir (J&K), is their unending ability to take Indian forces, their command structures, and the nation's political leadership by surprise. Even where sufficient tactical intelligence and indices of rational risk projection existed, the forces of aggression and terrorism were — and continue to be — able to strike with apparent impunity. The most dramatic case in point is the complex series of intelligence warnings relating to activities in and around Kargil, which preceded the eventual engagement in late May 1999, and which failed to generate any kind of effective response from the defence apparatus.[2]

This, of course, is not to suggest that all terrorist actions should or can be predicted and prevented. While intelligence operations do help thwart some terrorist strikes, it would be unrealistic to expect that all such events can be foreseen, irrespective of our levels of penetration into subversive networks. This is not only a consequence of the highly dispersed character of the organisation of terrorist activities, as well as of their conception and planning on, and launching from, foreign soil, but also of the simple physical and financial limits on intelligence structures and operations. The real failure, however, is not in the intelligence gathering mechanism, but in our inability to utilise large and discrete flows of intelligence to assess and evaluate the scale and direction of emerging threats, to maintain sustained vigilance in response to extended or diffuse threat perceptions, and to respond effectively when these are realised.

None of this reflects on our actual capabilities to frustrate Pakistan's proxy warriors from realising their objectives. Kargil was ample demonstration that the Indian forces, once aroused and mobilised, are more than adequate to put Pakistan in place. If separate evidence was needed regarding our abilities to confront internal security challenges with equal efficacy, it was provided in the nation-wide Republic Day celebrations and parades this year. There was ample evidence that disruption of these celebrations was a primary and major tactical and propaganda objective for the terrorists, and at least six suicide squads are known to have been sent into the Jammu region alone over the month preceding January 26, 2000. A significant increase in terrorist movements was detected in the days before the parades, including the arrest of a group of terrorists in possession of RDX and detonators in Delhi on January 16. But not a single incident of significance marred the celebrations at the hundreds of venues at which they were held right across the country.[3]

And yet, terrorists have been able to carry out as many as 13 attacks against heavily guarded security forces' establishments and camps since Pakistan's Kargil strategy collapsed in July-August 1999. These include the attack on the Badamibagh headquarters of the 15 Corps (September 12), the attack on the Army Headquarters at Srinagar in which the Defence PRO was killed (November 3), Army Headquarters, Baramulla (December 2), the J&K Police Special Operations Group (SOG) Headquarters at Srinagar, in which a DSP was among the 12 SOG personnel killed (December 27), and the attack on the Rashtriya Rifles Brigade Headquarters at Khannabal in Anantnag (January 12, 2000). In each case, the most alarming security lapses and inconceivable levels of carelessness and neglect heralded the terrorist attacks. At the SOG headquarters, for instance, the terrorists were simply allowed to drive unhindered into the heavily guarded campus since they were wearing Army uniforms. Evidently, basic security protocols were being ignored, since an attack on such a heavily guarded establishment was thought to be inconceivable — even after 11 such attacks had already taken place on other "secure" targets. The lesson, it appears, is that while we can mobilise our forces for well-defined or clearly predicted short term emergencies, our responses to the unexpected, or to unspecified threats, remain less than adequate.

IC 814 - The Paradigm of Failure

The critical failure of response to the hijacking of the Indian Airlines flight IC 814 occurred at the Raja Sansi Airport in Amritsar. Of course, the eventual and humiliating denouement at Kandahar can also be faulted on a number of grounds, the most obvious being the manifest loss of nerve on the part of the government's negotiators. However, little is still publicly known about the actual circumstances, negotiations and transactions at Kandahar, and it would, perhaps, be both unfair and unwise to judge the government's crisis responses on the basis of the fitful and often inaccurate information that is currently available. The debacle at Amritsar, however, is an entirely different kettle of fish, and although government sources have sought to project the "decision" to allow the hijacked plane to leave Raja Sansi Airport as a reasoned option — the best of a bad bargain that could easily have ended in a bloodbath for the hostages — this is far from the case. I had, at the time of the hijack crisis, repeatedly described the events at Amritsar as an unforgivable blunder that divested us of all effective options, and I have seen no evidence till date to force a revision of this opinion.

The fact is, the failures at Amritsar — and a majority of these emanated from New Delhi — were entirely avoidable and exemplify in extraordinary measure the institutional collapse that encounters each sudden or unforeseen crisis of internal security (indeed, perhaps, of governance at large) in India. In the absence of a credible or detailed public disclosure by the government, consequently, it is useful to trace out the sequence of events, on that fateful Christmas Eve, as we know them.[4]

- 4:52 p.m.: Delhi Air Traffic Control (ATC) receives a message from ATC Varanasi that the Airbus-300 plying on the Indian Airlines flight IC-814 has been hijacked.
- 4:56 p.m.: Confirmation is received when the pilot flashes the hijack code to the Delhi ATC. At this point of time radar information placed the plane over Lucknow. The Captain, D. Sharan, then makes radio contact and informs ATC that the hijackers are armed and their destination is Lahore. The information is communicated to the Crisis Management Group (CMG) comprising senior officials including the Cabinet Secretary, the Home Secretary and the Civil Aviation Secretary. Reports suggest that there was some delay in informing the CMG because telephone numbers had not been updated at the Delhi airport. The officials were also apparently unclear about what to do once they were contacted.

  What the CMG actually did for the next hour is uncertain and crucial to any analysis of the response. The Prime Minister who was flying back from Patna to Delhi was informed only at 5:20 p.m., after he landed. He reached his residence at 5:35 p.m. and summoned a meeting of his Cabinet colleagues. The CMG had still not assembled — its meeting reportedly convened shortly before 6:00 p.m. An hour had already been wasted without any action taken by the government or any of its agencies.
- 5:40 p.m.: The plane approaches Delhi. Reports indicate that though the pilot had said that he was heading for

Lahore, he was already trying to ensure that he landed at Amritsar. He brought the Airbus' speed down to 360-390 knots, well below the normal speed of around 460 knots. There is a certain point on the flight plan, point Ansari, where a pilot has to commit himself to heading either for Lahore or Amritsar. A Lahore bound flight veers left while the Amritsar bound flight must head right. The pilot, it was evident at this point, was trying to delay this decision.

A crucial fact in this context is that, from the time it was hijacked barely 20 minutes into the flight, till it landed in Amritsar, the plane was tracked closely on radar, its speed was known and a fair estimation of the amount of fuel remaining at the time it landed in Amritsar should have been available to the CMG, and should have been communicated to the authorities at Amritsar. The apparent failure to make these basic calculations available to decision makers at various levels had a crucial bearing on the subsequent response of the authorities.

- 6:15 p.m.: The plane reaches point Ansari and the pilot chooses to turn towards Amritsar.
- 6:18 p.m.: ATC Amritsar is first contacted by the pilot, "We are in contact with Opla (Lahore). Opla is not allowing us to land and we have only 40 minutes fuel. They are insisting us to go to Opla (sic) and they are not allowing us to land in Indian soil."
- 6:26 p.m.: Pilot informs ATC again, "We have fuel only for half-an-hour. Please coordinate with Opla. Please get us permission to land at Opla. They are very silly and they will kill us one by one."
- 6:31 p.m.: Pilot says that they have selected ten people to kill.
- 6:32 p.m.: Pilot says, "There is only 15 minutes of fuel left over. With this we can remain 15 minutes in the air. After that we don't have fuel. Make sure we land in Opla as they want to land in Opla and otherwise not anywhere in India."

Clearly, the pilot was doing all he could to make sure

the plane landed at Amritsar. He had made a choice that the ATC could interpret by observing the radar, even as he played along with the hijackers. From the transcript it is clear that more attention should have been paid to the accuracy of the information he was giving to decipher any subtext or signals he was sending, particularly with regard to the fuel remaining in the plane. Certainly, it should have been clear that what the pilot was mouthing was not to be taken at face value.

Specifically, at 6:18 p.m. he said he had 40 minutes of fuel left, at 6:31 p.m. he claimed to have only 15 minutes of fuel left. In 13 minutes he had supposedly lost 25 minutes of fuel. The plane finally landed at 7:01 p.m., half-an-hour after the pilot said he had only 15 minutes of fuel left. It should have been clear that his words were not reflecting, and were not intended to reflect, the true picture regarding the amount of fuel in the plane.

- 6:35 p.m.: The aircraft is now hovering over the Raja Sansi Airport, Amritsar, a full one hour and forty three minutes after the first report of the hijack was received by ATC Delhi. But even now, no clear response systems have been activated. It bears mentioning, here, that Amritsar had been the final or transitional destination of a majority of the twelve Indian commercial aircraft hijacked in the past, and should have been the most obvious and probable destination in the present case. While all airports within the flight capabilities of the hijacked aircraft should have been alerted for possible landing and response, Amritsar should have been in a state of high alert, with a clear Emergency Command and Communications system in place. As will be evident from the sequence of events below, this was far from the case.

  By this time, the Prime Minister's Principal Secretary Brajesh Mishra had finally joined the deliberations of the CMG at Delhi. Throughout this period, and the next hour or so, it is unclear what the PM and the Cabinet were doing.

- 7:01 p.m.: The plane landed and contact was established on the ground with the pilot. At this point the Senior Superintendent of Police (SSP), the district's Deputy Commissioner (DC), officials from the Border Security Force (BSF) as well as Inspector General of Police J.P. Birdi had reached the control tower. Airport Director V.S. Mulekar and senior aerodrome officer, Tarlok Singh, were already present there and Mulekar was the man who subsequently handled most of the communications with the aircraft. Two hours and nine minutes had passed since the authorities in Delhi were first informed of the hijacking. Clear indications had also been available for 45 minutes that the pilot was aiming to land the plane at Amritsar.

The plane landed on Tarmac 34 and came to a halt mid-way on the runway. The area is not well lit and is very far from the floodlit apron area of the airport. Visibility from the cockpit, officials confirm, would have been no more than 150 metres at best. The pilot conveyed the demand that the plane should be refuelled immediately, else the hijackers would start killing passengers. He also sent a coded message informing ATC that there were 5 hijackers on board. A message was also sent to Delhi asking for instructions. Reporters spotted Tarlok Singh outside the airport building, making preparations for refuelling.

To answer the question regarding what went wrong at Amritsar, we must begin with an inquiry on who was in charge. The State Crisis Management Committee (CMC), which included DGP Sarabjit Singh and IGP (Intelligence) M.P.S. Aulakh, was communicating with IG Commandos, J.P. Birdi who, in the absence of the zonal IG was asked to take charge. The Deputy Commissioner, is in the normal course of such a crisis, the man responsible for dealing with and authorising any action. He seems to have played virtually no role from here on. In addition to the SSP, the DIG Amritsar was also present.

- 7:05 p.m.: A man claiming to be G.Lal from the "Home Department" called up and asked about the situation at Amritsar. This man called once again with the same question. Who this person was is still to be established.

However, contrary to some newspaper reports, airport officials confirm that he gave no instructions regarding how the officials at the spot should tackle the problem.

- 7: 10 pm: The first contact between Amritsar and Delhi takes place, when the Cabinet Secretary calls up and speaks to the SSP. No specific instructions are issued, but the SSP is told to delay refuelling and ensure the plane does not take-off without the CMG's instructions. A short while later, Brajesh Mishra also speaks to the DIG and tells him that an all out efforts should be made to prevent the aircraft from taking-off.
- At this point, however, it is already clear that no one person was in charge at the ATC, Amritsar. The Cabinet Secretary was instructing the SSP, the PM's Principal Secretary was speaking to the DIG, the State DGP to the IG. The man actually talking to the pilots was the Airport Director V.S. Mulekar.

One source of confusion was certainly the lack of proper communication facilities at the airport. The ATC had no STD line to contact Delhi, and the mobile phones belonging to police officials were used to contact Delhi. Delhi may well have responded through the same channel. This is a confusion that could, and should, have been easily sorted out. It was not cleared up to the very end of the crisis. An official present at the ATC tower throughout the time when the plane was approaching and present at Amritsar clearly admitted that no one person was in charge. Specifically asked whether Birdi was handling things, he said, "He was present there, I wouldn't say that he was in-charge."

It should also be stressed that while subsequently defending their failure to prevent the plane from taking-off, the CMG and the State authorities cited various reasons — all of which had been conjured up after the event. Officials present at the ATC confirmed that, during the 48 minutes that the plane was at the Airport, no option to prevent its take-off was discussed by the officials at the ATC, and no specific directions were received from the superior authorities — specifically, the State CMC or the CMG at Delhi.

At this point it is also necessary to examine the rationale for delaying refuelling. All subsequent indications show that once the Indian Oil bowser had actually approached the plane, far more options would have been available to the ATC. The first was simply because of a fact that emerged in the media several days after the hijack, but which was known immediately to the authorities — that the airport lacked the proper ladder for refuelling an Airbus as no plane of this make currently lands at Amritsar. This in itself would have been sufficient reason in dallying over refuelling and there is no way the plane could have taken-off with the bowser connected to the plane.

The second is that the very mechanism that allows for the refuelling of a plane also allows its "de-fuelling", that is, the extraction of fuel from the tank. Once the bowser was in place, it could simply have dried out, and consequently immobilised, the plane.

In the aftermath, with the local and State authorities blaming the CMG, and the CMG returning the favour, it is also clear that once the Cabinet Secretary and the PM's Principal Secretary contacted officials in the control room, the local authorities immediately assumed a passive role. They were passing on information and awaiting instructions. In fact, just before the Cabinet Secretary called, the authorities were making preparations for refuelling — the only active decision they took during these 48 minutes. Existing evidence suggests a total lack of co-ordination between the State CMC at Chandigarh, the CMG at Delhi, and the officers present in the ATC — the last of whom were at the cutting edge of whatever action plan was devised. There is also some evidence that different officers at the ATC were separately receiving instructions from the CMG and the State CMC, and that there was no co-ordination of this information with the officers actually negotiating with the hijackers.

- 6:45 p.m.: Pilot first informs the ATC that the hijackers are armed with revolvers, AK-47 and grenades.
- 7:07 p.m.: Pilot repeats this claim, and, at around this time,

manages to convey a coded message to the ATC indicating that the hijackers are five in number.

- 7:11 p.m.: The panic is rising. Pilot says, "Now guns are on our head. Everyone will be shot down in another three to five minutes. Kindly please come refuel...."
- 7:15 p.m.: Pilot speaks again: "Why are you taking that much time. Guns are on our heads now."

The transcript over the next several minutes again requires close examination.

- 7:23 pm: "They are going to kill us any time. Please send the bowser. They have started killing now. Where is Oh.....! Where is the bowser now? Please tell us."
- 7:25 pm: "Where is the bowser? Where is the bowser (crying voice), *yaar*. He has started killing the passenger. Why don't you understand our problem. Where is the bowser *yaar*?...He has already killed a passenger now. Why don't you understand. Now we have stopped. Send the bowser fast. Please. Where is the bowser?"
- 7:42 pm: "Four passengers have been killed now. Why have not you responded. The bowser is not coming here. What is the problem?"

According to one of the district authorities present at the ATC, the impression conveyed by the pilot was that the hijackers were loosing their balance. These messages created an atmosphere of panic at the ATC. Contact was established with Delhi again but no clear instructions were received, the earlier instructions were repeated. Even as some of the officers rushed off to quietly brief the Press on the "four killings" on the plane, other officers present at the scene had doubts about the veracity of the claim. IG Birdi, in his Press briefing shortly after the plane took-off, stressed, among other things, that no shots had been heard by the policemen stationed within hearing distance from the plane.

His statement also provided confirmation of the fact that Punjab Police personnel had, indeed, moved on to the tarmac to within 300 metres of the plane.

Strangely, the authorities, while trying to justify their inaction had this to say, "One false move could have gravely endangered the lives of nearly 200 persons." They defended the lack of any active steps by saying that it was impossible to gauge the reaction of the hijackers, what they were armed with and how well trained they were. But from the above transcript it seems reasonably clear that the fact of four people apparently having been killed did not spur them to any urgency regarding refuelling.

They were obviously willing to waste four lives through delay and indecision (in retrospect they actually lost one life) over the refuelling, but were not willing to take direct action that would risk the lives of the passengers. This does not ring true. What it suggests is that they were working under certain (erroneous) assumptions. These would include the presumption that, with Lahore having refused permission and the plane left with barely any fuel, it could not go anywhere. The only way the plane could have taken-off, they felt, was if they went ahead with refuelling. The analysis of facts here was clearly incompetent, and was based primarily on the record of claims — which should have been seen to be inconsistent and deliberately misleading — made by the pilot at various stages before the landing.

Clearly, moreover, they were willing to risk lives, and they did, by trying to delay refuelling till the National Security Guard (NSG) arrived. Their second assumption also eventually proved to be miserably wrong. Indeed, they should have foreseen, or at least taken into account the possibility, that Lahore would, at some point of time, grant permission for the plane to land there. To place unqualified faith in Pakistan in such a situation is certainly less than wise.

Moreover, the inability to work out the actual amount of fuel remaining in the plane was just plain unprofessional. The amount should have been calculated to the last drop. In any case, since it is clear that they were willing to, and did, risk lives, there was nothing preventing action such as blocking the runway, or otherwise disabling the plane. The fact that the plane was taxiing on the runway for much of (though by no accounts all) the time does nothing to undermine possibilities of disabling or blocking the plane. Taxiing speeds were low, and the plane comes to a virtual standstill on each turn. There were more than ample opportunities to act, if the will and the clarity of vision and command had been there.

- 7:30 p.m.: The plane suddenly takes a half-turn and faces the North-South direction.
- 7:35 p.m.: Message from Delhi to the ATC that an NSG team had been dispatched. Specific instructions are repeated that the plane should be prevented from taking off. However, it is not clarified as to how this was to be done. A message is also sent to the DIG (BSF) in Amritsar with the same instructions. Three companies of the BSF are moved to the airport. Punjab Police personnel also enter the airfield and approach within 300 metres of the plane.
- 7:40 p.m.: Shortly before take-off, the plane takes a 180 degrees turn to face South. While passenger reports suggest that there is some truth in the CMG's claim that the plane was constantly turning on the tarmac, according to a very reliable source present at the ATC, the plane just made these two turns.
- 7:49 p.m.: The plane took-off surprising everyone at the Control Tower.

  According to an observer present there, "No one anticipated that the plane would take-off like that. We all knew the plane had hardly any fuel left, and certainly did not expect such a suicidal step." The plane had a near miss with the oil tanker, which had been stationed on the runway for refuelling. Sources make it clear that the tanker had been stationary at that point for at least the preceding ten minutes. No police official has yet confirmed the fact being now "leaked out" that trained policemen had been put on the bowser, and its movement towards the plane scared the hijackers.
- 8:15 p.m.: The NSG team lands at Amritsar — 26 minutes after IC 814 had flown out, one hour and fourteen minutes after it had landed at Amritsar, and a full three hours and

twenty three minutes after the first information of the hijack had been received at ATC Delhi. The team is headed by a Brigadier from the 52 Special Action Group and comprises 130 commandos.

According to sources, the commandos received information of the hijack at 6:10 p.m. at Manesar. It took them almost an hour to assemble at Delhi Airport, and they were ready for take-off on an Indian Air Force plane, at around 7:05 pm. Newspaper reports suggest that the failure of trained negotiators from intelligence agencies to reach the airport on time further delayed take-off by another half-hour. This is more than amazing — in a situation of extreme emergency a rapid response team sits waiting for a psychologist to arrive for half an hour, and it does not strike the decision makers that the latter could follow on another plane later, if needed. This is not an administrative failure, but an abject collapse of basic common sense. In any case, the one-hour delay between being informed and being ready to take-off itself speaks poorly of the efficiency of the NSG. Not to factor the distance to the Airport and the traffic on Delhi's roads into a rapid response plan displays an unacceptable level of incompetence.

These, of course, are mere details. The intention of the exercise of listing them here is not to fix individual responsibility on, or to blame, particular officials; this is not the objective of this paper, and would, in any event, be a futile exercise, since the same failures would only be repeated by someone else the next time round, when another — similar or dissimilar — crisis arises. It is at the level of a paradigm of response that the failures at Amritsar are important, and it is at this level that they need to be analysed if any effective structures of crisis management are to be forged out of our experience.

Shorn of detail, what were the generic failures at Amritsar?

(i) The first and most significant failure was the inability to establish an unambiguous and unique centre of command within reasonable time — and "reasonable time" in such a crisis, is to be measured in minutes, not hours. The failure here is institutional. A long and slow process of decay has undermined, disabled and, in many cases, destroyed the emergency response systems that were in place at various levels of governance, replacing them, by and large, by an anarchic system of charismatic leadership, where extraordinary individual initiative sometimes produces dramatic results. Charismatic and competent leaders, however, cannot be present for every one of the innumerable emergencies that arise with unfailing regularity in India. Consequently, most crises produce a conflicting reaction: on the one hand, an undignified jockeying for the centre position and for media projection, and, on the other, an abdication of responsibility by the majority of those who are required to act. One of the most effective institutions and processes of this abdication is the "committee" or sets of committees that "take over" — as they did in the present case — and play out a great charade of discussion, communication and management, while simply refusing to take decisive action. At the end of the day, even if the consequences are entirely disastrous — as they were in the present case — no one is responsible, since the decisions, or their lack, were "collective". At worst, some low level official at the site of the crisis can be sacrificed as the scapegoat of the hour. The situation is worsened infinitely by a long history of punishing officers who actually take action, while no penalties ever attach to "sins of omission" and acts of outright dereliction.

(ii) The second critical failure is that, even those who "took charge" — in the sense of arriving at the communication centres of the crisis management system that came into being out of the dynamics of the hijacking, and the moribund structures of systems past, i.e., the Raja Sansi Airport, the CMG at Delhi, and the CMC at Chandigarh — simply did not know what was to be done. Each began *de novo,* effectively trying to reinvent the wheel, with no guidelines, no reference to a historical context, and no structured system of emergency response.

(iii) The third critical failure was the inability to install or activate a clear line of communication with and between the various actors in the task. Conflicting and contradictory instructions were consequently being received through random and informal modes of communication — including personal cell phones — by various authorities at the Raja Sansi Airport, emanating in each case from sources that far outranked the officers in the field. Within the context of the existing political and administrative system, these circumstances would ordinarily divest local authorities of the will to initiate any action on their own initiative — though this should certainly not be the case. Moreover, the ATC official who was actually communicating with the pilot of the plane, and through him, with the hijackers, had no clear idea of the various information flows. Of course, the fact that even among those who were at the command centres of this management system, no one knew what was to be done, only compounded the problem further.

(iv) No system for providing adequate technical backup to decision makers was apparently in place till the end of the crisis. Simple but critical calculations — such as the available fuel in the plane — had clearly not been made. Nor were the technical and military options for immobilising the plane adequately clarified or explored. Individuals from non-technical backgrounds, with limited or no prior experience either of a crisis of this kind, or of other aviation or military emergencies, were evidently wracking their brains to figure out some sort of solution through the standard bureaucratic process of unending and ill-informed discussion.

(v) There was no context of a national policy on hostage or hijacking situations, or, for that matter, on terrorism in general, that could provide any kind of hint or guideline on the broad parameters of the resolution that was to be sought. The various decision makers were — as stated before — required to reinvent the wheel entirely on their own, right from the CMG at Delhi down to the officers struggling with the situation at the Raja Sansi Airport.

(vi) Rapid Deployment Forces located at Delhi failed to reach the focal point of the crisis in time. Had they done so, their very presence would have created a new dimension, multiplying available options manifold. Needless to say, the forces available at the Airport and in Amritsar lacked the capabilities necessary for the kind of operation that the NSG could have launched, and, despite their substantial presence fairly close to the plane, could not influence the 'equation' on the ground.

There were, furthermore, several aspects of the management of the adventitious or subsidiary crises that were ignored or bungled by the government. Some of these secondary crises established themselves within the first hours of the event, but persisted to the great detriment of the national interest throughout the crisis, and have survived into the aftermath. These related, in large part, to problems of co-ordinating media, public and international relations.

(vii) The first of these was a complete absence of a co-ordinated media response. From the very beginning of the crisis, the government and its officials spoke in a hundred conflicting voices, bringing its deliberations and decisions into the sphere of public debate at a time when restraint and sagacity — and not recrimination and the confused cacophony of ill-informed advice — were most needed. There was no system of media management, of the projection of a single, dignified and well-informed voice, reflecting a national government's sense of command and stability. Indeed, some of the highest offices of the land lent their authority and credibility to unconfirmed information that eventually proved false. If anything, the hijacking crisis underlined the fact that we have far too many amateurs in government — and that it is time that they were, at the very least, told to shut up.

In any crisis of this nature, it is imperative that an effective system be established to sift through the frenetic and contradictory flows of information, and that only what is confirmed should be released. This is not only a question of the government's credibility. Public perceptions are an integral input into the dynamics of decision making in these emergencies. And if these are distorted by disinformation and by deliberate falsehood, the possibilities of arriving at optimal decisions recede.

Take an example: the hijackers' claim, articulated through the pilot of IC 814, that they were armed with AK 47s, grenades and RDX was accepted as gospel and hastily communicated to every journalist in the vicinity. It was quoted as unqualified fact in every television channel even while the events of the hijacking were still unfolding, and was printed in every newspaper the next morning.

This perception had a powerful impact, not only on those who were charged with decision-making in this crisis, but also on our relations with a friendly country, which brings us to another aspect of subsidiary crisis management — the containment of unintended consequences in international relations. India heaped ignominy on Nepal and arbitrarily suspended flights to that country without even bothering to wait for the processes of an objective inquiry. Senior officials of the government pilloried the security arrangements at Tribhuvan International Airport without ascertaining the magnitude of the actual breach that had occurred. A breach had, of course, occurred — but the response was certainly disproportionate, and was based exclusively on the first aggregation of disinformation, sourced from the hijackers themselves. I cannot conceive of a less diplomatically sound course of action than what was adopted by India towards Nepal. Worse still, each element of this *disgracing* of Nepal was carried out in public, communicated to the media even as, if not before, it was communicated to that country's government.

(viii) A similar ineptitude characterised the handling of the relatives of the hijacked passengers. Part of the problem was, again, media management, as contradictory and exaggerated official and quasi-official statements fed the hysteria of the relatives. Of course, the conduct of a section of the relatives themselves was nothing less than disgraceful, but that cannot absolve the government of its own incompetence. A single, authentic and well informed source of the official position should have immediately been established to liase with the relatives, as also to provide an immediate channel of relief, so that they did not believe themselves to be abandoned, for hours at end, in the waiting lounges of the Airport. Suffice it to say, even to the very end of the crisis, an adequate and efficient system of information and relief for the relatives had not been established.

(ix) All the preceding factors combined into a single and devastating image of loss of control, of confusion and impotence that has continued to magnify in the aftermath of the crisis through the proliferation of manifestly puerile statements and suggestions in official quarters, and of empty political rhetoric posturing as policy.[5] These, indeed, have conceded to the hijackers a victory far greater than was merited by the release of three terrorists. The sheer confusion, the sense of visible frustration, and the direct and manifestly unsuccessful engagement of the highest offices in the country, both in the management and the aftermath of the hijacking, are the unintended consequences that are still to be fully evaluated, or even realised. Put yourself in the hijackers' place, and that of their sponsors, and try to imagine the sense of empowerment and satisfaction, not just of securing the release of three militants, but of having discomfited, and even humiliated, so many senior Indian leaders—including ministers and perhaps the Prime Minister himself. Imagine the sheer gratification of having inspired such a deep sense of failure and — as the pronouncements of the leaders of some political formations suggest[6] — even self-loathing, in the political leadership and the public at large. And consider the propaganda and recruitment potential of having created a feeling of bafflement and frustration in the Indian security forces to an extent far greater than ever before, greater even than the despondency or demoralisation that all the body bags over the past year had been able to instil in our fighting men. This, in fact, is what the terrorists actually achieved at the end of the hijacking — not just the release of three militants.

Proactivity: From a Slogan to a Policy

No nation and no army can win every battle — even against an inferior adversary. The constellation of local events and forces, the element of tactical initiative and surprise, sometimes combine with fortune to shift advantages in favour even of a weaker side. To this extent, the specific reverses that India suffered as a consequence of the blunder at Amritsar, and the subsequent and sub-optimal resolution of the hijacking crisis at Kandahar, have limited significance. To the extent, however, that a nation fails to correct the lapses of the past, the basic flaws in its strategic perspectives and institutions, however, it is condemned to repeat its mistakes at incremental costs to the national interest. At some point of time, the processes of attrition will carry it beyond the point of return or recovery, and the cumulative consequences, then, would be disastrous.

The evidence available suggests that we are currently set upon this course to catastrophe and lack the will and the vision to institute satisfactory correctives. In the month succeeding the hijack crisis, the spectacle of impotence and confusion was sustained at a high pitch by the government, with a number of ponderous declarations - entirely lacking in substantive content and originality — of a variety of "counter-terrorism initiative and policies". These included measures to 'improve' aviation security, including the hasty, ill-advised and entirely ad hoc announcement of the decision to post commandos on commercial flights;[7] the announcement by the Prime Minister of a Rs. 102.71 billion Central "agenda" for the Northeast, and an additional Rs. 14.2 billion towards reimbursements to the States of this region for expenditures on security;[8] and the announcement by the Ministry of Home Affairs (MHA) of a "new policy" for J&K.[9]

An analysis of the specific measures that comprise these various "policy initiatives" discloses nothing that is new. The aviation security measures have largely been ad hoc announcements, and a policy is currently being formulated. It would, consequently, be premature to comment on proposed measures. These, in any event, have only limited bearing on the specific probabilities of future attempts to hijack Indian commercial aircraft and do not, by and large, affect our arguments here.[10]

As regards the announcement of a 'development package' for the Northeast, this has become a routine reassurance ritual for every visiting Prime Minister to the region. As one commentator expressed it with some irony, "It is not yet a constitutional obligation but enjoys the force of convention."[11] In 1997, the then Prime Minister Deve Gowda's visit to the Northeast had also been accompanied by grand plans of economic reconstruction and the announcement of a Rs. 60 billion "package". I.K. Gujral, who succeeded Gowda shortly thereafter, also made a quick trip to the region, and announced another "package" worth Rs. 70 billion. Prime Minister Atal Behari Vajpayee has now clearly outbid his predecessors.

It is a different matter that such "financial grants" contain a substantial measure of financial jugglery, and that all the "developmental expenditure" of the past has only left the region poorer, with per capita incomes and other economic indicators registering steady declines. I have often stated that the only people who are enthused by the prospect of "developmental expenditure" in terrorism affected States are political leaders, bureaucrats and their favoured contractors, since a bulk of these funds end up in their private coffers. Some of these funds also flow, through a complex chain of collusion, compliance and extortion, to various terrorist groups — and eventually end up funding militancy. Their impact on the 'target groups' of the poor in the region remains negligible. However, the dogma of developmental funding as a "solution" to terrorism has never been challenged — despite the complete absence of supporting evidence — since it keeps most of the prominent players in the existing conflicts flush with funds.

The "new policy" on J&K is particularly significant in the present context. It constitutes a direct response — at least in part — to the hijacking, and is part of the effort to demonstrate the government's "will" to confront the mounting threat of the Pakistan-sponsored terrorist movement in the mountain State. According to reports, the main features of the new policy included:[12]

(i) Specialised battalions of Central paramilitary forces to be raised for counter-insurgency operations.

(ii) Counter-insurgency grids have been divided into 49 sectors as a part of a three-tiered control structure under the unified headquarters.

(iii) An additional unified headquarter is to be set up at Zojila.

(iv) Security in Srinagar city to be further 'beefed up'.

(v) Security forces have been asked to carry out round-the-clock operations.

(vi) Special operations are being launched with the help of retired soldiers and members of Village Defence Committees (VDCs). These would be integrated with the counter-insurgency grid for protection of civilians.

(vii) Sophisticated arms and modern communications equipment would be provided to the VDCs.

(viii) Special funds would be provided for border roads.

(ix) New job-generation projects will be put in operation in order to effectively deal with the problem of unemployment.

Every single one of these "new" measures has been the stock in trade of the government's "response to terrorism" in the wake of each new emergency, crisis, or major terrorist strike, and many of the measures mentioned are already part of existing policy. Only two of the decisions have the appearance of novelty or a shift in policy — but here again, the appearances are deceptive.[13] The first of these is the decision to substantially augment the number of sectors in the counter-insurgency grid by a process of vivisection. This is, at best, a tactical response, and certainly does not deserve the title either of a strategic shift or a policy initiative. The second is the decision to ask the SFs to carry out round-the-clock operations. Does this imply that the SFs have been functioning on a 9-to-5 workday over the past years of bloodshed in the State? Evidently not. Why then the fanfare that surrounded this "new policy"?

The fact is that the government was clearly suffering a crisis of credibility since the hijacking of IC 814. As the Minister for Home Affairs candidly, if inaccurately, asserted — the ruling Bharatiya Janata Party (BJP) perceives itself to have suffered as a consequence far more than the nation has.[14] It was, therefore, necessary to project a posture of aggressive determination and great activity in order to recover face — even if this was nothing more than a posture lacking all substance.

Unfortunately, these domestic compulsions notwithstanding, this was the worst possible course of action that could be adopted. The language in which the threat perceptions of the government were expressed as the context of the "new policy", and as these were interpreted by various leaders and commentators, not only increased the general perception of a loss of control by the government, but had the power to contribute directly to the demoralisation of the SFs. Worse still, the exaggerated projection of the "new policy" automatically raised unrealistic expectations of immediate results both among the general public and among the rank and file of the SFs — and these expectations will certainly not be fulfilled, given the very nature of the proposals. Inevitably, there would be another couple of dramatic strikes by the terrorists — no security force, policy or strategy can obviate this possibility under prevailing circumstances — and this entire house of cards will collapse on itself, creating a general sense of disappointment, betrayal and further demoralisation. In any event, the rubbishing of the new policy in innumerable editorials and articles had reinforced the general sense of confusion and vulnerability within days of the government's announcements.

What was needed in the aftermath of the hijacking, in the face of the rising tide of terrorist violence, the increasing incidence of attacks on the security forces, and the incontrovertible evidence of the Inter Services Intelligence's (ISI) involvement in terrorism and a wide range of criminal activities — including the massive injection of counterfeit currency into the Indian market — was not dramatic public declarations and postures in advance of the event, but unadvertised and critical policy shifts and a little imaginative action in the field. These would have created the successes that were needed, and the grounds for justifiable and lasting credit to the government. I have said this before, and will repeat it again: There is absolutely no substitute for success in the field. And this is where India appears to be, and is perceived to be, faltering.

I would be the last person to underestimate or understate the threat in J&K, or to deny that the situation has worsened significantly over the past months. Several grave dangers exist and have been augmented by new threats. The Indian SFs have suffered enormously under a barrage of direct and audacious assaults. This said, let me add that the situation is far from out of hand. India's fighting men have faced much worse in the past and have emerged victorious. The difference, however, is that, to do so, they must be allowed to operate under clear mandates, well-defined and internally coherent policies, and a leadership that exudes a sense of confidence and resolve. These, precisely, are the factors that have remained entirely elusive, despite decades of terrorism in an increasing number of theatres within the country, and despite a succession of governments reflecting a fairly wide ideological spectrum.

The greatest weapon in war is the human mind. Vast armies, "unbeatable" technologies and entire nations have been defeated by demoralisation. And this is the first step at which India is losing the present war. Better counter-terrorist strategies, improved systems of co-ordination, command and control, superior weapons, surveillance and communications technologies are all, certainly, needed. But the first element that must precede these, and that must be sustained throughout the conflict thereafter, must be a clearer understanding of public perceptions, projections and a coherent media policy. Feeding the prevailing sense of terror, helplessness and public distress does not strengthen the government or create a greater mandate for strong measures against the terrorists. That mandate already exists in adequate measure and has, in fact, been frittered away by the government at least on some occasions in the recent past.

This does not, of course, mean that a stoic and unyielding silence must be maintained by the government on all matters pertaining to terrorism. On the contrary, there is urgent need for the articulation of an authoritative and clearly defined position on the subject, and for convincing action to realise this position on the ground. Before turning attention to the character and content of such a position, and the actions consequent upon it, it may be useful to look at a few examples of the responses of some other nations to the challenges of a major terrorist strike or movement.

In 1974, in the wake of the Yom Kippur War, Israel was victim to a major terrorist onslaught that commenced in the spring that year. In addition to a number of smaller operations, these included at least a dozen major attacks including the ones at Nahariyah, Beit She'an, Shamir, Kiryat Sh'moneh and Ma'alot. The last two, involving the slaughter of women and children, were the worst shocks to the national conscience. In the Kiryat

Sh'moneh incident on April 11, 1974, three Arab terrorists first shot Eshter Cohen, a 40 year old woman, her 17 year old son, David, and her daughter, aged 14 in their apartment. They then moved through several other apartments in the building, lobbing hand grenades into some, and shooting indiscriminately at occupants in others. By the time Israeli soldiers caught up with them and shot them, they had killed 14 more Israeli civilians, including six children between the ages of two-and-a-half and 11. 16 men, women and children were wounded but survived, and some Israeli soldiers lost their lives as well.

Exactly a month later, however, the terrorists were to perpetrate an even greater outrage at the village of Ma'alot. At 3:00 in the morning, they first entered an apartment and shot a couple and their two children, a boy aged four and a girl aged five. The girl was the only survivor in this initial attack. The terrorists then went on to enter a schoolhouse where over a hundred high school students were sleeping. The children and their teachers were then herded into a hallway. Some of the children and one of the teachers managed to escape by jumping out of a window. The rest were held for over 14 hours. The terrorists, armed with Kalashnikovs and explosives, had issued a deadline that they would blow up the building if their demands — including the release of some 23 terrorists — were not met. The Israelis tried to negotiate the release of the hostages, but some confusion over a password and the terrorists' designated mediator brought the negotiations dangerously close to the deadline. Confronted with the possibility of all the hostages losing their lives, Israeli soldiers stormed the building. At this point, the terrorists opened fire into the crowd of children, hitting 84 of them. 22 of these were killed, and another three adults lost their lives. Prime Minister Golda Meir's statement before the Knesset five days after the outrage, is a model of dignity, of authority, of solemn — even noble — grieving, and of determination:

> The long list of victims of terrorism has now been swollen by our fine and innocent children... The blood of our children, the martyrs of Ma'alot, cries out to us, exhorting us to intensify our war against terrorism, to perfect our methods of operation, to concentrate our talents and

> resourcefulness, to persevere in the daring in seeking out the very heart of the terrorist nests wherever they may be.... The blood of the Ma'alot slain calls out to the world to desist from displaying any lenient attitude towards the terrorist organisations, their bases and their masters: to realise, while there is time, the peril stemming from the ideology and actions of... terrorism.[15]

In the months that followed, a counter-terrorism policy crystallised, a process that continued without interruption, alteration or any shift in emphasis or commitment, despite the fact that, less than a month later, a new government was sworn in under the leadership of Prime Minister Yitzhak Rabin. In his very first address to the Knesset, Rabin was to declare the identity of interests and intent with his predecessor government on the issue of terrorism, and to define the fundamental principle that became the foundation of Israel's policy thereafter: "The Government of Israel will not conduct negotiations with terrorist organisations whose declared goal is the destruction of the State of Israel."[16]

It is significant that this principle was articulated at a time when the memory of the Ma'alot incident, in which children were held hostage to secure the terrorists' demands, was fresh in the minds of the leaders of Israel. Yet, the government announced a policy of "no negotiations". "We prefer peace to new military victories," Prime Minister Rabin had said, "a stable peace, a just peace, an honourable peace, but not peace at any price."[17] The price Israel paid at Ma'alot was, indeed, terrible. But in the war against terror, the price of capitulation is even greater.

Out of these unequivocal declarations of intent, Israel forged the details of the structures and processes that would protect civilian lives, as well as inflict harsh deterrent punishment and reprisals on acts and sponsors of terrorism. Acts of terror targeting Israel continued, of course. But their intensity and their centrality to the Arab-Palestinian strategy waned, forcing a shift towards a negotiated settlement in which Israel engaged from a position of unwavering strength. The details of the specific measures adopted to force this shift merit a separate study and need not detain us here. What is significant in the present context is the fact that the underpinnings of these measures were a clear and utterly unambiguous statement of a national policy perspective on terrorism.

The threat perception with regard to terrorism in the United States of America is extraordinarily high, despite a relatively low incidence of terrorist incidents and casualties. A process of selective definitions, intentional blindness, and statistical inventions have allowed the US to perceive and seek to project themselves as the nation most at risk from this scourge, and one commentator goes so far as to assert that, "Historically, the United States has been the target of 32 per cent of all terrorist attacks worldwide, second only to Israel."[18] Speaking at the United Nations, President Clinton endorsed this perception of a nation under threat: "Because we are blessed to be a wealthy nation with a powerful military and a worldwide presence active in promoting peace and security, we are often a target... we know that many people see us as a symbol of a system and values they reject, and often they find it expedient to blame us for problems with deep roots elsewhere."[19] He generously conceded, nevertheless, that "it is a grave misconception to see terrorism as only, or even mostly, an American problem."[20]

The American part of the problem, however, is resolved through a pattern of harsh legislation and relentless reprisals that have made the US, at once, perhaps the most hated society among terrorist communities, and, equally, one of the safest among their potential targets. Thus, in the wake of the terrorist bombings of US embassy buildings in Kenya and Tanzania in August 1988, President Clinton ordered cruise missile strikes against alleged terrorist training camps in Afghanistan and a supposed chemical weapons plant in Sudan. It is a different matter that no judicial processes or open evaluation of evidence preceded these attacks. It was, moreover, not even the US case that the perpetrators of the embassy bombings were actually present in the "terrorist training camps" in Afghanistan. And the international media eventually discovered the "chemical weapons plant" in Sudan to be an innocent pharmaceutical company.

US action in this case did not end here. The bombing suspects were identified by an international investigation, apprehended in record time, and brought to America for trial — though the "chief conspirator," Osama Bin Laden, remains elusive. However, the international pressure, diplomatic, economic and covert, currently being exerted to bring this "fugitive" to American justice is a critical input in all US policy in Central and South Asia.

This is virtually a paradigm case of the application of the US Counter-terrorism Policy, defined succinctly and explicitly in the following principles:

> First, make no concessions to terrorists and strike no deals;
> Second, bring terrorists to justice for their crimes;
> Third, isolate and apply pressure on states that sponsor terrorism to force them to change their behaviour; and
> Fourth, bolster the counter-terrorism capabilities of those countries that work with the US and require assistancce.[21]

In addition, the Clinton Administration has defined the principles that would determine the objectives of US diplomatic efforts to secure the co-operation of all nations to:

> Deny terrorists safe haven and financial support, and pressure states that do;
> Co-operate in the extradition and prosecution of terrorists;
> Strengthen the Biological Weapons Convention and enforce the Chemical Weapons Convention;
> Increase airport security and control the manufacture and export of explosives.[22]

Another essential feature of the US counter-terrorism response is the degree of institutional consensus that prevails. The judiciary has ordinarily handed out maximum sentences, and even waived substantive provisions of US law to punish what is designated as terrorist crime. Thus, in the case of Aimal Kansi, the alleged killer of two CIA agents was virtually kidnapped in Pakistan, bundled onto a plane and brought to the US to face trial in violation of all the very stringent procedural constraints on wrongful arrest. In other cases, US Courts have been extraordinarily rigid, even pedantic, in their interpretation of civil rights and procedural protection against improper arrest — allowing some of the worst domestic crimes to go unpunished in cases where the police did not follow the stringent procedures prescribed for arrest or securing of evidence. All this, in the Kansi case, was simply brushed aside, and the perpetrator sentenced to death. The US, today, also has some of the harshest and most comprehensive anti-terrorist legislation in the world.[23] The Anti-Terrorism and Effective Death Penalty Act of 1996, for instance, prescribes the death penalty, or imprisonment of not less than 40 years even for conduct which directly or proximately causes personal injury or substantial risk of injury to any person, including any public safety officer performing duties. If a conduct results in death, the offender faces the death penalty, or imprisonment for not less than 20 years or life.[24] Minimum mandatory sentences are prescribed for most terrorist offences, leaving no room for equivocation or misplaced 'liberal' and 'human rights' posturing by the judiciary. There has, of course, been little attempt in the American judiciary to seek these escape routes when confronted by terrorist crimes. The World Trade Centre bombing in New York City resulted in the death of six persons. Each of the four perpetrators and the chief conspirator was sentenced to 240 years of imprisonment—with the last receiving an additional life sentence. None of them will again experience freedom in this lifetime.

It is, of course, a different matter that the US applies criteria that are entirely at variance with its own practices when terrorist activities are carried out in theatres far from its soil and when their victims are not US citizens. That, however, is not the issue here. Our present concern is with the measures that nations adopt to protect themselves against the scourge of terror, and in this, the US is a veritable pioneer, and recognises no constraints of morality or of international law and opinion. Indeed, the extent to which unconstrained use of force is sanctioned by society and the institutions of governance once a certain group of activities is designated a terrorist, or even an "un-American" activity, can be estimated by the massacre at Waco, Texas, in 1993. Here the Federal Bureau of Investigation (FBI) brought in tanks and initiated a violent and dangerous CS gas assault on a barricaded group of a millenneal religious sect, the Branch Davidians, resulting in the death of 74 people, including women and children.[25]

The US approach is rightly premised on the assumption that every unpunished terrorist attack diminishes its prestige and power in the international arena, and inflicts critical damage on 'US interests' abroad.

> Whenever a terrorist attacks a US target (be it civilian or military) America's reputation suffers in the eyes of many around the world. The implication is that the United States is not as strong, or as skilful, as America wants the rest of the world to believe it is. This is specially the case in cultures where reputation and the appearance of power count for much... As a result, terrorism can weaken relations with allies by intimidating or blackmailing a particular country into distancing itself from the United States or denying the US access to particular facilities.[26]

The approach also recognises an important distinction between anti-terrorism and counter-terrorism. The former comprehends the defensive measures used to reduce the vulnerability of individuals and property to terrorism, and recognises the limitations of such initiatives in combating terrorism since it would be physically and financially impossible to protect all potential terrorist targets through such defensive measures. Counter-terrorism, on the other hand, comprehends a wide range of offensive measures to prevent, deter and respond to terrorism.

With these perspectives, it is unsurprising that a counter-terrorism perspective is read into the institutional strategy of all related branches of government, not only the State, Justice and Defence Departments, but also other agencies that may be connected with the management of the consequences of a terrorist strike, such as the Health, Fire and Civil Administration. Moreover, an apex body, the Federal Emergency Management Agency (FEMA), prioritizes and co-ordinates all aspects of crisis management, including the identification of emerging threats, definition of response protocols, training and institutional structures.

Contours of a Counter-terrorism Policy for India

In the absence of a coherent vision of a nation's larger strategy, specific initiatives, especially where they are fire-fighting responses to current crises, tend to cancel each other out and often, in fact, prove counter-productive. To take a parallel, if one were to create a large number of random and unstructured defences on a battlefield, with no clear idea of the emerging pattern of engagement, of the imperatives of the terrain, of the relative strength of forces, and of the defined objectives of battle, we would find that these defences eventually become a hindrance to our own manoeuvres, rather than a shield against enemy attack. This is precisely the case that has arisen out of the innumerable, *ad hoc*, entirely unstructured and often contradictory actions and policy initiatives with regard to terrorism in India, and many of these actions and initiatives have now become the most significant obstacle to any coherent strategy of resolution.

The very first imperative of an effective policy on counter-terrorism, consequently, requires the definition of the basic principles on which all counter-terrorist action and policy are to be constructed. No such principles are reflected in our present policies, and I have no reason to believe that they exist. Once defined, these principles must be strictly adhered to, circumscribing the range and content of actions and negotiations that any government or official may engage in with regard to terrorists, or in situations of crisis generated by the actions of terrorists.

Several models exist for the identification of these basic principles,[27] but it is not sufficient simply to imitate these, or to adopt them verbatim from some other country. They would have to be based on a specific and objective evaluation of the character and magnitude of the threat of low intensity war and terrorism in this country. This may appear to be too obvious a point to require separate statement, but on closer scrutiny this is not the case. There is, in fact, a great deal of ambivalence that characterises the attitudes and perceptions of policy makers and those who shape opinions in this country, with regard to terrorism, and there exists a vast body of pseudo-sociological, political and economic analysis that seeks to justify terrorism or to underplay its enormity and impact. This stream of thought — actually an uncritical acceptance of politically fashionable postures — has influential supporters in various branches of government. It is, consequently, crucial that the objective dimensions of terrorism be explicitly and transparently evaluated, its dangers defined and documented, and an unequivocal national consensus be forged on the character and magnitude of this scourge, and the measures that are necessary and justified in order to confront it before we succumb to it.

This, however, is only the beginning of a long and relentless process. The Indian state, I have remarked in the past, must start educating itself on how it is to tackle individuals and groups trying to destroy the state. And it must learn how to arm and protect those who put their lives at stake in the defence of India's unity and integrity.[28] This will require a radical reformation of internal security forces and institutions, creating the skills, knowledge, attitudes and infrastructure necessary to confront the threat posed by terrorism and covert warfare. The parameters within which each agency of government must respond to such challenges will also have to be defined, specifically and in great detail. This would include the powers, the range of extraordinary actions permitted in these situations, and the applicable legal criteria and context of evaluation of these actions — whether these are the same as those applicable in peacetime or are to be akin to articles of war, or are to be redefined in terms of the new category of 'low intensity wars' — should be clearly determined and suitably legislated.[29]

These are only the preliminary conditions for an effective response to the challenge of terrorism — yet they demand a massive and unprecedented effort; an effort, moreover, which has to be exerted within a timeframe that grows shorter by the day if it is to have any hopes of success.

These timeframes of response are well illustrated by the US apprehensions of a biological weapons attack "within the next five to ten years". US officials concede, "We are a long way from being even modestly prepared," but simultaneously assert, "we're doing a lot more now than we did 12 months or even six months ago".[30] This is the urgency that attends a response to a threat that is expected to emerge in coming years in the future. The legislative response to cases of terrorism on US soil are also a case in point. Till 1996, the US had experienced only two major incidents of terrorism: the bombing of the Alfred P. Murrah Federal Building in Oklahoma in April 1995, where over 100 were killed; and the World Trade Centre bombing at New York, in which five persons were killed and over a thousand injured. Yet, by 1996, the Anti-Terrorism and Effective Death Penalty Act and a wide variety of other legislation had been passed, making the most comprehensive provisions not only for the effective prosecution and punishment of terrorist acts, but also for activities that helped finance, support or otherwise facilitate such actions.

By comparison, we are yet to set up systematic defences against the far greater threats that have already been realised and are currently undermining the rule of law, and even the possibility of civil governance, in a number of theatres of conflict in India. Fifty years after the first major terrorist movement in the country began, we are yet to have even a basic legislation to deal with the problem — the ill-drafted, and equally ill-fated Terrorism and Disruptive Activities Act, 1987, which was allowed to lapse in May 1995 without a whimper, being the only experiment in this direction. Thus, after tens of thousands of casualties inflicted by terrorists, and billions of rupees of property destroyed, as far as laws presently in existence in this country are concerned, there is no phenomenon that can be uniquely and legally identified as "terrorism", or be punished as such. For well over two years now, we have been speaking — just speaking — of a "proactive policy" on terrorism; yet the initiative remains squarely in the hands of the terrorists and their sponsors in Pakistan, and there is no evidence of even the basic framework of a policy in sight.

Even if institutions of governance succeed in shaking themselves out of their present torpor, they may find existing structures severely inadequate to deal with the problem. The first element of this structural failure is the co-ordination of efforts of the large number of institutions and forces that are pressed into service — or need to be so tasked — to tackle terrorism. I have recently drawn attention to the failure to effectively utilise even the available technological infrastructure, manpower and resources to fight terrorism.[31] This is only one aspect of the problem. The fact is, the efforts even of the SFs directly involved in the fight against terrorism are not adequately co-ordinated, and systemic and internecine conflicts undermine — even cancel out — a great deal of what is being done by different military, police and paramilitary organizations. The challenge of co-ordination, however, extends much further, to a wide variety of institutions and organizations that comprehend virtually every department of governance, but most prominently, the health, transport, communications, and emergency management services, science, technology and research institutions, the judiciary, the legislature, and civil administrations in terrorism affected areas. Evidently, no existing institution has the mandate or the capabilities to undertake such a task.

There is, consequently, an urgent need to set up a central agency for the co-ordination of all counter-terrorism efforts, initiatives and policies, so that the national interest and policy are realised through the vast multiplicity of discrete and apparently unrelated actions of the numerous divisions, departments and jurisdictions that currently exist.

Such an agency would also be tasked to carry out a continuous assessment and analysis of existing and emerging threats, to co-ordinate flows and maximise utilization of available intelligence from a multiplicity of sources, and to continuously define policies and protocols for response to each new area or pattern of terrorist activity, and to ensure that these are translated into action by the appropriate division and department of government. This agency should also be statutorily required to periodically apprise both the government and Parliament of prevailing threat perceptions, and the actions required to meet these.

It should be clear, in this context, that this central agency would not be the executive agency for counter-terrorism response, nor would it have the authority to intervene at the tactical and operational level. It would, however, define the strategic framework of counter-terrorism operations, devise protocols for response to a wide variety of possible threat situations, produce the training materials and structures for the creation of requisite proficiency in the execution of these protocols in concerned agencies and personnel, and generally put into place the systems that are required to safeguard the nation and its people against terrorism. The agency would also act as a clearing house for a great deal of inter-departmental and inter-agency dissemination of information, and as a pressure group to bring the policies and practices of various branches and departments of government into conformity with national counter-terrorism perspectives and policy.

Crucially, this agency must not be constituted along the pattern of existing "security advisory" fora, which have the essential character of government-sponsored debating societies, with no power of independent access to information, intelligence, or other resources for effective action.

Specifically, the central agency for counter-terrorism would be required to address the following tasks:

(i) *Project and continuously evaluate the essential elements of national counter-terrorism policy*: This function assumes that a national policy has already been defined by the national political executive — a task that can no longer wait for the constitution of a new institutional arrangement.

(ii) *Establish and continuously revise threat assessment criteria for all major threats*: This involves the definition and clarification of the analytic procedures to determine the threat of terrorism in various areas and regions, as also to specific installations, including defence and infrastructure installations and establishments. This would involve the analysis of inputs beyond conventional intelligence flows within government, and would reconcile these with information received from media and research resources, as well as from strategic and geopolitical analyses of the situation beyond the immediate threat of conflict. This process is critical because it would define certain objective parameters which would automatically mandate the activation of response protocols at various levels and in all concerned institutions and departments, with intervening discretionary or executive decisions — that is to say, without a 'judgement call' having to be made.

(iii) *Creation of standard emergency response protocols for all potential terrorist threats and actions*: This is a gigantic task that would, first, involve the identification of all such potential threats and their possible impact and crisis management requirements. Here, it is not only necessary to make provisions for existing threats, but also to continuously evaluate emerging technological and tactical shifts in order to ensure that the emergency response systems are geared to tackle these. For instance, I have already made this point specifically in connection with the possibility of a 'Chemical or Biological Weapons' (CBW) terrorist strike, or for the introduction of any 'Weapon of Mass Destruction' (WMD) into the terrorist arsenal - for which we are completely and visibly unprepared.[32] The actual contents of such response protocols would, of course, vary from situation to situation, but they would all have certain minimal features in common, and these would include at least the following:

(a) *Establishing crisis command and a clear chain of accountability*: As was amply clear from the confusion that followed the hijack of IC 814, this must be the first priority in any given situation of terrorist action or threat. The authority who is charged with commanding the emergency response must be clearly defined in the standard procedures — with an equally clear identification of a substitute in case of absence, death, inaccessibility or immobility on any grounds. The crisis command must be headed by a single individual, who would then be unequivocally accountable for the handling of all aspects of the situation.

(b) *Definition of graded minimal responses*: Each emergency or level of threat perception must automatically generate certain minimal and clearly defined responses by all agents on first information received, even if the crisis command centre is not yet fully activated or in contact. This refers not only to the activities of those who are directly connected to the security response aspects generated by the crisis, but to all support wings as well — such as media management, human relations management, emergency medical, fire, technical or other associated services, and, very crucially, the agencies charged with collecting and preserving evidence. This last is an aspect that is often neglected in the wake of major terrorist incidents, and in the process the possibility of building a body of evidence for the successful identification, apprehension and prosecution of culprits is diminished, and much crucial evidence, or many opportunities of generating such evidence, destroyed. It must be realised that the successful prosecution of terrorists is one of the critical elements in the successful war against terrorism, and in this regard the Indian record has been worse than disgraceful — though not entirely as a result of the failure of the apparatus for investigation and prosecution.

The idea of a mandatory "graded minimal response" is to ensure that local authorities are not directionless, paralysed, or constantly seeking the intervention of elusive 'higher authorities', in the face of a terrorist challenge, and that they are also accountable for having met — or for failing to meet — the requirements of a pre-defined and unambiguous protocol of responses. In addition, the existence of such unambiguous codes or protocols, protects subordinate officials from the process of 'scapegoating' that inevitably follows each botched up operation. The present system is biased in favour of non-performance — those who refuse to act are protected, but those who take an initiative, inevitably with the accompanying risks of failure, are humiliated and penalised. Once emergency response protocols are established for a particular genre of situations, however, a failure to respond in accordance with set codes would attract penalties.

As with every solution, there is a potential problem here. Rigid protocols can easily be reduced to a formalism that would protect officials without securing the intended results. If protocols are not to be transformed into avenues of escape by incompetent, under-motivated or corrupt officials, they would need to be constantly reviewed for weaknesses that lend themselves to such exploitation. Such continuous reviews are mandated also because of continuous technological and tactical developments, both within the national security community, and among the terrorists. Indeed, a measure of improvisation and flexibility will have to be built into the codes and protocols that are developed, even as if a guarantee of a minimum response. It is significant to note here that everything is expressed or implemented within a context, and the prevailing administrative and political atmosphere can undermine the impact and efficacy of any system that may be put in place. Every system needs to be backed by integrity and an honesty of purpose, and these are often lacking. Nevertheless, even with these qualifications, the impact of such systems would be salutary, to the extent that they would impose a degree of accountability even on the 'lowest common denominator' in the crisis response and counter-terrorism apparatus.

(c) *Emergency communications systems:* Once a terrorist action has taken place, or is believed to be imminent, exclusive and pre-designated systems of communications should automatically be activated between the command centre and all agents involved in the management of the emergency. No unauthorised lines of communication, or channels that are not mediated by the command centre, should have any role whatsoever, in crisis management.

(d) *Definition of incident priorities:* Within the context of the emergency response protocols, each genre of incident should contain a clear definition of the various priorities that must command the actions of the various agents. These priorities may include safeguarding the lives of SF personnel and civilians, protecting critical systems, stabilising the context of the incident, pursuit and apprehension of perpetrators, human impact and media management, estimation and containment of direct and secondary damage, etc. A clear definition of these priorities would facilitate the most efficient and rapid deployment of available resources.[33]

(e) *Definition of strategic goals and tactical objectives in the wake of an incident:* In addition to actions mandated by the minimal response protocol, the actions of local agents must be activated by clearly defined tactical and strategic objectives. These, in fact, provide the context of flexibility and human initiative that are integral to any effective response to a terrorist threat or strike. Once again, while these must be defined without dissimulation or vagueness, they would require continuous revaluation and adaptation in view of emerging situations.

(f) *Protocols for notification and co-ordination:* The responses of those agencies that make first contact with, or receive first information on, the terrorist act must include the issue of notifications and warnings, and an alert on all resources that may be required to deal with the emergency. Each level of threat, or character and magnitude of terrorist act must, consequently, be met with notification to all connected agencies and authorities at an appropriate level of the government hierarchy.

(iv) *Definition and inspection of physical security standards:* A comprehensive exercise needs to be carried out to define the required physical security standards and protocols for various civilian, government and security establishments, and thereafter, to ensure adherence to these standards. These standards, once again, would constitute minimal prescriptions, and institutions and establishments would have the discretion to exceed these, but not to fall short on their provisions. Subsidiary agencies may be required to inspect adherence to these standards on a regular basis. The central co-ordinating agency would, of course, be required to continuously review these standards in view of technological, strategic and tactical changes. Part of the task of defining physical security standards would also involve the identification of basic norms for the location, planning and security architecture of particular kinds of security and other potential target installations and establishments. The vulnerability of many security and critical infrastructural facilities is often structural and has to be tackled at the earliest stages of the development of these projects — commencing with the identification of their location. This has been a persistent failure, as has been borne out particularly by the vulnerability of a large number of security establishments that have been extraordinarily vulnerable to terrorist attack.

(v) *Definition of systems for co-ordination of forces and optimal sharing of intelligence between agencies and departments:* Many of the critical 'intelligence failures' of the recent past have been failures, not of the availability of intelligence, but of sharing, processing, or accessing the appropriate information at appropriate levels. Similarly, the continuous controversy over command and control systems in terrorism affected areas, and the unceasing jockeying for power and credit between the various arms of the SFs dedicated to the tasks of counter-terrorism, have been the cause of many of our recent reverses.

Evidently, the evolution of appropriate systems for the co-ordination of forces and the sharing of intelligence would need to be one of the most urgent priorities of the central co-ordinating agency on terrorism.

(vi) *Establishing training standards and providing curricula for all emergency response agencies:* Priority here would naturally go to appropriate training and curricula for the SFs engaged in counter-terrorism. A comprehensive review of current methods and practices is required to give our fighting men a clear understanding of the methods, motives and character of terrorist activities, and to create in them the ability to look at the situation from the perspective of the attacker. A better understanding of the weapons and technologies available to the terrorists and continuous improvements in counter-terrorism methodologies is also necessary. Irrespective of the costs of dissemination of this information, and the costs of training and re-training, these programmes must be undertaken. They would help save lives in our forces, create a decisive edge in the battle, and, in the long run, prove to be far more economical than prevailing practices that simply push in increasing numbers of poorly trained and motivated manpower into areas of conflict.

(vii) *Identification, co-ordination and management of legal, legislative and administrative issues arising out of counter-terrorism operations and challenges:* Counter-terrorism must be conceptualised not as a problem of the use of the SFs alone, but as a problem that concerns us all - not just the various institutions of governance, but the citizenry at large. A wide spectrum of constituent actions would be needed to create a comprehensive and effective response to this challenge, and the central agency would also have to accept responsibility for the identification and co-ordination of these elements.

(viii) *Development and revision of training curricula and programmes:* The creation of a wide range of emergency operational plans, protocols and security standards would, quite naturally, create corresponding demands for training and curricula in a wide variety of institutions. And the central co-ordinating agency would need both the resources and the infrastructure to produce these, or catalyse their production, as also to ensure their widest requisite distribution.

This listing is by no means exhaustive, nor can the elements within it be considered final. A wide variety of opinions would, quite naturally, be elicited by each of the proposals, and there are certainly new facets to the problem that will be exposed, and, indeed, that will be brought into being with each shift in terrorist strategy and tactics.

Nevertheless, the intention of the exercise here is to emphasise that it is now imperative that India's future responses to terrorism are far more scientific, systematic and consistent than they have been in the past, and that comprehensive and radical institutional and procedural changes are needed if this is to be achieved. The importance, indeed, criticality, of the personalised responses and charismatic leadership that have dominated our systems of crisis management in the past, needs to be minimised. Such responses and leadership have, of course, on occasion, contributed to the resolution of problems. But even where they succeed, they do great damage to the general systems of the institutional response, undermining the initiative and confidence of the large majority of officers, who then feel that a systemic solution is not possible, and that all crises demand the intervention of 'higher authorities' or high profile leaders. To the extent that such 'higher' intervention is usually not available in the immediate aftermath of a crisis, the state's responses are inevitably delayed, and necessarily inefficient. More often than not, however, such 'higher' interventions, ordinarily exercised from a safe and comfortable distance from the actual crisis, and on the basis of severely inadequate and inaccurate information streams, have lead to enormous failures, causing significant damage to the nation, and generating destructive processes of scapegoating and inane political rationalisation in their wake. It is now clearly time that a meaningful, flexible and effective institutional response is devised to the mounting challenge of terrorism in India.

NOTES AND REFERENCES

1. Kay C. Goss, *"America Preparing for the Consequences of Terrorism"*, a Presentation at the NATO Civil Emergency Preparedness Symposium at Moscow, April 22, 1997.
2. Cf. Praveen Swami, "The Kargil War: Preliminary Explorations", *Faultlines*, New Delhi, Vol. 2, July 1999, esp. pp. 29-40.
3. A bomb was detected opposite the Red Fort at Delhi just half an hour before the beginning of the parade. Four rockets were also fired, without any casualties, in the Jammu region. The only fatalities that occurred as a result of terrorist action on January 26, 2000 were in Assam, where militants reportedly shot dead three people in Bongaigaon District during an 18 hour general strike called by eight terrorist groups opposing the Republic Day functions. Cf. "Another Bomb Defused at Red Fort", *Pioneer*, New Delhi, January, 27, 2000; "Some Hiccups on Peaceful R-Day", *Times of India*, New Delhi, January 27, 2000.
4. Reconstructed from briefs by Hartosh Singh Bal, Senior Staff Writer, *The Indian Express*, New Delhi, and informal disclosures by a variety of sources who were connected with the management of the crisis.
5. Cf., K.P.S. Gill, "Government Demands Steel in the Soul", *Pioneer*, January 22, 2000.
6. "Freeing Militants to get Hostages shows Hindu Cowardice: RSS", *Indian Express*, January 6, 2000.
7. "Sky Marshals Aboard all Flights Now", *Indian Express*, January 6, 2000; *"Aviation force by Year-end"*, Tribune, Chandigarh, January 8, 2000.
8. "PM Announces Rs. 10,271 cr. Package for North-East", *Hindu*, New Delhi, January 23, 2000; "Centre okays Rs. 1,420 cr. to check N-E insurgency", Indian Express, January 22, 2000.
9. "Special Units to Tackle J&K Militancy", *Times of India*, January 18, 2000; "Govt. Draws Up 'War' Plan for Post-Kargil Kashmir", *Indian Express*, January 18, 2000; also see "Countering Terror", *Pioneer*, January 19, 2000, Manoj Joshi, "Kashmir Policy: Old Wine in New Bottle", *Times of India*,

January 19, 2000; and K.P.S. Gill, "Governance Demands Steel in the Soul", Pioneer, January 22, 2000.

10. Significantly, even as measures for improving airport security were being announced, there were reports that suggested that these had no bearing on the situation on the ground. Cf. Brajesh Upadhyay, "Alert Yes, but Airport Security is Lax", Times of India, January 5, 2000.
11. "Third N-E Package", Tribune, January 24, 2000.
12. "Special Units to Tackle J&K Militancy", *Times of India*, January 18, 2000.
13. This analysis of the "new policy" on Kashmir is based substantially on my article, "Governance Demands Steel in the Soul", Pioneer, January 22, 2000.
14. "Hijack Deal hurt BJP, not India: Advani", *Times of India*, January 4, 2000.
15. Statement to the Knesset by Prime Minister Meir, May, 20, 1974. Source: *www.israel-mfa.gov.il*.
16. Address in the Knesset by Prime Minister Rabin on the Presentation of his Government, 3 June 1974. Source: *www.israel-mfa.gov.il*
17. *Ibid.*
18. Intelligence Threat Handbook, May 1996, Section 4, reprinted by the Terrorism Research Centre, www.terrorism.com/terrorism/InterOperations.html. The absurdity of this evaluation is evident in the fact that it dates back to 1996. By this time, more than 11, 709 civilians and 1,781 security force personnel in Punjab (1981-1996), and over 5,411 civilians and 1,311 security personnel in Kashmir (1990-1996), had been killed by terrorists in just these two Indian provinces. Nevertheless, these exaggerated perceptions are integral to the US response to terrorism and help create the psyche of a society besieged, and the mandate for harsh counter-terrorism action.
19. Remarks by President Clinton to the Opening Session of the 53rd United Nations General Assembly at New York on September 21, 1998.
20. *Ibid.*
21. US State Department, *www.state.gov/global/terrorism*
22. *"President Clinton: A World Leader in the Fight Against Global Terrorism"*, The White House at Work, September 21, 1998, *www.whitehouse.gov*
23. This includes the very comprehensive Anti-Terrorism and Effective Death Penalty Act, 1996.
24. And "Life" it must be noted, means life. Not the maximum of 14 years and as little as eight and a half that it has been reduced to by a licentious penal regime in India.
25. Stuart A.Wright, "Anatomy of a Government Massacre: Abuses of Hostage-Barricade Protocols during the Waco Standoff", Terrorism and Political Violence, London, Vol. II, No 2, Summer, 1999, London, pp. 39-68.
26. "Flashpoints and Force Structures", Strategic Assessment, 1997, *www.ndu.edu/ndu/inss/sa97ch15.html*
27. For instance, the US Counter-terrorism Policy outlined above.
28. "Statement on the Death of Mr. A.S. Sandhu", Press Release, Chandigarh, May 24, 1997. Reported in all major Indian newspapers on May 25, 1997.
29. I have been repeatedly raising these and other issues with successive governments, starting with the Inder Kumar Gujral Government, vide my

letter dated May 30, 1997, to the present dispensation - evidently without any quantifiable impact on policy or action.

30. D.A. Henderson, Director of the John Hopkins Centre for Civilian Biodefence Studies, in "Bio-terrorism attack inevitable: US expert", *Asian Age*, New Delhi, February 6, 2000.
31. "Technology, Terror & a Thoughtless State," *Faultlines*, Vol. 3, October 1999, pp. 1-38.
32. K.P.S. Gill, " Technology, Terror & a Thoughtless State", *op. cit.*, esp. pp. 26-34.
33. And would obviate the ludicrous prospect of a rapid response force such as the National Security Guard sitting on a tarmac ready for take-off for over half-an-hour, waiting for a psychologist-negotiator to arrive, while a full-blown hijack endangered the lives of over 180 passengers and vital national security interests. Cf. the sequence of events relating to the hijack of IC 814 above.

NINE

Security and Development in India's Northeast: An Alternative Perspective

Ajai Sahni* *and* J. George*

Many profound theories have attempted to explain the proliferation of civil violence in general by reference to socio-economic and cultural developments such as response to feelings of intensifying deprivation and oppression or stresses engendered in States undergoing rapid modernisation. However, none of these theories can explain why, or under what precise conditions, people resort to terrorism rather than to other forms of violence.[1]

A broad stream of justification has marked the intellectual response to terrorism in India, and this tendency persists even today, after decades of strife have cost the nation thousands of innocent lives and billions of rupees towards the cost of counter-terrorism, and many billions more in terms of the developmental opportunities lost. There has been a great proliferation of "a false sociology of poverty, political neglect and whatever other stereotypical pop-psychological explanations... (we)... can invent to justify the unjustifiable."[2] At its worst, this trend finds its source in the propaganda of the terrorists and their front organisations; but even at its best, it is based, on the one hand, on a naivete that gives overwhelming credence to the political rhetoric and postures of extremist organisations, against all evidence of their actions or any objective analysis of the situation on the ground; and on the other, on an unexamined dogma that reduces all conflict and its resolution to developmental catechisms.

This last stream of economic determinism simultaneously asserts a kind of identity between causes and solutions, reducing the entire problem of the elimination of terrorism to a question of 'massive investment' in developmental projects in affected regions, which would magically eliminate both the source and all violent manifestations of discontent. This intellectual fashion has had a powerful — if fitful — influence, both on India's national policy, and on the pattern of demands raised by the governments (and indeed by the terrorists themselves) of various states afflicted by the scourge of terror. The result has been a massive — though usually *ad hoc* and erratic — allocation of resources by the centre to such states, particularly at times when a central government is under some political pressure to be seen to be responding 'effectively' or 'proactively' to terrorism.[3] In all such cases, little effort has been devoted to evaluating the utilisation or impact of such allocations in the past, and these actions are simply premised on the erroneous assumption that ending grievances will end terrorism.[4]

The dynamics of terrorism, however, acquires a character and autonomy entirely divorced from the paradigms of such naive determinism, resulting in a high rate of failure for all initiatives based on the conviction that terrorism can be made to disappear through appropriate developmental investments. Indeed, the only things that have been known to 'disappear' in most such cases, are all signs of the funds invested, and it is somewhat surprising that this dogma has persisted for such a long time in the complete absence of supporting evidence.

The following analysis, consequently, is premised on the assumption that, irrespective of underlying causes, objectives or ideology, once levels of violence and of general civil administrative collapse have exceeded certain parameters, they set into motions dynamics that is entirely autonomous and independent of the antecedent or 'triggering' mechanisms and motives. Consequently, no attempt is made to evaluate or analyse any such 'causal' factor in the emergence or development of any particular insurgency or terrorist movement.

Funding and Development in India's Northeast

The strife-riven states of India's Northeast are a case in point. It is commonplace to say that this region has remained an area of neglect for more than five decades since independence. From the point of view of national political consciousness, this is, perhaps, a correct evaluation. In the context of developmental allocations and a wide range of economic and social indices, however, this is far from the truth.

The states of the Northeast are ascribed a "special category" status by the Government of India, and the National Development Council (NDC), the apex body for the approval of Plan funding, earmarks 30 per cent of total Plan allocations for special category states as central assistance for State Plans. Significantly, these states receive 90 per cent of Plan assistance as a grant, and just 10 per cent as a loan, as against the norm of 30 per cent grant and 70 per cent loan for other states. Favoured treatment is also given by the Finance Commission with respect to the sharing of central tax revenues. Clearly, therefore, these states have not been made to suffer as a result of their resource endowments. The financial flow of funds to the Northeast, and the persistence of 'underdevelopment' against a backdrop of financial support from the Centre, consequently demand an examination of the decision making processes and patterns of resource allocation within these states.

In the first place (as Table 1 indicates) the financial support to these states from the central devolution (Planning and Finance Commissions), accounts for over 80 per cent of the per capita revenue receipts in this region. Secondly, developmental expenditure as a percentage of revenue expenditure ranges between a high of over 72 per cent (Arunachal Pradesh) and 60 per cent (Nagaland). Thirdly, capital expenditure as a proportion of total expenditure was, on an average, at least 10 percentage points higher than the national average. This is also the case if another avenue of capital/asset creation in the region, the per capita plan outlay, is considered. Simply put, these states, on the average, fare much better than the national average on each of these parameters.

This is also the case for a variety of socio-economic indices. Specifically, literacy rates in the region tend to be significantly higher than the national average, while population densities are significantly lower Table 2. Morbidity rates in the region are also well below the national average, at 94 per thousand as against the national average of 122, for short duration morbidity, and 3,076 per hundred thousand as against the national average of 4,578 for major morbidity.[5] Per capita incomes, at Rs. 5,070 per annum, are higher than the national average of Rs. 4,485, and the population below the poverty line, at 33 per cent, is less than the national figure of 39 per cent.[6] Even access to electricity, at 44 per cent of households, is marginally above the national average of 43 per cent;[7] as is access to a health sub-centre/hospital within five kilometres of the village, which stands at 47 per cent of villages in the Northeast, in comparison to the All India average of 41.2 per cent.[8]

There are, of course, a number of other parameters, the network of roads, industrial development, etc., on which these states lag far behind national averages.[9] But the image of grinding poverty that is often projected is inaccurate, and the 'social backwardness' that we ascribe to the tribes of this region is a heavily concept-dependent value judgement. Indeed, the character and equity of local institutions for village and self-governance in tribal societies tend to be far superior to the caste-riven, feudal panchayats in much of rural India, the status of women is certainly higher, and crimes against women dramatically lower than they are elsewhere in the country. Our impression of backward or 'primitive' tribal societies in the Northeast is cast, at least in some measure, in the mould of the market economy and its indices, and in the patterns of our cultural prejudices.[10]

To return, however, to the state of health of public finance in the region, it is notable that the ratio of development to non-development expenditure is declining despite increasing Central devolution, and the non-development expenditure as a percentage

TABLE 1
FUNDS FLOW PATTERN IN THE STATES OF THE NORTHEAST

State	*Percapita Net State Domestic Product (NSDP)*[1] *(Rs.)*	*Revenue Receipts Per Capita in 1995-96 (in Rs.)*					*Column (5 + 6) as percentage to Col. (7)) (%)*	*Develop-mental Expen-diture*[2] *(%)*	*Capital Expen-diture*[3] *(%)*	*Per Capita Outlay*[4] *(Rs.)*
		Own Tax Revenue	*Own Non-Tax Revenue*	*Tax Devo-lution*	*Central Grants*	*Total*				
(1)	(2)	(3)	(4)	(5)	(6)	(7)	(8)	(9)	(10)	(11)
Arunachal Pradesh	10205	82	866	1331	5774	8053	88	72.1	36.2	14936
Assam	6288	291	139	378	590	1398	69	65.6	11.4	836
Manipur	6914	140	229	835	2278	3483	89	66.1	22.4	4476
Meghalaya	7862	345	349	832	2038	3564	81	67.9	21.6	3960
Mizoram	9570	77	614	1656	6052	8399	92	70.8	19.5	9518
Nagaland	9758	158	260	1511	4020	5949	93	60.0	17.1	4692
Tripura	5083	161	129	766	2088	3144	91	67.9	19.1	3183
All States (Average)	9725	686	254	323	232	1494	37	61.5	15.2	1619

Source: Table 6 of Kurian, N.J. (1999) *"State Government Finances: A Survey of Recent Trends"*, Economic and Political Weekely, Vol. 34, No. 8-14, May, p. 1123.

Note: 1. NSDP in Rupees at Current Prices for 1995-96.
2. As a percentage of Revenue Expenditure in 1995-96.
3. As a percentage of Total Expenditure in 1995-96.
4. Realised in the Eighth Plan at 1991-92 Prices.

of total revenue expenditure has risen sharply. An analysis of budget papers for the period 1991-92 to 1998-99 for the seven states of the Northeast indicates that although the development to non-development expenditure ratio remains above unity, the gap is diminishing rapidly Table 3. This trend is confirmed by the estimates of non-development expenditure (NDE) as a percentage of total revenue expenditure. For example, in Nagaland and Tripura, NDE was consuming close to half of total revenue expenditure by 1998-99, up from a third in 1991-92. While increases in other states are smaller, the only exception to this rising trend isArunachal Pradesh.

TABLE 2
SELECT SOCIO- ECONOMIC INDICATORS IN THE NORTHEAST

State	*Population Density*	*Literacy Rate (%)*		
		Total	*Male*	*Female*
Arunachal Pradesh	10	41.59	51.45	29.69
Assam	286	52.89	61.87	43.03
Manipur	82	59.89	71.60	47.6
Meghalaya	79	49.10	53.12	44.85
Mizoram	33	82.27	85.61	78.6
Nagaland	73	61.65	67.62	54.75
Tripura	263	60.44	70.58	49.65
All States	274	52.21	64.13	39.29

Source: Economic Survey 1998-99, Govt. of India, Table 9.2: S-115

Note:
1. Population growth is annual exponential rate in per capita between 1981-91.
2. 0 - 6 years population is an percentage of total population.
3. Density is expressed as population per square Kilometre.
4. Literacy rate refers to population aged seven years and above.
5. WPR is work participation rate estimated as a percentage of total workers to total population.

The two main components of rising NDE are administrative services and interest payments, with the former consuming between 38 and 63 per cent of the total by 1998-99 Table 4. Of the administrative expenditure, policing consumes between 50 to 70 per cent of the total - this would appear to be reasonable in states characterised by high levels of civil strife. However, the role of the state police in counter-insurgency operations is severely limited in the Northeast, with the Army and the Central para-military forces carrying the brunt of the responsibilities for fighting terrorism. K.P.S. Gill's inference that there exists an extremely unfavourable ratio of operational to static and non-productive force in the state police would thus appear to be valid for this region as well.[11]

TABLE 3
REVENUE ACCOUNT DERIVATIVES

State	*Dev/NDE*		*NDE as % TR Exp.*	
	1991-92	1998-99	1991-92	1998-99
Arunachal Pradesh	2.92	2.53	29.25	28.31
Assam	3.00	1.78	25.00	35.92
Manipur	2.00	1.86	33.33	34.91
Meghalaya	2.56	2.11	28.11	32.19
Mizoram	3.13	1.91	24.19	34.42
Nagaland	1.76	1.21	36.27	45.16
Tripura	2.51	1.19	28.45	45.67

Source: Compiled by the authors.
Note: 1. Dev.: Development Expenditure.
2. NDE: Non-Development Expenditure.
3. TR Exp.: Total Revenue Expenditure.

TABLE 4
DISAGGREGATED VIEW OF NON-DEVELOPMENT EXPENDITURE, 1998-99
(as a percent of total NDE of Revenue Account)

State	*Interest (%)*	*Admn.Services (%)*	*Pension (%)*
Arunachal Pradesh	27.82	57.05	7.37
Assam	37.65	37.98	16.67
Manipur	28.69	45.00	18.35
Meghalaya	27.44	56.25	6.28
Mizoram	33.04	48.51	7.25
Nagaland	28.15	56.52	9.27
Tripura	22.54	63.22	9.86

Source: Computed by the authors.

A closer analysis of expenses within the Development Expenditure (DE) category also raises interesting questions, especially with regard to "general economic services" and including the sub-head "secretariat economic services." Secretariat economic services accounted for a mere 40 per cent of the total general economic services during 1991-92. By 1998-99, this proportion had increased to 80 per cent. Evidently, the maximum "development" taking place in this region is confined to the state secretariat's themselves.

If administrative expenses in both the NDE and DE categories are totalled, it is seen that they account for as much as 70 paise in every rupee of "development expenditure" in some of the seven states of the Northeast.

In addition to the substantial amounts of money that the states of the Northeast receive from the Centre are the large overdrafts from the Treasury that have become a routine practice in this region. The total amount available for development, over the years have, consequently, been very significant. In Assam alone, for instance, the Planning and Rural Development Departments had expended a total of Rs. 11.65 billion over the period April 1992 to February 1998, on Rural Development, with no visible impact on the ground, and no system of accountability for the funds so expended.

Where does all this money go? And can the cycle of terrorism ever be broken through such a strategy of massive investment in development?

The Blind Spots of Development Planning and Security Strategies

A simple and frequent answer to the first of these questions is often condensed into a single word: corruption. This appears to be a view that is gaining ground among officials at the Centre who now claim that the states of the Northeast are afflicted by levels of corruption that are higher even than those that prevail in the perennially sick state of Bihar. Evidently 'leakages'—as the diversion of public monies to private coffers is euphemistically referred to—are extraordinarily high in the Northeast, and this is one reason why "Development packages leave the people — all people — of militancy-affected states cold."[12] Indeed, the greatest enthusiasm for 'financial packages for the Northeast' is displayed only among the bureaucracy — both at the Centre and in the States - and by the nexus of politicians and contractors who will eventually and substantially benefit from these flows of funds. The 'corrupt elite' of the Northeast has thus frequently been accused of enriching itself at the cost of the common people and of the development of the region.

As with all reductionist explanations, however, this is just far too simple and ignores vast areas of complex linkages within the peculiar political, social and economic structures that have emerged under the shadow of terrorism. Before we address these, however, it is useful to look at another area of the dominating — and flawed — premises of counter-terrorism policy in India.

The thesis that developmental expenditure is the panacea to all violence — including terrorism — is often countered by a competing dogma, what is sometimes referred to as a 'law and order approach,' that emphasises the use of force to the exclusion of all other means, in order to restore the authority of government. This approach asserts that all issues of politics and development can be addressed only after terrorist depredations have been crushed. Thus, where the 'economic determinists' insist that development automatically generates a 'peace dividend' in the form of de-escalation of conflict and political violence, the opposing viewpoint argues that development is itself the 'peace dividend' that can arise only after 'law and order' has been imposed by the force of arms.

Both positions, of course, contain a germ of truth; neither, however, embraces its entirety. The fact is that substantial development has flowed into the Northeast; its impact on target populations has been negligible because of the corruption and violence of the prevailing politics. Much of this investment, moreover, has indirectly ended up financing militancy through the enveloping economy of extortion and collusion. On the other hand, despite as much as five decades of a 'military approach' in Nagaland, there has been no resolution of the basic issues, and violence invariably resurfaces after every transient spell of enforced or negotiated peace.

The difficulty is that, by and large, all analysis of conflict and development in the Northeast has (quite naturally) been defined in terms of available data, and the source of a bulk of this data has been the government. The character and content of this data is, consequently, defined by the settled practices and categories of the various statistical exercises carried out for the entire country, and tends to ignore the peculiar circumstances created by mass conflict in specific regions. A sensitive and responsive central bureaucracy would, of course, set into motion the processes of correction when it realised that the statistics on which it was basing government policies and actions were flawed - or at least not sufficiently comprehensive to provide an adequate and rational basis for decision-making. 'Sensitive and responsible bureaucracy,' however, is evidently an oxymoron, and no such entity has been reported to exist in India. "India's imperious, indolent and inept bureaucracy,"[13] by and large, prefers to conduct its deliberations and arrive at its decisions at a safe distance from the rough and tumble of the cutting edge of counter-terrorism operations, and to deal with problems that they 'understand' — mainly, sloganeering on poverty, underdevelopment and conventional civil disturbances. Their 'solutions', consequently, are also discovered in tried and tested — albeit entirely unsuccessful — strategies of massive 'development funding' and the shuffling around of existing forces from one theatre of civil strife to another. This is familiar, and consequently safe, territory where adequate precedents can be found to provide an alibi for every possible — and inevitable — failure. The fact that terrorists refuse to co-operate with their mindset and persist in continuously changing the rules of the game has yet to disturb this style of functioning, and no effort whatsoever has been made to document critical changes on the ground, and to fashion policies that would be relevant to the conditions actually prevailing.

There is, of course, one new pool of data that has emerged, as a result of the efforts of various security forces (SFs), but this is exhausted by comparative casualties inflicted by and on the militants and SFs, weapons possession and seizures, force availability and deployment, and a few other categories that have a direct bearing on tactical and strategic perspectives of the forces operating in the field. There have also been a few localised studies, usually by various research agencies and non-government organisations, tracing out the general impact of ethnicity and migration on the course of conflicts; however, while these have generated some debate, they are yet to have visible impact on policies.

We are, consequently, left with macroeconomic and public finance data, on the one hand, and with data on SF operations and terrorist strikes, on the other — and this naturally reinforces the prior predilection to interpret all events and define policies within the framework of the two conventional and competing models - 'economic determinism' and the 'law and order approach'.

Such analyses and policies inevitably ignore certain critical aspects of the unique social, economic, political and administrative processes and relationships that exist in the Northeast, and that inevitably emerge in areas afflicted by long periods of civil strife. The most significant among these is that insurgencies and terrorist violence, once they pass beyond a certain point, are invariably accompanied by a collapse of the institutions of civil governance — including the justice system - throughout the affected areas. These areas are, consequently, transformed into a shifting battlefield between the extremists and the SFs. Needless to say, the state's existing agencies of development have neither the power nor the will to reach out into this hazardous 'war zone'. In substantial measure, moreover, all critical activities, policies and decisions relating to the conflict are progressively taken over by the Central Government and are defined and co-ordinated by bureaucrats located thousands of miles away. Critically, as already noted, the shrinking role of the State Governments has historically been associated with disproportionate and increasing unproductive expenditures in administration.

It is within this context that the question of a 'corrupt elite' and of 'leakages' needs to be addressed. Here, we find, that the usual presumption of a clear opposition of interests between the government (and its officials and various agencies) and the militants is often unjustified. Indeed, complex collusive arrangements between various political groupings, administrators and officials, on the one hand, and different militant factions, on the other, are more the norm that the exception. Some of these 'collusive arrangements', in fact, are often institutionalised by the various secret or public 'peace agreements' that are forged, from time to time, between government negotiators and extremist factions. For instance, the allegedly 'comfortable' arrangement that had been arrived at, and that had persisted for over two and a half years, between the Centre (and its primary symbol in Nagaland, the Army) and the National Socialist Council of Nagaland-Isak Muivah (NSCN-IM), was briefly disturbed only when alleged NSCN-IM militants made an unsuccessful bid on the life of the State's Chief Minister, S.C. Jamir on November 29, 1999.[14] It was in the wake of this assassination attempt that Jamir exposed the farcical character of the Centre's 'peace accord', calling it a "licence to kill, threaten and extort." He added further, "This is just a ceasefire between the NSCN (Isak-Muivah) and the security forces and not a ceasefire with the people. Such a truce will only aggravate the situation."[15] It is significant that an elected state government in Nagaland has no role in the negotiations between the Centre and the militants operating in the state, and is, in fact, kept entirely ignorant of the character and content of ongoing negotiations.

Another aspect or form of collusion is exemplified by the 'arrangement' that the Arunachal Pradesh Chief Minister, Mukut Mithi, is widely believed to have arrived at with the National Socialist Council of Nagaland - Khaplang (NSCN-K). This Naga militant organisation dominates the Changlang and Tirap districts in his State. In order to dislodge the 19-year old Gegong Apang Government, intelligence sources disclose that Mukut Mithi and his supporters entered into an agreement with the NSCN-K, according to which the latter guaranteed that no candidate would contest any election against Mithi's Arunachal Congress for six years in the Changlang and Tirap districts; in return the MLAs and ministers thus elected unopposed would co-operate with the NSCN-K and follow their directions during this period. It was also clarified by the NSCN-K that the movement initiated for the demand of Union territory status for the Changlang, Tirap, Lohit and Dibang Valley districts was only for 'eye wash to the public'.[16]

The lines of collusion and opposition, of support and confrontation, are often not as clearly drawn. In Assam, both the ruling party, the Asom Gana Parishad (AGP) and the main militant organisation, the United Liberation Front of Asom (ULFA), trace their roots, motivation, ideology and leadership back to the same students' movement in the late Seventies. While the distance between the AGP Government and the ULFA has progressively grown over the years, linkages at a personal level between most ministers and various militant leaders and factions persist, and these play a very significant role in the state's politics.

Similarly, in Tripura there is growing evidence of a deepening nexus between the major political parties and extremist groups. The National Liberation Front of Tripura (NLFT) is alleged to have close links with the Congress (I), while the All Tripura Tiger Force (ATTF) is reportedly aligned with the ruling Left Front.[17] It is now increasingly clear that the militancy in the state is substantially supported and sustained by the political patronage received by these groups. In fact, this has been the case with every terrorist movement in all parts of the country, and the Northeast is far from an exception.

The progressive 'withdrawal' of civil governance and the network of collusive arrangements with militant factions are compounded by the emergence of widespread patterns of illegal economic activity that become the mainstay and motive of all insurgencies after what may be called their early 'ideological' stage. These include a thriving economy of extortion, smuggling, gun-running, narcotics, and an oligopolistic control over government contracts. Indeed, the various 'ideological' factions and rivalries within militant movements in the states of the Northeast are often thinly disguised 'turf wars' to retain or gain control over lucrative 'areas of influence', especially important routes of (illegal) cross border trade, including the drug trade.

The growth of this underground terrorist economy, backed by the disruptive power of the militants, distorts and inhibits the processes and growth of legitimate economic and developmental activities. In this context, it is also important to note that a wide variety of economic activities that were integral to the lives of the people of this region - including cross border trade, the use of a variety of forest products, some collective rights over land use, etc. — have, since Independence, suddenly (and from the point of view of the local populations, arbitrarily) been 'criminalised', forcing otherwise law abiding citizens into a collusive relationship with militants.

Within their areas of influence, moreover, militant groups gradually usurp a wide range of governmental functions, including the (albeit conditional) protection of life and property, and the provision of 'justice' to local communities. Militancy can, in fact, fruitfully (though only partially) be examined as a conflict to defend or expand monopolistic control over critical functions — economic and administrative — against all 'intruders', including the government, with militant groups taking on the character of a 'primitive state' in a situation of widespread anarchy.

These issues are widely - but randomly - commented upon, both within official circles and in the media. At a local level, they are, once again, fitfully factored in into the responses of various agencies of the state, including the SFs engaged in counter-terrorist operations. However, these processes are simply 'invisible' as far as the processes of developmental and strategic planning are concerned. This is what makes these processes irrelevant to the situation on the ground, and leads to an enormous and growing hiatus between the intention and the execution. Crucially, moreover, it circumscribes the range and spectrum of non-military interventions that could help to approach a resolution of the problem. Since the problem is not defined or understood in terms of the dynamics of the underground terrorist economy, and since the magnitude and proliferation of this economy are not quantified, the problem of terrorism and insurgency is looked upon, simply, persistently and obtusely, as a political, law and order, or developmental problem, with an inchoate layering of elements such as corruption or political collusion. In this, it would appear that far greater credence is given to the political postures and ideological pretensions of extremist groups than is merited by the reality. They are treated as political rebels or malcontents; or as, in some sense, representing - albeit by improper and illegal means — the democratic will and aspirations of the local communities. At worst, of course, they are projected as 'anti-national' elements working at the behest of foreign powers, a popular perception vigorously promoted by government agencies, but one that entirely ignores local dynamics. The fact, however, is that, at the leadership level, they would often be more accurately represented as criminal entrepreneurs. In their group dynamics, they bear close resemblance to the processes and operations of organised crime.

The moment terrorist movements are perceived, even in part, to have the character and dynamics of organised criminal enterprises, a critical shift occurs. Significantly, the glamour and glory attached to their identity as sub-national revolutionaries is compromised. This is significant at more than a psychological level. The image that dominates our minds today is of dedicated (though misguided) young men, heavily armed with sophisticated weapons, confronting the might of the state in bloody skirmishes. There is, of course, some truth in the image - young and heavily armed men are, from time to time, engaged in armed clashes with the SFs. But, as much of the preceding analysis suggests, the picture is entirely incomplete. The fact is that an overwhelming proportion of their activities — as with the activities of most contemporary organised criminal groups — are not predatory but collusive. That is, they are based on a continuing and symbiotic relationship of acquiescence between the 'terrorist entrepreneur', on the one hand, and government agencies, officials, enterprises and individuals whose primary businesses lie within the ambit of the law, on the other. In other words, their offences are, in substantial measure, "consensual in so far as they involve the active complicity of otherwise legitimate members of the larger society."[18] The greatest threat they pose is not the threat of arms, but of a more insidious subversion, based on their co-operation and competition both with governments whom they claim to oppose, and with the larger community within which they operate. A great deal of their power is based on their capacity to exploit legitimate business and financial activities, and their ability to corrupt government and law enforcement agencies. As the Secretary General of the United Nations declared in 1994, "The danger is the more pernicious because organised crime does not always confront the state directly. It becomes enmeshed in the institutional machinery. It infiltrates the state apparatus, so as to gain the indirect complicity of government officials... (it) poisons the business climate, corrupts political leaders and undermines human rights."[19] These are perceptions and concepts that are widely and progressively being applied to the analysis of organised crime, but are yet to be extended to the examination and containment of the criminal activities of terrorist conglomerates.

Such an extension puts powerful new tools into the hands of the state and its agencies. The one element that is not replaceable in the criminal enterprise — as in legitimate enterprises — is profit. Insurgencies today are being sustained by the enormous, almost unbelievable volumes of finances generated by their activities. Moreover, this is, by and large, easy money. In the initial stages of most terrorist movements, finances to fund activities are ordinarily secured through raids and robberies that demand some daring and involve a great deal of risk. In the subsequent 'settled' stage, where an area of influence or domination has been established, the money is much easier to come by. The ULFA, for instance, by 1990, found that their demands met with no resistance, and their revenues exceeded their own highest expectations:

> 'It was amazing, we asked for a little and they were prepared to go well beyond what we wanted,' said one ULFA leader. 'That was when we realised how soft the state was, how weak the businessmen were, how much black money they had, that they could pay up and still have enough for themselves.'[20]

As already stated, extortion and other outright criminal activities are not the only problem. The deeper problem is the inter-meshing of the legal with the illegal. An interesting example is the subversion of the Public Distribution System (PDS) in Assam. According to government sources, the subsidised essential commodities that are made available through the PDS are diverted to the open market, generating illegal revenues of an estimated Rs. 600 million per month, a large proportion of which reportedly accrues to the ULFA. The processes of this operation are exemplified by the diversion of the State's allocation of 40,000 tonnes of rice and wheat under the PDS. The difference between open market prices and the PDS price in 1998 was Rs. 4.00 per kilogram. Most of this rice is sold in the open market, and the 'premium' shared. Whole wheat is also distributed to consumers at an official rate of Rs. 5.00 to Rs. 5.50. Assam's monthly allotment of wheat till early 1998 was 30,000 tonnes, most of which was simply allocated to flour mills, many of which were directly owned by ULFA and Surrendered ULFA (SULFA) surrogates. The flour was then sold in the black market at a hundred per cent premium, generating illegal incomes estimated at about Rs. 100 million per month. Similarly, the PDS price of salt is Rs. 1 per kilogram; a bulk of the monthly allocation of 15,000 tonnes of salt is sold in villages at prices exceeding Rs. 3 per kilogram, generating illegal incomes estimated at Rs. 300 million. Villagers in Assam also pay up to four times the 'control price' for each litre of PDS kerosene oil.

'Rural development' is another lucrative sector, and it is estimated that as much as 70 per cent of all funds available to the State government in Assam under this head is systematically siphoned off under a well organised network of ULFA and SULFA cadres, contractors, civil servants and members of the political executive. According to official sources, of the total of Rs. 11.65 billion made available under this head during the period 1992-93 to February 1998, less than Rs. 4 billion went into legitimate schemes. There is little evidence of projects executed on the ground that supports the claim even of this fraction of expenditure. Critically, misappropriation of this scale in Assam is not possible without the direct collusion, both of the State government and of the ULFA leadership and its cadres.

These cases provide only anecdotal estimates of the total volume and range of financial activities in which insurgent groups in the Northeast are engaged.[21] No comprehensive data or estimates exist, but the totals would possibly dwarf the expenditure of many of the state government's departments.[22]

These revenues create enormous power and influence, especially through the direct capacity to give employment. SF sources indicate that the various underground groups offer recruits a remuneration, that is often several multiples of what is available to a recruit in the police or para-military forces, and is virtually inconceivable in any other entry-level salaried position in this region.[23] With significant levels of unemployment and under-employment, this creates decisive leverage with the local populations.

The control of these vast resources combines with a challenge to the state's presumed monopoly over the instrumentalities of violence, to undermine the fundamental legitimacy of governments. The progressive erosion of state authority is reflected in the government's inability, or perceived inability:

(i) to protect the lives and properties of the people;

(ii) to enforce the ordinary laws of the land (and the consequent and increasing dependence on extra-ordinary laws and force to sustain authority);

(iii) to reward and punish;
(iv) to collect taxes;
(v) to carry out functions of financial management with requisite credibility;
(vi) to enforce discipline among state employees;
(vii) to evoke a fear of sanctions.

The erosion of the government's legitimacy and authority is often paralleled by a simultaneous acquisition or ascription of legitimacy and authority to the 'revolutionary' groupings. In this, the insurgents have a decided advantage, in that they have much less to prove, and standards and expectations that are much lower than those applied to the established government and its agencies. Thus, a ragged band of a few 'soldiers', an occasional, dramatic, often crude demonstration of 'justice', random aid for individuals in distress or support to a village development project - such as the construction of a mud track (using voluntary labour from the village itself),[24] suffice to create the impression of a 'people's movement' committed to 'justice' and the alleviation of the poverty and misery of the larger population. The fact that a far greater number may benefit from government projects and programmes does not undermine the legitimacy of the rebels. The government is doing less than it is supposed and expected to do. Anything the terrorists do, exceeds expectations, and is a windfall. The parameters applied are simply not the same.

These factors have a critical bearing on the debate on the 'people's will' and 'loyalties'. As stated before, there is a tendency among terrorism's various, and sometimes well-intentioned, apologists to assert that such movements, in some sense, express the inchoate democratic will of the people. There have been times when this has seemed entirely credible - as, for instance, in the Punjab in the late 1980s, when it was widely believed that a large majority of the Sikh population, including Sikhs in the police and other government services, were strongly sympathetic to the movement for 'Khalistan'. This was a period of near complete anarchy, with the institutions of the state in disarray, and the SFs themselves in retreat. By 1992-93, however, the moment signs of the restoration of the state's power became visible, the 'sympathies' disappeared. Today, the 'tattered rump'[25] of the terrorist movement finds few defenders in Punjab, and sustained efforts at recruitment for a revival of the movement, backed by arms and liberal funding from Pakistan, have met with complete failure.[26]

The failure of the government to protect its citizens - and the (qualified and discriminatory) assumption of this function by the terrorists - is the crucial consideration in this determination of public response to the rival claims of 'legitimacy'. In Vietnam, an analysis of the comparative legitimacy of the South Vietnamese government and the Viet Cong during the Vietnam War identified the following determining factors: comparison of the relative risks of punishment; material contributions demanded; opportunities for reward; and the opportunities provided for meaningful activity provided by one supporting group or the other. The study concluded that the first of these factors, the perceived risk of death or other punishment far outweighed the others in importance.[27] As one commentator expressed it, "you can argue about whether security is 10 per cent of the problem or 90 per cent of the problem, but it's the first 10 per cent or the first 90 per cent."[28] The fact of the matter is that 'the people' are, except in rare and extraordinary circumstances, not particularly concerned about ideological niceties, and just wish to get on with life. This gives a natural advantage to those who most effectively threaten — or conversely, protect — them.

These, then, are the broad contours of the general administration, political and macroeconomic dimensions and dynamics in a situation of the widespread breakdown of law and order. However, it is not sufficient to document and analyse these elements. The microeconomic linkages and socio-political impact at the local and village level, on the one hand, and the intercourse between various individuals and factions within terrorist movements, on the other have extraordinary significance for policy. Many of the Centre's 'grand designs' for peace in the Northeast have floundered against the realities of these transactions. The example of the Union Ministry for Home Affairs' (MHA) 'surrender package' for militants is a case in point. The present scheme has been in force since April 1998. The wisdom of the scheme — which may well be interpreted as rewarding terrorists at the expense of law abiding citizens — is itself suspect, but this is not our present point. The scheme seeks to wean terrorists away from the path of violence by offering incentives and benefits to those who are ready to bid a 'farewell to arms', and targets "misguided youth and hardcore militants who have strayed into the folds of militancy and now find themselves trapped."[29] Under the 'give up and gain' criteria, a terrorist surrendering with weapons is given Rs 25,000 per rocket launcher or sniper rifle; an AK47/AK56 assault rifle secures Rs. 15,000; rates are similarly prescribed for pistols, grenades, rockets, remote control devices, explosive materials, etc. Each surrendered militant, moreover, would be paid a monthly stipend of Rs. 2,000. A 'rehabilitation package' also includes soft bank loans and vocational training.[30] The surrender scheme has created an entirely new category of nuisance - the Surrendered ULFA or SULFA - and has resulted in "growing criminalisation in Assam".[31] SULFA cadres now operate a flourishing extortion racket and intercede in all the other illegal and quasi-legal businesses that the ULFA also have a stake in. The only visible difference is that they have no declared political agenda - and this concession on their part has been sufficient for the state government and the Centre to adopt a live and let live policy towards them. No prosecutions have been launched against any surrendered militant, however serious the crimes he may have committed.[32] However, substantial revenues generated by the SULFA through their varied activities also flow to the ULFA - as also to their patrons in the political executive and state administration. If anything, the state's surrender policy has created and reinforced linkages between overground and underground formations.

Internecine strife between terrorist groups is also often related to a struggle for control over various financial operations and territories. Thus, the Kukis, who were once considered Nagas,[33] were later pitched into a fierce and bloody conflict with the latter. One of the major elements of the dispute was a 'turf war' to control the main drug route in the region, the highway linking Imphal to Myanmar, and its centre at Moreh.[34]

The examples above are random and it is not within the scope of this chapter to enumerate all aspects and cases of the wide spectrum of activities and linkages of the underground economy of terrorism. Indeed, at the present stage, reliable data on the subject is non-existent. It is, moreover, not the case that administrators and officials on the ground are ignorant of these cases, trends and incidents. Intelligence agencies regularly document the clandestine financial activities and linkages of underground operations. This flow of data, however, is discrete, and there has been no effort to organise and analyse it in a systematic manner. Moreover, the methodology of data and information acquisition suffers from a variety of inherent defects and biases. The cumulative impact of these factors is that the accuracy and utility of these information flows is suspect. More significantly, since long term trends at various levels of disaggregation are not available, the influence of these information flows on policy and strategy is negligible, and the primary response remains local and tactical.

Reconstructing the Bases of Planning for Peace

The premise is that no coherent and effective policies can be drawn up for the restoration of an abiding peace in, and for the enduring development of, the states of India's Northeast unless they factor in these various 'unorthodox' elements of the political, administrative and socio-economic conditions prevailing in this region. An obvious corollary is that the models and patterns of development that have been applied, or that have even succeeded in, other parts of the country, cannot mechanically be extended to this region.

Evidently, a massive exercise for the quantification and objective definition of the various trends, processes and linkages outlined above — or, perhaps more accurately, the broad categories generally identified, since the listing is by no means exhaustive — is, consequently, a precondition of any coherent or consistent approach. Specifically, the areas that such an exercise would minimally be required to cover would include:

(i) A study of the patterns of devolution, availability and utilisation of developmental resources to various state governments in the region, of the actual flow of funds, and of the impact of various existing projects and programmes on their target groups. Such a study would naturally entail the documentation of the viability of various programmes, as currently drafted, in situations of widespread terror.

(ii) A study of the functioning of the various institutions of civil governance in a situation of widespread breakdown of law and order, and the interaction between various arms of government in comparison with their constitutionally mandated relationship.

(iii) A study and comprehensive documentation of the dynamics and magnitude of the underground terrorist economy. This would include the analysis of the role of militant groups as providers of a range of 'goods', including administrative and quasi-judicial 'services', and their impact on local populations and institutions of governance.

(iv) A study of the character and pattern of counter-terrorism interventions by the state in various conflicts in the region, the role of the SFs, and their capacity or potential to substitute for the 'absentee state's' developmental agencies.

(v) A study of the status and functioning of existing and traditional institutions of local self-governance in situations of relative administrative anarchy in order to evaluate their potential as agents of development in the context of altered governmental interventions.

Needless to say, this is a tall order, especially in a situation of near administrative anarchy within the region, and the distinctly primitive systems of information management that exist in India's bureaucracy, even at the highest levels at the Centre. Nevertheless, even preliminary efforts to document the operations of the underground terrorist economy, and even to systematise existing information and data, and to accommodate the insights of this exercise within the planning process, would bear immediate fruits. Eventually, however, our actions can only be as effective as our perceptions and premises are accurate reflections of the situation on the ground.

NOTES AND REFERENCES

1. Paul Wilkinson, *"Terrorism versus Liberal Democracy: The Problems of Response,"* in William Gutteridge [ed.], The New Terrorism, London, Mansell Publishing Ltd., n.d., p. 8.
2. K.P.S.Gill, *"Injustice of Campaign against the Police,"* Pioneer, New Delhi, October 17, 1998.
3. Cf. pp. 19-20 in this Volume.
4. The evidence of the history of terrorist movements offers no support to such a thesis, and as Walter Laqueur unequivocally puts it, removing grievances will not end terrorism. Cited in N.O. Berry, *"Theories on the Efficacy of Terrorism"*, in Paul Wilkinson & A.M. Stewart [ed.], Contemporary Research on Terrorism, Aberdeen, Aberdeen University Press, 1987, p. 301. In any event, such investments have, in India, seldom succeeded even in addressing existing grievances, which is the basic rationale of the present analysis.
5. Abusaleh Sharief, India Human Development Report, New Delhi, Oxford University Press, 1999, pp. 136-136.
6. *Ibid.*, p. 7.
7. *Ibid.*
8. *Ibid.*, p. 189
9. Access to piped water - Northeast: 9%, All India: 25%. Villages connected by pucca road - Northeast: 21.2%, All India: 36.8%. *Ibid.* p. 7.
10. Some of these prejudices are defined by the living conditions and lifestyles of a minority of the most isolated of these communities. Others are the product of the relentless, insensitive and entirely uni-dimensional projection of these communities by the media (official and private) as a colourfully dressed people perpetually executing 'tribal dances'. This is roughly tantamount to stereotyping the entire people of Kerala on the dress and deportment of a Kathakali dancer.
11. K.P.S. Gill, *"Endgame in Punjab - 1988-93"*, *Faultlines*, New Delhi, Volume 1, May 1999, p. 20. Gill's assertion relates to a certain period of terrorism in the State of Punjab.
12. "Third N-E Package", *Tribune*, Chandigarh, January 24, 2000.
13. K.P.S. Gill, *"An Abyss of Anarchy,"* Pioneer, August 7, 1999.
14. "Jamir's Convoy Attacked", Hindu, New Delhi, November 30, 1999; "Jamir Beats certain Death", Pioneer, November 30, 1999.
15. "Shaken by Attack, Jamir rubbishes Talks," *Pioneer*, December 1, 2000.
16. While this account is based on intelligence sources, Gegong Apang confirmed the substance of these allegations in a Press Release, the contents of which appeared in Sentinel, Guwahati, on July 29, 1999. These allegations were subsequently refuted in a Press Release signed by 10 ministers and the Deputy Speaker of the State Assembly.
17. Cf. for instance, National Campaign Committee Against Militarisation and Repeal of Armed Forces (Special Powers) Act, Where 'peacekeepers' have declared war, New Delhi, April 1997, p. 70.
18. Thomas R. Naylor, "Mafias, Myths and Markets: On the Theory and Practice of Enterprise Crime", *Transnational Organised Crime*, London, Vol. 3, No. 3, Autumn 1997, p. 3.

19. Boutros Boutros Ghali, *"Statement at the Opening Session of the World Ministerial Conference on Organised Transational Crime at Naples,"* November 22, 1994.
20. Sanjoy Hazarika, *Strangers in the Mist*, New Delhi, Penguin, 1995, p. 187.
21. The reliability of these estimates is also, consequently, imperfect. To the extent that these estimates are based on intelligence reports received from various state agencies, moreover, they would tend to reflect certain systemic biases. But these are matters of detail, and they only reinforce the fundamental premise of this paper: that the entire underground economy of terrorism must be systematically documented and analysed, if it is to be dealt with under consistent and comprehensive counter-terrorism policies.
22. A crude estimate of the financial power of orgnanised crime - as distinct from terrorism - was provided recently after the arrest of a middle rung, though well connected criminal in Delhi. His assets were valued at a figure comparable to the annual budget of Delhi's police force. If anything, the proportionate strength and financial power of the major terrorist groups, some of which are virtually running parallel governments, would be greater. Cf., Arun Shourie, "Human Rights, Terrorism and Organised Crime", Asian Age, New Delhi, November 6, 1998.
23. This raises crucial questions of motivation. As K.P.S. Gill remarks, "It is a matter of great astonishment and of pride to me that these men (SFs) can still be motivated to confront and fight an enemy who is almost invariably better equipped and better compensated than they are. Indeed, the compensatory and welfare package and the working conditions offered to the 'soldiers' of organised criminal gangs and to terrorists, demonstrate a greater 'vision' in those who organise criminal activities than is manifested in the policies of the Indian state vis-_-vis its own defenders." Pioneer, October 17, 1998.
24. Hazarika, *op. cit.*, p. 188.
25. K.P.S. Gill, "Endgame in Punjab: 1988-93", *op. cit.*, p. 69.
26. Ibid., esp. pp. 66-67.
27. Robert A. Maranto, and Paula S. Tuchman, "Knowing the Rational Peasant: The Creation of Rival Incentive Structures in Vietnam", *Journal of Peace Research*, Oslo, Volume 29, No. 3, 1992, pp. 249-264.
28. J.P. Vann, cited in, Bradley R. Glitz, and Robert A. Maranto, *"Underclass Rationality and the Street Gang as Alternative Regime"*, Low Intensity Conflict and Law Enforcement, Kensington, MD, Volume 5, Number 1, Summer 1996, p. 96.
29. "Surrender Package for N-E militants", Hindu, November 24, 1999.
30. *Ibid.*
31. "Assam rebel surrender policy is flawed," Asian Age, November 18, 1999. See also, "Residents ransack SULFA dens", Hindu, October 5, 1999.
32. *Ibid.*
33. Sushil K. Pillai, "Anatomy of an Insurgency: Ethnicity & Identity in Nagaland," *Faultlines*, Vol. 3, October 1999, p. 41.
34. N.S.I. Narahari, *"Socio-ethnic Conflicts in the Northeast: Four Case Studies", Souvenir: Students Experience in Inter-State Living*, January 1997. p. 7.

TEN

Kargil: A Window of Opportunity

Sudhir S. Bloeria

During the first week of May 1999, Pakistan unleashed a storm of unprecedented magnitude in the little known Kargil area of Jammu & Kashmir (J&K). Even though India has been inured to, and conditioned by, the last one decade of Pakistan-inspired proxy-war in the State, these belligerent incursions across the Line of Control (LoC) came as a rude shock, taking both the government and the security forces completely by surprise. It took India over two months to clear this transgression. Operations involved considerable concentration of troops with over one thousand soldiers killed or wounded and strenuous diplomatic effort and enormous costs. There have been differing accounts of the Pak forces' occupation of Indian territory, but one observer has comprehensively summed them in these words:

> The Pakistan army had established posts on seven prominent features dominating the National Highway - the lifeline connecting Kashmir valley to Ladakh. The closest feature was Tololing located barely two km from the highway and about four km from the Line of Control. Tololing is so close to the highway that a medium machine gun with a range of 1,800 meters is enough to stop vehicular movement. What the Rajputana Rifles troops discovered atop this dominating feature were well prepared bunkers with roofs made of corrugated

galvanised iron (CGI) sheets as also long angle iron pickets to erect obstacles. The Pakistanis had separate bunkers for living and gun positions. Since these were located on the reverse slopes, artillery firing was not so effective. 'It was good work, good planning. It would have taken them three to four months to build,' said an officer".[1]

Since May 1999 there has also been criticism as well as analysis of the failure of the army and the intelligence agencies to detect the occupation of Indian territory by Pakistan, and the handling of the Kargil Operation, in all its manifestations, by the Government. Some defence analysts and strategic thinkers maintain that the Indian response to the challenge posed by Pakistan was, once again, muted and lacking in the sting that such an adventure should have attracted.

The Region

Whatever the other manifestations and fall out of these incidents have been, Kargil emerged as a prominent entity on the national scene and briefly captured and held world attention as well.

Kargil, with a geographical area of 14,036 square kilometres, is one of the two districts of the Ladakh region of Jammu & Kashmir, the other being Leh. It has an estimated population of eighty-one thousand,[2] and is subdivided into two *tehsils*, seven blocks, 65 *panchayats* and 129 villages. Kargil is the only town in the district.

The Kargil district was carved out in Ladakh in June 1979, and shares boundaries with Leh in the East, Himachal Pradesh in the South, with Doda, Anantnag and Srinagar touching its western confines. Towards the North lie the Pakistan occupied territories of what are called the Northern Areas, including Skardu and Gilgit. The majority of the population is Shia Muslim, with very few Sunnis, as is the case in the northern areas as well. The Buddhists come next and are concentrated in the Zanskar *tehsil*. The district presents a composite tapestry of Balti, Ladakhi, Purki, Dardi, Zanskari and Shina cultures. Irrespective of their ethnic identities all these communities speak the *Kargali* language with ease.

Considering the cold desert conditions, mountainous terrain and difficulties of communication, infrastructure and civic services in Kargil district are relatively well developed. All but three of the 129 villages have been provided with drinking water and 79 villages are electrified; there are 478 kilometres of surfaced and 198 kilometres of un-surfaced roads, connecting 92 villages. 358 educational institutions are functioning in the district and there are 97 health institutions, including one district hospital and six primary health centres (PHCs).[3] As in the rest of the Ladakh region, the terrain is mostly rocky and mountainous with heights ranging from eight thousand to eighteen thousand feet above mean sea level, mostly barren and devoid of any vegetation, with greenery existing only in valleys and patches irrigated by fast flowing streams. The main population concentration, as also the cultivable area, is in the Suru Valley, which is drained by the Suru River. The district receives snowfall varying between two and five feet, with hardly any rainfall. Drass is said to be the second coldest inhabited place in the world, after Siberia in Russia.

Before 1947, Kargil was part of the erstwhile Ladakh Wazarat, which included areas of the present Leh and Kargil districts and the Skardu area. Gilgit in the North was a separate administrative unit. This entire Himalayan highland region was generally known as the Northern Areas, extending right up to the Karakoram Pass.[4] The strategic importance of this region had been realised by the British over a century ago in the context of Russian expansionist ambitions towards the South of their empire. Lord Curzon called Gilgit one of the Northern gates of India. Describing its importance, E.F. Knight, who had travelled in the region in 1891, wrote, "Gilgit, the northernmost outpost of the Indian Empire, covers all the passes over the Hindoo Koosh, from the easternmost one, the Shimshal, to those at the head of the Yasin river, in the West..."[5] Now, whatever position we take with regard to the debatable lands beyond the Hindoo Koosh, there can be no doubt as to what our course of action should be on the southern slope. Our influence should at least extend up to that great mountain range which forms the natural frontier of India. It is necessary for the safeguarding of our Empire that we should at any rate hold our side of the mountain-gates; but unless we looked to it, Russia would soon have both sides under her control.[6] Kashmir has been called the northern bastion of India. Gilgit can be described as her farther outpost. And hard by Gilgit it is that, in an undefined way, on the high Roof of the World - what more fitting a place! - The three greatest Empires of the Earth meet - Great Britain, Russia, and China."7 The Defence of India Plan prepared in the 1920s considered these areas to be of "vital importance".[8]

Most of the Northern Areas in this strategic region, consisting of a huge land mass of more than seventy thousand square kilometres of what was J&K territory, was illegally occupied by Pakistan in 1947. The occupation followed a successful revolt against Maharaja Hari Singh by the Gilgit Scouts, supported by two British Officers, on October 31, 1947. Ever since, fully realising its strategic importance, Pakistan, has never loosened her grip on the region. Significantly, the entire recent operation by Pakistani forces in the Kargil sector was carried out from bases and training centres spread in Pakistan's Northern Areas around Gilgit and Skardu, with the forward base at Olthingthang.

Successive Pakistani Governments, over the past five decades, have ruled this area with an iron hand leaving its inhabitants without political identity, civil rights or even constitutional status. Large populations of Afghan and Pakhtoon settlers have been inducted into the region to alter the demographic Shia character of the region.

In stark contrast, policy framers in India appear to have failed to realise the importance of the Northern Areas from a national security perspective and practically no efforts were made to regain Skardu and Gilgit during the 1947-48 conflict with Pakistan. In fact, even Leh and Kargil were saved from Pakistani occupation by skin of the teeth.[9] This area continued to be neglected subsequently as well, which has resulted in major gaps in India's knowledge of the Northern Areas. Indian intelligence was better informed on Pakistan Occupied Kashmir (PoK), but had difficulty in collecting human intelligence in the Northern Areas.

Unfortunately, till recently, not only successive Governments but also the intelligence community itself gave low priority to this area, even in terms of strengthening technical intelligence capabilities.[10]

The single-minded pursuit by Pakistan of its disruptive designs and the less than adequate Indian response has not been confined to the Kargil-Gilgit region alone, or to the period of, and immediately preceding, the Kargil War. The pattern has, unfortunately, been consistent in respect of the entire J&K area, right since 1947. To understand the full implications of Pakistan's Kargil misadventure an over view of the contours of Indo-Pak conflicts since Independence is necessary.

Pakistan's Involvement since 1947

Pakistan was born on August 14, 1947, a "moth eaten, truncated" country emerging out of political chaos, economic ruination, colossal transmigration, and dripping in the blood of communal violence. The Muslim League, which was responsible for the country's creation, and its leadership headed by Mohammad Ali Jinnah, also laid the foundations of the evils that have since afflicted that nation. Jinnah concentrated all effective power in the hands of the Governor General, a post he chose to occupy himself, thereby heralding the beginning of authoritarian rule, a legacy that persists. The country has been under a military dictatorship for more than half of its independent existence. Two other developments have simultaneously taken place with comparable consistency: an ever increasing dependence on foreign aid, both economic and political, and a continued devaluation and erosion of democratic norms and constitutional propriety. These trends have severely undermined Pakistan's state structure. In spite of internal problems, financial difficulties and a fragile political edifice, however, Pakistan has been constantly, and consistently, focusing on gaining control of the J&K state through any means possible.

Unlike most of the rulers of the princely states in India, Maharaja Hari Singh of J&K found it difficult to decide on the issue of accession before the formal lapse of British paramountcy. Instead, he made the offer of a 'standstill agreement' to both India and Pakistan, on 12 August 1947. No agreement was signed with

India prior to the State's accession on 26 October 1947. However, a standstill agreement was executed with Pakistan. Postal and telegraph facilities in the state were placed under the control of the Pakistan Government, which also promised to continue the existing arrangement by which the state imported rice, wheat, cloth, ammunition, kerosene oil and petrol from West Punjab. However, Pakistan's rulers had soon put into operation plans to force the Maharaja to accede to Pakistan. The strategy for achieving this was a multi-pronged approach based on armed invasion, subversion of the Muslim population—including military personnel—and economic blockade of the state.

The invasion of Kashmir by tribals was meticulously planned, carefully timed and competently executed. The main attack, *Operation Gulmarg,* was planned and launched by the Army Headquarters of Pakistan. The British Commander-in-Chief of the Pakistan Army personally signed the orders within a few days of the creation of Pakistan. The main force consisted of tribals from the North West Frontier, who were organised into units of about 1000 each, called *Lashkars,* under the command of their respective Chiefs called *Maliks;* Pakistani Army personnel joined these tribals as stiffeners. Each *Lashkar* was provided with an army Major, a Captain and ten Junior Commissioned Officers (JCOs). Major General Akbar Khan, who was given the code name Tariq,[11] assisted by Brigadier Sher Khan, commanded the entire force. The operational plan envisaged six Lashkars to advance along the main road from Muzaffarabad to Srinagar via Domel, Uri and Baramulla. Two Lashkars each were to make subsidiary moves from Haji Pir Pass to Gulmarg and Tithwal to Handwara, Sopore and Bandipore, with the twin objectives of securing large chunks of territory as also to protect the flanks of the main column. The D-day for Operation Gulmarg was fixed as October 22, 1947.[12]

The main attack was launched, as planned, on the night of October 21/22, 1947, at Muzaffarabad. The raiders made a dash for Baramulla and Srinagar. A valiant and courageous rearguard action by Brigadier Rajinder Singh,[13] Chief of Staff of the State Forces, and a handful of his men delayed the advance of the hostiles by four crucial days. This gave the Indian Army time to land its troops in Srinagar on the morning of October 27, after

Maharaja Hari Singh had signed the Instrument of Accession. The Indian Army fought some spirited actions around Srinagar city, the most noteworthy being the battle of Budgam and Shalteng. These actions resulted in the complete rout of the hostiles, who were chased by the Indian Army to Uri and beyond.

During the summer of 1948, Pakistan tried to enlarge the area of conflict by opening two more fronts in Gurez and Ladakh. In a bold and wide sweep, its forces struck simultaneously at Drass and Kargil, and launched a drive towards Leh. Gilgit was by then already under Pakistani occupation and the Skardu garrison was effectively surrounded. The latter finally gave up on August 14, 1948, after a resistance lasting over six months. State Forces very thinly defended all three. Kargil was captured on May 19, while Drass was occupied a little later. By the second fortnight of May, the hostiles were practically knocking at the doors of Leh and had simultaneously reached Machoi near the mouth of Zojila.[14] The entire Ladakh, Baltistan and Gilgit region had, thus, fallen into the raiders' hands, with the exception of Leh to its East. The bid to capture Zojila and roll down from there into the Valley was made towards the last week of May, when '1 Patiala' took up the defence of Zojila, together with a Company of '6 J&K Infantry' already stationed there.[15] There was no change in the position prevailing in the Valley during the latter part of 1948. With the Indian advance stalled at Uri and Tithwal, Muzaffarabad remained an elusive target. Indian successes in the Ladakh area, however, were more notable. In a significant operation, brilliantly planned and heroically executed, the Indian troops broke the Pakistani stranglehold over Zojila on November 1, 1948, with an almost super-human effort, conducting tank operations beyond 11,000 ft. and fighting in temperatures as low as minus 20°C. This success was quickly exploited by moving further to recapture Drass on 16 November, and Kargil on 21 November, 1948. Another Indian column had proceeded from Leh and, brushing aside enemy resistance in Nimu and Khaltsi, joined with their own troops at Kargil on November 24. With this link up, the Leh and Kargil areas had been saved from falling into Pakistan's hands. Skardu, the rest of Baltistan and the entire Gilgit region, however, could not be retrieved and remain under Pakistani occupation.

With India accepting the UN proposals for a cease-fire and Pakistan following suit, hostilities came to an end at midnight on December 31/January 1, 1949. India had lost over a third of the J&K State's territory amounting to 78,114 square kilometres. This included the strategic region of Baltistan-Gilgit in the Northern highlands, Muzaffarabad district in the Jehlum Valley, Mirpur District of the Jammu division, and half of the Poonch Jagir - a tremendous loss by any standards.

During the entire period of conflict the Indian government always gave an impression that it was dealing with Pakistan at two different levels. At worst, Pakistan was an adversary in the limited context of J&K; in other matters, the dealings between the two countries continued at the normal pace. The transfer of substantial amounts of money to Pakistan, as well as the flow of defence material to that country continued - even while the two armies were engaged in open combat in one part of India. Not even once, during the entire period of operations, did the Government of India initiate any move by which Pakistan could feel threatened for her misadventure in J&K. On the contrary, it appears that efforts were made to reassure the adversary that the entire conflict would remain localised. Not even a threat was held to strike at the vulnerable areas of Pakistan outside J&K. Even within the State, i.e., within Indian territory, the Indian Air Force (IAF) was made to operate with its hands practically tied behind its back.

The second war with Pakistan, again caused because of her obsession with J&K, took place in 1965 when the military dictator Ayub Khan was at the helm of affairs. His adventurism was matched equally by his fiery and impulsive foreign minister Z.A. Bhutto. Both had convinced themselves of their military superiority, and the operation was to be, in a way, a repeat enactment of the 1947-48 bid. The guerrilla infiltration by Pakistanis into J&K, planned under the code name *Operation Gibraltar*, was noticed on August 5, 1965. Effective and vigorous counter action by the Indian Army followed and a large number of infiltrators were eliminated or arrested. The dismal end of *Operation Gibraltar* failed to deter Ayub Khan and Z.A. Bhutto, and in fact had an opposite effect. With General Moosa, the Pakistani Commander-in-Chief, they decided to launch a full-scale invasion along the cease fire line. In response, the Indians attacked and occupied the tactically important and heavily defended Haji Pir Pass on August 24. On the morning of September 1, 1965, the Pakistani forces launched a massive armoured thrust, backed by a large-scale infantry assault and heavy shelling in Chhamb in the Jammu sector. Pakistan had launched *Operation Grand Slam* as a last and desperate gamble.

India gave a befitting reply across the International Border, striking Pakistan in the Lahore-Sialkot sector on September 6. In the ensuing seventeen days, the Indian forces reached the outskirts of Lahore and of Sialkot City. The subsequent declaration of ceasefire, and the events that followed, however, were to prove that the ignoble performance of Pakistan's military machine was more than counter balanced by its impressive performance in the field of foreign relations and diplomacy. Pakistan not only managed to retrieve her lost territory but also got back the strategic Haji Pir Pass.[16]

The 1971 war between India and Pakistan was occasioned by latter's internal problems with her Eastern wing, and the all consuming desire of the ruling classes of Pakistan to perpetuate its stranglehold on that less fortunate territory. The ruling elite, with Bhutto as the leader of the largest political party in West Pakistan, were not prepared to allow Mujib-ur-Rehman, a Bengali, to form the government at the centre despite the clear victory of the Bengali dominated Awami League in the national elections. The story of Bhutto's intransigence, the army's brutal repression and the civil war in East Pakistan, which led to the creation of Bangladesh, is well known. The two-nation theory, founded in the genteel living rooms of Uttar Pradesh, was finally laid to rest in the paddy fields of Bangladesh.[17]

During this conflict, major operations were conducted in J&K, particularly in the Jammu sector where the Pakistanis again took the initiative by attacking the Indian forces on December 3, and succeeded in occupying the areas right up to the Munnawar Tawi, including the village of Chhamb. In the Kargil sector, Indian troops succeeded in capturing some important enemy posts overlooking Kargil town,[18] thus removing the threat to the Srinagar-Leh Highway, as also to the town itself, which was under direct observation from the posts on this feature.

After the fiasco of 1971, resulting in the loss of its eastern wing and the defeat of its armed forces, Pakistan's prestige, with its economy and military capacity, touched rock bottom. Nevertheless, the abundance of petro-dollars in West Asia and Pakistan's deft use of the Islamic card helped stabilise her economy within a few years. During this period, Pakistan's flirtations with democracy proved short-lived and the Army once again assumed control of the country in July 1977. General Zia ul Haq ruled his country with an iron hand during the following eleven years, till his death in an air crash. Out of his own acute religious beliefs, as also the domestic compulsions of containing the deteriorating internal situation, Zia actively encouraged the spread of fundamentalist and sectarian organisations within Pakistan and later outside the country as well. The Russian intervention in Afghanistan in December 1978 and the rise of Ayotullah Khomeni in Iran towards the beginning of 1979, once again, brought into emphasis Pakistan's role as a 'front line state' and the most favoured ally in the eyes of the United States and her global interests. These factors further helped Pakistan consolidate her economy and build up military capabilities. The Inter Services Intelligence's (ISI's) considerable and active involvement in organising and sustaining anti-Soviet resistance by armed groups in Afghanistan provided Pakistan with enormous supplies of unaccounted arms and explosives, slush money and expertise in organising and spreading armed insurgency, an experience that was applied with telling effect in the Indian Punjab.

The experience gained in organising and sustaining militancy in Punjab was synthesised with the lessons learnt in the two abortive attempts to annex J&K in 1947-48 and in 1965. A blue print of activities, as outlined in what has been revealed as *Operation Topac*, was prepared and set into motion by the beginning of 1988. It aimed at creating disturbances in the State by appealing to the Muslim sentiments of the population. The magnitude of activities acquired a new scale in order to enlarge the base of sympathisers. Pakistan provided arms, explosives and training to the militants to begin a new round of insurgency. The third - and by far the most sinister and cunning - attempt to annex and appropriate the State of J&K had commenced.[19]

Pakistan-inspired militancy erupted during the middle of 1988 and gathered momentum slowly, assuming full-blown proportions by the beginning of 1990. This low-cost proxy war thrust on India by Pakistan has inflicted untold miseries on the people of the State, and a tremendous strain on the resources of the nation and on the Indian Security Forces. From January 1990 to the end of September 1999, 43,305 incidents of terrorist violence had taken place in the State, resulting in the death of 11,307 civilians, 10,429 militants and 1962 security forces personnel.[20] Forceful counter measures by the security forces, and the increasing alienation of the local population from the militants, brought the situation sufficiently under control to ensure the peaceful conduct of Parliamentary and State Assembly Elections in 1996. With the installation of a popular government, whatever little support the militants could muster amongst the local population shrank further to insignificance. This was a serious setback for Pakistan, and delivered an almost terminal blow to the apparatus of militancy that had so assiduously been built by the ISI. With the local elements amongst the militants decreasing progressively, Pakistan embarked on an alternative course, inducting foreign mercenaries in ever-increasing numbers. By 1997-98 the command and control of militancy had been taken over by these mercenaries, mostly belonging to Pakistan and Afghanistan, with a smattering of militants from countries including Sudan, Lebanon, Iran, and some of the Central Asian Republics. These *mujahideen* received their training and indoctrination in the fundamentalist seminaries - *madarsas* - of Pakistan. The experience of the *Taliban* experiment in Afghanistan was now being applied in J&K. This shift of emphasis from local to foreign elements, who were undoubtedly better trained, experienced, and more committed, did raise the levels of violence and the frequency of clashes with the security forces. But the primary objectives of disrupting the life of the people and discrediting the elected government were not realised. Even after sustained efforts of over a decade, Pakistan had not achieved anything beyond hurting and alienating the people of the State. It was against this backdrop that Pakistan appears to have focussed her attention on Kargil.

Kargil: The Response to Pakistan's Machinations

Pakistan's repeated attempts to establish a foothold amongst the people of Kargil and subvert their loyalties to the nation have been thwarted by the local population right since 1947. In 1948, the raiders had occupied almost the entire Kargil area for few months, but they were not able to get any support or co-operation from the locals. The spontaneous welcome and enthusiasm that greeted the Indian liberating forces amply demonstrated the attitudes of the population. Pakistan made no further attempts in this area, even in 1965 when large-scale infiltration was engineered along almost the entire length of the ceasefire line in rest of the State. During the 1971 Operations, a couple of villages were part of the area where the Indian Army had made advances. The response of the people of these villages towards the Indian troops, as also the civil administration, was sufficient indication of their sense of relief on having become part of India again.[21]

A bulk of the population of Kargil is very religious, professing an orthodox Shia faith. They have nothing in common with or sympathies for, the rulers of Pakistan. On the contrary they have always mistrusted and disliked them. There is no commonality between the *Kargalis* and the people of Pakistan apart from religion. Even this tenuous link does not create much leeway because of the deep Shia-Sunni divide. In fact, the Kargil population is of the same stock as the people of Baltistan. The oppressive rule Pakistan has perpetuated in the entire Northern Areas since 1947, has alienated the Kargil population even further. For the interpretation of the tenets of their faith, the people of Kargil have traditionally looked up to the famous Islamic institutions and renowned theologists in Iraq.

Against this backdrop, Pakistan's *modus operandi* for infiltration across the LoC in the Kargil area could not conform to the pattern that has been followed in other parts of the State. Tactics such as creation of cells comprising sympathisers among the local population, subversion of local youth, and use of fundamentalist front organisations to undermine the sentiment of the local population did not precede infiltration in Kargil. Instead, infiltration was effected without any support whatsoever from the locals. Indeed, clear evidence exists to show that Pakistani troops entered the area and occupied positions in such a manner as to deliberately avoid any contact with the local population. Over the past decade the people of Kargil have shown no interest in Pakistani designs on Kashmir, and the stray attempts made by the militants to use the Kargil territory for infiltrating into Kashmir have also failed, with heavy loss of men and equipment to them. This has probably been the most important reason why Pakistan's troops initiated and sustained intensive artillery attacks on Kargil town and the villages around it over the last few years, with considerable damage to life, limb and property in the area. The Pakistani shelling from across the LoC assumed serious proportions during 1998 and rose to a crescendo in the autumn of that year. According to an analyst, "Kargil town itself was devastated, and 17 civilians lost their lives. In a desperate attempt to ensure that the conflict did not escalate to the point where it would sabotage nascent efforts for a *rapprochement* with Pakistan, the Indian Army Chief, General V.P. Malik, is believed to have been instructed to ensure that his troops did not retaliate Pakistani fire with heavy caliber guns, including the 155-mm Bofors howitzers."[22]

Towards the latter half of 1998, Pakistani firing and shelling had seriously disrupted the life of the local population, especially between Drass and Kargil, and more so of the people of Kargil town.[23] Certain stretches of the road between Drass and Kargil, where Pakistan observers could see the traffic on the road, were so systematically brought under enemy fire that almost the entire vehicular movement on these stretches used to take place in the dark, with all lights, including the tail lights of vehicles, switched off. Kargil town wore a deserted look, and few shops would open even during the day. Shopkeepers and people working in government offices would move for safety to adjoining villages as soon as night fell and the local population's resentment against Pakistan had reached an all-time high. The shelling from across the border continued, at considerable intensity, till the end of October, tapering off thereafter to a practical standstill during end-November 1998. It picked up again only as the crisis broke out in May 1999.

Operation Vijay

It is now evident that Pakistani Army regulars along with the *Lashkar-e-Toiba* and the *Hizb-ul-Mujahideen* were responsible for crossing the LoC and occupying important heights as well as areas of tactical importance, right from the Mushkoh Valley to Chorbat La in Batalik and beyond and to Turtuk in the North. Though the exact timing of this ingress and occupation, and the preparation of defences in respect of each of the positions occupied, is yet to be reliably determined, it is safe to assume that this was done during autumn of 1998 and spring of 1999. Ironically, at the time of the Lahore-Bus-Diplomacy, and the meeting between the Indian Prime Minister and his Pakistani counterpart, in February 1999, considerable effort and resources of the Pakistan Army had already been expended towards creating trouble across the LoC in the Kargil sector. The confrontation between the Indian Army and Pakistani forces, which commenced in early May 1999, continued for two and a half months and even threatened a much wider conflagration at certain points, before the situation was defused in the second fortnight of July. During this period, the Indian Army, under *Operation Vijay*, used air power for the first time since 1971, although on a restricted scale and under considerable constraints. The salient features of the Kargil confrontation during this period comprise the following elements.

Trouble began on May 5 when two army patrols in the snow-clad Yaldor area in the Kargil region spotted a group of men, apparently from PoK. A larger patrol, which went to crosscheck, was ambushed and lost four soldiers.[24] A week later, based on the reports of the number of patrols sent along the LoC in this sector and on the basis of aerial reconnaissance, the army realised that the ingress by Pakistanis was fairly large and widespread on the ridges and areas of tactical importance in Mushkoh valley and facing Drass, Kaksar, Kargil and Batalik. Tentative Indian attempts to clear some of the positions attracted heavy bombardment by Pakistani artillery. The army also realised that, apart from the extensive scale of the operation, the Pakistani soldiers were not there with the narrow intention of infiltration, but had established regular positions with attendant defences and fortifications in most of the locations. Clearly, the situation was extremely serious from the Indian point of view although the extent of the Pakistani intrusion had not yet been fully realised.

By the middle of May, the army was discovering fresh Pakistani-held positions on an alarmingly regular basis spanning the entire Kargil sector; from the Mushkoh valley in the West to Chorbat La in the East.[25] Overseeing these operations, the 15 Corps Headquarters acknowledged that, by May 20, the Indian forces had lost 15 soldiers, with another 30 injured. 40 infiltrators had also been reported killed in the operations till that date. As the clashes between the two forces increased with the attendant intensity of shelling across the border, civilian life in the area was totally disrupted. Drass and eleven villages surrounding it were completely deserted. The Kargil town and villages around it registered a migration of more than 50 per cent of the population to safer areas, further south in the Suru Valley. The Chief Minister of Jammu and Kashmir, Farooq Abdullah, flew into Kargil on 18 May to reassure the local population, supervise relief work, and ensure an efficient functioning of the civil administration.[26] On May 25, the country's Cabinet Committee on Security met for the first time to review the prevailing situation.[27] More than 50 Indian soldiers were, by then, dead.[28]

The situation in Kargil entered a new phase when the IAF was brought in, though on a limited scale in a ground support role, on May 26. MiG fighter-bombers and helicopter gunships struck twice on that day against enemy formations in the Drass sector. All the targets engaged by the IAF were well on the Indian side of the LoC. The air strikes continued into the next day. Two MiG aircrafts were lost, with one MiG-27 M crashing after its pilot ejected following engine trouble; Pakistan captured Ft. Lt. Nachiketa, the pilot.[29] A MiG 21, on a location and rescue mission, was shot down and the pilot, Sq. Ldr. Ajay Ahuja, was captured and shot in cold blood. The IAF also lost one Mi-17 helicopter gunship and four crew the following day, after which attack helicopters were withdrawn from air operations and Mirage 2000s were pressed into service for aerial reconnaissance and special missions. The Mirages pounded the positions of the infiltrators with telling effect, especially in the Mushkoh valley using laser-guided rockets and cluster bombs. The Mirages superior avionics helped evade the Stinger missiles that had threatened earlier operations. The use of the Airforce came at a critical moment in the operations, when the Army's actions against the enemy were just picking momentum. The air strikes boosted the morale of Indian soldiers, with an opposite and desired impact on the enemy, even as they helped soften targets for eventual reoccupation by the infantry.

In addition to the deployment of the IAF, the Indian Navy was also put on high alert, and a certain repositioning of its ships undertaken, even though no occasion arose to use the fighting capabilities of India's sea power. Towards the end of May, the Indian Navy's strike elements were moved from the Eastern to the Western seaboard, and during the first week of June most of the Eastern Fleet was also moved to the Arabian Sea. These steps were intended to avoid any surprises and convey the kind of strategic threat that the Indian Navy could pose to Pakistan. The moves caused substantial concern in Islamabad.[30]

By June 6, troops and logistic build-up by the Army had been sufficiently achieved to launch effective counter-strikes in Kargil and Drass sectors with the immediate aim of clearing the threat to the vital line of communication on the Srinagar-Leh highway. June 9 was a dark day in the ongoing conflict when the mutilated and tortured bodies of Lt. Saurav Kalia and five others were received from Pakistan. These six Indian soldiers had been missing since May 14 while on a patrol in the Kaksar sector. "It was clearly aimed at causing a national outrage and provoking India further. It was just the most recent example of Pakistan's determination to prolong its Kargil offensive and escalate the war on Kashmir's borders and focus international attention on the dispute."[31]

The Indian counter-offensive produced its first significant result in the capture of Tololing Peak in the Drass Sector on June 13. It was on the same day that Prime Minister Vajpayee visited Kargil. He and his entourage had a near escape from Pakistani shelling. On July 2, Naik Inayat Ali of Pakistan's 5 Northern Light Infantry was captured in Batalik sector, providing concrete and irrefutable proof, if any proof was needed, of the Pakistan Army's presence and involvement on the Indian side of the LoC. By the beginning of July, considerable headway had been made in Mushkoh valley and Drass Sectors. However, the progress in Kaksar and Batalik was comparatively less, even though the army had maintained constant pressure.

American efforts to defuse the tension between India and Pakistan, and disengage the two armies, had started on June 15, with President Clinton urging Prime Minister Sharief to withdraw his country's forces from Indian territory. During the next three weeks intense diplomatic activity followed, including a visit by General Zinni to Islamabad. American pressure, widespread condemnation from the world community including China, and the Indian forces' gradual but unmistakable advances forced Nawaz Sharief and the Pakistan Army to back off. On July 11, Pakistani elements began retreating and the Indian territory was reportedly fully vacated on July 16, 1999. Two days before this, the Indian Prime Minister declared *Operation Vijay* a success.

In any military conflict it is almost impossible to exactly find out the resources used by the contending parties, and only rough estimates are possible. One report, quoting Lt. Gen. Krishan Pal, General Officer Commanding (GOC) 15 Corps, mentioned that, in all, nine battalions, including two teams of 9 Para, were deployed in Drass and Mushkoh sub-sector, six battalions in Batalik, while one battalion was used in Kaksar.[32] Pakistani manpower in this sector appeared to be in the range of eleven battalions, including Pakistan Army regulars, Northern Light Infantry Units, SSG troops and mercenaries.

The Indian Army also reportedly deployed 300 artillery pieces, including 100 Bofors guns. The IAF logged 550 strike missions, 150 reconnaissance missions and 500 escort missions. Besides, 2185 chopper sorties were also conducted. The cost of the conflict in monetary terms, for India, has been projected at Rs. 11.1 billion. In terms of manpower, the most precious national resource, 407 soldiers were killed, 584 injured and six are missing. Pakistani casualties were estimated to be at 696 killed.[33] In the final analysis, identifying the most important assets, a war-veteran of this area wrote, "Kargil proved that both young officers and the Bofors were a winning factor".[34]

The Assessment

Expert comments on and analyses of the Kargil operations have ranged between high praise for the Indian forces and stinging criticism of the failure of commanders and units in not being able to track enemy ingress sufficiently in advance and take immediate counter measures. The higher direction of operations, both at the military as well as the political level, also came under criticism. It would be useful to go through some representative samples of the post-operations assessment made by experts in the field. According to a former Vice-Chief of the Army Staff:

> Local commanders also ought to have been maintaining contact with the local village communities who have excellent information on any unusual movements in the area. I am totally mystified and perplexed as a military professional, how something of this kind could have happened. Frankly it is incredible — I am unclear whether there were helicopter patrols in winter, which we used to have in our time. If there were such patrols they should have certainly spotted something — I cannot believe a thousand to two thousand infiltrators could not be detected by routine physical patrolling.[35]

In a similar vein, Prem Shanker Jha, pointed out that the Indian Intelligence "has at least one and possibly two operatives in Switzerland; it failed to get even an inkling of Pakistan's purchase of 40,000 pairs of snowboots, ultra-light rucksacks, down-filled parkas and snow goggles last summer. Similarly, if it has an operative in Baltistan, that operative must have been fast asleep. For, the Pakistanis were improving roads and strengthening bridges to the LoC and building supply camps at its base all last summer." He also pointed out a serious gap in Indian armament, thus: "It is not only that Pakistani soldiers were far better equipped. It is that 80 per cent of all our deaths occurred in Pakistani artillery fire we couldn't suppress, as the army lacked a counter battery, or weapon-locating radar (WLR, which Pakistan has had for 15 years)."[36] K.Shankar Vajpai has opined that we cannot afford to handle security with our habitual slackness.[37] Another view on the enemy forces indicates:

> Pakistan relied primarily on troops from the Northern Light Infantry... because soldiers of this regiment are mostly young

> local men from the mountainous regions of Skardu, PoK, Baltistan, Gilgit and the North West Frontier Province. They are fully acclimatized to military activities at high altitudes. They were ordered to shed their uniform, put on *salwar kameez*, grow beards and wear skullcaps. Regular Pakistani army officers and soldiers carried out most of the military operations. Pakistan had also deployed squadrons of its helicopters and artillery to give cover to the military offensive. The Forces Commander, Northern Areas (FCNA) and the higher command of the 10th Corps of the Pakistan Army provided command and control and back-up for the military operation. We are dealing with a Pakistan army, which is a force indoctrinated in religious dogma and extremism without commitment to normal military norms.[38]

There may be important lessons for us in these observations. Commenting on Pakistan's strategy, Lt. Gen. V. R. Raghvan (Retd), former Director General of Military Operations, stated: "In this conflict Pakistan has chosen a ground or theatre of operations where India's military might cannot be brought to bear. It is not possible for India to use its strike Corps, tank divisions or air force to full advantage in these mountainous heights. The second factor to be borne in mind is that Pakistan's gambit of using a small element of its regular force with huge ballast of irregulars has succeeded in drawing a minimum of three Indian Divisions into a small pocket of Drass to Batalik."[39]

> The Pakistani perspective on this conflict is also interesting: The finest institution in this land, the bedrock of our existence, is now directly under attack because an initiative was not fully thought out as to possible consequences. More than a hundred officers and men of this magnificent army have paid a terrible price in blood for this negligence. On the other hand, though belated, we have begun to recognise the sacrifice and valour of the Northern Light Infantry (NLI). This was a must. No single unit of our Army has inflicted such damage on men, morale and equipment of the Indians in their history as the NLI has done, a handful holding at bay

> for weeks a force at least sixty to seventy times their strength. They deserve battle honours collectively and recognition of their valour individually. Though in sacrificing their life and limb they took a tremendous toll of the enemy in many times their own dead and wounded, because of mishandling the Indians have turned their military disaster on the ground into a victory in the media.[40]

Former Pakistan Army Chief General Aslam Beg has said that those who thought Kargil a misadventure "are cowards, the *mujahideen* have acted in a calculated way. Now it will be difficult for the international community and India to push Kashmir under the carpet".[41]

The Indian army, in addition to the lack of resources in the initial stages as well as the extremely difficult task of dislodging a determined adversary from well defended mountain heights, had to reckon with other disadvantages. Ideally the army would have adopted the "encircle and squeeze" tactic to evict intruders. "But it [had] strong orders not to cross the LoC into PoK which mean[t] that it [could not] really cut off the Pakistan army's supplies to the intruders at many of the key ridges. Also given the inhospitable terrain, which is almost like Siachin, the Indian army was initially ill prepared to take up such a large scale intrusion. Almost half of its front line troops were without what is known as "Glacier Clothing" to withstand extreme weather in the high reaches and fresh supplies took time in coming. Equipment malfunctioning and accuracy of fire was affected."[42] K. Subrahmanyam, the noted defence analyst, commented thus, on the higher direction of the national security issues:

> Kargil proves that national security cannot be handled as a part time vocation. It requires full time attention of a National Security Advisor and a fully and adequately manned National Security Council Secretariat and well-coordinated procedures to ensure that there are no lapses in intelligence assessment, policy formulation and purposeful direction in matters relating to country's security. That calls for a total revamping of our national security set up, which has to be undertaken after the elections.[43]

He also showered high praises on the leadership qualities of young officers who led from the front and took casualties disproportionate to average ratios, in terms of officers to *jawans*, in normal infantry battles, a view that was widely echoed.[44]

An Overview

Going by the deliberate nature of the defensive positions that the Pakistani troops had prepared in a number of places that they had held on the Indian side of the LoC, it is abundantly clear that the decision to cross the LoC and occupy territory on the Indian side was not taken in a hurry, but was a deliberate and calculated move. An enterprise of such proportions, which is likely to have long-term and serious implications on Indo-Pak relations, could only have been put into operation with the authority of the highest levels in Pakistan, both military as well as civililan, as Nawaz Sharief was not a push-over Prime Minister. The apparently calculated strategy appeared to be aimed at flogging dying militancy in Kashmir as also to put J&K back on the international agenda.

The Kargil operation was meticulously planned by the Pakistan Army and effectively executed. Its timing appears to have been motivated by Pakistan's acquisition of an overt nuclear status. It is no accident that the trans-border movement and occupation of territory by militants sent across by Pakistan, duly backed by troops without the involvement and support of the local population, had taken place for the first time after 1965. This view is supported by Maj. Gen. (Retd) Afsir Karim:

> The likelihood of a conventional war between India and Pakistan had gradually receded over the years due to India's growing in military superiority in conventional warfare and Pakistan's involvement in Afghanistan. The newly acquired nuclear capability of India and Pakistan has, however, changed the situation. Pakistan now feels confident enough to violate the LoC in strength without fearing serious reprisals or enlargement of the conflict. Pakistan is now secure that India cannot enlarge the conflict and attack Pakistan's heartland as it did in 1965.[45]

Irrespective of the motives and resources put behind the endeavours in the Kargil sector by Pakistan, the fact that Indian troops in that area were completely taken by surprise is a matter that cannot be overlooked. Obviously, something has been seriously amiss both at the strategic as well as the tactical level. The planning, briefings and preparations for operations of such nature and magnitude take months and a number of individuals and agencies do get involved at various stages. Also, troops would have had to be moved, equipped and trained for operations at such heights, and in difficult terrain. Equipment and supplies would have been moved and stocked at bases at Astore, Skardu and forward locations. That all this was done without any of the Indian intelligence agencies - Research and Analysis Wing, Intelligence Bureau and Military Intelligence - learning of it is a telling comment on the monumental failure on this count. These three premier agencies, apart from a few other minor players in the field, do have fairly significant resources and assets across the border. Each one of them must now have initiated appropriate corrective measures, but Kargil should also provide the impetus for co-ordinated functioning and better interaction between these agencies; something that has been lacking in the past.

Apart from the complete failure of the intelligence gathering mechanism, two other modes of collecting such information, viz. aerial surveillance and field patrolling were certainly not pressed into service to the desired extent. For these lapses and shortcomings, responsibility has to be shared by officers from the Unit Commander-level, upwards. There could be some justification in not being able to detect the movement of Pakistani troops in certain pockets on such a wide front, during the months of February or March, when movement on foot is extremely difficult. There is no valid reason for the infantry failing to get an inkling of the enemy's activities, which took place before the onset of winter, in 1998. Something as basic as routine patrolling to cover the front and inter-post contact patrolling had been either overlooked or not conducted with seriousness and requisite professionalism. Inappropriate and avoidable public controversy between the GOC, Leh Division, and the Commander of the Kargil Brigade also damaged the Army's image.

It is also surprising that even a fortnight after the Pakistani ingress was noticed on May 5, 1999, the army was not able to comprehend the serious nature of the infiltration and its motives. At this stage it appeared that the army knew nothing about the scale and character of the intrusion and even less about the structure of the war that was to follow. Furthermore, the GOC 15 Corps claimed that, 'the situation was local and would be defeated locally.' These observations were made at the Unified Headquarters meeting in Srinagar, on May 19, 1999, chaired by the State's Chief Minister. In fact, the CM's appreciation of the situation was nearer the truth. He opined that the 'recent infiltration was not a short-term plan but a sinister design of Pakistan aimed to isolate certain areas and cut off Kargil-Leh from the Valley, as was being done in Rajouri-Poonch area,' and that 'these were not mere militants but supported by some Pakistani regulars too'.[46]

The infiltration appears to have taken place in two phases. The first, and the deliberate one, must have commenced sometime during the summer of 1998 and culminated in preparation of regular defences, stocking and arrangements for occupation of these new posts during the long and harsh winter. In the next phase, the intruders either took possession of some of the Indian positions vacated during the winter, before these could be re-occupied by Indian troops, as per established routine, or moved forward and laterally from the prepared defences to enlarge the arc of infiltration.

It, however, does go to the credit of the army that after the details of infiltration became available and the seriousness of the incursions became evident, it reacted swiftly and decisively, not taking any further chances. According to reliable sources, almost five additional brigades were moved into the area of conflict, along with elements of specially trained commandos. Enough artillery, comprising field guns, howitzers, multi-barrel rocket launchers, etc., were positioned and used with telling effect. The logistics and administrative back up for such large-scale movement and maintenance thereafter were managed competently.

During the entire period of the conflict the media was given unprecedented access to the field of operations, in addition to regular briefings held at New Delhi down to local formation headquarters. The electronic media, with its extensive coverage, brought the war virtually to peoples' homes. The movement of such a large body of troops into Kargil necessitated the shifting of a number of units, which were engaged in the counter insurgency operations, from the Valley. Although some additional battalions of the Border Security Force and the Central Reserve Police Force were inducted, these were fewer in number and their impact poorer. Thus, Pakistan's moves in Kargil did seriously jeopardise the efficacy of the security forces' drive against militants, giving the ultras the necessary time to regroup and rework their strategy. The increased activity and effectiveness of the militants' strikes in the Valley and some parts of the Jammu division can, in no small measure, be attributed to this aspect.

The presence of men from certain militant organisations operating along with Pakistani troops in Kargil has introduced a new element into the ten-year-old militancy in the State. The Indian state will now have to contend with Islamic fundamentalism and the Afghan factor. It is well known that the Islamization of the Pakistan Army was assiduously undertaken by General Zia-ul-Haq, and that officers recruited during his time are now occupying middle-level positions, motivated and guided by some of the top generals. The Pakistan Army's involvement in Afghanistan has been quite substantial and has continued over a long period. This has further strengthened its links with fundamentalist forces. According to some analysts, there is a speculation that the Pakistan Army may be creating an entity within itself, composed of Afghans, which may come in handy for use in J&K or other areas. This would enable Pakistan to harass India, and, at the same time, claim that it is not involved.[47] Masood Khalili, who represents the exiled Afghan Government in New Delhi, feels that the same combination of Pakistan's forces, under its Inter Services Intelligence's control and Arab mercenaries operating with the inspiration of Osama bin Laden, are fighting in both Kargil and Kapisa.[48] Indian defence planners will have to take into account factors such as the Afghan links of the Pakistani Army and also the fact that it is imbued with religious fundamentalism. Having tested the waters in Kargil, such a misadventure by Pakistan cannot be ruled out in other isolated valleys like Gurez-Tilel, Machhil and Tangdar.

In the ten years of terrorist activities in Kashmir, Pakistan had never attempted such a venture, and this strategic shift demands a re-examination of India's approach towards Pakistan. An incoherent policy must make way for a cogent policy.[49] Such a re-examination does appear to be under consideration and the Government of India had instituted an inquiry into the events that led to Pakistan's incursions into Kargil. If these developments result in a comprehensive reassessment and reappraisal of the entire gamut of India's policies towards Pakistan the crisis in Kargil could well prove to be a window of opportunity.

The Options

India has had to deal with Pakistan as a difficult neighbour and a source of constant trouble, mostly an irritant, but at times downright dangerous. It would be a useful exercise to take a broad overview of developments, particularly over the last ten years and the more recent Kargil conflict, to analyse and understand the broad contours of policy formulations and the pursuit of India's national objectives in relation to Pakistan. The Indian response to the Kargil intrusion must be understood in the overall perspective of ongoing militancy in J&K, as well as the continuing stand-off in the icy-heights of Siachen. According to a former Chief of the Indian Army:

> As part of its prolonged *jihad* against India, peace is perceived as a temporary phase, to last only until preparations for the next round can be made. We must heed this strategic lesson of the last fifty years, and plan our long term national security — Pakistan's hostility will stay with us for a long time and the nation must be prepared to sleep next to its weapons for the foreseeable future.[50]

Any country dealing with an inimical neighbour has a number of options, which can be resorted to, singly or in combination. These include diplomatic, economic and military measures. A panoramic appraisal of India's dealings with Pakistan during the last fifty years indicates that India has depended upon diplomatic initiatives and accepted norms of international behaviour far too much and far too long. Commencing with India's recourse to the

United Nations in January 1948, down to the involvement of the US President in June 1999, it has been a long and tortuous journey down the diplomatic alley. Indian diplomatic endeavours and negotiations in relation to Pakistan have primarily resulted in perpetuating the *status quo*, with the end result weighed in favour of Pakistan. The fact is, diplomacy can be used as an effective tool to safeguard national interests only if it is backed by credible military strength. Besides, a clear signal needs to be sent to the adversary that military means would be used, where necessary. There is, thus, an urgent need for a fundamental shift in India's application of diplomacy as a tool for securing vital national interests.

The military option must, of course, be kept open. At the same time, India can continue to explore ways and means to achieve its goals of stalling, blunting and neutralising Pakistani machinations in diplomatic encounters at different international gatherings, UN fora and multilateral groupings. This is in addition to a strategy of diplomatic containment and isolation of Pakistan through closer ties with Iran, the Central Asian Republics and Russia, as these countries are adversely affected by Islamic terrorism.

The Kargil episode also unmistakably points towards the growing dangers of Pakistan's Afghan connection and its dangerous implications for India's security. In a way, Kargil has been an extension of the policy pursued in Afghanistan by Pakistan's rulers over the last two decades. Pakistan has not only been able to put its creation, the *Taliban*, in a pre-eminent position of power in that state, but is also on the threshold of acquiring the much needed strategic depth that it lacked so far. Pakistan is also indulging in wishful thinking, hoping that it may have finally solved one of its abiding problems — the Durand Line dividing the two countries which no Afghan ruler or government has ever accepted for over a century. Even during his most difficult period, Najibullah did not accept Pakistan's demand for the recognition of the Durand Line. India has always maintained extremely cordial relations with all the governments and rulers in Afghanistan, with the exception of the *Taliban*. Kargil must act as a catalyst and prompt India to make all efforts to become a major player in Afghanistan's affairs and, to that extent, revamp its Pakistan policy and make it an integral part of its Afghanistan policy. Such a focus can help wean Afghanistan away from Pakistan and deal a blow to the main centre of Islamic fundamentalism, drug trafficking and international terrorism that this region has become. The anti-*Taliban* forces and elements could be taken as allies in this endeavour. There are also reports that the *Khalq* and *Parcham* factions of yesteryear have not been entirely obliterated, even amongst the *Taliban*.

Apart from managing to divert a good number of Indian units and formations to the Kargil sector, Pakistan's exertions there have imposed a very high economic cost on India. India cannot afford to let the troop deployment in this area cause depletion in its strike and reserve forces, beyond a short period. The raising of more units is, consequently, inevitable, with attendant logistics, cost and efforts required for occupation, maintenance and fighting at such heights and in extreme climatic conditions. The cost of suitably clothing and outfitting a single soldier is estimated at Rs.200,000. Added to this would be the cost of the establishment of a requisite number of border posts, hardware in terms of guns, vehicles and equipment. These troops will also require special devices like night vision gadgets, battlefield radar, satellite surveillance, etc. to operate in that area. According to one estimate, the total cost would be in the range of Rs.24 billion annually. Against this, the additional expenditure by Pakistan in this field would be practically negligible. This asymmetrical situation must change and India needs to engage Islamabad in an arms race by raising its defence expenditure from 2.3 per cent to 4 per cent of GDP. This will force Pakistan either to spend nearly 70 per cent of its budget on defence, or reach an accommodation with India. The Soviet Union's example shows that while nuclear bombs and ballistic missiles may secure the country from external aggression, they cannot prevent internal discontent.[51]

General Parvez Musharraf, Pakistan's military ruler, announced in mid-December 1999, that Pakistan's defence expenditure would be reduced by Rs. 700 billion. This may have been a statement made for the benefit of the international community, specifically international lending agencies, which have been blowing a whistle on Pakistan. Purely in terms of national economic indicators, India is in a much better position than ever before to enhance its defence budget. After a decade of nearly 6 per cent growth, India is strong enough to take on Pakistan both on the battlefield and in the market place. After years of persistent economic troubles, and now in the throes of a serious balance of payments crisis, Pakistan will have to pay an unaffordable price to wage a larger war.[52] Instead of continuously reacting to Pakistan, therefore, forcing an increase in the allocation of her scarce financial resources to its security apparatus would be far more effective.

To any informed observer and analyst, Pakistan is at best an enigma. A nation created on the basis of religion has already been divided by a nationalist movement in its Eastern part. None of the four provinces in West Pakistan supported its creation almost till the mid-1940s. The official language of Pakistan, Urdu, is not the spoken dialect of any of its provinces. Right from the beginning, Punjab has ruled over the other provinces. Not only the religious minorities but Muslims professing a faith different from the orthodox *Sunnis* are treated as second class citizens and feel unsafe. A significant number of lives have been lost, some even while offering prayers in mosques, in the clashes between the protagonists of militant elements of the *Shia* and *Sunni* sects. Baluchs, Sindhis, Muhajirs and even the Saraiki segment of Punjab are all restive against Punjabi domination; the list is endless and so are the centrifugal tendencies inherent in Pakistan. If this country has been consistently trying to create problems for India by manipulating a small section of the latter's population, it is time that it was paid back in the same coin.

In addition, and even more importantly, India should be prepared to use the military option and send clear signals to this effect. According to Lt. Gen. Satish Nambiar (Retd), India should buy time, make up the deficiencies in equipment, spares, etc., fine-tune plans and prepare to launch the offensive at a time and place of its choosing. India has reacted to Pakistani moves for far too long. Things now have to be done in such a manner as to make Pakistan react to our moves. Whether this entails crossing the LoC or the international border is an option that should remain open.[53] The GOC of 15 Corps has also spoken in a similar vein emphasising that Pakistan is not going to stop its anti-Indian activities. It wants to carry on with the low-cost war, which has already become a great burden on India. Unless India raises the costs for Pakistan, in whatever way it chooses, it will be very difficult to put an end to this low-cost war. The covert war is lucrative for Pakistan, both militarily and strategically.[54]

India has depended excessively on the sympathy of the international community by presenting itself as a victim and hoping for some kind of reward, which has not come its way. In fact, at each important turn of events effecting India's national security, India emerged as the net loser. Every nation has to take measures to secure its own interests. The more a nation asserts itself, the more it is respected in the contemporary world. India should be prepared to act decisively, retaliate comprehensively and make any adventure on the part of the adversary prohibitively expensive. K. Subrahmanyam has succinctly outlined this approach: "What India has to focus on is how to deal with this militarised polity with nuclear weapons, sponsoring cross-border terrorism, being obsessed with Islamic extremism and harbouring a visceral hatred for India. Till now India has largely been on the defensive with Pakistan taking the offensive on the Kashmir issue. A time has come when India has to take the initiative."[55]

The Strategy

In essence, India should realise the limitations of diplomacy and international support to its cause and vital national interests in light of the experience of the past fifty years. India needs to give a fresh look to the ties and linkages with Afghanistan and the friendly elements there, aiding, supporting and bolstering them. It must be remembered that the security of the Indian landmass is best ensured on the *Karakoram* and the *Hindu Kush* and that Afghanistan is necessarily a very valued ally there. India should make Pakistan spend so much on her defence effort that the economy gets a shattering blow, in a befitting response to the latest cost escalation forced due to Kargil operations, as also the militancy for last ten years in the Valley. India should wrest the initiative from Pakistan in all security-related matters in the future. "So far the lesser state is in the driver's seat."[56] Lastly, India should follow an active policy along the LoC and plan and prepare to strike at a point of her choosing, which would yield maximum results.

The Kargil conflict gave India an opportunity that it was unprepared to turn to its advantage. India should be ready in the next round to secure optimum results. Pakistan will certainly create another opportunity. At this stage, India can make deep penetration strikes to register its military superiority as well as national resolve and drive home an unmistakable lesson in language that is understood, that the cost of tampering with its security would be prohibitively high. Other attendant measures on diplomatic initiatives and costs can be taken in tandem with this decision.

In forecasting aggressive postulations the Indian planners will be faced with the choice of concentrating the main thrust of the military forces on the international border, the PoK or the Northern Areas. In so far as the international border is concerned, efforts and resources utilised can give us the benefit of hitting at Pakistan's war machine and making a serious dent. But the long-term benefits may not be very tangible, as international pressures would make India withdraw from the territory that might fall in its hands, as has happened in the past. Pakistan's nuclear capability is also a relevant factor. It might well be the first to mount a nuclear strike and argue before the world that, as a much smaller country, it had to do so for its own sheer survival. Irrespective of the retaliatory measures that India might take, the damage to India's armour and personnel would be very considerable.

In PoK, any Indian advance would have the advantage of bringing the territory under India's control. But this is an area where the Pakistan Army would react very strongly - this has been the pattern right from the beginning. Pakistan occupied the *Haji Pir Pass* at the first possible opportunity during the winter of 1947-48. In the offensives in the Tithwal sector, in June 1948, the only position occupied by the Indians across the *Kishanganga* river was Ring Contour, which was taken back by Pakistani troops in a determined counter-attack. Similarly, during the Indian forces' bid to recapture Muzaffarabad in the summer of the same year, an important feature, *Pandu*, was captured, facilitating further advance. Pakistani troops made strenuous efforts in recapturing that hill position, thereby stalling India's advance towards Muzaffarabad. Pakistan has always considered PoK as vital for its security. In April 1948, Lt. Gen. Gracey, the then Commander-in-Chief of the Pakistan Army, explained Pakistan's interest in this area:

> An easy victory of the Indian Army, particularly in the Muzaffarabad area, is almost certain to arouse the anger of tribesmen against Pakistan for its failure to render them more direct assistance and might well cause them to turn against Pakistan... If Pakistan is not to face another problem of about 750,000 people uprooted from their homes; if India is not to be allowed to sit on the doorsteps of Pakistan to the rear and on the flank, at liberty to enter at her will and pleasure; if civilian and military morale is not to be affected to a dangerous extent; and if subversive political forces are not to be let loose within Pakistan itself, it is imperative that the Indian Army is not allowed to advance beyond the general line Uri-Punch-Nowshera.[57]

By employing different means, including military, diplomatic and personal influences at that time, the British establishment in India ensured that the Indian advance was checked precisely along this line. Since then, the importance of PoK has considerably increased from Pakistan's point of view. The Mangla Complex has to be protected, and this region is proximate to its nuclear establishments and the capital Islamabad. The mountainous terrain and difficult communication in PoK would make a significant Indian advance there a difficult proposition. The population composition and its negative attitude towards India would also be a factor that has to be taken into consideration.

The third possible sector where an Indian advance could be considered is the Northern Areas. It is the nomenclature given to the huge land mass - more than seventy thousand square kilometre of the State's territory - illegally occupied by Pakistan in 1947. It comprises the Himalayan tableland of Baltistan, Gilgit and areas further North. The people of the Northern Areas are directly ruled by the Centre from Islamabad - a regime that has been harsher and more degrading to human dignity, life and property than the Pakistan's control over PoK. Successive governments, over the past five decades, have followed a policy that left its inhabitants with no political identity, civil rights or even constitutional status. They are denied the right to vote, have no legislature and do not have access to justice in the form of appeals to the High Court or the Supreme Court.

The Northern Areas have been divided into five districts, namely Gilgit, Skardu, Diamer, Ghizer and Ghanche; the sixth unit being Hunja-Nager. The administration is practically headed by the Joint Secretary, Ministry of Kashmir Affairs in Islamabad, with the help of six officers, all non-natives and deputed from outside. These apart, other officers include the Commissioner, the Inspector General of Police, the Deputy Commissioner, the Judicial Commissioner and the Chief Engineer, Public Works Department. The Northern Areas are being ruled under the provisions of Frontier Crimes Regulations, left behind by the British, who considered the locals as half savage and half criminal. With a population of 1.5 million, literacy is dismally low at 14 per cent for males and 3.5 per cent for females. There is one school for 4,000 children and one doctor for 6,000 people; protected drinking water outside important towns is a dream and more than two-thirds the population has no access to electricity.

Deprivation of the rights of the people, a deteriorating economy and subjugation, coupled with active efforts of the government to alter the demographic pattern by settling increasing numbers of persons from the North West Frontier and Afghanistan, have made the local population restive. *Shias* and *Ismailis* form the bulk of the population of the Northern Areas. With the rise of Sunni fundamentalism and the *Talibanisation* of Pakistan, they have been subjected to increased discrimination based on sectarianism. Lately, there have been signs of social tension manifested periodically in various forms, especially since the summer of 1996.

Contrary to Pakistan's sustāined interest in the Northern Areas and the realisation of its strategic importance, the Indian interest in this region has always been peripheral. During the 1947-48 operations, little attention was paid and military resources were not made available to wrest the region back from Pakistani occupation. Even during the subsequent decades, Indian intelligence agencies have not tried hard enough to create assets there. This, in spite of the fact that the local population has not been very favourably disposed towards the rulers in Islamabad.

Thus, in comparison to the international border and PoK, the political situation and the ground conditions in the Northern Areas are far more conducive to a determined military push, as and when required. The Pakistani misadventure in Kargil has given an opportunity to India to increase its military presence in the Ladakh region, to which Pakistan cannot make any objection. Force levels has already been raised to a Corps Headquarters, with three Infantry Divisions. Land communications on the Indian side are much better. According to Lt. Gen. Moti Dhar, former Vice Chief of the Army Staff, 'Pakistan has very poor and stretched lines of communication in this area. We always used to consider Kargil an excellent theatre of offensive operations for India because of its superior communications infrastructure. The fact that we have a highway there should be seen as an asset than a cause for concern.'

The infrastructure created and installations developed here could be used to increase the build up to the desired level and use the present deployment as a springboard for future operations. Of course, considering the terrain and the difficulties of living and fighting at high altitudes and bleak mountain tops, the troops staying there and those who would be required to undertake operations there would have to be specially trained and suitably acclimatised. The usefulness of stepping up the enrolment of the local population in the forces can hardly be over- emphasised. The fighting qualities of the Ladakh Scouts and local troops, right since 1947, and more recently during Kargil operations, have been amply proved.

In the Ladakh area, Suru and Nubra Valleys could be developed as bases and launching pads for offensive operations into the Northern Areas. Another alternative from the Valley side can be the Gurez-Burzil Pass-Deosai plateau axis. In fact, Gen. Thimaya had planned *Operation Snipe* in the summer of 1948 to recapture Skardu along this line, pushing ahead from Gurez. For this purpose, he had asked for a brigade to be maintained by air for one week. Since that was not made available Gen. Thimaya's plan was not executed.[58] Moreover, the willingness of Pakistan's generals to commit resources for the defence of the Northern Areas, by shifting forces from the hinterland, is also in serious doubt.[59]

Pakistan's much vaunted nuclear capabilities would pose minimum danger to the Indian troops operating across the Northern Areas, as compared to those operating in the other two sectors. Moreover, due to the terrain, the damage to the Indian forces would be so little that Pakistan would have to think twice before launching a nuclear first strike as the Indian response would inflict much greater and unacceptable destruction.

Apart from physical preparations, the Indian Army will also be required to change its tactics and mindset for achieving success. For too long, Indian response to Pakistani unorthodox tactics and unconventional use of forces has been in the form of traditional and predictable set-piece moves. Even during the last eleven years of militancy in J&K, the Army's efforts to meet Pakistani terrorism have not indicated adequate appreciation of non-traditional and unorthodox tactics on the part of the troops. Beyond doubt, Kargil has proved the bravery, leadership qualities and fighting spirit of Indian soldiers and young officers. An appropriate change of mindset and due support from higher commanders would be a pre-requisite for making bold forays into Indian territory being illegally held by Pakistan since 1947. India's ultimate aim should be to not only teach a lesson to the constant acts of aggression by Pakistan but also to push its borders Northwards to the natural frontiers of India.

Summation

Who has been the winner in this conflict and where do we go from here? India can consider the outcome in Kargil only in a limited sense and of pyrrhic nature. The adversary was not defeated, and no territory was gained. India was only able to get its territory vacated, that too, not all of it, at the point of the bayonet, and at an enormous cost in terms of men, material and money. For Pakistan, it has been much less costly and affordable to even induce it to undertake similar adventures in the future, unless the cost of any such rash actions are raised beyond acceptable limits to the perpetrator. The pattern established from 1947 onwards and refined during the last decade will continue to be followed. The events at Kargil should make India reassess its dealings with Pakistan. This can only happen if unambiguous signals are sent—that the nation's patience has reached a threshold.

The proxy war launched by the ISI in the State of Jammu and Kashmir since 1988 culminated in the Kargil conflict.

Pakistan's adventure in Kargil has been condemned by the world at large. The USA exerted pressure on Pakistan to withdraw its forces from Indian territory, which it subsequently did. Despite these, Pakistan has not shown any let up in its efforts to continue to create problems in J&K.

The taking over of the reigns of power in Pakistan by the military once again may or may not be attributable to its involvement in Kargil. But, the future course of action is likely to be pursued even more resolutely by Pakistani agencies involved in fomenting trouble on the Indian side. This has been amply proved and the process goes on.

In spite of its small size, weaker economic base, internal dichotomy and smaller armed forces, Pakistan has initiated three wars against India, followed by a decade-old militancy in J&K leading to the Kargil conflict, and has come out as a net gainer. This has been achieved through a combination of artful use of guerrilla tactics and conventional warfare, a highly skilled pursuit of foreign policy, coupled with diplomatic finesse.

Pakistan came to realise very early that it pays to be aggressive and belligerent. It is pursuant to this realisation that it has succeeded in only retaining its illegitimate gains of 1947-48 and repeating the policy of adventurism in 1965, and, then, again in the current round. In the proxy war launched by the ISI in the State in 1988, the operating principle was to mislead the youth, subvert the civilian population and keep the Indian forces bleeding, so that political and public opinion in India would buckle under constant losses and accept the futility of the holding on to the State. A failure to achieve its primary aim seems to have spurred Pakistan into going ahead with the Kargil misadventure; the onslaught on India's security continues unabated. As has been once again confirmed recently by Indian military authorities, the incidence and viciousness of militancy in India has increased after the army took over in Pakistan.[60]

What should be of particular concern to Indian policy makers is that there has been a paradigm shift in Pakistan's hostility towards India. In the beginning, the anti-India tirade was more or less confined to the ruling elite, but over the decades, an increasing segment of the population is getting sucked into this phenomenon. Presently, large sections of its civil society, political and religious organisations, the military, the intelligence and scientific community are irrational, and motivated by a burning desire to teach India a lesson. These irrational elements advocate what they call the doctrine of permanent *jehad* against India, till India breaks into "a million pieces" (to quote Qazi Hussain Ahmad, the Amir of Jamait-e-Islami Pakistan).[61] The underlying philosophy of Pakistan's current phase of onslaught on India's security interests was amply summed up by Mushahid Hussain on 18 May, 1991, when he said, "Pakistan has apparently adopted in regard to Kashmir an Afghan model, essentially a protracted war which has made Kashmir into a bleeding wound for India, raising the political, military and psychological costs of its occupation".[62]

In contrast, India's responses have been passive, reactive and defensive. India has not only lost much of its territory but also failed, more than once, to take advantage of its military strength in forcing a lasting solution to the problem during the conflict in 1947-48, and repeated the same attitude in 1965 by returning the *Haji Pir Pass*. Even being the decisive victor in the 1971 war, India's magnanimity was boundless and unilateral. As in the military field, India's position at the United Nations, and with the world community, has continuously been defensive and reactive. If India wanted to teach a lesson to Pakistan and pay it back in the same coin, a window of opportunity had certainly been created by the Kargil episode to launch a massive and coordinated campaign against terrorists. India failed to wrest the initiative and militants are striking once again in J&K, with considerable regularity and effectiveness. According to KPS Gill, "The terrorist handlers in Pakistan must be congratulating themselves on the success of their current strategy as the death toll in Jammu and Kashmir mounts, and as the terrorists deliver blow after blow against the morale of the security forces".[63] According to analysts, there has been persistent worsening of the ratio of security force to militant casualties. This ratio has declined from 1:5.79 in 1997, through 1:4.54 in 1998 and further to 1:3.20 in 1999. Worse, with the thinning out of the security forces, in the wake of Kargil and subsequent escalation in Pak-backed terrorist activity, this ratio fell to 1:2 in June 1999.[64] The time has come to call Pakistan's bluff. Indian riposte should be quick, effective and decisive.

In all the problems that have been created for India by Pakistan, the Pakistan Army has been a common denominator. It has also been a constant factor in the power equations in Pakistan, even when civilians were governing the country. The army's influence over the government and the people of Pakistan has been has been all-pervasive. Under General Parvez Musharraf, the Government of Pakistan and the army are going to be even more inimical to India's security interests. The army is more fervently committed to *jehad* against India than any other section in Pakistan. India should do well to remember that the power there has now fallen to the architect of the Kargil conflict. The crying need for India is to take urgent and effective steps to control Pakistan's mischief making capacity. This has been brought out by an editorial in the *Times of India*, in these words:

> A society which does not feel a sense of threat after the loss of over twenty thousand lives over ten years of terrorism directed by a neighbouring state, after having fought a limited war involving more than 450 fatalities, and after being continuously engaged in a proxy-war, is bound to be subjected to further acts of terrorism and aggression. Its complacency and casualness actually ask for it.[65]

As a socicty, government and nation, India has not only not taken any firm action against Pakistan, whenever it was forced to take arms against it, India has not shown any willingness to fight to the finish or take the fight into the enemy's camp; India has constantly displayed a lack of ruthlessness. The age-old and ancient Indian psyche of fighting the war along certain time honoured principles and rules has done incalculable harm down the ages, and continues to afflict it even today. This must change. Chanakya, the great Indian strategist, had once said that except in matters of the security of the State, means are as important as ends. As a nation India never desired or worked towards the destruction of Pakistan; but to keep it intact at its own peril would certainly not be a sensible proposition. Preservation of Pakistan's integrity and its survival as an independent nation in friendship with India is certainly a desirable objective to work for, but not at the cost of India's own security, integrity and its very existence. India should, therefore, be prepared to take bold initiatives, decisive action and conclusive exertions in the next round, an opportunity that may present itself quite soon.

Kargil has caused India a lot of anguish; it has also stirred its soul. Kargil can now become a defining moment, a watershed and a new beginning, spreading a beacon to the new avenues and opportunities that lie before this nation. The sacrifices of those who died for the nation and the mourning of those left behind cannot be allowed to go in vain.

NOTES AND REFERENCES

1. Dinesh Kumar, *Times of India* (New Delhi), July 16, 1999.
2. This is the estimated population in 1991 as no Census was conducted in J&K State due to disturbed conditions. The population figures of this area during 1981 Census were 61,990.
3. Information Department, Government of Jammu and Kashmir, *District Profiles*, Srinagar, 1998, pp. 381-82.
4. In fact, the territories of the Princely State of J&K extended to areas beyond Gilgit and included principalities like Chitral, Hunza, Nagar, Chilas, etc.—including some areas even North of the Karakoram Pass.
5. E.F. Knight, *Where Three Empires Meet*, London, Longmans Green & Co., 1919, p. 290, p. 289 and p. vii.
6. *Ibid.*, p. 289.
7. *Ibid.*, p. vii.
8. Defence of India Policy Plans, New Delhi, Orient Longman, 1963, p. 23.
9. S. S.Bloeria, *Battles of Zojila* - 1948, New Delhi, Har Anand, 1996, p. 174.
10. B. Raman, *Frontline* (Madras), July 30, 1999.
11. Tariq is the name of a legendary military commander who led Arab forces into Spain in the Seventh century. On landing on the coast of Spain he had burnt his boats to spur his troops to fight for victory. As is evident in his book, *Raiders in Kashmir*, General Akbar Khan (he was, in fact, a Brigadier then) relished his code name.

12. S.N. Prasad and Dharam Pal (eds.), *History of Operations in Jammu and Kashmir* (1947-48), New Delhi, Government of India, Ministry of Defence, 1987, pp 17-19.
13. Brigadier Rajinder Singh was posthumously awarded the first Maha Vir Chakra of independent India.
14. In the native language "Zojila" means "Path of Blizzards," a befitting name for the Pass, as would be sufficiently evident after studying its topography. Also, the Zojila is known by other names such as Seojila, Baltal Kotal, Dras Pass, Zogila and Swaje La, etc. In the great Himalayan mountain range starting from Mount Everest in the East to Nanga Parbat in the West, Zojila is the lowest depression at 11,578 ft. above mean sea level. All other passes are over 14,000 ft. For the major part of the year, all these Passes, including Zojila, remain closed due to snow and avalanche.
15. 1 Patiala, under the spirited command of Lt. Col. Sukhdev Singh, Vr. C., MVC, fought a series of successful actions against the enemy, earning six MVCs and 12 Vr. Cs. during its six months-stay at Zojila.
16. Haji Pir Pass is an important military feature and its occupation also implies the availability of an alternative land route between Jammu and the Kashmir Valley, via Poonch.
17. Tariq Ali, "A General Paralysis," *Sunday* (Calcutta), Vol. 11, No. 4, August 14-20, 1983.
18. The most important of these heights was a mountaintop known as 13,620—the figure being the height in feet of the feature. This ensured the security of Kargil town as well as the Leh-Srinagar road in that sector. This height, in fact, was so near to Kargil town that it was jokingly said that any Pakistani sitting with binoculars at that post could become a referee in the badminton match being played in the officers' mess of the Brigade Headquarters at Kargil.
19. S.S. Bloeria, *Pakistan's Insurgency vs. India's Security*, New Delhi, Manas, 2000, pp. 93-94.
20. Data provided by J&K Police.
21. I was SDM, Kargil, in 1974 and had interacted with these people on a number of occasions. My observations are based on sustained contact with them.
22. Praveen Swami, "The Kargil War: Preliminary Explorations", *Faultlines* (New Delhi), Vol. 2, May 1999, p. 31.
23. I was on a visit to Leh and Kargil during September 1998, and was witness to the damage caused as I travelled by road from Srinagar.
24. Romesh Vinayak, *India Today* (New Delhi), May 11, 1999, p. 31. According to Praveen Swami, *Frontline*, July 30, 1999, p. 7, local grazers established the first physical contact with Pakistani troops and regulars in the Kargil sector on Jubbar heights, on May 3.
25. Praveen Swami, "The Kargil War: Preliminary Explorations", *op. cit.*, p. 4.
26. In fact, J&K Chief Minister Farooq Abdullah made a number of visits to Kargil during the two-and a-half months of the conflict. His frequent on-the -spot study of the situation helped restore confidence amongst the local population and exerted a salutary pressure on the civil administration so that it carried out its functions fairly well under exceptionally trying circumstances.

27. Praveen Swami, "The Kargil War: Preliminary Explorations", *op. cit.*, p. 6. According to Praveen Swami, this meeting took place a day after Farooq Abdullah visited New Delhi to beg the Prime Minister to take the Kargil issue seriously. "It says not a little about the chaotic management and poor strategic appraisal that characterised this period".
28. *Ibid.*, p.14.
29. On June 3, 1999, Pakistanis returned the Indian pilot 'as a gesture of goodwill'.
30. The United Service Institution (USI) Director, Lt. Gen. (Retd.) Satish Nambiar, cited in S. Kalyanaraman, "Beyond Kargil: Compilation of a Panel Discussion", USI Journal (New Delhi), Vol. 129, No. 537, July-September 1999, p. 333.
31. Manoj Joshi and Raj Changappa, *India Today*, June 21, 1999, p. 21.
32. Dinesh Kumar, *Times of India*, July 19, 1999.
33. Swapan Dasgupta, in *India Today*, July 26, 1999, p. 32.
34. Personal communication from Brig. Sukhdev Singh Retd),Vr. C., M.C, who commanded 1 Patiala during the historic battles for Zojila in 1948, October 15, 1999.
35. Lt. Gen. Moti Dhar (Retd), quoted in *Frontline*, August 27, 1999, pp. 22-23. Gen. Dhar also commanded a brigade in Ladakh area and had been the Brigade Major of the Kargil Brigade.
36. *Outlook* (New Delhi), August 9, 1999, p. 34.
37. *Times of India*, June 12, 1999.
38. J. N. Dixit, in *Indian Express* (New Delhi), July 22, 1999.
39. Lt. Gen. (Retd) Satish Nambiar, cited in S.Kalyanaraman, "*Beyond Kargil: Compilation of a Panel Discussion*", *op. cit.*, p.336
40. Ikram Sehgal, *The Nation*, 31 July, 1999, as reported in *Times of India*, August 1, 1999.
41. Sunil Narula, in *Outlook*, June, 21,1999, p.99.
42. Joshi and Changappa, *op. cit.*, p.26.
43. *Times of India*, July 26, 1999.
44. Personal communication from Brig. Sukhdev Singh, *op. cit.*
45. *Times of India*, June 4, 1999.
46. Praveen Swami, in *Frontline*, September 10, 1999, pp. 33-34. The quotes have been supported by photocopies of the minutes of the UHQ meeting.
47. Lt. Gen. (Retd) Satish Nambiar, cited in S.Kalyanaraman, "*Beyond Kargil: Compilation of a Panel Discussion*", *op. cit.*, p. 347.
48. Cf. Mahendra Ved, *Times of India*, August 31, 1999.
49. Amit Baruah, in *Frontline*, June 5-18, 1999, p. 15.
50. Gen. Shankar Roy-Chowdhury (Retd.), former Chief of the Army Staff, in *Times of India*, June 20, 1999.
51. Mohan J. MAlik, in *Hindustan Times* (New Delhi), September 21, 1999.
52. Sanjay Baru, in *Times of India*, July 14, 1999. It has been estimated that during 1995-98 India's GDP rose 7 per cent after inflation while Pakistan's rose at 3 per cent.
53. Lt. Gen. (Retd) Satish Nambiar, cited in S. Kalyanaraman, "*Beyond Kargil: Compilation of a Panel Discussion*", *op. cit.*, pp. 334-335.

54. Lt. Gen. Krishan Pal, quoted in *Frontline*, August 27 , 1999, p. 36.
55. *Times of India*, November 1, 1999.
56. Bharat Karnard, "A New Strategy for the LoC & Low-intensity Warfare in Kashmir", *Faultlines*, Vol. 2, 1999, p. 118.
57. Lt. Gen. Vijay Madan, "Jammu and Kashmir Operations, 1947-48: The other version", USI Journal, July-September, 1992, p. 315.
58. S.N. Prasad and Dharam Pal (eds.), History of Operations in Jammu and Kashmir (1947-48), *op. cit.*, pp. 349 and 367.
59. Bharat Karnard, "A New Strategy for the LoC & Low-intensity Warfare in Kashmir", *op. cit.*, p. 124.
60. Daily Excelsior (Jammu), January 4, 2000, quoting Maj. Gen. H.S. Kanwar, Chief of Staff, Headquaqrters, 16 Corps. While briefing the newsmen he said ever since the Army take over, Pakistan has further intensified its proxy war in Jammu and Kashmir. Today, the entire equation has changed and Pakistan's intelligence agency, ISI is even more responsive to the Army. This change over at the top had a direct bearing and has given a major boost to the insurgency in the State.
61. B. Raman, Institute for Topical Studies, Chennai, 18 August 1999.
62. Quoted by A.G. Noorani, in *Statesman* (Calcutta), September 21, 1999. Mushahid Hussain has been a leading media person of Pakistan, an ideologue of Pakistan Muslim League and was Nawaz Sharief's Information Minister in his last government.
63. *Daily Excelsior*, November 23, 1999.
64. Praveen Swami, "The Kargil War: Preliminary Explorations, *op. cit.*, p. 42.
65. *Times of India*, January 3, 2000.

Index

Abandonments/desertions
- by police (Scales of), 61

Abduction (Sanjay Ghose), 90
Access to International
- platforms by terrorist/ separatists, 91, 93

AGP/ULFA (Roots), 306
Air Offensives, 103-104
- consequences, 104

Airforce losses
- (Ahuja), 103

AIR Srinagar Case, 161, 163
AISSF (All India Sikh Students Federation), 31, 55
Akali's
- in power,
- leadership,
- attitude on terrorism, 31
- split, 33

Amnesty (MNF), 235
American Role to Diffuse Kargil, 335
American Supreme Court on hostile audience, 173-74
American/Western Goodwill
- reliance, 145

Anti-terrorist Legislation
- (absence), 13

Anti/Counter Terrorism
- distinction, 279

Anup Chetia (ULFA), 91-92
- and his alias (legal wrangle), 92-93

ARC (Aviation Research Centre)
- and Surveillance, 126-27

Army vs Mujahideen, 148
Arms Arsenal
- accessibility, 9

Arming the Volunteers
- (Punjab), 50

Army
- inducting/deployment (Punjab), 72, 74

Army Schemes
- counter insurgencies, 231

Army (Indian)
- counter insurgency warfare, 214

Aslam Beg Gen (Pak)
- on Kargil, 338

Attitudes vs Technological
- competence Kargil, 188

Authorised Representatives
- harbouring separatists, 91

Babari Masjid Crisis, 62
Balance of Terror, 132
Babbar Khalsa International, 78, 162
Babbar Sukhdev Singh
- killing, 78

Badamibagh H.Q. Attack, 259
Bains Committee, 32
Barnala Government, 32
- tenure, 33
- dismissal, 34

Bangladesh
- terrorism in, 10

Batalik Assault, 104, 106
Beant Singh, 76
Bhindranwale, 27, 29

murder, 27, 56
associates, 35
capture, 30
Bhutto Ali (arrest), 135
Bihari's Killings (Punjab)
Mann's statement, 58
Biological Weapons
nations having, 202
Blair House Summit, 116
Boer War Concentration camps, 237
Brahma Avtar
Singh, 47
Brajesh Mishra, 113
British Case Law
on unlawful
assembly, 174
British Counter Insurgency
Strategy, 220-21
Brigades in position
(Kargil), 105
BSF high altitude
positions, 131
BSF/CRPF in Kargil, 342
Bulletproof Jacket, 187, 196
cost of, 199
Bureaucratic
indifference, 188
response to challenges, 185
understanding, 184

Casualties
of police (Punjab), 25
civilians/police/
terrorists, 70
reductions, 53
CAT (Convention Against
Torture), 86
Candidates supported by
terrorist organizations, 65
CBW (Chemical or
Biological Weapons), 284
CCS (Cabinet Committee on Security),
103
Central agency to Co-ordinate
counter terrorism, 284
CERD (Convention on the
Elimination of Discrimination),
86
Cellular Phone
technology, misuse, 184
Centre's Strategy
Punjab, 31
Change in Tactices (terrorists), 51
Chandra Shekhar
on safe passage (Kargil)
109-110
government, 62—63
Civilian casualties, 66-67
Clinton to Nawaz Sharief
on Kargil withdrawal, 335
Collusion/opposition - centre/state, 306
Cologue G-8 Summit, 113
Communal differences, 13
Communal divisions/ bias in
police, 41-42
Command Centre
of terrorist organizations, 66
Comprehensive Test
Ban Treaty, 146
Comprehending Conflict
costs, 153
Command (Question of)
French, British, 222-23
Confronting Internal Security
challenges, 252
Consequences of Terrorism, 11
Conviction in Terrorist
cases, 12-13
Correction Process (initiated
by author), 42
Counter Terrorist
measures - Punjab, 24
strategies, 73, 76
operations, 183, 303-304
initiatives, 199
policy/principles, 280
Counter Insurgency Warfare
American approach, 218
factors, 211, 239
modern approach, 217
principles, 220
Courts Omissions/Commissions, 167
CSCE (Conference on
Security and Cooperation
in Europe), 89-90
Cuban Revolution
lessons, 217

Dangers and Alternative
scenarios, 203
Damdami Taksal, 49, 64
Declaration of Khalistan, 32

Defeat of Terrorism
in Punjab, 24
Defence Academies, 214
Dereliction of Duty, 12, 46
Development Planning/
Expenditure, 302
Destabilising Karachi, 152
Deterrence Paradigm, 201
theory, 202
Dress Code for Women
(terrorists), 162
Directions to be Explored
(Punjab terrorism), 205

Economic Neglect
-the North-East, 19
ECOSOC (Economic
and Social Council) UN, 85
Election Announcement, 55
Election Issue (playing up), 55
Election
boycott, sabotage, 75
1992-impact, 76
End of Terrorism
in Punjab and
status of killings
(numbers), 28, 36, 81
Encounter/Fellings, 79
Enquiry into Intelligence/
military failures, 100
Escalation of Violence, 72
External Intelligence
Agencies, 152
Extremist Isolation, 213

Farooq Abdullah
Kargil visit, 333
Failure Responsibilities, 185
Fact Finding Committees, 59
Failure of Police Leadership
(Punjab), 45
Finances Generated
by terrorists, 310
Fire (movie) Furore, 164-65
Firearms (Use of), 187
Firepower Capability
measurement, 187, 219
First Phase of Kargil
operations, 103
Fleeing to Pakistan, 81
Freedom of Speech (suppression),
19, 164, 172
and violence, 169
imposition, 164, 169
threats to peace, 168
FSL (Forensic Science
Laboratories), 194-95
Forecasting Aggressive
postulations, 348

Gandhi Rajiv
support to Chandraswami
government, 63
George Fernandes, 109
pronouncements, 109-110
assumptions, 111
Give up and Gain
criteria for terrorists, 314
Golden temple
surrender to terrorists, 32
search order, 32
Gorbachev Prophecies, 11
Grouping of Villages, 225
Government Failure
areas of, 312-13
Grouping of Villages, 225
Gun-power (Punjab)
terrorist vs forces, 34
Gurcharan Singh Tohra, 62
attempted killing of, 62
Guerilla tactices/warfare,
in insurgency, 216-17

Hari Singh Maharaja, 323
Helicopter Surveillance, 103
Hind Samachar Group
(protection Punjab), 177
High Altitude Positions
occupation of by army, 130
Human Rights
Activists masquerading
as, 59
Bodies Criticism of Police, 61
Issues, 85

IAF in Kargil, 333-34
Ideologies of India, 132
ICRC (International
Committee of the Red
Cross), 90
Impending Victory (Khalistan), 71
India
the case of, 10-11

Incidents of Killings
by terrorists, 57
of Policemen, 60
Infirmity of Institutions
-the case of Pakistan, 13
India's Approach to
disputes with
neighbours, 142
India's Response to
Kashmir, 354
Indian Casualties
Kargil, 335
Indian Manpower/
weapon power
Kargil, 335
Intelligence Operations, 48
after Black Thunder, 44
International Covenants
of Human Rights, 86
Internationalization
of Kargil, 112, 145
of Kashmir, 124
Intelligence
lapses Kargil, 128
v/s assessment
lapse, 131
operations, 252
Intercepts of Conversation
(Pak army), 111-12
Innovations
technological
types, 195-98
impact, 198
Insurgencies
India, 212
Mizo, 212
Militant Response, 215
Iridium Technology, 184
Islamic Fundamentalism,
203-204
Israel Terrorism, 273-75
ISI
and proxy war, 353

Jaswant Singh
on the Kargil
Conflict, 144
Jammu and Kashmir
Light Infantry, 105
J & K Partition
perception of
Pakistan, 117
Jodhpur Detenues, 35
Jubbar Heights
and first contact
with Pakistan
troops, 101
capture of, 106

Kargil War, 17-18, 99
Kashmir perspective, 18
objectives explanations, 116
Post (era), 191
and equipment upgradation, 191
accounts of Pakistan forces
occupation, 319-20
Region, 320-22
the first encounter, 332
assessment, 336
lessons, 337
Indian/Pakistan
perspective, 337-38

Labh Singh General
(KLF), 47
Ladakh Scouts, 351
Lahore Bus Diplomacy, 332
LIC (Low Intensity
Conflict), 219
Longowal, 31
assassination, 32
LoC (Line of Control),
147
Low Intensity Warfare
technologies, 190
LTTE (Liberation of
Tamil Tigers Elam), 91

MAD (Mutually Assured
Destruction), 201
Malik, Gen V.P., 113, 156
hints on attack, 113
hints on failures, 126
orders on non-escalation, 125
Manchanda, M.L.,
murder, 78, 162-63
Manochahal
talks proposal, 63
Mann, Simranjit Singh, 55, 72
release, declaration,
55, 57
Mao's Strategy
guerrilla warfare, 216

Mid-term Elections (Punjab)
 participation, boycott,
 aborting, 64-65
Migration, 156
MIG losses, 103
Military
 force-abuse of, 19
 outcomes - alternatives, 113
 options, 346
Mishra, R.K., (emissary), 116
Mizo
 military campaign, 19
 insurrection, 225
 villages - resettlement,
 240, 243
Mobilization of Crowds, 59
Mobile cum Naka Contingents, 40
Morale of Terrorists (decline in), 53
Mopping up Operations, 81
Mountain Footwear, 188
Mushkoh Valley, 332
 confrontation,
 assault, 104-106
Musharraf-Zinni Negotiations,
 116-17
Musharraf Gen, 111-12
 355-56
Muttahida Quami Movement
 (MQM), 152
Muslims in India,
 156-57
MNF (Mizo National Front)
 claim for separate
 set-up, 244-46
 declaration, 243

Narasimha Rao Government,
 65, 71
NAM
 and human rights fora, 89
Nawaz Sharief's Marginalization,
 114
National Conference
 recasting as Muslim
 communal force, 136
Negotiations with Militants, 64
Nepal Conflict, 10
New
 policy (J&K). 270-71
 strategy, 147
NGOs Lending Danners
 to individuals, 88
Niaz Naik (Sharief's envoy), 115
NLF (Northern Light Infantry),
 337
North-East India
 terrorism, 27
North-East
 conflict analysis, 303
 insurgency, 311

OOTW (Operations Other
 Than War), 9
Operation Accomplishment,
 232
Operation Blanket, 234
Operation Black Thunder,
 32-33, 36, 65
 aftermath, killings,
 36-37, 47
Operation Blue Star,
 30, 35
Operation Gibraltar, 326
 Gulmarg, 324
 Grand slam, 327
 Night Dominance, 79
 Rakshak, 64, 73
 Satsriakal, 233
 Snipe (Thimaya's), 351
 Topac, 332
 Vijay, 332
 Woodrose, 30
Ore Oru Gramathile
 film censorship case,
 169, 171, 173, 175-76
OSCE (Organization for
 Security and Co-operation
 in Europe), 89
Options for India (post-Kargil),
 343

Pakistan
 as centre of
 terrorism, 10
 case of infirmity, 13
 might behind
 Punjab terrorism, 68
 reaction to J&K elections, 329
 modus operandi of infiltration,
 330
 strategy/game plan, 143-44
 second War with, 326

1971 War, 327
involvement in Kargil, 323
militancy, 329
direct intervention (terrorism) 190, 195
aggression by, 205
military presence-evidence,106
Panthic Committees, 48-49, 71
Partisan Activities of Human Rights groups, 94
Partition criteria, 155
Patrols to investigate insurgency, 102
Petro-Islam dollars, 137
PHRO (Punjab Human Rights Organization), 63
POK
control by, 350
political situations, 351
advances in, 349-50
Pokharan II
& J&K future, 129
aftermath, 127, 201
nuclear tests, 100
Police
criticism, 68
paralysis/deriliction/ immobilization in Punjab, 29, 39-40
atrocities (stories), 59
Political Solution
philosophy, 34, 55
Politicization of Human Rights Forum, 89
Press Code, 163
Propaganda and campaign and desertion among forces, 52
Protection of election candidates, 74
Professional Agencies, 73
Proxy War, 353
Public Distribution System
diversion for ULFA, 310
Punjab
experience, 221
institutional collapse, 12
studies on, 17
police- action
terrorism
political factor, 26-27
final crushing, 34
Public
response to terrorists, 51
campaign by terrorist Groups, 57-58

Ratio of Security Force personnel to militants killed, 134
RAC (Regional Autonomy Committee) Report, 117
threats, recommendations impact, members, 118-20
Ray, Siddharth Shankar, 34
Rajputana Rifles, 104, 320
Reduction in Killings, 74
Reconciliation Issue (Hindu/Islam), 154
Reluctance among Punjab police, 28
Removal/transfer from Punjab (author's), 64
Restructuring on regional identity (J & K) proposal, 123
Response Proposals for terrorists
threats, 284-85
features, 285-88
Resettlement
of villages, 230
strategy, 234, 238
armies, 237
Revulsion against terrorists, 51
Reorganizing the army, 151
Reversal of Trends, 80
Retreat of Pakistan, 108
Ribeiro Julio, 35
Rode, Jasbir Singh, 35

SAM (Surface to Air Missiles)
use by terrorists, 126
Saurabh Kalia's patrol, 102
Safe Passage, 109-110

arbat Khalsa, 32
andhu Harminder Singh
(AISSF)
release, declaration, 57
ıartaz Aziz, 111-12, 121
ıarvanan Maj
body recovery, 104
ıGPC (Shiromani
Gurdwara Prabandhak
Committee), 32
ıecurity Standards, 288
ıearching/Combing Opeations,
47-48
ıevere Options, 153
ıhifting/hybernation of
terrorist organizations, 74
ıhimla Accord, 148
ıikh
sentiments/representation
against terrorism, 68
casualties, 69
ıingh, V.P. (government), 56
and reversal of gained
ground, 56-57
uncoherent policies, 62
collapse, 63
Sikh Aspirations,
and terrorism, 26
Sihota Maj Gen,
warning, 129
South Asia, 9
Special Operation, 47
Speech, 177
Special Cell, 194-95
SPAC (Shiromani
Panthic Action
Committee), 77
Sub-Commission for
Protection of Minorities,
85-86
Special Forces Command,
151
units recruited
area, 152
Surrender by
militants
negotiations, 53

Targets
of security force
personnel, 134
of terrorism, 11
of police and
families, 60-61
Terrorism
future, 20
killings Punjab (numbers), 28
Punjab (crushing of), 47
Organizations (Punjab), 48
Leaders (fellings), 79
Activity (post—Kargil), 133
Terai Region (UP)
moving of terrorists, 51
Tiger Hills
assault, 104
skirmishes, 107
Tipnis, A.Y., Air Marshall, 103
Tololing Heights - capture, 104
Transfer/Appointment in
Punjab (Author's), 28, 37
Two Nation Theory, 13

ULFA
PDS diversion
to, 310-11
abduction, 90
unreliability of
police force, 25
Unpreparedness
Kargil, 126
United Nations
General Assembly
Resolution, 142-43
Unfinished agenda
(partition), 139
United Nations Military
Observer Group of
India & Pakistan
(UNMOGIP), 150
Uniform Service
contempt of, 186
Unconventional Weapons,
access, 206
Upgradation of Weapons,
(Punjab), 38-39, 50
Unpopular Speech
Right to, 172
Upgradation Plan
Post-Kargil, 191-92
Problems, 192-93
United States
condemnation of Pakistan, 114

diplomacy, 123
Vietnam bombings, 218
terrorism, 276
counter terrorism policy, 277-78

Vajpayee A.B.,
on nuclear doctrine, 132
VDC (Village Defence
Committees), 213
Victims of Terrorism, 10
Volting Percentages, 75

War of the Minds of Men, 176
War of Kashmir
Causes, 155
Warning by Intelligence
Bureau, 128
WASO (Wide
Area Surveillance
Operations), 102
Weaponry Changes
among terrorists,
52-53
Weapons
technologies, 184
in CRPF, 186
authorization
for use, 187
Weapons of Mass
Destruction (WMD), 285

Yaldor Assault, 107

Zaffarwal Directive
to Mann, 57
on talks, 63

Zinni
visit to Pakistan, 115, 335